MATERIALS AND METHODS IN ELT

MATERIALS AND METHODS IN ELT

A TEACHER'S GUIDE
Third Edition

Jo McDonough,
Christopher Shaw
and Hitomi Masuhara

WILEY-BLACKWELL

A John Wiley & Sons, Ltd., Publication

This third edition first published 2013
© 2013 John Wiley & Sons, Inc

Edition History: Blackwell Publishing Ltd (1e, 1993 and 2e, 2003)

Wiley-Blackwell is an imprint of John Wiley & Sons, formed by the merger of Wiley's global Scientific, Technical and Medical business with Blackwell Publishing.

Registered Office
John Wiley & Sons Ltd, The Atrium, Southern Gate, Chichester, West Sussex, PO19 8SQ, UK

Editorial Offices
350 Main Street, Malden, MA 02148-5020, USA
9600 Garsington Road, Oxford, OX4 2DQ, UK
The Atrium, Southern Gate, Chichester, West Sussex, PO19 8SQ, UK

For details of our global editorial offices, for customer services, and for information about how to apply for permission to reuse the copyright material in this book please see our website at www.wiley.com/wiley-blackwell.

The right of Jo McDonough, Christopher Shaw, and Hitomi Masuhara to be identified as the authors of this work has been asserted in accordance with the UK Copyright, Designs and Patents Act 1988.

Library of Congress Cataloging-in-Publication Data

McDonough, Jo.
  Materials and methods in ELT : a teacher's guide / Jo McDonough, Christopher Shaw, and Hitomi Masuhara. – Third edition.
       pages   cm
  Includes bibliographical references and index.
  ISBN 978-1-4443-3692-4
  1. English language–Study and teaching–Foreign speakers.   I. Shaw, Christopher.
II. Masuhara, Hitomi.
  PE1128.A2M383 2013
  428.0071–dc23

                                                                    2012020859

A catalogue record for this book is available from the British Library.

Cover image: 3D Blue background © CTRd/Stockphoto
Cover design: Nicki Averill Design

Set in 10.5/12.5 pt Sabon by Toppan Best-set Premedia Limited

6   2016

Contents

List of Figures

Preface to the Third Edition

This third edition of *Materials and Methods in ELT: A Teacher's Guide* has been extensively revised and updated to provide teachers of English as a foreign language (EFL) with a contemporary account of major trends in English language teaching (ELT) materials and methodology. It is based on the same rationale as the first two editions in that we hope it will be equally useful to teachers who are following a scheme of study in language teaching methodology or applied linguistics as well as to classroom teachers of EFL around the world who wish to keep abreast of developments in the field. The overall aim of the book is to provide a synthesis between 'principle' and 'practice', by making links between background issues – views of language, psychological bases of language learning – and the practical design of materials and methods.

The first edition of *Materials and Methods in ELT* appeared in 1993 and the second in 2003. During that time we have received extensive feedback from teachers in many parts of the world, and we have tried in this new edition to incorporate that feedback. The revisions for this third edition, undertaken by Hitomi Masuhara working with the original authors, are substantial, though the overall format remains essentially the same, as does the hands-on approach and supportive voice. By the end of the book, we hope that readers will have the necessary skills to understand the most common design approaches for teaching materials, to evaluate critically the principles upon which they are based and to assess their relevance to their own teaching context. It is also our hope that readers will gain some insight into materials and methods within educational frameworks that may differ from their own.

We have divided the book into three parts. The five chapters in the first part relate to the area of materials and syllabus design by looking at the *principles* on which materials and methods are based. This includes a description of educational frameworks relevant to all ELT practitioners, an analysis of the communicative approach and the wide range of developments that have followed it, a 'pair' of chapters on evaluating and adapting materials, and a completely new chapter on technology in ELT, written specially for this book by Diane Slaouti of the University of Manchester. In part II of the book we attempt to relate to each individual language skill in turn the principles discussed in part I, finishing with a chapter that looks at different ways of achieving effective skills integration in teaching materials. The third and final part of the book focuses largely on different methods of organizing the resources and management of the classroom, including a variety of classroom structures and interaction patterns, in particular group and pairwork and the concept of the individual learner. We then focus increasingly on the teacher by looking at classroom observation techniques and in the final chapter on teachers' roles and possibilities for professional development in the contemporary ELT context.

For this edition, references have been totally updated for all chapters, as have illustrative samples from current and representative teaching materials. There is up-to-date discussion of developments that have taken place since the second edition. The original chapters 2 and 3 have been amalgamated and rewritten, taking a more historical perspective for the analysis of the impact of communicative approaches and exploring current approaches in more detail than before.

Our final goal in writing this book remains that of enabling readers to become better informed about contemporary ELT methods and materials by providing a relatively compact reference package that incorporates practical 'operational' tasks into the text with the desired outcome that readers will have the skills to make informed judgements about their present and future classroom practice.

Jo McDonough, Christopher Shaw
Colchester
Hitomi Masuhara
Southport
March 2012

Acknowledgements

The authors and publisher gratefully acknowledge the permission granted to reproduce the copyright material in this book:

Chapter 2:
P. Kerr and C. Jones 2007, *Straightforward Intermediate Student Book*. Macmillan. © P. Kerr and C. Jones 2006. Published by Macmillan Publishers Ltd. Reprinted with permission of Macmillan Publishers Ltd. All rights reserved.

Scanned pages from A. Tilbury, T. Clementson, L. A. Hendra, D. Rea, A. Doff, *English Unlimited Elementary Coursebook* with e-Portfolio. Cambridge University Press, 2010, pp. 2–3. Reprinted with permission of Cambridge University Press.

Scan of contents pages from A. Clare and J. Wilson, *Speakout Intermediate Student Book*. Pearson Longman, 2011. Reprinted with permission of Pearson Education Ltd.

Coursebook map from *Outcomes Upper Intermediate* 1E, Dellar/Walkley, Heinle/ELT, 2011. Copyright © 2011 Heinle/ELT, a part of Cengage Learning, Inc. Reproduced by permission. www.cengage.com/permissions

Chapter 6:
Exercise 7b, c and d on pp. 66–7 from H. Puchta, J. Stranks and P. Lewis-Jones, *English in Mind Level 5 Student's Book*. Cambridge University Press, 2008. © Cambridge University Press 2008. Reprinted with permission.

Excerpt from *Life of Pi* by Y. Martel. Copyright © 2001 by Y. Martel. This material may not be reproduced in any form or by any means without the prior written permission of the publishers. Reproduced with permission of Houghton Mifflin Harcourt Publishing Company, Random House of Canada Limited, Westwood Creative Artists Ltd, and Canongate Books UK.

Illustration of the book cover *Life of Pi* by Y. Martell, illustration by A. Bridge. © A. Bridge, reprinted with kind permission of the illustrator.

L. Clanfield and A. Jeffries, p. 111, *Global Pre-Intermediate Student Book*. Oxford: Macmillan Education. Text © D. Crystal, Instruction © L. Clanfield and A. Jeffries 2010, Design and Illustration © Macmillan Publishers Limited, 2010. Reprinted with permission of Macmillan Publishers Ltd. All rights reserved.

p. 98 Wellar/Walkley/Hocking *Innovations Intermediate* 1E. © 2004 Heinle/ELT, a part of Cengage Learning, Inc. Reproduced by permission. www.Cengage.com/permissions

E. Glendinning and B. Holmstrom, *Study Reading, A Course in Reading Skills for Academic Purpose*, 1992, excercise from pp. 104–5. © Cambridge University Press. Reprinted with permission of Cambridge University Press.

J. A. C. Brown, *The Social Psychology of Industry*, p. 186. London: Penguin 1954. Reprinted with permission of Penguin Books UK.

p. 113, Wellar/Walkley/Hocking *Innovations Intermediate* 1E. © 2004 Heinle/ELT, a part of Cengage Learning, Inc. Reproduced by permission. www.Cengage.com/permissions

Colchester Evening Gazette for *Paying to learn: is it snobbery?*

Chapter 7:
p. 36, Wellar/Walkley/Hocking *Innovations Intermediate* 1E. © 2004 Heinle/ELT, a part of Cengage Learning, Inc. Reproduced by permission. www.Cengage.com/permissions

Extract from p. 30, *New Cutting Edge Intermediate Students' Book* by S. Cunningham and P. Moor, Pearson Longman, 2005. Reprinted with permission of Pearson Education Ltd.

Unit 14 pp. 147–8, *Just Right Upper Intermediate - Teachers Book* 1E by J. Harmer and C. Letherby. Published by Heinle/ELT. Reprinted with permission of Cengage Learning Inc. www.cengage.com/permissions

Chapter 8:
16.1 from *Market Leader Upper Intermediate Coursebook* by Cotton, Falvey and Kent, Pearson Education, 2001, p. 157. Reprinted with permission of Pearson Education Ltd.

p. 382 J. Angouri 'Using textbook and real-life data to teach turn taking in business meetings'. In N. Harwood (ed), *English Language Teaching Materials. Theory and Practice*. Cambridge University 2010. Reprinted with permission of Cambridge University Press.

'The Bully Asleep' by J. Walsh, from *The Roundabout By the Sea* by J. Walsh published by OUP 1960.

Speaking 6A from p. 39 *Speakout Intermediate Students' Book* by A. Clare and J. Wilson, Pearson Education, 2001. Reprinted with permission of Pearson Education Ltd.

Chapter 9:
Writing Portfolio of Unit 4 p84 C. Davies, F. Tup, and D. Aziz. 2003. Life Accents. © Times Media Private Limited in Singapore Reprinted with permission of Marshal Cavendish International (Singapore) Pte Ltd

Chapter 10:
'Water Conservation' activity written by B. Tomlinson. Unpublished. © B. Tomlinson. Reprinted with kind permission of the author.

p. 52 from G. Duran and G Ramaut, 'Tasks for absolute beginners and beyond: developing and sequencing tasks at basic proficiency levels'. In K. van den Branden (ed), *Task-Based Language Education: From Theory to Practice*. Cambridge University Press, 2006. Reprinted with permission.

p. 62 from G. Duran and G. Ramaut, 'Tasks for absolute beginners and beyond: developing and sequencing tasks at basic proficiency levels'. In K. van den Branden (ed), *Task -Based Language Education: From Theory to Practice*. Reprinted with permission of Cambridge University Press.

Figure 'A hole in your hand' taken from a task-based syllabus for Dutch Language education at the level of secondary education, from *KLIMOP+TATAMI*, Centre for Language and Education, Leuven. Reprinted with permission.

Figure and activity 'A gruesome performance taken from a task-based syllabus for Dutch Language education at the level of secondary education, from *KLIMOP+TATAMI*, Centre for Language and Education, Leuven. Reprinted with permission.

'Focus on writing: project work', from pp. 148–9 from A.-B. Fenner, and G. Nordal-Pedersen. *Searching 9, Learner's Book*. © Gyldendal Norsk Forlag AS 2008. Printed by permission.

Chapter 12:
'Openings' by B. Tomlinson, Penguin 1994. © B. Tomlinson, Reprinted with permission.

Figure 8.3 on p. 193 from Christine Goh 'Listening as process: learning activities for self-appraisal and self-regulation'. In N.l Harwoods (ed), *English Language Teaching Materials: Theory and Practice* (2010). © Cambridge University Press, 2010. Reprinted with Permission.

Chapter 13:
pp. 48, 50–1, 126–8 of D. Lubeleska and M. Matthews 199 in the booklet accompanying, Andrew Bampfield, *Looking at language Classrooms*. © Cambridge University Press. Reprinted with permission of Cambridge University Press.

Transcript between T and S1 and transcript between T, S1 and S2, from pp. 31–2, Chapter 2 by I.-K. Ghosn in B. Tomlinson and H. Masuhara (eds), *Research for Materials Development in Language Learning*, 2011. London: Continuum. ©Irma-Kaarina Ghosn. Reprinted with the kind permission of the author and by kind permission of Continuum International Publishing Group, a Bloomsbury company.

Every effort has been made to trace copyright holders and to obtain their permission for the use of copyright material. The publisher apologizes for any errors or omissions in the above list and would be grateful if notified of any corrections that should be incorporated in future reprints or editions of this book.

Part I

Topics in the Design of Materials and Methods

1

The Framework of Materials and Methods

1.1   Introduction: Setting the Scene

(Graddol (2006: 22), in his study of global trends surrounding English, comments: 'On the one hand, the availability of English as a global language is accelerating globalization. On the other, the globalization is accelerating the use of English'. He refers to a statistical projection of the number of learners: '. . . there could be around 2 billion people simultaneously learning English in the world's schools and colleges and as independent adults. Nearly a third of the world population will all be trying to learn English at the same time' (Graddol, 2006: 101).

As the need intensifies for social, economic and technological communication at a global level, so English language teaching has been diversifying. For example, English teachers may be engaged in teaching

- English as a Foreign Language (EFL) – English taught outside English speaking regions.
- English as a Second Language (ESL) – English taught inside English speaking regions to non-native learners.
- English for Young Learners (EYL) – English taught as an additional language to very young to young learners up to, normally, primary level.
- English for Specific Purposes (ESP) – English taught for specific occupational purposes such as English for medicine and for business.

Materials and Methods in ELT: A Teacher's Guide, Third Edition.
Jo McDonough, Christopher Shaw, and Hitomi Masuhara.
© 2013 John Wiley & Sons, Inc. Published 2013 by John Wiley & Sons, Inc.

- English for Academic Purposes (EAP) – English taught to those who wish to study at institutes of higher education.
- Content and Language Integrated Learning (CLIL) – English taught in cross-curricular programmes in which content subjects and language are taught at the same time.

Whichever varieties of English language teaching we are engaged in, teachers of English are members of an established worldwide profession. Wherever we work, we share many assumptions about what we do; we prepare and use teaching materials and classroom methods and techniques based on similar, or at least comparable, principles. Yet, despite this commonality, it is not unusual for teachers to report a sense of isolation from colleagues in other countries, and even in different areas of their own country. Another attitude that is sometimes expressed is that the teaching situation in our country, or school, is unique, with its own special problems and difficulties. There is some justification for these feelings, of course: many teachers work in geographical isolation, and may not have access to channels of professional communication (journals, conferences, in-service training courses); different countries have widely differing educational systems and philosophies, resulting in teachers being subject to different expectations and pressures.

In this chapter we shall take some time to look beyond our individual teaching circumstances to what can be thought of as a professional 'common core'. This has relevance to all teachers, whether we work in a Japanese high school, a Mexican university, a private language school in Spain, a Chinese polytechnic, a Turkish secondary school, a Zairean college – this list could go on indefinitely. We shall argue that the idea of a 'common core' is also useful whether our materials and methods are selected by us or specified by the educational authorities. It is, then, broadly made up of two kinds of factors: firstly, of the various wide-ranging criteria on which decisions about language teaching programmes are based, and secondly, on the pedagogic principles according to which materials and methods are actually designed. We shall take these two kinds of factors together and refer to them as the shared framework.

In what follows, this notion of a 'framework' is set out in a little more detail. We then subdivide it under the two headings of 'context' and 'syllabus', both exploring their general implications and trying to relate them as we do so to our own familiar and specific teaching situation.

1.2   The Framework: Context and Syllabus

In simple terms, the overall goals of a language teaching programme usually derive from an analysis of the reasons why a group of learners in a particular environment needs to learn English: these goals may be stated in general, educational, or very specific terms. They may, on the one hand, be set out in the large-scale categories of a national language policy with many associated implications for the development of the curriculum. For instance, the aim of English language teaching in Malaysia was earlier stated to be 'to create a society that is able to utilize the language for effective communication as the need arises, and as a key to wider experiences. For those furthering their studies, the skills learned should become an instrument with which they may cope with the necessities of using the language'. The new guidelines for language teaching in Japanese schools include such statements as 'to develop understanding of language and culture through a foreign language . . . to develop a positive attitude towards communication in a foreign language, and a basic practical communication ability in hearing and speaking'. Alternatively, at the other end of the scale, a course may be organized to address a particular learning need for, say, the identifiable purposes of a small group. For instance, a course may be designed 'to meet the needs of learners who need to improve their ability to communicate when socializing, telephoning, making business presentations and taking part in meetings', or 'to help international postgraduate students in English-medium universities develop the writing skills necessary for writing dissertations'.

There is, then, a whole spectrum of possibilities for defining the goals of language teaching, for a country, an age group, a whole school, a class or an individual; and whether for general educational purposes, business, scientific development, cultural appreciation or many other reasons.

> 1   Is there an explicit statement of the goals of the language programme on which you work? If so, what are its primary aims?
> 2   If there is not such a statement, try to draft one that represents your own understanding of the goals.

To define what is meant here by 'framework' we start from the view that materials and methods cannot be seen in isolation, but are embedded within a broader professional context. This is represented in figure 1.1, which shows in a very simplified form the typical stages of planning an English language programme.

Whether goals are stated in terms of a national language policy, or in the more specific environment of, say, a particular school or college, the possibilities for actually implementing them will be directly related both to the learners themselves – their needs, characteristics and so on – and to the whole educational setting in which the teaching is to take place. Obviously, as we shall see in our subsequent discussion, goals need to be realistic for each circumstance. There is little use, for example, in planning for a multimedia

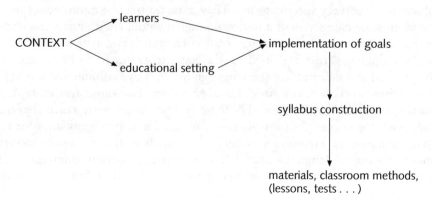

Figure 1.1   The framework of language teaching.

course if appropriate equipment is unavailable or unreliable, or in making too many general assumptions about classroom methodology. The statement of goals, then, related to the learners and conditioned by the setting, leads to the selection of an appropriate type of syllabus content and specification. The broad syllabus outline will in turn have direct implications for the more detailed design and selection of materials and tests, the planning of individual lessons and the management of the classroom itself. Clearly this logical planning sequence is an idealization of what is often a less well-defined procedure, where 'set' materials may linger behind aims that have been reformulated and updated, or conversely where new syllabus types may be ill-matched to existing educational objectives. The logical sequence will nevertheless be used as a reference point for discussion, and as a starting point for the exploration of individual teaching circumstances.

   Let us now look at the most important contextual factors involved in planning, and then at the key types of syllabus from which actual courses are derived.

Contextual factors

In the preceding section, we took a broad view of 'context' and included both learners and setting under this heading. Let us examine each of these in turn in a little more detail.

Learners   It is possible to identify a number of important learner characteristics or 'variables' which, as we have suggested, influence planning decisions and the specification of goals. The relative importance of these variables, and their effect on programme design, obviously depend to a certain extent on some of the situational factors to be discussed in the next section. For example, a pupil's mother tongue may be more, or less, significant depending on whether more than one native language is represented in the classroom, or perhaps on the educational philosophy of that particular environment.

For the moment we can list here the key characteristics of 'the learner', indicating how they might affect planning and noting that they form part of our common frame of reference as language teachers, wherever we work. Some of these are characteristics of whole groups or subgroups of learners; others are individual and less open to generalization. Again, some can be known in advance and incorporated at the initial planning stage, in principle at least. Others are more appropriately assessed in the classroom environment itself, and as such are more obviously susceptible to teacher reaction and influence.

We consider the learner's

- *Age:* this will particularly affect topics chosen and types of learning activity, such as the suitability of games or role play.
- *Interests:* as with age, this may help in the specification of topics and learning activities.
- *Level of proficiency in English:* teachers will wish to know this even where their classes are based on a 'mixed proficiency' principle rather than streamed according to level.
- *Aptitude:* this can most usefully be thought of as a specific talent, in this case for language learning, as something that learners might show themselves to be 'good at', perhaps in contrast to other subjects in a school curriculum. (It can be measured by formal aptitude tests, although they are not very frequently used.) The relationship between aptitude and intelligence is not clear, and is certainly not direct.
- *Mother tongue:* this may affect, for instance, the treatment of errors or the selection of syllabus items – areas of grammar or vocabulary and so on.
- *Academic and educational level:* which help to determine intellectual content, breadth of topic choice or depth to which material may be studied.
- *Attitudes to learning*, to teachers, to the institution, to the target language itself and to its speakers. This is directly related to the following point.
- *Motivation*, at least in so far as it can be anticipated. Obviously a whole range of factors will affect this.
- *Reasons for learning*, if it is possible to state them. With school-age pupils this may be less significant than with many adult learners, where it is often possible to carry out quite a detailed analysis of needs.
- *Preferred learning styles:* which will help in the evaluation of the suitability of different methods, for instance, whether problem-solving activities could be used, or whether pupils are more used to 'rote learning', where material is learned by heart.

- *Personality:* which can affect methodological choices such as a willing acceptance of role play and an interactive classroom environment, or a preference for studying alone, for example.

Many of these factors will affect the learners' needs (for a recent book on needs analysis see Long, 2005), and this issue will recur in the relevant sections of subsequent chapters.

Setting   That aspect of the context that we refer to as *setting* is to be understood here as the whole teaching and learning environment, in a wide sense: it is the factors falling under this heading that will determine whether the aims of a language programme, defined with reference to the learners' needs and characteristics, are actually feasible and realistic. In certain situations, the setting itself may be so significant that it provides the foundation for the specification of aims. This might be the case, for instance, in a country with a single political or religious ideological base, where the education system is primarily an expression of that ideology. In the majority of circumstances, however, the setting is more likely to condition the way in which goals are carried out, and indeed the extent to which they can be.

For most EFL/ESL teachers, therefore, the following factors, in some combination and with varying degrees of significance, will influence course planning, syllabus design, the selection of materials and resources, and the appropriateness of methods:

- *The role of English in the country:* whether it is a regular means of communication or primarily a subject taught in the school curriculum, where, in turn, it may or may not be the first foreign language. This relates to the linguistic environment, and to whether English is spoken outside class in the community or alternatively never heard.
- *The role of English in the school*, and its place in the curriculum.
- *The teachers:* their status, both at national and institutional levels, their training, mother tongue, attitudes to their job, experience, expectations (for a discussion of teachers' needs and wants, see Masuhara, 2011). This topic will be taken up in detail in the final chapter of this book.
- *Management and administration:* who is responsible for what level of decision, particularly which are the control points for employment of staff, budgets, resource allocation and so on. Additionally, the position of teachers in the overall system needs to be understood, as does the nature of the hierarchy in any particular institution.
- *Resources available:* books and paper, audio-visual material (hardware and software for cassette and video), laboratories, computers, reprographic facilities and so on. Design and choice of teaching materials will

be particularly affected by resource availability, as will the capacity to teach effectively across a range of language skills.

- *Support personnel:* administrators, secretaries and technicians, and their specific roles in relation to the teaching staff.
- *The number of pupils* to be taught and the size of classes. Overall numbers may affect the total number of teaching hours available, and the large class problem is a very familiar one in many settings worldwide.
- *Time* available for the programme, both over a working year (longitudinally), and in any one week or term (intensive or extensive). Many teachers would also consider that time of day is a significant factor.
- *Physical environment:* the nature of the building, noise factors, flexibility of tables and chairs, size of room in relation to size of class, heat and cold, and so on.
- *The socio-cultural environment:* this can often determine the suitability of both materials and methods. For example, some textbooks contain topics inappropriate to the setting, and some classroom methods require an unacceptable set of teacher and learner roles.
- *The types of tests used*, and ways in which students are evaluated: assessment procedures may, for example, be formal or informal and subjective. They may also be external, in the form of a public or national examination, or internal to the institution and the course.
- *Procedures (if any) for monitoring and evaluating* the language teaching programme itself. This kind of evaluation may be imposed by 'senior management', or alternatively agreed between teachers as colleagues.

Hedge (2000) covers similar points, classifying them into social, educational, pupil and teacher variables. Nation and Macalister (2010) discuss these factors as environment analysis with three major elements: learners, teachers and situation. Holliday (1994, 2005) is particularly concerned with the need for methodology to be *appropriate* to its socio-cultural context, not inappropriately transplanted from a different – and often more privileged – system. We will discuss this in Chapter 11 and, to a certain degree, Chapter 12.

Teachers are affected, directly and indirectly, by all these variables. Some they may be able to influence or even control: for example, the deployment of resources and materials, or the pacing of work within an overall timescale. Others, of course, arise from decisions taken far removed from a teacher's day-to-day professional life, perhaps at Ministry level, or at an earlier point in the country's educational history. Whatever their source, it is the teacher who is in the 'front line' – attempting to promote learning and fulfil the stated goals against the background of a complex network of interrelated factors. The grim reality described by Gaies and Bowers (1990: 176), with large classes, low motivation, inadequate coursebooks, poorly trained teachers, lack of resources, heavy workload and the pressure of exams may still be realities in many teaching contexts (e.g. Hu, 2003; Pham, 2007 to name two). The conclusion in Gaies and Bowers (1990) still sounds pertinent that 'by coming to grips not only with new ideas but with the evidence of what happens when they are introduced into the local context, [teachers] equip themselves with the tools for establishing an appropriate methodology that can set realistic national objectives for teacher training and education' (181). We will discuss in more detail in Chapter 14 how changes and innovation affect teachers and how teachers may manage their self-development while seeking support.

Consider the following short case study of a fairly typical teaching environment. Note how the factors associated with the learner and the teaching situation can affect the organization of the language programme, the materials, the teachers and the methodology. For instance, most aspects are determined by decisions taken at some distance from the teacher, although teachers' views may have some effect. Again, the classes are on the whole conditioned by the examination system, but a minority of pupils are able to select classes in line with their own interests, which in turn means that teachers may be less bound by coursebooks and able themselves to be more autonomous in choice of materials and methods. In other words, there is a complex set of factors in operation, and the teacher in the classroom is the focus of a variety of pressures and influences, both direct and indirect.

Teacher X   works in a secondary school, with pupils ranging in age from 12 to 16. She teaches 30 periods a week, two of which are options selected by older pupils according to their interests. Course materials consist in the main of set textbooks graded according to age and proficiency level and focused heavily but not exclusively on accuracy. Materials are written by a Ministry of Education team according to Ministry guidelines, and teachers' opinions are solicited annually by an Area Language Teaching Adviser. It is government policy to revise materials every eight years.

Average class size is 40 pupils. The pressure of the examination system ensures satisfactory attention, though – since there is little opportunity for travel – learners do not readily perceive the relevance of learning materials to their own lives.

The school has a language laboratory and a very small collection of books (mainly stories) written in English. Classrooms are basic but adequate. Very few supplementary English language teaching materials are available, though teachers are encouraged to make their own small-scale resource materials, and to share ideas at local teachers' centres. The school has one computer, so far without Internet access.

This teacher has been to Britain once, on a three-week summer school. She corresponds regularly with an English schoolteacher.

1 Now examine your own teaching environment in a similar way. First list the characteristics of your learners and of the teaching situation.
2 Then decide which are the more significant of these, and try to plot the patterns of cause and effect that they set in motion. For example, how are your classroom materials selected? To whom are you responsible? What possibilities do you have for innovation, or for professional development?
3 Finally, you might like to consider what kinds of changes in your teaching situation would have the strongest effect on your role as a teacher – a change in your status? Smaller groups? More time? The possibilities are many.
4 Discuss your analysis with colleagues, both with those working in the same environment and, if possible, with others from different backgrounds. Keep a note of your analysis: it will be helpful to refer to it again in subsequent chapters.

The syllabus

We can now assume that the goals of an English language programme have been set out and that the contextual factors affecting its implementation have been established and understood. The next step in the task of planning is to select a type of syllabus relevant to the learners for whom it is intended, appropriate to the situation and which fulfils the aims as closely as possible.

The 'syllabus' can be seen for our purposes as the overall organizing principle for what is to be taught and learned. In other words, it is a general statement as to the pedagogical arrangement of learning content. Richards and Rodgers (2001) have proposed a useful framework for the comparison of language teaching methods that illustrates the place of the syllabus in programme planning. Their model has three distinct levels, which they term *approach*, *design* and *procedure*, and is intended to show the relationship between the theory and practice of language teaching as an 'interdependent system'. Briefly, 'approach' is the most general level, and refers to the views and beliefs – or theories – of language and language learning on which planning is based. The most obvious example here is a view of language described as a set of grammatical structures. The next level, 'design', is where the principles of the first level are converted into the more practical aspects of syllabuses and instructional materials. It is here that decisions are taken about the arrangement of content to be taught and learnt, the choice of topics, language items to be included in the programme and so on. Finally, 'procedure' refers to techniques and the management of the classroom itself.

The English language teaching profession nowadays has available a range of different types of syllabus from which a choice will be made for a specific situation. So however diverse our teaching contexts, our courses will be based on one, or a combination of, these principles of organization. Although syllabuses typically are written and published documents, their circulation is often restricted to the particular situation for which they have been drawn up. Therefore, one of the simplest ways of surveying the types of syllabus available is to examine the contents pages of published English language teaching textbooks, because they reveal the underlying principles and assumptions on which the writers have based their material. At one and the same time, they tell us something both about the approach and the design adopted, thus bringing together principle and practice in a directly observable way.

This is not a book about syllabus design as such, and it will not be necessary or appropriate to analyse each syllabus type in depth here. References to more detailed discussion are given at the end of the chapter, and the next chapters will examine the major areas of current debate. Let us simply try to identify the key principles of syllabus organization by examining the types of contents page most often found in the materials we use, because these distinctions will be the foundation for our discussion of 'design and procedure' in the remainder of the book.

> Look at the coursebook(s) that you use most frequently. With which of our samples in figure 1.2 does the table of contents in your own material compare most closely?

The first of these obviously is organized according to a list of grammatical structures and is one that will readily be recognized by most English language teachers. The second is based on the communicative and interpersonal uses to which language is put and, in contrast to the formal structural system of the first type, highlights what people do through language. It is normally referred to as a 'functional' syllabus. This design principle is often found together with the other list of items in the same box: they are technically called 'notions', a term used to describe the rather general and abstract categories a language is able to express, such as concepts of time and place. For convenience – and in line with common practice – they will be placed together here, and the syllabus as a whole designated 'functional-notional'. The most important distinctions between this on the one hand and the so-called structural syllabus on the other will be taken up in the next chapter.

(1) Simple past; irregular verbs The passive Formation of adverbs Type 3 conditionals Gerunds and infinitives	(2a) Making suggestions Asking for directions Giving advice Introducing yourself ---- (2b) Location Duration Ability
(3) In the restaurant At a hotel In the post office At a garage	(4) Making notes from a talk Reading for information Using a dictionary Writing an exam answer
(5) Space travel Intelligence tests Smoking The weather	(6) Language focus: question forms Vocabulary: meeting people Skills: speaking, reading, listening Task preparation: listen to people meeting Task: interviews Task: follow-up

Figure 1.2 Principles of syllabus organization. (Adapted from *Cutting Edge* by Cunningham and Moor, 1999.)

The third sample presents a set of everyday situations or 'settings'. The fourth focuses on language skills, and is concerned with what learners do as speakers, listeners, readers, writers. The fifth uses topics or themes as its starting point. The sixth invokes the concept of task, discussed in Chapter 2.

We can now identify six broad types of syllabus:

1   grammatical or structural
2   functional-notional
3   situational
4   skills-based
5   topic-based
6   task-based

It is, of course, unusual to find just one of these as the only organizing principle, in isolation from others, and before leaving this discussion of syllabus types, two final explanatory points must briefly be made.

First, most syllabuses are based on a combination of two or more of the types we have illustrated. Some, like this one, for example, may have a 'primary' and a 'secondary' organizing principle:

At the bank: question forms
At a garage: imperatives
At a hotel: present perfect

Indeed, many situational and topic-based syllabuses are part of a broader pattern of this kind, where a grammatical point to be taught is linked to an interesting theme or practised in a 'real-world' setting rather than learnt mechanically and outside any context. Other syllabuses are multilayered, using several different principles (ideally) interwoven in a systematic way:

Talking about holidays
Requesting information
Question forms
At the travel agent
Listening and role play
Intonation practice

This deliberately is a somewhat extreme example, but it does show how topics, functions, structures, skills, situations (and pronunciation practice) can be brought together.

The second point to bear in mind here is the need to distinguish between the syllabus itself and what we might call a 'syllabus inventory'. The inventory is simply a list of the contents to be covered in the language programme, whether that is a list of functional or grammatical items, or of skills, or of topics and situations. The 'syllabus' is the way in which that content is organized and broken down into a set of teachable and learnable units, and will include consideration of pacing, sequencing and grading of items, methods of presentation and practice, and so on.

> Examine the list on the following page, which shows a number of different types of learners and teaching situations. Work with a colleague if possible, and select two or three of them to look at in a little more detail.

Where?	Who?	Why?
China: university of technology	Undergraduates	Reading purposes: English is a library language
Turkey: secondary school	School pupils	Part of general school curriculum
Britain: university	Postgraduates in various subjects	To follow postgraduate studies after one year English
An English town: secondary school withdrawal class	Refugees, newly arrived	Language survival
France: evening class	Mixed group: retired people, housewives	Tourism and general purposes
London: private language school	Young adults from the Middle East (male)	To do engineering in further education
Japan: university	Undergraduates	To be tourist guides for foreign visitors
Malaysia: technical institute	Post-'O'-level student	To enter higher education in Australia

1 Try to decide what you think might be the most important factors to do with the learners and the setting for the situations you have chosen. For example, you may think that learners' proficiency levels, or attitudes to English, are significant, and that class size and resources are the key elements affecting the teaching situation.

2 Consider the kind of syllabus that might be selected as the most appropriate in each case, bearing in mind the stated learning purpose. It does not matter if you are not personally familiar with these kinds of teaching context. They are quite representative, and the task here is to practise applying and integrating some of the principles that we have been discussing in this chapter.

1.3 Conclusion

This chapter has discussed the background against which teaching materials and classroom methods evolve. Our professional activities as language teachers are not carried out in a vacuum, and planning a successful language programme involves much more than mere decisions about the content and presentation of teaching materials. Although we work in specific situations with specific groups of learners, according to a specified set of aims, our work can be described along a number of shared and generalizable dimensions. These dimensions are the characteristics of learners, the range of factors in the teaching situation itself, and the syllabus types available to us as a profession. The differences lie in the relative importance of these factors and the choices that are made.

1.4   Further Reading

1 Harmer, J. (2007b): Chapter 8 discusses planning and syllabus design.
2 Jolly, D. and Bolitho, R. (2011): 'A framework for materials writing' describes real cases of how teachers developed materials and discuss principles and procedures.
3 Nation, P. and Macalister, J (2010): *Language Curriculum Design*. This is a recent addition to the literature on the whole process of curriculum development.

2

Current Approaches to Materials and Methods

2.1 Introduction

In the previous chapter we examined in very general terms the most common types of syllabus organization for English language teaching. We also noted that these syllabus types form an essential component of the framework within which objectives are specified according to the learners, teachers and contexts, and within which the details of language teaching programmes are set out. This happens, as we have seen, according to certain principles and with various possibilities for combination. It is the purpose of the present chapter to take a closer look at the methodology and materials design that have influenced changes and innovations in English language teaching in recent years. We will start by discussing the 'communicative approach' with its underlying principles as they constitute the foundation for the approaches and materials that have followed.

The present chapter uses a selection of recent courses in order to examine the design perspectives that they demonstrate. We shall take some fairly popular courses available on the general market, partly on the argument that if a course is used frequently, then its users probably find it relevant and appropriate. It is not the intention to carry out an evaluation of their inherent quality, but rather to follow through developments and identify trends, in particular the so-called multi-component syllabus and the various current interests (e.g. English as lingua franca, task-based course design, emphasis on intercultural competencies, use of corpora and technology). Readers will

Materials and Methods in ELT: A Teacher's Guide, Third Edition.
Jo McDonough, Christopher Shaw, and Hitomi Masuhara.
© 2013 John Wiley & Sons, Inc. Published 2013 by John Wiley & Sons, Inc.

again be invited to contextualize the discussion by commenting on materials familiar to them. We shall concentrate particularly on organization and coverage, and on views of learners and learning underpinning current materials, including the growing interest in learner strategies.

> Try to characterize the approaches to materials design that the following two tables of contents represent.
>
> Compare them with the textbook(s) you most frequently use: are your materials close to either of these approaches?

Lesson	Grammar	Vocabulary	Functional language	Pronunciation
1A Double lives p6	Stative & dynamic verbs Present simple & present continuous	Verbs with two meanings		
1B Britishness p10	Subject & object questions	Self-image		
1C First impressions p12		Describing people	Describing people	Intonation (lists)
1 Language reference p14				
2A Journeys p16	Present perfect & past simple 1	Phrasal verbs (separable & inseparable)		Word linking
2B Down under p20	Present perfect & past simple 2			
2C Getting around p22		Verb collocations (travel)	Travel	
2 Language reference p24				
3A Dream homes p26	Modals of obligation, permission & prohibition (present time) *Make, let & allow*	Accommodation		
3B Bedrooms p30	Modals of obligation, permission & prohibition (past time)	Verb collocations (sleep)		
3C Dinner date p32		Conversation fillers	Requests	Intonation (requests)
3 Language reference p34				
4A Luck of the draw p36	Past simple & past continuous	Idioms (taking risks)		*Was & were*
4B Coincidences p38		*Both & neither*	Talking about similarities & differences	
4C Twists of fate p40	Past perfect simple	Time linkers Injuries		
4 Language reference p44				
5A Hard sell p46	Comparatives 1 Comparatives 2	Adjectives (advertising) Adjectives (negative prefixes)		/s/, /z/ & /ʃ/
5B The office p50	Comparing nouns	Office activities		
5C Paperwork p52		Office supplies	On the phone	
5 Language reference p54				
6A Summer holiday p56	Future 1 (future plans) Future 2 (predictions)	Holidays 1 Holidays 2		
6B Perfect day p60	Present tenses in future time clauses			
6C Travel plans p62		Collocations with *sound*	Indirect questions	Word stress
6 Language reference p64				

	Reading & Listening	Speaking	Writing (in the Workbook)
1A	R *Liars!* L Radio review of TV programme: *How Michael Portillo became a single mum*	Discussing what people are most likely to lie about Talking about yourself *Did you know?* British political parties	A description of a best friend
1B	R *Are you British enough?* Devising a quiz about culture in your country	Discussing answers to a British culture quiz	
1C	L Three conversations in an office	Talking about first impressions	
2A	R *Lawyer gives up job to cycle around South America* L/R Three unusual journeys	Discussing travelling Talking about a film or book of a long journey	A description of a town or city
2B	R An excerpt from a web diary about a trip round Australia	Talking about Australia Planning a journey across your country	
2C	L Three conversations about trying to get somewhere	Talking about daily transport *Did you know?* New York & London taxis	
3A	R *Paradise Ridge* L Interviews with residents talking about disadvantages of living in Paradise Ridge L Interviews with people who live in unusual homes	Discussing where you live Designing a luxury holiday home	Advantages and disadvantages
3B	R *6 things you probably didn't know about beds and bedrooms*	Talking about sleeping & dreaming	
3C	L Three conversations at a dinner party	Describing a recent dinner party *Did you know?* Food in Britain	
4A	R *Lottery winners and losers*	Inventing a story about a lottery winner	A narrative: Lottery winner
4B	L Conversation: discussing things in common	Identifying & discussing coincidences	
4C	R *The world's luckiest man* L Three bad luck stories	Inventing a bad luck story *Did you know?* Superstitions in Britain	
5A	R *Catch them young* L A phone call: credit card telesales	Planning & presenting an advertisement for a mineral water Carrying out a market research survey	An advertisement
5B	R *Office stereotypes*	Planning an office party	
5C	L Ordering office supplies over the phone	Roleplay: phone conversation ordering office supplies *Did you know?* London's Mayfair district	
6A	R Questionnaire: *What kind of holiday person are you?* L Six short interviews at the airport	Roleplay: making plans with other holiday makers Planning a holiday for a family group	An extract from a holiday brochure
6B	R *Emerald Tours*	Discussing the perfect day out *Did you know?* Cork–European capital of culture	
6C	L Enquiring about flights over the phone	Discussing the different ways men & women think	

LESSON	GRAMMAR/FUNCTION	VOCABULARY	PRONUNCIATION	READING
UNIT 1 IDENTITY page 7 ▣ Video podcast I What does *family* mean to you?				
1.1 Who do you think you are? page 8	question forms including subject versus object questions and questions with prepositions	family	intonation patterns in question forms	read and understand a text about a BBC programme that reveals family histories
1.2 Men and women page 11	review of verb tenses: present and past simple versus present and past continuous	relationships; collocations with *take, get, do, go*	stressed syllables	read a BBC blog about the differences between men and women; read and answer a questionnaire about what women really think
1.3 Tell me about yourself page 14	talking about yourself	interview advice; phrases to introduce questions		read tips on successful interviews
1.4 Second Life page 16		things you can do in Second Life; phrases to describe an avatar		
UNIT 2 TALES page 19 ▣ Video podcast I When is it OK to tell a lie?				
2.1 Fact or fiction? page 20	present perfect versus past simple	types of story; focus on prepositions (with expressions of time, nouns and fixed expressions)	strong and weak forms of the present perfect	read a text about whether Hollywood films use fact or fiction
2.2 What really happened? page 23	narrative tenses	the news		read an article about conspiracy theories; read short news stories
2.3 I don't believe it! page 26	telling a story	collocations with *say* and *tell*; sequencers	polite intonation	read a text about how to tell if someone is lying
2.4 Hustle page 28		crime collocations; narrative phrases		
UNIT 3 CONTACT page 31 ▣ Video podcast I Can new technology help communication?				
3.1 You're going where? page 32	the future (plans): the present continuous, *going to, will, might*	communication	*going to* in fast speech	read an article about teenage communication
3.2 Getting connected page 35	the future (predictions): will, might, may, could, going to, *likely to*	future time markers; idioms		
3.3 In other words … page 38	dealing with misunderstandings	types of misunderstandings; phrases to clarify/ask someone to reformulate	intonation: dealing with misunderstandings	read a short story about a misunderstanding
3.4 The virtual revolution page 40		internet communication; phrases for discussing preferences		
UNIT 4 JOBS page 41 ▣ Video podcast I Is your job a 'dream job'?				
4.1 Millionaires page 44	modals of obligation: *must, have to, should*	personal qualities; confusing words		read an article about millionaires; read and do a survey about whether you have got what it takes to be a millionaire
4.2 Dream job page 47	*used to* and *would*	strong adjectives	stressed syllables	read about childhood dreams; read job advertisements
4.3 That's a good idea page 50	reaching agreement	business collocations; phrases to give opinions, comments on other opinions and suggestions	sentence stress	read about a programme called *The Apprentice* broadcast on the BBC
4.4 Gavin and Stacey page 52		office conversation; phrases to describe routines		
UNIT 5 SOLUTIONS page 55 ▣ Video podcast I Are you good at solving problems?				
5.1 Machines page 56	comparatives and superlatives	technology	main syllable stress in words/phrases	read an article about how technology changed the world; read an essay about the advantages and disadvantages of technology
5.2 Ask the experts page 59	question tags	words related to questions; wors building: adjectives	falling/rising intonation in question tags	read a book review
5.3 It's out of order page 62	polite requests	problems and solutions	polite intonation in requests	read a short text about PC anger in the workplace
5.4 Top Gear page 64		presentation phrases to describe a machine		
IRREGULAR VERBS page 127 LANGUAGE BANK page 128 VOCABULARY BANK page 148				

LISTENING/DVD	SPEAKING	WRITING
listen to someone describing their family history	talk about family events: talk about people in your life	write an email of introduction; learn to use formal and informal styles
listen to a set of instructions and do a test	discuss the differences between men and women	
listen to a set of interviews; learn to understand and use DVD-word responses	talk about type of interviews and interview experiences; role-play an interview	
The Money Programme: Second Life: watch and understand a documentary about life online	discuss and create a new identity	write answers to a questionnaire
listen to a radio programme about important roles in films	talk about life experiences; talk about your life story	
listen to news reports	talk about an important news story/event	write a news report; learn to use time linkers: *as soon as, while, during, until and by the time*
listen to people telling anecdotes; learn to keep a story going	tell a true story or a lie	
Hustle: watch and listen to a drama about a burglar and a famous painting	discuss fictional crime dramas; tell a narrative	write a short newpaper article
	discuss attitudes now in comparison to ones you had earlier in life	write messages; learn to use note form
listen to predictions about the future of communication	talk about how things will change in the future	
listen to telephone conversations involving misunderstandings	learn to reformulate and retell a story about a misunderstanding; role-play resolving a misunderstanding	
The Virtual Revolution: watch and understand a documentary about the impact of the internet	talk about communication preferences	write a memo
	discuss the qualities needed for different jobs; complete a survey and discuss the results	
listen to two people describing dream jobs gone wrong	talk about past habits	write a covering letter; learn to organise your ideas
listen to people making decisions in a meeting	learn to manage a discussion; participate in a meeting and create a business plan	
Gavin and Stacey: watch and understand a comedy programme about a man's first day in a new job	describe a day in your life	write about daily routines
	discuss how technology has changed the world; talk about different types of transport and their uses	write an advantages versus disadvantages essay; learn to use discourse markers
listen to peole answering difficult general knowledge questions	do a short general knowlege questionnaire; answer questions on your area of expertise	
listen to conversations about technical problems: learn to respond to requests	role-play asking and responding to requests	
Top Gear: watch and understand a programme about a race between a car and two people	present and describe a new machine	write an advertisement for a new machine

COMMUNICATION BANK page 158   AUDIO SCRIPTS page 164

Source: A. Clare and J. Wilson, Contents pages from *Speakout Intermediate Student's Book*. Pearson Longman, 2011. Reprinted with permission of Pearson Education Ltd.

2.2   Communicative Language Teaching and Its Influences

The communicative approach challenged the prevailing structural view of language and language teaching in the 1960s and innovated many aspects of course design, incorporating insights into language use, language learning and teaching from the 1970s to the early 1980s. Some of the principles of the communicative approach have come to be an explicit or implicit part of English language teaching in the everyday professional lives of teachers in many parts of the world. Communicative design criteria permeate both general coursebooks and materials covering specific language skills as well as the methodology of the classroom. For example, the two tables of contents we have looked at in the previous section include familiar categories of grammar, vocabulary and pronunciation. These categories were the norm in coursebooks in the 1960s, and they are still widely used. Categories such as 'function/functional language' and the four skills show the influence of the communicative approach from the 1970s onwards. What we are now seeing is the influence of both the structuralism of the 1960s and the communicative approach of the 1970s and 1980s in the materials of the new millennium, so they continue to influence our classroom teaching today. Richards and Rodgers (2001: 151) state:

> Communicative Language Teaching (CLT) marks the beginning of a major paradigm shift within language teaching in the twentieth century, one whose ramifications continue to be felt today. The general principles of Communicative Language Teaching are today widely accepted around the world.

What kinds of paradigm shift took place in the 1970s? What are the general principles of Communicative Language Teaching (CLT)? Before exploring the implications of CLT for materials and methods, it is worth reiterating the point that CLT is an 'approach' in the sense that it represents 'a diverse set of principles that reflect a communicative view of language and language learning and that can be used to support a wide variety of classroom procedures' (Richards and Rodgers, 2001: 172). This means that how exactly these principles are realized as materials, methods and classroom procedures depends on how the fundamental tenets are interpreted and applied.

We need to be aware that CLT as an approach has evolved over the years. For example, Richards and Rodgers (2001) identify three stages in its development:

> Since its inception CLT has passed through a number of different phases as its advocates have sought to apply its principles to different dimensions of the teaching/learning process. In its first phase, a primary concern was the need to develop a syllabus that was compatible with the notion of communicative competence. This led to proposals for the organization of syllabuses in terms of notions and functions rather than grammatical structures (Wilkins, 1976).

In the second phase, CLT focused on procedures for identifying learners' needs and this resulted in proposals to make needs analysis an essential component of communicative methodology (Munby, 1978). In the third phase, CLT focused on the kinds of classroom activities that could be used as the basis of a communicative methodology, such as group work, task-work, and information gap activities. (Prabhu, 1987)

It is neither appropriate nor possible within the scope of this book to set out all the many ramifications of 'the communicative approach': inappropriate, because our main intention is to look at its impact on learning, teaching methodology and materials today rather than at the theory and background in themselves; impossible, because the concept covers a potentially vast area touching on many disciplines (philosophy, linguistics, sociology, psychology and anthropology). There are several readily available works for teachers interested in an overview of the historical accounts and various debates that took place in the 1980s–1990s (e.g. Richards and Rodgers, 2001; McDonough and Shaw, 2003).

It is vital, however, to revisit the fundamental tenets of communicative approaches because they constitute the foundations of post-communicative approaches and materials. We would now like to explore what we think are the most significant factors within the broad concept of the 'communicative approach' as the background to the main discussion of this chapter. As a whole, CLT shifted the goal of language teaching from mastering linguistic properties (e.g. pronunciation, vocabulary, grammar) to that of acquiring communicative competence. There are some variations regarding what exactly constitutes communicative competence depending on views of the nature of the language system and its functions (Hymes, 1972; Halliday, 1975; Wilkins, 1976) and emphasis on different theoretical insights (Canale and Swain, 1980). Larsen-Freeman and Anderson (2011: 115) provide a concise description of communicative competence: 'In short, being able to communicate required more than linguistic competence . . . – knowing when and how to say what to whom. The shift in focus towards the "real-world" use of language required considering the dimensions of context, topic, and roles of the people involved. In methodology and materials such a new paradigm led to revisiting our view of language and how it is used, how a language may be learned and how it can be taught'. We shall restrict ourselves here to trying to show those implications that have most helped to form the kinds of teaching materials we work with and our attitudes to managing our classrooms. As we go through this section, we suggest from time to time some points for you to consider in relation to your own experience, both of language and teaching.

Implication 1

In its broadest sense, the concept of 'being communicative' has to do with what a language has the potential to mean, as well as with its formal grammatical properties. The research of the 1970s laid the foundations for this view, which is particularly associated with the work of Wilkins (1976) originally carried out for the Council of Europe. Wilkins proposed two categories of communicative meaning: 'notional' (or 'semantico-grammatical') and 'functional'. The distinction between these two terms is clearly set out by Johnson (1981). 'Notions' are rather abstract concepts – frequency, duration, dimension, location, quantity and so on – which in English are closely related to grammatical categories. So, for instance, expressing 'frequency' involves tense selection and certain adverbial constructions. ('They often used to visit friends'; 'I talk to my students regularly', for example.) 'Functions', on the other hand, refer to the practical uses to which we put language, most usually in interaction with other people. Johnson suggests that, to find out the function of any particular utterance, we can simply ask, 'what was the speaker's intention in saying it?' (Johnson, 1981: 5). For example, a short statement like 'I'll do that!' could be an offer of help, but it could also be a warning, if the speaker believes that the other person is likely to be in danger when trying to carry out some activity; while 'Do you smoke?' could be a straightforward enquiry, perhaps asked during a medical examination, or it could be an indirect request for a cigarette. Other functional categories often found in teaching materials include making requests, greeting, making suggestions, asking for directions, giving advice. Having awareness of communicative functions helps learners to understand the fact that communication could break down if they only focus on linguistic (semantico-grammatical) meaning and ignore the intended use of the utterance (i.e. function) by the speaker. For example, imagine that a person struggling to open a door with a lot of luggage turns around and asks your student, 'Can you open the door?' If your student gives a grammatically correct answer 'Yes, I can' without taking any action it could cause offence as the answer shows lack of understanding of the embedded function of 'making a request'.

> Think of some more examples of functions in English and the grammatical structures related to them. You could also think about comparable patterns in your own language.

The semantic criteria outlined here have obvious implications for the design and organization of teaching materials. Let us consider a simple conversational statement like 'Give me your telephone number'. This could, of course, be an order, if spoken by a policeman to a motorist who has committed a traffic offence. However, if said, with suitable intonation, to an acquaintance, it could be a suggestion about a way of getting in touch. Or 'If you don't sit down, there'll be a problem' could be interpreted as either

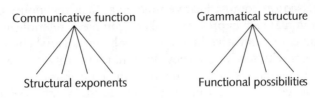

Figure 2.1   Form and function.

threatening or helpful. In other words, a grammatical structure can in principle perform a number of different communicative functions – an imperative might, for example, be a command or a suggestion, a conditional might be selected to threaten, to warn or alternatively to give advice.

The converse relationship also holds, where a single function can be expressed in a number of different ways. To make a suggestion, for instance, we can choose to say, 'You should . . .', 'You ought to . . .', 'Why don't you . . . ?', 'You'd better . . .', 'I think you should . . .', 'Have you thought of . . . ?', and undoubtedly there are several other possibilities. (In the Council of Europe's terms (van Ek, 1977), these structural items are referred to as 'exponents' of a particular function.) Figure 2.1 summarizes the relationships.

In more traditional teaching materials, this complex form–function relationship tends to be simplified, often implying a one-to-one correspondence, so that 'interrogatives' are used for 'asking questions', 'imperatives' for 'giving commands', 'conditionals' for 'making hypothetical statements' and so on. From a communicative perspective, this relationship is explored more carefully, and as a result our views on the properties of language have been expanded and enriched. However, there are a number of pedagogic problems associated with this approach to materials design, particularly to do with the sequencing of the language to be practised.

> How do your teaching materials handle the relationship between grammar and communicative function? Are communicative functions taught at all? If so, is a 'function' taught together with several grammatical forms, or just one? Alternatively, is a 'function' just used as an example where the main focus is on teaching grammar?

Materials developers in the 1970s and 1980s faced a dilemma. On the one hand, if they followed a traditional grammar syllabus, how should functions be incorporated? The same sentence could have various functions, depending on how it is used. On the other hand, if the main spine of the syllabus is based on communicative functions, each function would involve different grammatical expressions. The complex relationships between grammar and communicative functions may be too overwhelming for beginners or learners with low proficiency. We will revisit this issue when we look at some current coursebooks. Meanwhile, the contribution of CLT deserves our acknowledgement in setting communication as the goal of language education and in identifying the roles of functions as well as linguistic structures.

Implication 2

Real-world language in use does not operate in a vacuum, and this is the second implication of the communicative approach. When we give advice, we do so to someone, about something, for a particular reason. If we are invited, it is by someone to do something, or to attend something. So in addition to talking about language function and language form, there are other dimensions of communication to be considered if we are to be offered a more complete picture. These are, at least

1   Topics, for example, health, transport, work, leisure activities, politics and so on.
2   Context or setting, which may refer to both physical and social settings, and may therefore include personal conversation and business discussion as well as the more traditional 'situations' such as travel or medical or leisure-time settings.
3   Roles of people involved: whether, for example, stranger/stranger, friend/friend, employee/boss, colleague/colleague, customer/person supplying a service.

Two short and simple examples will serve to illustrate this:

a   Can I have a kilo of those red apples, and three lemons please?
b   Anything else?
c   That's all, thanks.
d   £1.50 please.

a   This is really good, but a bit expensive.
b   Manchester restaurants are much cheaper.
c   Who's paying?

Language function and language form, then, do not operate in isolation but as part of a network of interconnected factors, all of which need to be taken into account in materials that use a communicative concept as their design principle. Based on a large amount of data from spoken language known as a 'corpus', Carter et al. (2011) and O'Keeffe et al. (2007) explain how spoken grammar is distinctly different from written grammar. There are also principles of conversation (McCarten and McCarthy, 2010) in which social interactions play an important role. We will elaborate on this point in Chapter 8, Speaking Skills.

Alongside this there is often a stated requirement for 'authenticity' – a term that loosely implies as close an approximation as possible to the world outside the classroom, in the selection both of language material and of the activities and methods used for practice in the classroom. The issue of 'authenticity' has been somewhat controversial, and there is no space here to go into the complexities of the argument: for readers who wish to do so, Mishan (2005) offers an extensive discussion on the relationship between teaching materials and the concept of authenticity. After reviewing 30 years of debate on authenticity including the relationship with Internet technology, she lists

> . . . a set of criteria 'by which the authenticity of texts' might be assessed in the context of language learning materials design:
> 1   Provenance and authorship of the text
> 2   Original communicative and socio-cultural purpose of the text
> 3   Original context (e.g. its source, socio-cultural context) of the text
> 4   Learners' perceptions of and attitudes to the text and the activity pertaining to it. (Mishan, 2005: 18)

In relation to the notion of authenticity, CLT has recently provoked a debate in relation to the perceived clash between the source culture and that of the adopters' cultures (Holliday, 1994; Kramsch and Sullivan, 1996; Holliday, 2005). As Pham (2007:196) puts it, echoing Kramsch and Sullivan (1996), 'What is authentic in London may not be authentic in Hanoi'. Taking the reality outside into the classroom invites discussion of the intercultural appropriacy of introducing language use in different contexts together with the accompanying methodology. We will discuss this issue in Chapter 11. It was CLT that pioneered attempts to capture the reality of language use and to introduce it into classroom materials.

Implication 3

Once we move away from the idea that mastery of grammar = mastery of a language, we are obliged at the same time to move away from evaluating our learners' proficiency on the basis of accuracy alone. It is undoubtedly desirable that their language production should be as 'correct' as possible, but we have seen that grammaticality also takes place in a wider social and communicative context. The implication here is that we should concern our-selves not only with accuracy of form, but also with appropriacy in relation to the context. This derives in part from Hymes's view of language as includ-ing 'what a speaker needs to know in order to be communicatively competent in a speech community' (Richards and Rodgers, 2001: 70). The communica-tive approach has therefore led to a broadening of the criteria by which language proficiency is defined. We now have the concepts of appropriacy as well as accuracy, communicative as well as grammatical competence, use as well as usage (Widdowson, 1978).

For teaching purposes, these considerations clearly lead to a rethinking of attitudes to, and the treatment of, learners' grammatical errors. For example, if a learner tries to buy a train ticket by saying 'Give me a ticket to London (please)', or writes to a college for information with the phrase 'Send me your prospectus', he may show satisfactory mastery of language form, but he is offending certain forms of sociolinguistic behaviour. We may say, 'What?' to a friend we have not understood, but we would be advised to say, 'Pardon?' to the boss; 'Shut the door, will you?' may be appropriate within the family, but 'Excuse me, would you mind closing the door?' for a stranger on the train (example from Littlewood, 1981: 4). We can also look at 'error' from another perspective, and ask whether to prefer *'Please could you to send me your prospectus?' or *'Can I have six air letters, please?' to the choice of an imperative form. (* is a symbol used to denote grammatical inaccuracy.)

We can see from this that the notion of error is no longer restricted only to incorrect grammar or perhaps choice of vocabulary. If 'being communicative' includes also paying attention to context, roles and topics, then it is logically possible to make an error at any of these levels. It is even possible – though this can only be mentioned in passing – to make 'cultural' errors: an English person's way of thanking someone for a present is to say, 'You really shouldn't have done that', readily interpretable as a reprimand by a giver who is not familiar with the normal response. (See also Cook, 1989: 123–5, for other examples and Bartram and Walton, 1991.)

The extent to which error types are significant depends very much on particular teaching situations, and on the objectives of specific programmes. It is certainly not possible to make generalizations, and what may be tolerated in one case may be unacceptable in another. But even a partial acceptance of communicative criteria will allow for a certain amount of creativity and exploration in language learning, and this will inevitably extend the frame-work in which errors are evaluated. Chapter 9, Writing Skills, offers more detailed discussions on what may constitute so-called 'errors' and various ways of providing error feedback. See also Chapter 8, Speaking, in which we look at the use of language in oral interactions and the characteristics of English as a lingua franca, or world Englishes in relation to changing notions of 'correctness'.

Implication 4

Materials based on an approach to teaching that takes mastery of the formal system of a language as its major objective are likely to use the grammatical concept of the sentence as the basis for exercises. We may find, for example, the instruction 'Put the verb in infinitive form into the present perfect' or 'Join each pair of sentences with a relative pronoun', followed perhaps by 10 numbered sentences. Not much real-life communication proceeds strictly according to such fixed patterning. A letter to a friend, for instance, is unlikely to be only a string of sentences:

I went to the USA.
I went to New York.
I saw the Statue of Liberty.
I flew by Concorde.

Nor does this conversation sound natural, although, like the letter, it practises some useful verb structures, and the questions and answers are at least related:

Where did you go for your holidays? I went to New York.
What did you do? I saw the Statue of Liberty.
How did you travel? I flew by Concorde.

A concept of communication does not have to be based on sentence-level criteria, and it can allow language to be described, and language learning to take place, over longer stretches. In principle it can handle whole conversations, or paragraphs, or even longer texts. In recent years, a number of categories for describing language have been developed that are not based on sentence-level criteria, but on the broader notion of 'discourse'. There is a large and growing background literature on 'discourse analysis', and a detailed explanation of these categories is outside the scope and intention of this book. Essentially, the notion gives us the possibility of showing how different parts of a text or a conversation or any stretch of language are interlinked. This may be, for example, by cross-referencing with pronoun use or definite articles; by semantic links across items of vocabulary; by markers of logical development ('however', 'therefore', 'so', 'because' and the like); by ellipsis in conversation (the 'short answers' of coursebook practice); and by substitution ('this is my book, yours is the other one'). This is usually referred to as the concept of 'cohesion', whereby relationships between different elements in a text (written or spoken) are made explicit. Alternatively, a 'text' in this sense may be described in terms of its intention and its thematic coherence, in simple terms whether it 'makes sense' or not. It is important to note that a stretch of language may be 'coherent' even if it contains no explicit markers of cohesion; and conversely may be 'cohesive' but make no sense. A useful summary is provided in Nunan (1999: ch. 4). Celce-Murcia and Olshtain (2000) have devoted a whole book to showing how notions of discourse have practical applications in teaching.

Implication 5

Particularly in the early phase of the 'communicative revolution', it was sometimes assumed – mistakenly – that the approach was only really valid for teaching the spoken language, when learners needed to make conversation in English. The assumption is an understandable one, since face-to-face interaction is the most obvious kind of communication with other people, and learners were and are increasingly felt to need oral skills, given the greater opportunities for travel and for communication with English speakers visiting their countries.

It is important to realize that 'communicative' can in fact refer to all four language skills. We can look at this in two different ways. Firstly, we can divide the 'four skills' into 'productive' (speaking and writing) and 'receptive' (listening and reading) and practise them separately. It is possible to do this successfully from a communicative perspective, as we shall see in Part II of this book. However, treating the skills discretely can also lead to a concern for accuracy in production and an emphasis, in comprehension, on the grammatical characteristics of written and spoken material. More usefully, we can group together the oral/aural skills of speaking and listening, and the 'paper skills' of reading and writing. In both cases, we have a giver and a receiver of a message, and the ways in which the information in the message is understood by the receiver is an integral part of the communication. This is true whether we think of a brief exchange, a letter, a book, or an extended discussion. Possibilities of this kind for exploring the four skills, and integrating them with each other, will be examined in more detail in Part II.

> How do you interpret the idea of 'communicating in English' for your own learners? What, in other words, are their particular 'communicative needs', and to what extent are each of the 'four skills' important?

Implication 6

Finally, the term 'communicative' itself has been used in relation to teaching in two distinct though related ways, and this apparent ambiguity has sometimes been a source of confusion. Firstly, as we have seen from a number of the implications outlined in this section, the concept can refer to a view of the nature of language, leading to the procedures that have been detailed for a 'functional' analysis of language. In other words, language is seen to have inherent communicative as well as grammatical properties.

Secondly, a communicative approach also implies a concern with behaviour, with patterns of interaction as well as linguistic content. Morrow (1981) makes a simple and useful distinction between the 'what' – the contents of a language programme – and the 'how' – the ways in which that content might be learned and taught. This behavioural 'how' would cover the kinds of activities we carry out and the tasks we perform, such as writing a letter, or an essay, or talking to a friend, at a meeting, to a stranger and so on. We shall see in the next two parts of the book how such activities can be implemented in the classroom (1) in terms of the framework of skills and activities that we use for language learning activities, and (2) in the various possibilities available for structuring and managing the classroom itself.

Thompson (1996) looks at some of these implications from a different angle, arguing that considerable confusion still surrounds clear definitions of CLT, leading to four fundamental misconceptions, namely that (1) CLT means not teaching grammar, (2) CLT means teaching only speaking, (3) CLT means pairwork, which means role play, and (4) CLT means expecting too much from the teacher. We will discuss these controversies in more detail in Chapter 11.

More recent materials have reacted in various ways to and against the communicative movement of the 1970s. However, the main principles, with varying degrees of change and modification, have had a lasting impact on materials and methods that should not be underestimated. As Thompson (1996: 14–5) puts it: 'CLT is by no means the final answer. . . . But whatever innovations emerge, they will do so against the background of the changes brought about by CLT. . . . Certain of them are too important to lose: the concern with the world beyond the classroom, the concern with the learner as an individual, the view of language as structured to carry out the functions we want it to perform'.

1   Look at the syllabus guidelines for your own situation, if they are available. Are claims made there for 'communicative' objectives? Since it is the teacher who has to interpret them, how are the general objectives translated into your everyday classroom reality? (If you are working in a group of teachers from different backgrounds, you might like to compare your observations with those of others.)

2   How does your coursebook deal with the following issues?
   • What is the role of grammar in the unit?
   • What language skills are practised?
   • To what extent does the unit deal with (1) communicative functions as properties of language, (2) communicative behaviour and activities?
   • How large are the stretches of language that learners are asked to deal with? How much of the language practice is concerned with the manipulation of sentence structure?
   • Do learners have any freedom to 'create' meanings and language for themselves? Can they in any sense 'be themselves', and talk about their own interests, wishes, needs?

2.3   Some Claims for Current Materials

In the previous section, we have looked at the impact of CLT and its implications for materials and methods. We have also considered some controversies and debates. An obvious question, when discussing developments in materials design after CLT, is whether the influences can be detected in current materials after many debates and the test of time. Nunan (1999: 2) thinks that 'contemporary practice represents an evolution, and . . . the best practice incorporates the best of "traditional" practice rather than rejecting it'. We need, then, to ask to what extent current materials show evolution while retaining the best legacies. Let us now look at the kinds of claims that are being made, taken from the blurbs of a number of published global coursebooks (italics are ours):

• 'It enables you to learn English *as it is used in our globalized world*, to *learn through English* using information-rich topics, and to learn about *English as an international language*'.
   '. . . offers a comprehensive range of *interactive digital components for use in class, out of class and even on the move*. These include *extra listening, video material and online practice*'. (Clandfield and Jeffries, 2010)

• 'With its *wide range of support materials*, it meets the *diverse needs of learners* in *a variety of teaching situations* and helps to *bridge the gap between the classroom and the real world*'. (Clare and Wilson, 2011)

- '*Natural, real-world grammar and vocabulary* help students to *succeed in social, professional and academic settings*'. (Dellar and Walkley, 2010)
- '. . . is an *integrated skills* series which is designed to offer flexibility with *different teaching and learning styles*'.

   '*fully integrated grammar, skills and lexical syllabuses* provide a balanced learning experience'

   '*Contextualised vocabulary* focuses on *authentic real-world language*'

   '*Clearly structured grammar presentations* are reinforced with *extensive practice*'

   '*Free MP3 files* for all activities in the Student's Book *available online*'. (Harmer, 2012)
- '. . . prepares learners to *use English independently for global communication*'.

   '*Real life* every step of the way . . . practical *CEF goals at the core of the course* . . . *achieving purposeful real life objectives* . . . language that's natural and dependable – *guaranteed by the* . . . *Corpus* . . . *Authentic audio throughout* builds learners' ability to *understand the natural English of international speakers*'.

   '*Building global relationships* . . . develop learners' *intercultural competence as a "fifth skill"*, leading to a *more sensitive and more effective communication* . . .'. (Rea et al., 2011)

It is not difficult to identify some mainstream communicative themes in this selection – authentic real-world language, diverse needs of learners, integrated skills, effective communication in various settings. At the same time, there clearly are a number of further elements here. We find more explicit statements about English as an international language; reference to the communicative goals of the Common European Framework (see below, Section 2.6; use of corpora; use of technology in providing multimedia components; contextualized vocabulary and grammar; and mention of 'learning styles' and strategies in learning as well as learner independence). For convenience, we shall now divide these claims into two broad and related areas: content and learning. Several of them come together in the phrase 'the multi-component syllabus', which we shall explore in the first of the next two sections.

2.4   Organization and Coverage

Multi-component syllabus

Teaching materials following a traditional structural approach typically appear as an ordered list of grammatical items – perhaps

1   Simple present active
2   Present continuous
3   Simple past

and so on. There is here a single organizing principle that provides the material to be taught and learned in each unit or section of the course. However, it is likely that learners will not only be expected to formulate rules and manipulate structures in a vacuum; they will probably be given a situation or a topic as a context for practice. In other words, even traditional materials may have a primary organizing principle (structures) and a secondary one (topics or situations) – see the discussion of syllabus in Chapter 1. We might, say, teach the present perfect by asking our students about things they have done or places they have visited; regular activities and habits are often used to teach the simple present. Earlier in this chapter we saw how the development of the communicative approach not only consolidated a two-tier arrangement (functions and structures), but also opened up the possibility of the principled inclusion of other 'layers' of organization (functions, structures, roles, skills, topics, situations), although, with some exceptions, this was not fully explored in the materials of the time. It is in the last 20 years or so that the idea of a multilayered syllabus has begun to be more explicitly and systematically addressed.

The Tables of Contents on pp. 35–38 – referred to as a 'Map' – are two examples of a multi-component syllabus approach. What do you notice? What kinds of categories of content does each coursebook offer? Note down some of the similarities and differences you find between the two maps.

	Goals	Language	Skills	Explore
1 pages 6–13	**Media around the world** ⊜ talk about entertainment media ⊜ talk about habits ⊜ express preferences ⊜ talk about information media ⊜ evaluate ideas ⊜ make recommendations ⊜ describe a book or TV show ⊙ **Target activity** Describe a book or a TV show	**Vocabulary** Habits and preferences p6 Talking about facts and information p8 Evaluating and recommending p9 Describing books and TV shows p10 **Grammar** Talking about the present p7 **Pronunciation** Common pairs of words 1 p7	**Listening** TV and radio habits p6 What's on TV? p7 Four people describe books and TV show p10 **Reading** Can you believe what you read? p8 **Writing and speaking** Media habits p7 **Speaking** Is it true? p9 Make recommendations p9	**Across cultures** Intercultural experiences **EXPLOREWriting** ⊜ write a book review for a website **Look again**◌ Spelling and sounds: /f/
2 pages 14–21	**Good communication** ⊜ talk about methods of communication ⊜ express opinions ⊜ talk about using the Internet ⊜ speculate about the present and future ⊜ speculate about consequences ⊙ **Target activity** Discuss an issue	**Vocabulary** Expressing opinions p15 It's + adjectives p15 Using the Internet p16 Expressing probability p17 Speculating about consequences p18 **Grammar** will, could, may, might p17 **Pronunciation** Sentence stress p15	**Listening** Keeping in touch p14 Eric and Graham discuss a management decision p18 **Reading** Online friendships p16 Email Survival Guide p18 **Speaking** Express opinions p15 Socialising online p17 Is it likely? p17	**Keywords** so, such **EXPLORESpeaking** ⊜ ask for clarification ⊜ clarify what you're saying **Look again**◌ Spelling and sounds: /tʃ/
3 pages 22–29	**Success** ⊜ talk about a business idea ⊜ talk about hopes, dreams and ambitions ⊜ talk about abilities ⊜ talk about achievements ⊜ take part in an interview ⊙ **Target activity** Sell an idea	**Vocabulary** Talking about a business idea p23 Hopes, dreams and ambitions p23 Abilities p24 Facts and feeling p26 **Grammar** Present perfect and time expressions p25 **Pronunciation** Schwa /ə/ p23	**Listening** I've always wanted to … p23 I'm most proud of … p25 Olga's 'easybag' p26 **Reading** Inventors: karaoke; the iPod p22 What is intelligence? p24 **Speaking** Business ideas p23 Your hopes, dreams and ambitions p23 Your achievements p25	**Across cultures** Attitudes to success **EXPLOREWriting** ⊜ take notes **Look again**◌ Spelling and sounds: /s/
4 pages 30–37	**What happened?** ⊜ talk abou accidents and injuries ⊜ explain how something happened ⊜ talk about natural events ⊜ describe a dramatic experience ⊜ say how you feel about an experience ⊙ **Target activity** Describe a dramatic experience	**Vocabulary** Accidents and injuries p31 Saying how something happened p31 Natural events p32 Adverbs for telling stories p33 Common verbs in stories p34 **Grammar** Narrative verb forms p32 **Pronunciation** Groups of words 1 p33	**Listening** Ouch! Five accidents p31 Stories: tsunami; eclipse p32 Megan's accident p34 **Reading** Why so clumsy? p30 **Speaking** Quiz: Safety first p30 What happened? p31 Retelling a story p33	**Keywords** over **EXPLORESpeaking** ⊜ Refer to an earlier topic or conversation **Look again**◌ Spelling and sounds: /k/
5 pages 38–45	**A change of plan** ⊜ discuss plans and arrangements ⊜ make offers and promises ⊜ talk about something that went wrong ⊜ talk about changes of plan ⊜ catch up with old friends' news ⊙ **Target activity** Attend a reunion	**Vocabulary** be supposed to, be meant to p38 no chace, no way p41 Catching up p42 **Grammar** Future forms p38 Future in the past p41 **Pronunciation** Common pairs of words 2 p39	**Listening** Locked out p38 Pierre and Munizha talk about fate p40 Maggie's story p41 Carolina and Iqbal catch up p42 **Reading** True Story competition p40 **Speaking** Ask a friend for help p39 Changes of plan p41	**Across cultures** Saying no **EXPLOREWriting** ⊜ make offers and promises in emails or letters ⊜ refer back in emails or letters **Look again**◌ Spelling and sounds: /r/

	Goals	Language	Skills	Explore
6 pages 46–53	**Let me explain** ⊚ give advice ⊚ talk about how you manage money ⊚ give detailed instructions ⊚ give reasons for advice ⊚**Target activity** Give expert advice	**Vocabulary** Linking expressions p46 Multi-word verbs: managing money p47 Using equipment p48 Giving reasons p50 **Grammar** Verb + -ing p49 **Pronunciation** Linking consonants and vowels p49	**Listening** Vishal phones a computer helpline p48 Managing money p50 **Reading** How I lived on £1 a day pp46–7 Misunderstandings p48 **Speaking** Are you good with money? P47 Give instructions p49 Give advice p49	**Keyword** *mean* **EXPLORESpeaking** ⊚ say you don't understand ⊚ ask for help ⊚ explain something **Look again** ○ Spelling and sounds /ɔː/
7 pages 54–61	**Personal qualities** ⊚ describe qualities you need for different activities ⊚ describe personality ⊚ make comparisons ⊚ say how a person has influenced you ⊚**Target activity** Talk about people who have influenced you	**Vocabulary** Personal qualities p55 Matching people to jobs and activities p55 Personality p57 Describing someone's influence p58 **Grammar** Comparing p49 **Pronunciation** Contrastive stress p49	**Listening** Interview with a dancer p55 Five different pets p56 Tara talks about her role models p58 **Reading** Interview: Carlos Acosta p54 Pets and their owners p56 **Writing and speaking** 5–minute interviews p54 **Speaking** Match people to jobs p55 Compare people you know p57	**Across cultures** Roles in life **EXPLOREWriting** ⊚ compare and contrast two alternatives ⊚ organise ideas 1 **Look again** ○ Spelling and sounds /iː/
8 pages 62–69	**Lost and found** ⊚ talk about attitudes to possessions ⊚ describe objects ⊚ talk about unexpected travel situations ⊚ discuss options and decide what to do ⊚ make deductions ⊚**Target activity** Find something at lost property	**Vocabulary** Multi-word verbs: tidying and cleaning p63 Discussing products p63 Travel situations p64 Describing objects p66 **Grammar** Modals of deduction and speculation p65 **Pronunciation** Emphatic stress p65	**Listening** Alice and Javier's nightmare journey p64 Lost property p58 **Reading** Declutter your life! p62 **Writing and speaking** Freecycle P63 **Speaking** Travel problems P64 Find your way home p65	**Keyword** *have* **EXPLORESpeaking** ⊚ describe objects you don't know the name of ⊚ use vague language to describe things **Look again** ○ Spelling and sounds /ɑː/
9 pages 70–77	**Make up your mind** ⊚ describe problems in the home ⊚ discuss solutions ⊚ talk about decision-making ⊚ discuss the consequences of decisions ⊚ negotiate ⊚**Target activity** Reach a compromise	**Vocabulary** Problems in the home p70 Discussing problems and solutions p71 Decision-making p72 Negotiating p74 **Grammar** Real and unreal conditionals p73 **Pronunciation** Groups of words 2 p73	**Listening** What shall we do? p71 A new business p73 Flatmates p74 **Reading** Blogs: domestic disasters p70 Six Thinking Hats p72 **Speaking** Solve domestic problems P71 Discuss decisions p72 Consequences p73	**Across cultures** Dealing with conflict **EXPLOREWriting** ⊚ write a web posting explaining an argument ⊚ organise ideas 2 **Look again** ○ Spelling and sounds /ɜː/
10 pages 78–85	**Impressions** ⊚ talk about memory ⊚ talk about what you remember ⊚ talk about complaining ⊚ complain about goods or services ⊚ ask for a refund or replacement and explain why ⊚ make a complaint politely ⊚**Target activity** Resolve a dispute	**Vocabulary** Remembering an event p78 Problems with things you've bought p80 Softeners p82 **Grammar** Verb patterns p79 Present perfect simple and progressive p81 **Pronunciation** Intonation in questions p81	**Listening** Hiromi witnesses a crime p78 Complaining in different countries p80 Mariah makes a complaint p80 Good neighbours? p82 **Reading** The problem with witnesses p79 **Speaking** Can you remember … ? p79 Complain about something you've bought p81	**Keyword** *of* **EXPLORESpeaking** ⊚ add comments to say how you feel **Look again** ○ Spelling and sounds /uː/

Source: A. Tilbury, T. Clementson, L. A. Hendra, D. Rea and A. Doff, From *English Unlimited Elementary Coursebook* with e-Portfolio, pp. 2–3. Cambridge University Press, 2010. Reprinted with permission of Cambridge University Press.

	In this unit you learn how to
01 MY FIRST CLASS p.8	• ask and answer common questions • maintain a conversation • talk about language learning experiences • tell stories
02 FEELINGS p.14	• talk about how you feel – and why • give responses to news • use stress and intonation more effectively • ask double questions
03 TIME OFF p.20	• describe interesting places • ask for and make recommendations • talk about problems • talk about the weather
04 INTERESTS p.26	• talk about free-time activities • talk about sports • talk about music • pronounce, and understand, groups of words
Review 01 p.32 **Writing 01** p.120 **Writing 02** p.122	This Review unit revises units 1–4 Introducing yourself Short emails
05 WORKING LIFE p.36	• talk about jobs • talk about what jobs involve • add comments using *That must be*
06 GOING SHOPPING p.42	• describe things you buy • describe clothes • compare products • make, and respond to, recommendations
07 SCHOOL AND STUDYING p.48	• describe courses, schools, teachers and students • use different forms of a word • talk about different education systems • talk about possible future plans
08 EATING p.54	• describe different dishes and ways of cooking food • explain what is on a menu – and order • describe restaurants
Review 02 p.60 **Writing 03** p.124 **Writing 04** p.126	This Review unit revises units 5–8 Stories Making requests

Grammar	Vocabulary	Reading	Listening	Developing conversations
• Question formation • Narrative tenses • Other uses of the past continuous	• Learning languages • Language words	• 'Language policy a disaster' says head teacher	• Getting to know people • Explaining why you were late	• Asking follow-up questions • *John was telling me ...*
• *be, look, seem* etc • *-ing / -ed* adjectives • The present continuous • Present continuous / simple questions	• Feelings • Adjective collocations	• It only takes Juan Mann to save the world!	• How's it going? • How's it going at work?	• Response expressions • Making excuses
• Present perfect questions • The future	• Places of interest • Holiday problems • Weather	• Workers can't bank on holidays	• Deciding where to go sightseeing • Talking about your holiday plans	• Recommendations
• Frequency (present and past) • Duration (past simple and present perfect continuous)	• Evening and weekend activities • Problems and sports • Music	• The playlist of your life	• Did you have a good weekend? • A martial art	• *Are you any good?* • Music, films and books
• Rules: *have to, don't have to, can* • Rules: *allowed to, supposed to, should*	• Jobs • Workplaces and activities • *be used to, get used to*	• Terrible jobs not a thing of the past	• What does your job involve? • Rules at work	• *That must be ...*
• *must*	• Describing souvenirs and presents • Clothes and accessories	• Shop till you drop!	• Negotiating prices • Comparing mobile phones • The best way to buy tickets for a gig	• Avoiding repetition • Responding to recommendations
• *after, once* and *when* • Zero and first conditionals	• Describing courses • Forming words • Schools, teachers and students	• Learning to be happy	• Describing how a course is going • Different aspects of education	• *How's the couse going?*
• *tend to* • Second conditionals	• Describing food • Restaurants • *Over-*	• Food for thought	• Ordering dinner in a peruvian restaurant • Conversations about restaurants and food	• Describing dishes

Source: H. Dellar and A. Walkley, Coursebook map from *Outcomes Intermediate 1E.* Heinle/ELT, 2011. Copyright © 2011 Heinle/ELT, a part of Cengage Learning, Inc. Reprinted with permission. http://www.cengage.com/permissions

At first sight both maps seem complex, if rich, views of materials design, because several (in this case, eight) syllabus possibilities are in play. Not only do the details have to be specified for each individual organizing principle, but the principles themselves then have to be linked in a systematic way that does not leave the learner faced with a number of separate lists of items. A more straightforward way of looking at this kind of multi-component syllabus is to see it in terms of a merging of two broad approaches. One of these is concerned with a view of language in use, and includes categories of function, context and language skill. The other is a version of a more formal linguistic syllabus, which comprises elements of grammar, pronunciation and vocabulary. Obviously these two approaches are not mutually exclusive: pronunciation and vocabulary, for instance, can both be practised in a context of use, or alternatively can be rehearsed in isolation. What a multi-component syllabus does is to build on a range of communicative criteria at the same time as acknowledging the need to provide systematic coverage of the formal properties of language. Bailey and Masuhara (2012) report a successful case in a global coursebook of combining the two strands in a coherent way. Earlier in Implication 1 in Section 2.2, we pointed out that CLT materials in the 1970s and 1980s had problems with the complex relationship between structural (semantico-grammatical) syllabuses and communicative function syllabuses. A similar conflict between the two strands was noted in Bailey and Masuhara (2012) in three out of four global coursebooks published between 2011 and 2012.

Take a close look at the two maps in pp. 35–38 again.

Take one specific unit from each of the two maps. Consider the following points:

1 Is there a particular communicative target with a real-life outcome? Or are the targets contextualized exercises of structures or lexical chunks?
2 Do different components cohere in terms of objective of the unit?

The emphasis on lexis

One of the areas that has recently received considerable attention in approaches to materials design is that of vocabulary or lexis. The teaching of vocabulary is a very large topic, and we shall restrict ourselves here to commenting briefly on its role in some current coursebooks. (For more discussion, see Chapter 6 for more details; see also Chapter 12 of Richards and Rodgers, 2001 and McCarten and McCarthy, 2010). Most of us – whether as learners or teachers – have experience of classrooms where practising vocabulary means learning lists of words, not always in relation to a real-world context and sometimes in the form of two columns, with a mother tongue equivalent for the foreign language word. We have probably noticed that vocabulary approached in this way is not always efficiently remembered and reused. It is typical of many current coursebooks that they are concerned (1) to rationalize vocabulary as content, in other words, to establish a principled framework and a set of contexts within which vocabulary development can take place, and (2) to base teaching on an understanding of the psychological mechanisms whereby people learn and remember lexical items. We shall comment on the background to the second of these in the next section. As far as the first point is concerned, we can note that it is unusual to find merely a list of words to be learned by rote: the multi-syllabus concept means that vocabulary is selected according to the other dimensions on which the materials are built. For example, English Unlimited (Rea et al., 2011) sets a target activity in each unit, based on one of the communication goals of the Common European Framework of Reference. Take as an example Unit 7 in which the target activity is to 'Talk about people who have influenced you'. The vocabulary sections appear as supporting parts in the sequence of integrated skills activities. The activities are meaning-focused and personalized. There is a lot of meaningful and varied exposure to lexical chunks in relation to personal qualities in roles in work or in life, which gradually prepare learners to achieve the target activity of the unit.

For most of us 'vocabulary' also means using a dictionary. A new dictionary for learners of English was published in 1987. The dictionary is called COBUILD, which stands, rather technically, for the 'Collins [Publisher] – Birmingham University International Language Database'. It is based on an extremely large corpus of language of billions of words, stored on a computer database. Sources of data are both the spoken and written language, and include magazines, books, broadcasts, conversations and many more. The philosophy of the dictionary is to provide 'above all a guide to ordinary everyday English', and frequency of occurrence is a key criterion for inclusion. It focuses particularly on the most common 2000–3000 words, the 'powerhouse of the language', and the examples given in the dictionary entries are taken from the source material. McCarten and McCarthy (2010), after giving an overview of corpus-based coursebooks, discuss how corpora can be used for building a syllabus of lexical chunks as well as single words to help the learners learn the language for communication. They also consider limitations and offer some guidelines in developing corpus-based materials.

The task-based approach

Approaches to task-based learning (TBL) can be seen as a significant further evolution of CLT, both in terms of views of language in use and the development of classroom methodology. Although teachers have been operating with the notion for some time, it is only in recent years that frameworks have become more explicit and formalized. J. Willis (1996: 23) offers a simple definition: 'tasks are always activities where the target language is used by the learner for a communicative purpose . . . *in order to achieve an outcome*' (italics added). In other words, TBL is goal-oriented, leading to a 'solution' or a 'product'. Nunan (1989, cited in Nunan, 1999: 25) makes a further distinction between 'real-world' and 'pedagogical' tasks, the latter defined as 'a piece of classroom work that involves learners in comprehending, manipulating, producing, or interacting in the target language while their attention is focused on mobilizing their grammatical knowledge in order to express meaning, and in which the intention is to convey meaning rather than manipulate form'.

Despite this emphasis on communication and interaction, it is important to note that the TBL approach is concerned with accuracy as well as fluency. It achieves this most obviously through the TBL framework, which has three key phases:

1   the pre-task phase, which includes work on introducing the topic, finding relevant language and so on
2   the task cycle itself
3   language focus.

As Willis (1996: 55) notes, 'to avoid the risk of learners achieving fluency at the expense of accuracy and to spur on language development, another stage is needed after the task itself'. TBL, then, takes a holistic view of language in use. Willis also offers an extensive set of suggestions for task possibilities, from simple to complex, and also shows how mainstream textbooks can be adapted to introduce tasks. A simple task may require learners just to make lists (e.g. 'the features of a famous place'); more complex tasks may incorporate simulation and problem-solving, such as how to plan a dinner menu on a limited budget (Willis's examples) (see also Willis and Willis, 2007 for updates or more examples of tasks). Nunan (2004) and Ellis (2010) also argue that Second Language Acquisition studies support the validity of TBL.

In this section we have discussed the principle of the multi-syllabus, have shown how some coursebooks have highlighted lexical chunks as one particular area of design, and have commented on the task-based approach as an important area of development. In the next section we shall turn our attention to ways in which current approaches view the learners themselves.

2.5   Learners and Learning

There are a number of ways in which current coursebook design is concerned in general terms with a perspective on 'the learner', as well as with the language material itself. These ways can be grouped as follows:

1   Although the majority of learners study in the environment of a whole class, and often in a large one, an analysis of the characteristics of learners as individuals can offer a helpful view on the construction of materials and methods.
2   Learners will naturally need to engage in the process of both comprehending and producing language. In doing this they use a range of strategies, some of which are probably shared by all language users, whether learning a foreign language or using their mother tongue.

The first of these perspectives is normally characterized by the concept of 'individual differences'; the second is studied under the headings of both language acquisition and learning strategies. Both perspectives have come into some prominence as factors affecting materials design, and we shall briefly survey each of them in turn.

Learners

In the previous section on the organization and content of current materials, we did not discuss in any detail the selection of topics for language learning, whether for discussion, or comprehension or writing. We have chosen to start this section with them because they are the most obvious way in which learners' needs and interests can be taken into account. Here is a small selection of themes taken from some of the coursebooks used as examples in the preceding section. You might like to consider whether such topics would be relevant for your own learners, and whether learning context determines topic choice. For instance, materials appropriate for students in an English-speaking environment – social situations, travelling, everyday 'survival' – may not be applicable in other educational settings, and vice versa:

Travelling	Shopping	Success and failure
School and studying	Music and singing	Driving
Food and drink	Health and illness	The environment
Dreams and fears	Television	Technology
Money	Racism	Leisure time
Relationships	Education	Getting old

Topics in this form are listed as content, as material to be covered. Masuhara et al. (2008), in their review of eight global coursebooks, welcome the efforts made towards valuing learner engagement in the selection and treatment of topics.

1 Do you think the topics listed on page 42 would be appropriate or engaging for your students?
2 Look at the materials you use in your classes. Do you think the topics are engaging for your students?

Topics, of course, are by no means the only way in which attention can be paid to the learners themselves. Although for most teachers, especially those faced with big classes, the goal of large-scale individualization of instruction may not be a very realistic one, some differences between learners can be taken into account in a limited way. Chapter 12 of this book will explore the possibilities in more detail. Here we shall simply highlight the 'individual differences' that appear to be significant in current materials.

Researchers in the psychology of second language learning have investigated a number of learner characteristics that have implications for the language classroom. An understanding of such characteristics, or 'variables', can make it possible for teachers and materials designers to adjust and vary certain aspects of the classroom to allow for the different individuals in it. Dörnyei (2005) provides an extensive review of studies on individual differences and considers key learner variables including:

- Personality: learners may be quiet, or extrovert, for instance
- Motivation: learners may have chosen to learn; they may be obliged to take a course or an examination; they may or may not perceive the relevance of material
- Attitude: learners have attitudes to learning, to the target language and to classrooms
- Aptitude: some people seem more readily able than others to learn another language
- Preferred learning styles: some learners are more comfortable in a spoken language situation, others prefer written material
- Intelligence.

We are not concerned here with the relationships between these factors. This is an interesting and complex issue and we will discuss it at some length in Chapter 11 of this book.

Some of the dimensions along which individuals vary, IQ measures for example, do not have an obvious effect on language learning potential. Others are difficult to measure, and certainly to change: it is not normally considered part of a teacher's role to try to adjust students' personalities. Yet others, such as motivation, can more obviously be affected by the learning environment. What we should note, in other words, is that some individual differences can have an influence on language instruction, and others can be influenced by it. A distinction also needs to be made between the possible effects of the coursebook and those of the structure and management of the classroom itself.

Several of the English language teaching materials now available attempt to incorporate some consideration of learner characteristics into their methodology. As far as variables differentiating between learners are concerned, mention is made most frequently of differences in learning styles. The pedagogic response to this is to allow in a principled way for variety, especially in content and in language skills, and to build in suggestions for variability in pacing – the speed at which learners are able to work through the material. Pacing, in turn, implies a concern for aptitude, a factor that interests all teachers even if no formal measurement of aptitude is available. We also find reference to the importance of understanding learners' attitudes. Students may have expectations, perhaps about the role of correction, or about pronunciation, and ignoring them will certainly have an adverse effect on motivation.

As mentioned earlier, most of the teaching we do is to learners in a class with others, so all materials necessarily have to be a compromise, as do teachers' interpretations of materials. With the development of technology, learning modes are changing: self-access centres, learning through the Internet or making use of mobile technology. We will discuss different ways of encouraging learning in Chapter 5 in relation to the use of technology in learning and in Chapter 12 in relation to individualization, learner autonomy, self-access learning and learner training.

> Taking the individual differences discussed in this section, to what extent do you think they influence your own teaching, and how far can you, as a teacher, influence them? Compare your observations if possible with someone who works in a different educational environment.

Learning processes and strategies

Some readers will be familiar with the terms 'learning' and 'acquisition'. The purpose of this subsection is simply to introduce what have arguably been the most significant approaches to materials design and classroom practice in recent years. Details of learning skills and processes in particular are the subject of much of Part II of this book; and the strategies work is taken up again in Part III, in the discussion of learner autonomy and learner training.

This can be considered as typical of an earlier approach to reading comprehension where the text might, for example, be about the life of a famous person, and the questions are there to find out whether the text has been understood. ('Mr X was born in Edinburgh in 1835'. Question: 'When was Mr X born?') Such a format is more like a test of comprehension, and does not itself teach the learners any strategies for understanding the passage. Alternatively, learners were often required to translate the English text into their mother tongue. Despite new ways of analysing and describing language material, it took some time for our profession to turn its attention to the psychology of learning, particularly in relation to the comprehension skills of reading and, subsequently, listening. A 'test' or 'translation' method clearly tries to check that learners have understood a particular piece of language, but does little to develop techniques that can be transferred to other texts. Currently, then, there is a growing concern to ensure that practice is given in activating these generalizable skills that are believed to represent underlying (even universal) processes for all language users. Thus the reading skill, for instance, as we shall see in Chapter 6, is seen in terms of a number of different 'subskills', such as reading for general information, scanning, skimming and so on. These subskills or strategies can then be used as the basis for specific tasks and exercises in a lesson. It is important to note that 'comprehension' is therefore no longer just a way of doing more grammar practice using a text, but opens up a perspective on psychological text-processing mechanisms.

Let us look at how some current materials make use of this perspective. The subskills of comprehension most frequently found are

1   Reading/listening for the general idea, or 'gist'. In relation to reading, this is sometimes referred to as 'skimming'.
2   Looking for specific items of information (or 'scanning' for details).
3   Predicting or anticipating what is coming next.
4   Making inferences or deductions when a 'fact' cannot simply be identified.

These skills are practised through a number of exercises and techniques. For example, we find various activities to be carried out before reading; activities that require different groups in the class to share different information; questions in the middle of a text to help with anticipation; and true–false questions that require learners to combine two or more parts of a text before they can answer. Overall we can observe that different kinds of texts and different reasons for reading or listening can be allowed for in the methodology used. The aim is not primarily to ensure that every word and every grammatical structure are understood – there are more efficient ways of doing this – but to equip learners with useful and transferable skills.

Finally, we should comment on a further dimension of the concept of a 'skill'. The kinds of strategies discussed above have developed from general work in the psychology of language processing which need not necessarily be applied to questions of language learning. Most teachers are also concerned with the conscious skills their students need in order to learn as efficiently as possible. With this in mind, we find that increasing attention is being paid to two related areas. The first of these is usually referred to under the heading of 'study skills', the second of 'learning strategies'.

Study skills can be thought of as a range of learnable and practical techniques that help students to adopt more effective methods of study. In the area of English language teaching known as English for Academic Purposes (EAP), the concept is very well developed, particularly for students studying their own specialism through the medium of English where a mastery of a large number of academic-related skills is very important. In terms of general English coursebooks, study skills have a more restricted scope. Take the skill of using a monolingual dictionary. Learners are taught, for example, to understand the different parts of a dictionary entry, to select relevant information from a longer entry, and to recognize the significance of word parts, especially prefixes. Other skills include keeping a vocabulary book containing definitions and examples in English as well as (or instead of) the mother tongue equivalent, and sometimes the wider reference skills involved in using the different sections – contents page, index and so on – of a textbook.

The second area – learning strategies – owes much to research that analyses the components of successful language learning and offers definitions of a 'good language learner'. 'Success' is thought to be based on such factors as checking one's performance in a language, being willing to guess and to 'take risks' with both comprehension and production, seeking out opportunities to use strategies, developing efficient memorizing strategies, and many others. Many current materials draw on this research, and incorporate practice in 'good learner' strategies across all language skills, often asking learners to be explicit about their own approach to learning so as to be able to evaluate its efficiency for them.

The available literature on learning strategies has grown enormously in recent years, covering strategies and skills, methods for researching strategy use, universality and individuality, strategy 'teachability' and so on. Clear discussion of various aspects of strategy research of particular interest to the language teacher can be found in Oxford and Lee (2008). Griffiths (2008b) provides an extensive historical overview of attempts to classify and define strategies and investigates their commonality.

There has only been space here to look briefly at approaches to materials design drawn from various aspects of the literature on the psychology of language learning. We conclude the chapter by commenting on a rather different focus altogether.

2.6 Related Developments

When we reviewed the claims of current global coursebooks in Section 2.3 above, we noted the influence of changes that have been taking place around English Language Teaching.

Firstly, we are seeing a dramatic spread of English as a lingua franca or world Englishes (Graddol, 2006, 2010; Kirkpatrick, 2010; Jenkins et al., 2011). English as a lingua franca is currently seen as a common currency, as it were, to enable communication at global level, be it face to face or through digital means. As Graddol (2006, 2010) predicts, the perception of the significance of English as a lingua franca may be different in years to come, indeed various world Englishes or different languages may claim dominant status. At the moment, however, English seems to be viewed as one of the necessary skills that can lead to social, academic and economic success. Many countries seem to have adopted or be interested in adopting Content and Language Integrated Learning (CLIL) (i.e. a cross-curricular approach for learning content through a target language) and/or Teaching English to Young or Very Young Learners to enhance English language education. This situation challenges the foundations of traditional views of 'what constitutes good English'. As Jenkins et al. (2011: 284) put it:

> From an ELF perspective, then, once NNSEs are no longer learners of English, they are not the 'failed native speakers' of EFL, but – more often – highly skilled communicators who make use of their multilingual resources in ways not available to monolingual NSEs, and who are found to prioritize successful communication over narrow notions of 'correctness' in ways that NSEs, with their stronger attachment to their native English, may find more challenging.
>
> NNSEs may, for example, code-switch in order to promote solidarity and/or project their own cultural identity; or they may accommodate to their interlocutors from a wide range of first language backgrounds in ways that result in an 'error' in native English (Jenkins et al., 2011: 284).
>
> NB
> ELF: *English as lingua franca*
> NSE: *Native Speaker of English*
> NNSE: *Non-Native Speakers of English*

This new perspective of English as Lingua Franca affects potentially all sorts of aspects of English Language Teaching including assessment. We explore this issue in more detail in Chapter 8 in relation to speaking skills.

Secondly, related to English as Lingua Franca (Jenkins et al., 2011) or World Englishes (Kirkpatrick, 2010), is the issue of intercultural sensitivity. Earlier in this chapter we have discussed how CLT, which originated in Western Europe under the initiative of the Council of Europe, received criticism as the cause of intercultural conflict during the implementation of its materials and methodology in many parts of the world (see Chapter 11 on this issue; see also Holliday, 1994, 2005). The problem may have more to do with the way CLT was implemented rather than inherent defects of the approach. The importance of intercultural sensitivity and accommodation is becoming important in this globalized world.

Lastly, the global development of World Englishes and the demands for English as a Lingua Franca sits alongside the diversification of learners and learning contexts. We see at least two interesting issues emerging. One is concerted efforts to establish a system, as in the case of the Council of Europe's Common European Framework. The other is the necessity for teachers including those in training to be able to evaluate, adapt and develop their own approaches in the form of principled materials based on their own judgement and experience.

All the global coursebooks we sampled in Section 2.3 in this chapter use the levels specified by the Common European Framework of Reference (CEFR). This framework was the product of collaboration to ensure the mobility of people and ideas within the member countries of the Council of Europe. The mission of the Language Policy Division of the Council of Europe is to improve the provision of language education and to promote linguistic and cultural diversity and plurilingualism. CEFR is a tool for the planning and assessment of language learning so that qualifications can be mutually recognized and policies can be coordinated. It has become widely accepted as the standard for grading an individual's language proficiency across European languages (Council of Europe, 2001: 24; updates on their website at http://www.coe.int/t/dg4/linguistic/Cadre1_en.asp). A comparison with various other examination levels can be obtained from http://en.wikipedia.org/wiki/Common_European_Framework_of_Reference_for_Languages. What is remarkable about CEFR is that the syllabus, methods and assessment are designed to cohere with each other. Methods and assessment specifications in CEFR are written as general suggestions and recommendations. The specification allows methodologists and examination developers to seek ways for the optimal realization of ideals. It would be interesting to see if the common yardstick expressed in terms of skill capabilities can usefully be applied to teachers and learners in different contexts.

The case of CEFR may seem like a distant dream to teachers working on their own in resource-poor conditions. With diversified teaching contexts and learners with different variables, teachers are more likely to face a situation where there are no ready-made materials. Chapter 14 discusses various approaches to teachers' own professional development. Tomlinson (2003a) provides useful chapters for those teachers who are interested in finding out the principles and procedures of materials evaluation, adaptation and development. The section named 'Beyond Approaches and Methods' in Chapter 19 of Richards and Rodgers (2001) gives useful advice in developing teacher autonomy.

2.7   Conclusion

This chapter firstly considered the contributions of Communicative Approaches to English Language Teaching. It then discussed a number of important growth areas in materials since the 'communicative revolution' of the 1970s. We looked first at the concept of a multi-component syllabus, where a number of components are interwoven, touched on the lexical syllabus and examined the current focus on TBL. We then commented on the increasing interest in various areas of the psychology of language learning and language use, both in the characteristics of individuals and in underlying processes and strategies. Clearly not all coursebooks incorporate all the elements that have been covered here, and it would probably not be appropriate for them to do so. They are design principles, and cannot have equal and universal applicability: as we have seen, different teaching situations have different requirements and expectations. The next two chapters in this part of the book will discuss procedures for evaluating and adapting general design criteria for specific contexts. The final chapter in Part I will look at how teachers can take advantage of various technologies in their classrooms.

If you were to design the syllabus, materials and methods for a specific course, what would your syllabus look like? What kinds of methods or approaches are you going to use? Can you design a unit based on your syllabus?

2.8   Further Reading

1 Griffiths, C. (ed) (2008a): *Lessons from Good Language Learners*. This provides an overview of strategy research and its applicability to teaching.
2 Lightbown, P. and N. Spada (2006): *How Languages Are Learned*, 3rd edition. A good introductory book for prospective teachers to understand the field of second language learning.
3 Ortega, L. (2009): *Understanding Second Language Acquisition*. A readable book on the field of second language acquisition.
4 Tomlinson, B. (ed) (2003): *Developing Materials for Language Teaching*. Provides a useful collection of chapters that will guide teachers in evaluating, adapting and developing materials.
5 Willis, D. and J. Willis (2007): *Doing Task-based Teaching*. Contains definitions, discussion of principles and procedures, and many practical examples.

3

Evaluating ELT Materials

3.1 Introduction

The ability to evaluate teaching materials effectively is a very important professional activity for all English as a Foreign Language (EFL) teachers, and
in this chapter we shall examine the reasons why teachers need to evaluate
materials in the first instance. We shall then move on to discuss the criteria
that can be used to evaluate materials by suggesting a working model which
we hope will be an effective one to use for teachers working in a variety of
contexts. The model that we suggest is based on the view that it is useful for
us as teachers to perform an external evaluation of materials first of all in
order to gain an overview of the organizational principles involved. After
this we move on to a detailed internal evaluation of the materials to see how
far the materials in question match up to what the author claims as well as
to the aims and objectives of a given teaching programme.

3.2 The Context of Evaluation

Let us look at why we need to evaluate materials in the first place. For the
term evaluation, we take Tomlinson's (2003c) definition: 'Materials evaluation is a procedure that involves measuring the value (or potential value) of
a set of learning materials'. It is probably reasonable to assume that there are
very few teachers who do not use published course materials at some stage

Materials and Methods in ELT: A Teacher's Guide, Third Edition.
Jo McDonough, Christopher Shaw, and Hitomi Masuhara.
© 2013 John Wiley & Sons, Inc. Published 2013 by John Wiley & Sons, Inc.

in their teaching career. Many of us find that it is something that we do very regularly in our professional lives. We may wish at this stage to make a distinction between teaching situations where 'open-market' materials are chosen on the one hand, and where a Ministry of Education (or some similar body) produces materials that are subsequently passed on to the teacher for classroom use on the other.

The nature of the evaluation process in each of these scenarios will probably differ as well. In the first type of situation teachers may have quite a large amount of choice in the materials they select, perhaps being able to liaise freely with colleagues and a Director of Studies/Principal with respect to this material. However, there are many situations around the world where teachers in fact get a very limited choice or perhaps no choice at all, and this second scenario mentioned above may well obtain for teachers who are 'handed' materials by a Ministry or a Director and have to cope as best they can within this framework. This situation will more than likely involve teachers in an understanding of why the materials have been written in such a way and how they can make effective use of them in the classroom. For the vast majority of teachers working in the first situation, that of having a good deal of choice in the selection of appropriate materials, writing their own materials can be very time consuming and not necessarily cost-effective; hence the need to be able to discriminate effectively between all the coursebooks on the market. Today there is a wealth of EFL material available, with literally hundreds of new, commercially available titles appearing every year in English-speaking countries. Wider choice means more need for evaluation prior to selection. In response to such a demand, there are some journals which have regular reviews of recently published materials (e.g. *ELT Journal*, *Modern English Teacher*, *English Teaching Professional*, *TESOL Journal* and *RELC Journal*). *Modern English Teacher* includes a section called 'A Book I've Used', which consists of reviews by practitioners reporting their post-use evaluation of coursebooks. Most of the reviews are about specific textbooks or courses, but the *ELT Journal* sometimes includes survey reviews of a number of current textbooks of the same sub-genre (e.g. Tomlinson et al., 2001; Masuhara et al., 2008).

Another fairly typical factor to consider is that teachers or course organizers are often under considerable professional and financial pressure to select a coursebook for an ELT programme that will then become the textbook for years to come. Added to this pressure is the fact that in many contexts, materials are often seen as being the core of a particular programme and are often the most visible representation of what happens in the classroom. Thornbury advocates teacher independence from coursebooks; for instance, writing their own materials (Thornbury 2000, 2005; Meddings and Thornbury, 2009), but the reality for many is that the book may be the only choice open to them. The evaluation of current materials therefore merits serious consideration as an inappropriate choice may waste funds and time, not to mention the demotivating effect that it would have on students and possibly other colleagues.

For some teachers, the selection of a good textbook can be valuable, particularly in contexts where the assimilation of stimulating, authentic materials can be difficult to organize. Other teachers working with materials given to them by a Ministry or similar body will clearly have some different issues to contend with. They may, for example, have to work with materials they find very limiting, and will probably need to resort to adapting these materials as best they can to suit the needs of their particular context. (See Chapter 4 for a full discussion of materials adaptation.) Even though such teachers will not have to evaluate to adopt materials, they may well be interested in evaluation as a useful process in its own right, giving insight into the organizational principles of the materials and helping them to keep up with developments in the field. This in turn can help the teacher to focus on realistic ways of adapting the materials to a particular group of learners where pertinent. Tomlinson and Masuhara (2004) explain how evaluation criteria can be developed by teachers articulating their beliefs on language learning for their students within their contexts and then using them together with learning principles from the literature for the evaluation, adaptation and development of materials. Masuhara (2006) uses an example of an adaptation process that involves the use of self-developed evaluation criteria. She demonstrates how teachers can deepen their critical and creative awareness required for developing principled materials through adaptation.

We have assumed that as teachers we all use published teaching materials. What do you feel are the reasons for this? What are teaching materials expected to achieve and how might they do it? Could we ever teach a foreign language without published materials? Is it ever possible for everything we need for a course to be contained in one textbook?

No textbook or set of materials is likely to be perfect, and there does not seem as yet an agreed set of criteria or procedures for evaluation (see critical reviews of the evaluation literature in Tomlinson, 2012a; Mukundan and Ahour, 2010). This is inevitable 'as the needs, objectives, backgrounds and preferred styles of the participants differ from context to context' (Tomlinson, 2003c: 15). We nonetheless need some model for hard-pressed teachers or course planners that will be brief, practical to use and yet comprehensive in its coverage of criteria, given that everyone in the field will need to evaluate materials at some time or other. We hope to do this by offering a model that distinguishes the purpose behind the evaluation – be it to keep up to date with current developments or to adopt/select materials for a given course.

As Mukundan and Ahour (2010) argue, evaluation procedures should not be too demanding in terms of time and expertise and must be realistically useful to teachers. For those who are interested in analysing the literature on evaluation, Tomlinson (2012a) provides a critical review covering the period from the 1970s to the present day.

In the first instance, teachers may be interested in the evaluation exercise for its own sake. For example, we may wish to review all the materials that have come out during a given period of time and require some criteria with which to assess these materials (see Masuhara *et al.*, 2008 for an example of this sort of evaluation for adult courses). In doing this, we may of course find materials suitable for adoption/selection at some future date. For teachers wishing to select, however, there is no point in doing a full evaluation for selection purposes if a preliminary evaluation can show that those materials will be of little use for a particular group.

We thus examine criteria in two stages; an external evaluation that offers a brief overview of the materials from the outside (cover, introduction, table of contents), which is then followed by a closer and more detailed internal evaluation. We cannot be absolutely certain as to what criteria and constraints are actually operational in ELT contexts worldwide and some teachers might argue that textbook criteria often are very local. We may cite examples of teachers who are involved in the evaluation process. One teacher from a secondary school in Europe is able to 'trial' a coursebook with her students for two weeks before officially adopting it. Some secondary school teachers in Japan team-teach their classes with native speakers and are able to evaluate materials jointly with them. However, as we pointed out in Chapter 1, we are attempting to look at areas where our professional framework shares similar interests and concerns, and with this in mind, the criteria that we shall examine here will be as comprehensive as possible for the majority of ELT situations on a worldwide basis. Of course the evaluation process is never static; when materials are deemed appropriate for a particular course after a preliminary evaluation, their ultimate success or failure may only be determined after a certain amount of classroom use (while- and post-use evaluation).

1   In Chapter 1 we looked at the educational framework in which we all work. With reference to this, you might like to think about who actually evaluates materials in your educational system; that is, what is the role of published materials and therefore the role of evaluation? Do teachers do it (by themselves, jointly with other teachers/students?), or does the Ministry of Education choose or write the materials for you?

(Continued)

2   You might also like to think about the criteria you used to select the ELT materials you are using at the moment. Or, if you did not select the materials, think about the criteria you would use. Discuss your answers with a colleague if at all possible. Did you select the same criteria? Note down your answers because we shall refer to them again at the end of this chapter to see how far the criteria you mention overlap with ours.

3.3   The External Evaluation

In this central stage of the model we have included criteria that will provide a comprehensive, external overview of how the materials have been organized. Our aim is basically that of examining the organization of the materials as stated explicitly by the author/publisher by looking at

- the 'blurb', or the claims made on the cover of the teacher's/students' book
- the introduction and table of contents

that should enable the evaluator to assess what Tomlinson (2003c: 16) calls analysis in that 'it asks questions about what the materials contain, what they aim to achieve and what they ask learners to do' (Littlejohn, 2011 makes a similar distinction). We also find it useful to scan the table of contents page in that it often represents a 'bridge' between the external claim made for the materials and what will actually be presented 'inside' the materials themselves. At this stage we need to consider why the materials have been produced. Presumably because the author/publisher feels that there is a gap in the existing market that these materials are intended to fill: so we shall have to investigate this further to see whether the objectives have been clearly spelt out. To illustrate what we mean, here is an example of one such 'blurb' taken from a well-known EFL textbook published in 2012:

. . . an integrated skills series which is designed to offer flexibility with different teaching and learning styles. Fun for learners to use and easy for teachers to adapt . . .
- Fully integrated grammar, skills and lexical syllabuses provide a balanced learning experience
- Engaging topics motivate students and offer greater personalization
- A wide range of approaches exploit different learning styles
- Clearly structured grammar presentations are reinforced with extensive practice
- Contextualized vocabulary focuses on authentic real-world language

- A variety of listening and speaking activities develop learning fluency
- Learner training throughout the Student's Book and Workbook maximizes skills development.

It appears that this textbook is aimed at intermediate level students with different learning styles and different levels of motivation who will benefit from learner training. This textbook also seems to be designed for flexible use and to offer an integrated learning experience covering grammar, lexis and skills. Later, when the evaluator investigates the organization of the materials she will have to ascertain whether or not this is really the case.

Let us see the types of claim that can be made for materials in the introduction. The following example is part of the introduction taken from a recent EFL series. We have italicized certain terms and key concepts that we feel need further investigation:

- Tasks and activities are designed to have a *real communicative purpose* rather than simply being an excuse to practise specific features.
- We have placed a special emphasis on representing *an accurate multicultural view of English as it is spoken today.* Many courses still represent the English-speaking world as being largely UK- and US-based. Considering the fact that there are now more non-native English speakers than native, we have also included a variety of accents from a wide range of countries and cultures.
- Throughout the Student's Book, *learner autonomy* is promoted via clear cross-referencing to features in the Workbook and elsewhere. Here students can find all the help and extra practice they need.

We can deduce from this that the claims made for the materials by the author/publisher can be quite strong and will need critical evaluation in order to see if they can be justified. From the 'blurb' and the introduction we can normally expect comments on some/all of the following:

- The intended audience. We need to ascertain who the materials are targeted at, be it teenagers aged 13 and upwards or adults, for example. The topics that will motivate one audience will probably not be suitable for another.
- The proficiency level. Most materials claim to aim at a particular level, such as false beginner or lower intermediate. This will obviously require investigation as it could vary widely depending on the educational context.
- The context in which the materials are to be used. We need to establish whether the materials are for teaching general learners or perhaps for teaching English for Specific Purposes (ESP). If the latter, what degree of specialist subject knowledge is assumed in the materials?
- How the language has been presented and organized into teachable units/lessons. The materials will contain a number of units/lessons, and their

respective lengths need to be borne in mind when deciding how and if they will fit into a given educational programme. Some materials will provide guidelines here such as 'contains 15 units, providing material for 90–120 hours of teaching'. In other words, the author expects that between 6 and 8 hours will be required to cover the material.

* The author's views on language and methodology and the relationship between the language, the learning process and the learner.

In many cases the date of publication of the materials will be of importance here. For materials written over the last 20 years or so designed to fit into a multi-component syllabus or corpus-based lexical syllabus, we might expect the author to make claims about including quite a large amount of learner involvement in the learning process. This will require investigation. For example, the materials may claim to help the learner in an understanding of what is involved in language learning and contain various activities and tasks to develop this.

> Look at the 'blurb' and the introduction to the materials you typically use. Also look back at the 'blurbs' we examined in Chapter 2. What kinds of information do they give you?

To give an overview of some typical 'blurbs', we have selected a range of examples taken from EFL coursebooks. We may notice how certain 'key' words and expressions come up time and time again.

> As you are reading them, note down some of the claims that are made for the materials that you would want to investigate further in the next (internal evaluation) stage.

1 'It enables you to learn English as it is used in our globalized world, to learn through English using information – rich topics and texts, and to learn about English as an international language'.
2 '. . . offers a comprehensive range of interactive digital components for use in class, out of class and even on the move. These include extra listening, video material and online practice'.
3 'Natural, real-world grammar and vocabulary help students to succeed in social, professional and academic settings'.
4 '. . . is a goals-based course for adults, which prepares learners to use English independently for global communication'.

When evaluating materials, it is useful to keep a note of these claims, which we can then refer back to later in the process. Other factors to take into account at this external stage are as follows:

- Are the materials to be used as the main 'core' course or to be supplementary to it? This will help to evaluate their effectiveness in a given context as well as the total cost. It may be that sheer economics will dissuade the evaluator from selecting these particular materials, especially if they are not going to be the core part of the course.
- Is a teacher's book in print and locally available? It is also worth considering whether it is sufficiently clear for non-native speaker teachers to use. Some teacher's books offer general teaching hints while others have very prescribed programmes of how to teach the material including lesson plans. Non-availability of the teacher's book may make the student edition difficult to work with.
- Is a vocabulary list/index included? Having these included in the materials may prove to be very useful for learners in some contexts, particularly where the learner might be doing a lot of individualized and/or out-of-class work. Some materials explicitly state that they are offering this: 'student's book with an introductory unit, 40 double-page units, 4 self-check units, . . . an interaction appendix, a vocabulary appendix with phonetic spelling, a list of irregular verbs, and a listening appendix', and the claims made are worthy of investigation. The table of contents may sometimes be seen as a 'bridge' between the external and internal stages of the evaluation and can often reveal useful information about the organization of the materials, giving information about vocabulary study, skills to be covered, additional interactive digital materials and so on, possibly with some indication as to how much class time the author thinks should be devoted to a particular unit. Consequently, it is often useful to see how explicit it is.
- What visual material does the book contain (photographs, charts, diagrams) and is it there for cosmetic value only or is it integrated into the text? Glossy prints in the published materials seem to make the book appear more attractive. It is worth examining if the visual material serves any learning purpose (see Hill, 2003 for an example of an evaluation of visual materials); that is, in the case of a photograph or a diagram, is it incorporated into a task so that the learner has to comment on it/interpret it in some way?
- Is the layout and presentation clear or cluttered? Some textbooks are researched and written well, but are so cluttered with information on every page that teachers/learners find them practically unusable. Hence a judicious balance between the two needs to be found. Tomlinson (2003c) suggests that we also include clarity of instructions and stipulate which activity goes with which instruction as part of the overall concept of the layout of the materials. The potential durability of the materials is another

important factor in teaching contexts where materials may be selected for several groups over a period of years. Factors such as paper quality and binding need to be assessed.

- Is the material too culturally biased or specific?
- Do the materials represent minority groups and/or women in a negative way? Do they present a 'balanced' picture of a particular country/society? It is possible that the content of some materials will cause offence to some learners. The investigation by Bao (2006) into teaching materials shows how textbooks may be 'biased' in subtle, and in some cases not so subtle, ways in their representation of ethnic background.
- What is the cost of the inclusion of digital materials (e.g. CD, DVD, interactive games, quizzes and downloadable materials from the web)? How essential are they to ensure language acquisition and development?
- The inclusion of tests in the teaching materials (diagnostic, progress, achievement); would they be useful for your particular learners?

During this external evaluation stage we have examined the claims made for the materials by the author/publisher with respect to the intended audience, the proficiency level, the context and presentation of language items, whether the materials are to be core or supplementary, the role and availability of a teacher's book, the inclusion of a vocabulary list/index, the table of contents, the use of visuals and presentation, the cultural specificity of the materials, the provision of digital materials and inclusion of tests.

After completing this external evaluation, and having funds and a potential group of learners in mind, we can arrive at a decision as to the materials' appropriacy for adoption/selection purposes. If our evaluation shows the materials to be potentially appropriate and worthy of a more detailed inspection, then we can continue with our internal or more detailed evaluation. If not, then we can 'exit' at this stage and start to evaluate other materials if we so wish, as figure 3.1 illustrates.

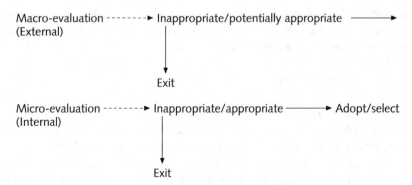

Figure 3.1   An overview of the materials evaluation process.

3.4 The Internal Evaluation

We now continue to the next stage of our evaluation procedure by performing an in-depth investigation into the materials. The essential issue at this stage is for us to analyse the extent to which the aforementioned factors in the external evaluation stage match up with the internal consistency and organization of the materials as stated by the author/publisher – for, as we saw in the previous section, strong claims are often made for these materials. In order to perform an effective internal inspection of the materials, we need to examine at least two units (preferably more) of a book or set of materials to investigate the following factors:

- The presentation of the skills in the materials. We may want to investigate if all the language skills are covered, in what proportion, and if this proportion is appropriate to the context in which we are working. Are the skills treated discretely or in an integrated way? The author's presentation and treatment of the skills may conflict with the way in which we wish to teach – if the skills are presented too much in isolation, for example. If they are integrated, is this integration natural? (See Chapter 10 for a discussion of integrated skills.)
- The grading and sequencing of the materials. This criterion is an important one and merits some investigation as it is not always patently clear what the principle is. Some materials are quite 'steeply' graded while others claim to have no grading at all.

   In this example the materials are based on a lexical frequency count: 'The course is in three levels, each covering about 100 hours of classwork, and each level is complete in itself. Together they cover the most useful patterns of 2500 of the most frequently used words in English. Book 1 covers the first 700 of these . . . .' Sometimes the grading of the materials will be within the unit, other materials will be graded across units allowing a progression of difficulty in a linear fashion. Other materials claim to be modular by grouping a set of units at approximately the same level. In cases where there is virtually no grading at all – 'Most of the units do not have to be taught in any particular order . . .' – we have to investigate the extent to which we think this is true, and how such a book would suit our learners.
- Where reading/'discourse' skills are involved, is there much in the way of appropriate text beyond the sentence? As teachers we sometimes find that materials provide too much emphasis on skills development and not enough opportunity for students to learn to use those skills on extended reading passages.
- Where listening skills are involved, are recordings 'authentic' or artificial? We need to ascertain whether or not dialogues have been specially written, thereby missing the essential features of spontaneous speech.

- Do speaking materials incorporate what we know about the nature of real interaction or are artificial dialogues offered instead?
- The relationship of tests and exercises to (1) learner needs and (2) what is taught by the course material. Where these are included as part of the materials, we need to see if they are appropriate in context.
- Do you feel that the material is suitable for different learning styles? Is a claim and provision made for self-study and is such a claim justified? With the growth of interest in independent learning and learner autonomy, many materials will claim that 'self-study modes' are also possible. From the knowledge that we have of our learners, we will need to assess this particular claim.
- Are the materials engaging to motivate both students and teachers alike, or would you foresee a student/teacher mismatch? Some materials may seem attractive for the teacher but would not be very motivating for the learners. A balance therefore has to be sought. At this stage it is also useful to consider how the materials may guide and 'frame' teacher–learner interaction and the teacher–learner relationship. Rubdy (2003: 45) proposes three broad categories that are essential for evaluation:
  1 The learners' needs, goals and pedagogical requirements
  2 The teacher's skills, abilities, theories and beliefs
  3 The thinking underlying the materials writer's presentation of the content and approach to teaching and learning respectively.

In the internal evaluation stage we have suggested that as evaluators we need to examine the following criteria: the treatment and presentation of the skills, the sequencing and grading of the materials, the type of reading, listening, speaking and writing materials contained in the materials, appropriacy of tests and exercises, self-study provision and teacher–learner 'balance' in use of the materials.

3.5   The Overall Evaluation

At this stage we hope that we may now make an overall assessment as to the suitability of the materials by considering the following parameters:

1 The usability factor. How far the materials could be integrated into a particular syllabus as 'core' or supplementary. For example, we may need to select materials that suit a particular syllabus or set of objectives that we have to work to. The materials may or may not be able to do this.
2 The generalizability factor. Is there a restricted use of 'core' features that make the materials more generally useful? Perhaps not all the material will be useful for a given individual or group but some parts might be. This factor can in turn lead us to consider the next point.

3   The adaptability factor. Can parts be added/extracted/used in another context/modified for local circumstances? There may be some very good qualities in the materials but, for example, we may judge the listening material or the reading passages to be unsuitable and in need of modification. If we think that adaptation is feasible, we may choose to do this. (Refer to Chapter 4 for a full discussion of materials adaptation.)

4   The flexibility factor. How rigid is the sequencing and grading? Can the materials be entered at different points or used in different ways? In some cases, materials that are not so steeply graded offer a measure of flexibility that permits them to be integrated easily into various types of syllabus.

The following remarks illustrate the types of comments that teachers have made to us regarding the suitability of certain published ELT materials for their teaching situations:

> There is a wide variety of reading and listening material available but the speaking material is not very good and is too accuracy based. I would therefore have to add something in terms of fluency. The book is usable and could be adapted, but given the cost factor I would prefer to look for something else.
>
>   The materials are very good. I was looking for something that would present the skills in an integrated way and would make a connection with the real lives of my students. I checked the 'blurb', the table of contents and made a detailed inspection of several units. On the whole the author's claims are realized in the materials. Consequently, I could use this as a core course with very few adaptations.

Thus, when all the criteria that we have discussed have been analysed, we can then reach our own conclusions regarding the suitability of the materials for specified groups or individuals, as the aim of this final stage is intended to enable the evaluator to decide the extent to which the materials have realized their stated objectives. Even after the internal evaluation we still have the option of not selecting the materials if we so wish. (Refer back to figure 3.1.) This is usually avoided, however, if we undertake a thorough internal inspection of the material outlined above. But once materials have been deemed appropriate for use on a particular course, we must bear in mind that their ultimate success or failure can only be determined after trying them in the classroom with real learners. Tomlinson (2003c) discusses the often overlooked areas of while- and post-use evaluation. While-use evaluation involves trying to evaluate the value of materials while using them through teaching them and/or observing them being taught (see Chapter 13 for a full discussion). Jolly and Bolitho (2011) describe case studies in which students' feedback during lessons provided useful evaluation of materials and led to improvements of the materials during and after the lessons. Tomlinson

(2003c) suggests various while- and post-use evaluation questions. Post-use evaluation is the least explored but is potentially the most informative as it can provide information on not only the short-term effects but also those of durable learning. Such while- and post-use evaluation would also have the advantage of enabling teachers to reflect on their practice, which links very closely with the small-scale action research notion that has gained wide currency in the last decade. (Refer to Chapter 14 for a full discussion of the teacher.)

1   At the beginning of the chapter we asked you to note down some criteria you would use to evaluate materials. Now refer back to those criteria. How far do they match the ones we have mentioned? Are any different?

2   Now take a coursebook or set of ELT materials unfamiliar to you and put into operation the criteria we have examined in this chapter.

3.6   Conclusion

In this chapter we have suggested that materials evaluation can be carried out in two complementary stages, which we have called the external and internal stages. We then outlined and commented upon the essential criteria necessary to make pertinent judgements with reference to ELT materials in order to make a preliminary selection. We suggested that this particular model should be flexible enough to be used in ELT contexts worldwide, as it avoids long checklists of data and can operate according to the purpose the evaluator has in evaluating the materials in the first place. We also suggested that materials evaluation is one part of a complex process and that materials, once selected, can only be judged successful after classroom implementation and feedback.

3.7   Further Reading

The following contain useful information on materials evaluation:

1   McGrath, I. (2002): *Materials Evaluation and Design for Language Teaching.*
2   Mukundan, J. and T. Ahour (2010): A review of textbook evaluation checklists across four decades.
3   Tomlinson, B. (2003c): Materials evaluation.

4

Adapting Materials

4.1 Introduction

The main concern of all the chapters in this part of the book has been to examine the principles on which current teaching materials and classroom methodology are built. This chapter looks at some of the factors to be considered in the process of adapting teaching materials within particular classroom environments where there is a perceived need for change and manipulation of certain design features. There is clearly a direct relationship between evaluating and adapting materials, both in terms of the reasons for doing so and the criteria used: this chapter can therefore usefully be seen as forming a pair with Chapter 3. We shall first set the scene for a discussion of adaptation by looking at ways in which the concept can be understood. We shall then try to enumerate some of the reasons why teachers might need to adapt their teaching material. Finally, in the main part of the chapter, these reasons will be examined in terms of the procedures typically used in adaptation.

4.2 The Context of Adaptation

A straightforward starting point for considering the relationship between evaluation and adaptation is to think of the terms 'adopting' and 'adapting'. We saw in the previous chapter that a decision about whether a particular coursebook should be used in a specific teaching situation can be taken on

Materials and Methods in ELT: A Teacher's Guide, Third Edition.
Jo McDonough, Christopher Shaw, and Hitomi Masuhara.
© 2013 John Wiley & Sons, Inc. Published 2013 by John Wiley & Sons, Inc.

the basis of a number of evaluative criteria. These criteria, formulated as a set of questions to ask about the materials, provide answers that will lead to acceptance or perhaps rejection. For instance, typical questions concerned aspects of 'skills', different ways in which language content is handled, and the authenticity of both language and tasks. However, a decision in favour of adoption is an initial step, and is unlikely to mean that no further action needs to be taken beyond that of presenting the material directly to the learners. It is more realistic to assume that, however careful the design of the materials and the evaluation process, some changes will have to be made at some level in most teaching contexts. As Tomlinson points out:

> Most materials, whether they be written for a global market, for an institution or even for a class, aim to satisfy the needs and wants of an idealized group of target learners who share similar needs and levels of proficiency . . . . No matter how good the materials are, they will not by themselves manage to cater to the different needs, wants, learning styles, attitudes, cultural norms and experiences of individual learners. (Tomlinson, 2006: 1)

Adaptation, then, is a process subsequent to, and dependent on, adoption. Furthermore, whereas adoption is concerned with whole coursebooks, adaptation concerns the parts that make up that whole.

An important perspective on evaluation – though of course not the only one – is to see it as a management issue whereby educational decision-makers formulate policy and work out strategies for budgeting and for the purchasing and allocation of resources. In this sense, teachers do not always have direct involvement: they may well influence decisions about whole textbooks only if they are part of a Ministry of Education team concerned with trialling or writing materials, for example. Others, perhaps, may be invited to make suggestions and comments as part of a corporate process of materials selection, but even then, the final decision will be taken at a managerial point in the school hierarchy. A far more widespread, and necessary, activity among teachers is therefore that of adaptation, because the smaller-scale process of changing or adjusting the various parts of a coursebook is, as we shall see, more closely related to the reality of dealing with learners in the dynamic environment of the classroom.

This said, let us remind ourselves of another major and persuasive reason for evaluating textbooks even in a context where teachers have little direct say in decision-making. Evaluation as an exercise can help us develop insights into different views of language and learning and into the principles of materials design, and is something we do against the background of a knowledge of our learners and of the demands and potential of our teaching situation. It is difficult to see how the dependent activity of adaptation can take place without this kind of understanding – how can we change something unless we are clear about what it is we are changing?

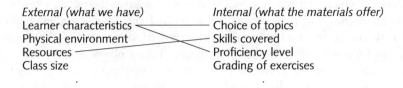

Figure 4.1 Matching external and internal criteria.

With this wider perspective in mind, and as a starting point for thinking about the process of adaptation, it will be useful to extend a little the criteria put forward in Chapter 3 under the headings of 'external' and 'internal' (see figure 4.1). External factors comprise both the overt claims made about materials and, more significantly for the present chapter, the characteristics of particular teaching situations. Internal factors are concerned with content, organization and consistency. For instance, teaching materials may be coherent but not totally applicable in context. In this case, internal factors are acceptable, but there is an external problem. Alternatively, materials may be largely appropriate for the teaching situation, so external factors are met, but show signs of an inconsistent organization – an internal problem. Thus, to adapt materials is to try to bring together these individual elements under each heading in figure 4.1, or combinations of them, so that they match each other as closely as possible.

Madsen and Bowen refer to this matching as the principle of 'congruence': 'Effective adaptation is a matter of achieving "congruence" . . . . The good teacher is . . . constantly striving for congruence among several related variables: teaching materials, methodology, students, course objectives, the target language and its context, and the teacher's own personality and teaching style' (Madsen and Bowen, 1978: ix). This view is echoed in more recent publications on adaptation (McGrath, 2002; Islam and Mares, 2003; Tomlinson and Masuhara, 2004). McGrath points out that 'non-compatibility' is inherent when the materials are not written for particular teaching and learning contexts (e.g. learner needs and wants, syllabus). He also argues for the benefits of adaptation: appropriate and relevant adapted materials are likely to increase learner motivation and therefore contribute to enhanced learning. Tomlinson and Masuhara point out that adapting materials can not only contribute to the learners' learning but also to the teachers' enjoyment of teaching.

The final point in this section is frequently overlooked, perhaps because it is so much a part of our everyday professional practice that we are unaware of its implications. Adaptation tends to be thought of as a rather formal process in which the teacher makes a decision about, say, an exercise that needs changing, and then writes out a revised version for the class. In fact, although the concept of adaptation clearly includes this kind of procedure, it is also broader than this. Adapted material does not necessarily need to be written down or made permanent. It can be quite transitory: we might think of the response to an individual's learning behaviour at a particular moment, for instance, when the teacher rewords – and by doing so adapts – a textbook explanation of a language point that has not been understood. The recognition of the short-term needs of a group may similarly require teachers to 'think on their feet' by introducing extra material, such as a grammatical example or some idiomatic language, from their own repertoire in the real-time framework of a class. Madsen and Bowen make the point clearly:

> the good teacher is constantly adapting. He adapts when he adds an example not found in the book or when he telescopes an assignment by having students prepare 'only the even-numbered items'. He adapts even when he refers to an exercise covered earlier, or when he introduces a supplementary picture . . . . While a conscientious author tries to anticipate questions that may be raised by his readers, the teacher can respond not merely to verbal questions . . . but even to the raised eyebrows of his students. (Madsen and Bowen, 1978: vii)

To focus only on these kinds of activities would obviously not give us a complete picture of the concept of adaptation, because it would be necessary at some stage to extend and systematize its possibilities. Nevertheless, it is worth noting that the task of adapting is not an entirely new skill that teachers must learn.

---

1   Before you read on, consider the materials you use most frequently: to what extent do you feel they need, in principle, to be adapted? Try to note down the main aspects of change or modification you think are necessary or at least desirable.

2   It will also be useful to think about adaptation from the point of view of the source of your materials. Are they commercially produced and widely used internationally; are they designed at national level by your Ministry of Education; or are they perhaps more localized, produced by a team of teachers for a particular area or school?

3   If possible, share your comments with other teachers. You could also discuss the scope you have for adapting materials – do you have time? Is it acceptable to do so in your teaching situation? Are you required to adapt?

In this part of the chapter, we have tried to show that adaptation is essentially a process of 'matching'. Its purpose is to maximize the appropriacy of teaching materials in context, by changing some of the internal characteristics of a coursebook to suit our particular circumstances better. We shall now look in more detail at possible reasons for adaptation and at some of the procedures commonly used.

4.3 Reasons for Adapting

We have just asked you to consider your reasons for needing to make modifications to your own materials, and some of the changes you would wish to make. These reasons will depend, of course, on the whole range of variables operating in your own teaching situation, and one teacher's priorities may well differ considerably from those of another. It is certainly possible that there are some general trends common to a large number of teaching contexts: most obviously there has been a widespread perception that materials should aim to be in some sense 'communicative' and 'authentic'. Nevertheless, it is worth bearing in mind that priorities are relative, and there is no absolute notion of right or wrong, or even just one way of interpreting such terms as 'communicative' and 'authentic'. It is also the case that priorities change over time even within the same context. For instance, decontextualized grammar study is not intrinsically 'wrong' in a communicatively oriented class, just as role play is not automatically 'right'. Nor does a need to adapt necessarily imply that a coursebook is defective.

It will be useful to compare your own reasons with those in the following list. The list is not intended to be comprehensive, but simply to show some of the possible areas of mismatch ('non-congruence') that teachers identify and that can be dealt with by adaptation:

- Not enough grammar coverage in general.
- Not enough practice of grammar points of particular difficulty to these learners.
- The communicative focus means that grammar is presented unsystematically.
- Reading passages contain too much unknown vocabulary.
- Comprehension questions are too easy, because the answers can be lifted directly from the text with no real understanding.
- Listening passages are inauthentic, because they sound too much like written material being read out.
- Not enough guidance on pronunciation.
- Subject matter inappropriate for learners of this age and intellectual level.
- Photographs and other illustrative material not culturally acceptable.

- Amount of material too much or too little to cover in the time allocated to lessons.
- No guidance for teachers on handling group work and role-play activities with a large class.
- Dialogues too formal and not representative of everyday speech.
- Audio material difficult to use because of problems to do with room size and technical equipment.
- Too much or too little variety in the activities.
- Vocabulary list and a key to the exercises would be helpful.
- Accompanying tests needed.

Undoubtedly much more could be added to this list, but it serves as an illustration of some of the possibilities. All aspects of the language classroom can be covered: the few examples above include (1) aspects of language use, (2) skills, (3) classroom organization and (4) supplementary material. Cunningsworth (1995) seems to generally agree with the list above but adds learner perspectives to his list such as expectations and motivation. Tomlinson and Masuhara (2004:12) summarize what factors may trigger feelings of incongruence among teachers. They categorize the sources as

- teaching contexts (e.g. national, regional, institutional, cultural situations)
- course requirements (e.g. objectives, syllabus, methodology, assessment)
- learners (e.g. age, language level, prior learning experience, learning style)
- teachers (e.g. teaching style, belief about learning and teaching)
- materials (e.g. texts, tasks, activities, learning and teaching philosophy, methodology).

Islam and Mares (2003) discuss principles and procedures of adaptation and provide three scenarios (i.e. materials for public junior high schools in Japan, materials for an adult language school in Spain, materials for university English as a second language in the United States) and their more learner-centred adapted version for each case. Some practical and useful examples of adaptation using task-based learning can also be found in Willis and Willis (2007), who also offer some articles on Task-Based Teaching and lesson plans on their web site (http://www.willis-elt.co.uk). Saraceni (2003) advocates learner-centred adaptation and explores this promising new area. She reports that there is very little, if any, literature showing how exactly students could be involved in the adaptation process. She argues that learners as well as teachers should develop awareness of principles of learning and materials design through adapting and evaluating courses. She then proposes a model of adapting courses and provides an example of materials in which activities are designed to be adapted by the learners.

4.4   Principles and Procedures

The reasons for adapting that we have just looked at can be thought of as dealing with the modification of content, whether that content is expressed in the form of exercises and activities, texts, instructions, tests and so on. In other words, the focus is on what the materials contain, measured against the requirements of a particular teaching environment. That environment may necessitate a number of changes that will lead to greater appropriacy. This is most likely to be expressed in terms of a need to personalize, individualize or localize the content. We take 'personalizing' here to refer to increasing the relevance of content in relation to learners' interests and their academic, educational or professional needs. 'Individualizing' will address the learning styles both of individuals and of the members of a class working closely together. 'Localizing' takes into account the international geography of English language teaching and recognizes that what may work well in Mexico City may not do so in Edinburgh or in Kuala Lumpur. Madsen and Bowen (1978) include a further category of 'modernizing', and comment that not all materials show familiarity with aspects of current English usage, sometimes to the point of being not only out of date or misleading but even incorrect. Islam and Mares propose and explain some additional principles including 'Catering for all learner styles', 'Providing for learner autonomy', and 'Making the language input more engaging' (Islam and Mares, 2003: 89–90). Tomlinson and Masuhara (2004) demonstrate how incorporating systematic as well as impressionistic evaluation helps adaptation to be more principled and coherent. They also show how the principles of evaluation as part of the adaptation process can be different from those for selection and adoption purposes.

In this section we shall now look at questions of procedure – at the main techniques that can be applied to content in order to bring about change. There are a number of points to bear in mind. Firstly, this can be seen as another kind of matching process or 'congruence', where techniques are selected according to the aspect of the materials that needs alteration. Secondly, content can be adapted using a range of techniques; or, conversely, a single technique can be applied to different content areas. For example, a reading passage might be grammatically simplified or its subject matter modified, or it can be made shorter or broken down into smaller parts. The technique of simplification can be applied to texts, to explanations and so on. Thirdly, adaptation can have both quantitative and qualitative effects. In other words, we can simply change the amount of material, or we can change its methodological nature. Finally, techniques can be used individually or in combination with others, so the scale of possibilities clearly ranges from straightforward to rather complex. All these points will be raised again in the discussion of individual techniques.

The techniques that we shall cover are as follows:

Adding, including expanding and extending
Deleting, including subtracting and abridging
Modifying, including rewriting and restructuring
Simplifying
Reordering

Each will be briefly introduced, and a few examples given. There are implications for all of them in Parts II and III of this book where we consider language skills and classroom methodology. Readers interested at this stage in more detailed examples of procedures for adaptation are referred to the 'Further reading' at the end of this chapter. The first references have broadly similar lists of techniques, and offer a large number of worked examples.

1   When you have finished reading through the discussion of techniques, select one or two of them and consider their application to any materials with which you are familiar.
2   It will be useful at this stage to work on a small scale, taking single-content areas, such as an exercise, a text, or a set of comprehension questions.

Adding

The notion of addition is, on the face of it, straightforward, implying that materials are supplemented by putting more into them, while taking into account the practical effect on time allocation. We can add in this simple, quantitative way by the technique of extending, and might wish to do this in situations such as the following:

- The materials contain practice in the pronunciation of minimal pairs (bit/ bet, hat/hate, ship/chip) but not enough examples of the difficulties for learners with a particular L_1. Japanese speakers may need more l/r practice, Arabic speakers more p/b, Spanish speakers more b/v and so on.
- A second reading passage parallel to the one provided is helpful in reinforcing the key linguistic features – tenses, sentence structure, vocabulary, cohesive devices – of the first text.
- Our students find the explanation of a new grammar point rather difficult, so further exercises are added before they begin the practice material.

The point to note here is that adding by extension is to supply more of the same. This means that the techniques are being applied within the methodological framework of the original materials: in other words, the model is not itself changed.

Another, more far-reaching perspective on addition of material can be termed expanding. Consider these possibilities:

- The only pronunciation practice in the materials is on individual sounds and minimal pairs. However, this may be necessary but not sufficient. Our students need to be intelligible, and intelligibility entails more than articulating a vowel or a consonant correctly. Therefore, we decide to add some work on sentence stress and rhythm and on the related phenomenon of 'weak' and 'strong' forms in English. A further advantage is that students will be better able to understand naturally spoken English.
- If there is insufficient coverage of the skill of listening, the reading passage provided may also be paralleled by the provision of listening comprehension material, using the same vocabulary and ideas but presented through a different medium, making sure that it is authentic in terms of the spoken language.
- Although the new grammar material is important and relevant, the addition of a discussion section at the end of the unit will help to reinforce and contextualize the linguistic items covered, particularly if it is carefully structured so that the most useful points occur 'naturally'.

These kinds of additions are not just extensions of an existing aspect of content. They go further than this by bringing about a qualitative as well as a quantitative change. Expanding, then, as distinct from extending, adds to the methodology by moving outside it and developing it in new directions, for instance, by putting in a different language skill or a new component. This can be thought of as a change in the overall system. Note that there are some minor terminological issues between writers on adaptation techniques (e.g. McGrath, 2002; Islam and Mares, 2003; Tomlinson and Masuhara, 2004). For example, McGrath advocates that creative addition involving qualitative changes should be called 'exploitation'. What matters, however, is not so much the art of categorization but that teachers can make creative use of the techniques described in their own adaptations.

Finally in this section, it is worth pointing out that additions do not always have to be made onto the end of something. A new facet of material or methodology can be introduced before it appears in the framework of the coursebook. For example, a teacher may prepare the ground for practice in an aspect of grammar or communicative function determined by the syllabus through a 'warm-up' exercise involving learners talking about themselves and their everyday lives.

Deleting or omitting

Deletion is clearly the opposite process to that of addition, and as such needs no further clarification as a term. However, although material is taken out rather than supplemented, as a technique it can be thought of as 'the other side of the same coin'. We saw in the previous section that material can be added both quantitatively (extending) and qualitatively (expanding): the same point applies when a decision is taken to omit material. Again, as with addition, the technique can be used on a small scale, for example, over part of an exercise, or on the larger scale of a whole unit of a coursebook.

We shall refer to the most straightforward aspect of reducing the length of material as subtracting from it. The following kinds of requirements might apply:

- Our pronunciation exercises on minimal pairs contain too much general material. Since our students all have the same mother tongue and do not make certain errors, many of the exercises are inappropriate. Arabic speakers, for example, will be unlikely to have much difficulty with the l/r distinction.
- Although a communicative coursebook has been selected as relevant in our situation, some of the language functions presented are unlikely to be required by learners who will probably not use their English in the target language environment. Such functions as 'giving directions' or 'greetings' may be useful; 'expressing sympathy' or 'ordering things' may not.

Deletion in these cases, as with extending, does not have a significant impact on the overall methodology. The changes are greater if material is not only subtracted, but also what we shall term abridged:

- The materials contain a discussion section at the end of each unit. However, our learners are not really proficient enough to tackle this adequately, since they have learnt the language structures but not fluency in their use. The syllabus and its subsequent examination does not leave room for this kind of training.
- Students on a short course are working with communicative materials because of their instrumental reasons for choosing to learn English: some of them wish to travel on international business, others plan to visit a target language country as tourists. The lengthy grammatical explanations accompanying each functional unit are therefore felt to be inappropriate.

Addition and deletion often work together, of course. Material may be taken out and then replaced with something else. Where the same kind of material is substituted, as for instance one set of minimal pairs for another, the internal balance of the lesson or the syllabus is not necessarily altered. The methodological change is greater when, for example, grammar practice is substituted after the omission of an inappropriate communicative function, or when a reading text is replaced by a listening passage. This takes us directly into the next section.

Modifying

'Modification' at one level is a very general term in the language applying to any kind of change. In order to introduce further possibilities for adaptation, we shall restrict its meaning here to an internal change in the approach or focus of an exercise or other piece of material. It is a rather important and frequently used procedure that, like all other techniques, can be applied to any aspect of 'content'. It can be subdivided under two related headings. The first of these is rewriting, when some of the linguistic content needs modification; the second is restructuring, which applies to classroom management. Let us look at some examples of each of these in turn. You will undoubtedly be able to think of many more.

Rewriting   Currently the most frequently stated requirement for a change in focus is for materials to be made 'more communicative'. This feeling is voiced in many teaching situations where textbooks are considered to lag behind an understanding of the nature of language and of students' linguistic and learning needs. Rewriting, therefore, may relate activities more closely to learners' own backgrounds and interests, introduce models of authentic language, or set more purposeful, problem-solving tasks where the answers are not always known before the teacher asks the question. Islam and Mares (2003) provide an extensive discussion and examples for making textbooks more learning-centred through rewriting.

It is quite common for coursebooks to place insufficient emphasis on listening comprehension, and for teachers to feel that more material is required. If accompanying audio material is either not available, or cannot be purchased in a particular teaching context, then the teacher can rewrite a reading passage and deliver it orally, perhaps by taking notes from the original and then speaking naturally to the class from those notes.

Sometimes new vocabulary is printed just as a list, with explanatory notes and perhaps the mother tongue equivalent. We may wish to modify this kind of presentation by taking out the notes and writing an exercise that helps students to develop useful and generalized strategies for acquiring new vocabulary. Equally, a text may have quite appropriate language material for a specific group, but may not 'match' in terms of its cultural content. For example, a story about an English family, with English names, living in an English town, eating English food and enjoying English hobbies can in fact be modified quite easily by making a number of straightforward surface changes.

A last example here is that of end-of-text comprehension questions. Some of these are more like a test, where students can answer by 'lifting' the information straight from the text. These questions can be modified so that students have to interpret what they have read or heard, or relate different sections of the text to each other. Chapter 6 looks at these kinds of tasks.

The point was made in the introduction to this chapter that content changes are not always written down. Adaptation of linguistic content may just require rewording by the teacher as an oral explanation.

Restructuring   For many teachers who are required to follow a coursebook, changes in the structuring of the class are sometimes the only kind of adaptation possible. For example, the materials may contain role-play activities for groups of a certain size. The logistics of managing a large class (especially if they all have the same L1) are complex from many points of view, and it will probably be necessary to assign one role to a number of pupils at the same time. Obviously the converse – where the class is too small for the total number of roles available – is also possible if perhaps less likely.

Sometimes a written language explanation designed to be read and studied can be made more meaningful if it is turned into an interactive exercise where all students participate. For instance, it is a straightforward matter to ask learners to practise certain verb structures in pairs (say the present perfect: 'Have you been to/done X?'; or a conditional: 'What would you do if . . . ?'), and it can be made more authentic by inviting students to refer to topics of direct interest to themselves.

Modifying materials, then, even in the restricted sense in which we have used the term here, is a technique with a wide range of applications. It refers essentially to a 'modality change', to a change in the nature or focus of an exercise, or text or classroom activity.

Simplifying

Strictly speaking, the technique of simplification is one type of modification, namely, a 'rewriting' activity. Since it has received considerable attention in its own right, it is considered here as a separate procedure. Many elements of a language course can be simplified, including the instructions and explanations that accompany exercises and activities, and even the visual layout of material so that it becomes easier to see how different parts fit together. It is worth noting in passing that teachers are sometimes on rather dangerous ground, if a wish to 'simplify' grammar or speech in the classroom leads to a distortion of natural language. For example, oversimplification of a grammatical explanation can be misleadingly one-sided or partial: to tell learners that adverbs are always formed by adding '-ly' does not help them when they come across 'friendly' or 'brotherly', nor does it explain why 'hardly' cannot be formed from 'hard'. A slow style of speech might result in the elimination of the correct use of sentence stress and weak forms, leaving learners with no exposure to the natural rhythms of spoken English.

However, the main application of this technique has been to texts, most often to reading passages. Traditionally, the emphasis has been on changing various sentence-bound elements to match the text more closely to the proficiency level of a particular group of learners. Thus, for instance, we can simplify according to

1   Sentence structure. Sentence length is reduced, or a complex sentence is rewritten as a number of simpler ones, for example, by the replacement of relative pronouns by nouns and pronouns followed by a main verb.
2   Lexical content, so that the number of new vocabulary items is controlled by reference to what students have already learned.
3   Grammatical structures. For instance, passives are converted to actives; simple past tense to simple present; reported into direct speech.

These kinds of criteria form the basis of many of the published graded 'simplified readers' available for English language teaching.

Simplification has a number of further implications. Firstly, it is possible that any linguistic change, lexical or grammatical, will have a corresponding stylistic effect, and will therefore change the meaning or intention of the original text. This is particularly likely with literary material, of course, but in principle it can apply to any kind of text where the overall 'coherence' can be affected. Widdowson (1979) goes into these arguments in more detail. Secondly, some teaching situations require attention to the simplification of content when the complexity of the subject matter is regarded as being too advanced. This could be the case for some scientific explanations, for example, or for material too far removed from the learners' own life experiences. Thirdly, simplification can refer not only to content, but also to the ways in which that content is presented: we may decide not to make any changes to the original text, but instead to lead the learners through it in a number of graded stages. We shall come back to this notion of 'task complexity' in the chapters on reading and listening comprehension.

Reordering

This procedure, the final one discussed in this section, refers to the possibility of putting the parts of a coursebook in a different order. This may mean adjusting the sequence of presentation within a unit, or taking units in a different sequence from that originally intended. There are limits, of course, to the scale of what teachers can do, and too many changes could result, unhelpfully, in an almost complete reworking of a coursebook. A reordering of material is appropriate in the following kinds of situations:

*   Materials typically present 'the future' by 'will' and 'going to'. However, for many learners, certainly at intermediate level and above, it is helpful to show the relationship between time reference and grammatical tense in a more accurate way. In this example we would probably wish to

include the simple present and the present continuous as part of the notion of 'futurity', perhaps using 'Next term begins on 9 September' or 'She retires in 2015' as illustrations.

- The length of teaching programme may be too short for the coursebook to be worked through from beginning to end. It is likely in this case that the language needs of the students will determine the sequence in which the material will be taken. There is little point in working systematically through a textbook if key aspects of grammar, vocabulary or communicative function are never reached. For instance, if the learners are adults due to study in the target language environment, it will be necessary to have covered several aspects of the tense system and to have introduced socially appropriate functions and frequently used vocabulary.
- Finally, 'reordering' can include separating items of content from each other as well as regrouping them and putting them together. An obvious example is a lesson on a particular language function felt to contain too many new grammar points for the present proficiency level of the learners.

4.5   A Framework for Adaptation

There are clear areas of overlap among the various techniques discussed in this section, but it would be beyond the scope of this chapter to try to cover all the combinations and permutations. The intention here has been to offer a workable framework into which the main possibilities for adaptation can be fitted (not to offer some 'how to do' recipes, which are well covered elsewhere). Figure 4.2 shows how the considerations on which the principle of adaptation is based fit together:

1   Choose some materials with which you are familiar, or any others you would like to work with. (If you do not have any to hand, look back at the unit reprinted at the end of Chapter 2.)

2   Decide on any features of the material you would like to change because it is not entirely suitable for your own teaching situation.

3   Referring as much as possible to the techniques we have been discussing, draw up some suggestions for how to adapt the material to achieve greater 'congruence'.

4   If possible, discuss with other colleagues the reasons for your decisions.

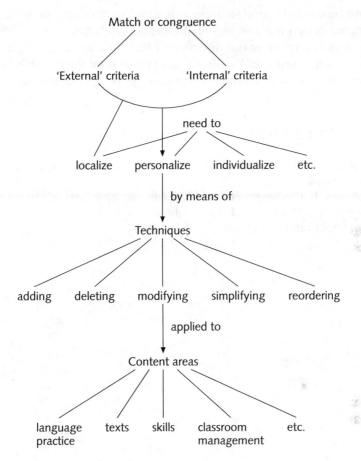

Figure 4.2 A framework for adaptation.

4.6 Conclusion

At one end of the scale, adaptation is a very practical activity carried out mainly by teachers in order to make their work more relevant to the learners with whom they are in day-to-day contact. It is, however, not just an exercise done in self-contained methodological isolation. Like all our activity as teachers, it is related, directly and indirectly, to a wider range of professional concerns. Adaptation is linked to issues of administration and the whole management of education, in so far as it derives from decisions taken about material to be adopted. Further, the need to adapt is one consequence of the setting of objectives in a particular educational context. Finally, adaptation can only be carried out effectively if it develops from an understanding of the possible design features of syllabuses and materials.

This chapter completes our discussion of the principles on which materials and methods are based. In Part II, we shall show how some of these principles have been expressed in relation to the concept of language skill.

4.7   Further Reading

1   McGrath, I. (2002): Chapter 4 discusses how coursebooks might be adapted with some examples.
2   Tomlinson, B. (2006): Localising the global: matching materials to the context of learning. In J. Mukundan, 1–16. Tomlinson shows practical ways of how global coursebooks can be localized.

5

Technology in ELT

Diane Slaouti

Our aim in this chapter is to explore relationships between technology and language teaching and learning. This is not to suggest that technology 'does things better'. We need to maintain a healthily critical stance, reflecting on how the potentials we identify might play out in our own practice and in the specific contexts in which we teach. Salaberry (2001: 51), reflecting on developments in technologies and the roles that they have played in language teaching, provides us with two useful questions which are central to this exploration:

- What technical attributes specific to the new technologies can be profitably exploited for pedagogical purposes?
- How can new technologies be successfully integrated into the curriculum?

In this chapter, we firstly invite you to reflect upon your own use of technologies. We then provide a brief overview of recent developments, and move on to explore ways in which we might harness specific technologies for specific purposes in our language classrooms. We will illustrate some of this thinking through examples of tasks and particular language learning resources.

5.1 The Teacher and Technology

Historically, we have looked for understandings of how technology 'fits' with current language learning paradigms. Warschauer and Healey (1998)

Materials and Methods in ELT: A Teacher's Guide, Third Edition.
Jo McDonough, Christopher Shaw, and Hitomi Masuhara.
© 2013 John Wiley & Sons, Inc. Published 2013 by John Wiley & Sons, Inc.

rehearsed these periods of development. Early form-focused, question-response drills that can be easily programmed for computer-based practice were in line with behaviourist methodologies in the 1960s and 1970s. A shift towards meaning-focused communicative methodology brought attention to learner choice, opportunities to explore language through programmes which presented learners with language in context (concordancing, text manipulation) or provided opportunities to receive feedback on their language use. The development of the Internet and broader communication opportunities, they argued, saw us move into what they termed a phase of integrative computer-assisted language learning (CALL), drawing on sociocognitive views of learning, where authentic task and text are central, and teachers draw on tools such as word processors and the Internet to put learners into positions in which they use technology for authentic activity.

While this historical analysis provides us with a way of understanding how different technologies, and more specifically their use, reflect pedagogical thinking, it has been critiqued as not easily reconcilable with neat phases in time by Bax (2003). There is a good deal of overlap and just as teachers make use of eclectic approaches with different learners, Bax argues that technology use needs to also be understood in relation to a teacher's intentions and role, and where it is used in the curriculum. He describes technology as being 'restricted', focusing on aspects of the language system with minimal interaction with other students, often reflecting individual language practice; 'open', which involves teachers choosing particular tools and tasks to focus learners on language in context and cognitive processes; and 'integrated', where learners move back and forth to computer-based activities as an integrated part of their learning. Bax suggests that fully integrated technology use might be described as 'normalised' (Bax 2003, 24), where the technology has to a large extent become 'invisible'. CALL then ceases to deserve specific labelling, just as we would never think of talking about the pen in any special way.

You may identify various technologies as normalized into your daily lives or indeed in your professional practice. However, it is also difficult to talk about technology or even computers in such a sweeping way, applicable to all contexts. How technology is integrated into teachers' practice is very much related to a number of issues that we have to acknowledge as we explore this area. Access to specific technologies and how your institution supports their use is clearly important. Personal confidence in using technology is also a factor in teachers' decision-making. Our learners, their specific needs, and their own expectations of technology use are also powerful influences on eventual technology use. Most importantly, these factors interact with our beliefs about the teaching and learning of English to form a powerful filter to ideas that we read about and engage with.

Before you read further, reflect on your own technology use.

- What technologies would you say are 'normalized' in your own daily life?
- What technologies would you say are 'normalized' in your learners' daily lives?
- Do you make use of any of the technologies you list in (1) and (2) for language teaching or learning?
- If so, which technologies are they? Do you use them for the same purposes?
- Do you use technologies you have not listed in (1) or (2) for language teaching or learning?
- What influences your decisions to use or not to use different technologies for language teaching?

5.2 The Technologies

We will now look at this developing field.

Exploring terms and technologies

As you read this chapter, we cite various technologies with which you may be more or less familiar. Use your search skills to check out named instances; tap into shared knowledge at Wikipedia http://www.wikipedia.org/.

To further explore specific terms, a useful search strategy for you and your learners is the **define:** function in google. For example:

Define: Web 2.0 returns a list of definitions and links to the sites which have provided these.

Mobile technologies, wireless networking, increasingly compact computers such as palm tops are all representative of the ways in which technology has become potentially integral to our lives. It may be that a good number of the technologies you have identified as 'normalized' in your personal usage include various communication tools. The whole area of computer-mediated communication has developed at speed with an array of synchronous tools such as Messenger programmes (e.g. MSN and Yahoo), telephony software such as Skype (http://www.skype.com) and video conferencing, and asynchronous communication through bulletin boards or forum spaces, BLOGs and email. With the arrival of the 'social web' (see Karpati, 2009) and applications which provide a locus for group exchange and activity such as Ning and Facebook, google docs, Twitter, social networking and collaboration have taken on new meaning.

We also need to remember that many technologies are still with us as they were 20 years ago, only with a 'new look'. Research into the use of word processing in language learning has a long tradition (e.g. Piper, 1987; Pennington, 1996; Slaouti, 2000). The word processor has not gone away; newer iterations simply provide evermore sophisticated functions, and increasing integration with other tools, including the Internet. However, there are new kids on the block; what is known as Web 2.0, which describes the second generation of Web structure, allows us not only to read content disseminated via the Internet but also write to the Web as well. This means that we can interact with others in more open structures, freely publishing and editing content. The wiki is one such structure, and perhaps the most well-known example is *Wikipedia*, the encyclopaedia which all can construct. Through a wiki, users can contribute to text generation in distributed contexts as immediately as working with a word processor on a local computer; the texts generated might be an assembly of words, pictures and links to audio and video and other files capable of being hyperlinked; those texts can be freely edited; in turn those edits can be tracked and decisions reversed, if judged preferable.

Another technology with an interesting history is video. With the arrival of digital video we have begun to see renewed interest with interesting research into Second Language Acquisition (SLA) and DVD use (e.g. Tschirner, 2001; Gruba, 2004); attention to video as an authentic resource again (Sherman, 2003); DVD feature films and language learning (King, 2002). Moving online, *YouTube* seems to be a first port of call for many teachers searching for video content. Of course as with all unmoderated online content, this needs a discerning teacher eye to identify extracts for meaningful use. In response to this, however, in line with the ways in which Web 2.0 content can be shared and manipulated, an intriguing tool is Safeshare TV (http://www.safeshare.tv/). This allows teachers to not only link to or display a YouTube clip without surrounding distractions, but also to set specific start and end points within the whole to create more usable chunks. And of course with respect to video production, there is renewed interest in putting the technology into the learners' hands to produce their own multimedia texts, viewable in a myriad of ways including local movie clips (using, for example, Windows Moviemaker or Apple's iMovie) or online podcasts and vodcasts. Voicethread (http://voicethread.com), for example, a Web 2.0 tool described as 'conversations in the cloud', facilitates collaborative, multimedia text generation allowing learners to simply upload photos or videos and create a storyboard, adding further text, written or audio. More than this display, however, these texts are open to comment from peers, teachers, family, and interested others. Learners immediately have a real audience for their language endeavours.

In all of these examples so far, we are already recognizing the ubiquity of the World Wide Web. Not only is this a huge library of authentic content, but its significance in terms of how it mediates our access to learning materials has to be acknowledged. Our print coursebook is not yet redundant, but published English language teaching (ELT) packages may contain a traditional book and some form of Web-based supplement. This latter may be downloadable or interactive to be used online; see, for example, Cambridge ESOL (http://www.cambridge.org/gb/elt/students/zones/item2325598/ESOL/). As with other supplementary material, online content may be used to extend whole class activity or be targeted for independent learning. Some such activities allow for flexibility in use; take for example, *New English File* (OUP) which includes topic-based reading which a learner can 'gap' for themselves (elt.oup.com/student/englishfile/intermediate). Learner use of staples such as dictionaries or a thesaurus seems to change in contexts where the use of the Web is encouraged. These are in turn in constant development, providing what print can never do in one resource. In the online Cambridge Advanced Learner's dictionary, for example, learners find UK and US pronunciation files, a link to a visual thesaurus, a topic-based smart thesaurus. Try for example http://dictionary.cambridge.org/dictionary/british/tomato.

Furthermore, the online dissemination of language learning activities, ideas, tips among our professional community means there is usually something to be found to fit a particular need. This may be thematically linked content in different media formats such as this around St. Patrick's Day in Ireland (http://www.britishcouncil.org/learnenglish-central-magazine-st-patrick.htm) from the British Council's *LearnEnglishCentral*; or this around breaking news items http://breakingnewsenglish.com/; it may be content addressing a particular skill such as Podcasts in English at http://www.podcastsinenglish.com/index.shtml or providing language practice opportunities. Learners preparing for Cambridge examination, for example, can find specific needs addressed at Flo Joe's http://www.flo-joe.co.uk/ or Splendid Speaking's http://splendidspeaking.podomatic.com/.

Technology is clearly bringing expanded opportunities to learners both within and beyond the boundaries of our language classrooms. Understanding how technology impacts on language teaching practice might, therefore, also be appreciated in terms of a potential shift in locus of activity. That developing locus of activity increasingly reflects technology use in the world beyond the context of language learning, whether physical or virtual; that technology use in turn also relates to contexts of language use. Figure 5.1 illustrates these shifts from locally accessed technologies to those that

There are, of course, too many resources to do justice to in one chapter. However, as you locate and bookmark your own favourites, consider the potential of these resources on the Web as an enormous self-access centre for your learners. This self-access centre is indeed huge, and we need to ask ourselves 'How do I provide the support my learners need to make the most of these resources'?

How am I helping learners to locate relevant resources?

Would it be useful to explore some form of 'online class tool' to direct my learners towards relevant resources, for example, a class web site, blog, virtual learning environment such as *Moodle* (http://moodle.org/) or *Nicenet Classroom Assistant* (http://www.nicenet.org/)?

How are my learners organizing their learning resources locally (e.g. bookmarking as a vital digital literacy)?

Am I encouraging strategies to record their onscreen learning (e.g. taking notes, saving URLs, keeping a learning blog)?

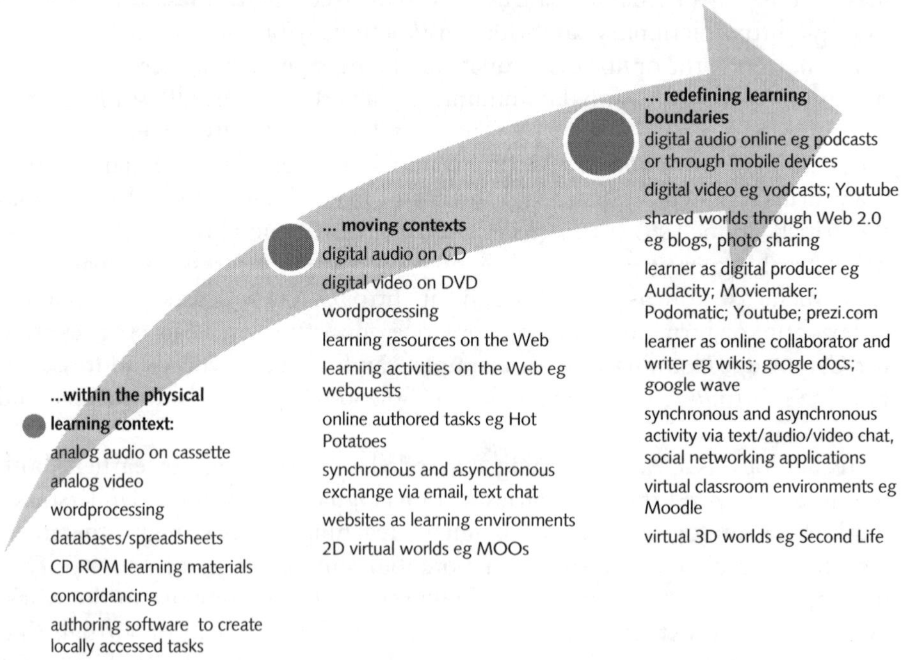

... redefining learning boundaries
digital audio online eg podcasts or through mobile devices

digital video eg vodcasts; Youtube

shared worlds through Web 2.0 eg blogs, photo sharing

learner as digital producer eg Audacity; Moviemaker; Podomatic; Youtube; prezi.com

learner as online collaborator and writer eg wikis; google docs; google wave

synchronous and asynchronous activity via text/audio/video chat, social networking applications

virtual classroom environments eg Moodle

virtual 3D worlds eg Second Life

... moving contexts
digital audio on CD

digital video on DVD

wordprocessing

learning resources on the Web

learning activities on the Web eg webquests

online authored tasks eg Hot Potatoes

synchronous and asynchronous exchange via email, text chat

websites as learning environments

2D virtual worlds eg MOOs

...within the physical learning context:
analog audio on cassette

analog video

wordprocessing

databases/spreadsheets

CD ROM learning materials

concordancing

authoring software to create locally accessed tasks

Figure 5.1   Shifts in technology use.

transitioned classroom and Internet-facilitated activity to current online technologies that redefine the boundaries of language learning.

5.3　Views of Technology

To help us explore how we might think about these technologies in relation to language learning activities, we will first of all look to a well-rehearsed metaphor, that of the 'tutor, tutee, tool'. Developed by Taylor (1980), its relevance for language learning was first explored by Levy (1997). (See also Hubbard and Siskin, 2004, and Levy and Stockwell, 2006, for more recent discussions.) The 'tutor' view sees software as having a teacher 'built' in, so there will be instructions, support and feedback in the material itself. This describes language practice software on CD ROMs or DVDs or accessed on teacher and publisher web sites. The tutee metaphor sees the computer at the control of the learner and thus requires the user to programme the computer in some way. An often-cited example is LOGO, a programming language used with robots or other devices. School learners may be familiar with the 'Turtle', for example, a robot which can be made to move in different directions, if programmed successfully. The concept of 'tool' is adapted from more generic software. This is the kind of software we might use on a daily basis, a word processor, or a Web browser, or other tools that enable us to complete a specific task. We would see a search engine such as google or a wiki or a blog in this category. Meskill (2005: 33) points to two implications of this metaphor:

> Like other human tools, computers can be used to assemble, construct, attach, detach, disassemble, connect and fashion products. Like other tools their use influences the ways we think, behave and communicate.

While tools are 'content neutral', the influence on thinking is an interesting dimension. A word processor may simply be seen by some as a rather sophisticated typewriter; it comes into its own as a problem-solving tool, supporting the process of text composition. Tools can, therefore, scaffold thinking or problem solving, and the term 'mindtool' refers to these attributes (Jonassen, 2000). Tools such as spreadsheets, concordancers, databases, mindmapping software such as Inspiration (http://www.inspiration.com) carry heuristic qualities, to enable learners to think their way through to a solution or outcome.

The notion of tool is thus associated with authentic endeavour. It relates to views of language teaching as empowering learner autonomy, that is, the ability for learners to take their knowledge and apply it for the purposes they require. Thinking about purpose, there is a further dimension to what tools allow us to do. Yes, they are workhorses that allow us to generate and revise text, process and display numerical information, access and retrieve information. However, if these workhorses, and if the encounters with language to which they give access are increasingly part of our learners' real-world interactions, we need to look at the particular skills and awareness that make for empowered use. These are encapsulated in the term 'electronic literacy', defined by Warschauer (2002: 455) as including:

> computer literacy (i.e., comfort and fluency in keyboarding and using computers), information literacy (i.e., the ability to find and critically evaluate online information), multimedia literacy (i.e., the ability to produce and interpret complex documents comprising texts, images, and sounds), and computer-mediated communication literacy (i.e., knowledge of the pragmatics of individual and group online interaction).

The increasing interest in developing electronic literacy as part of language learning processes reflects the growing emphasis in the world of work on knowledge over industrial production and on key or transferable skills. As 'social computing' (e.g. wikis, BLOGs, Facebook, Twitter) has developed, it is the construction of connections between people that has also come to the fore. In this major development, online community is central and the Web has become a world to share in both read and write mode.

We will consider Web 2.0 tools within the following discussion, and return to its specific implications at the end of this chapter. Before we come to that point, we will look to create some connections between technology use and aspects of our practice as language teachers which have been explored earlier in this book.

5.4   Computers and Reading

Our first set of connections revolves around shifting understandings of computers and reading from cognitive and sociocognitive perspectives. Writing in 1987, Jones and Fortescue (p. 31) identified three ways in which the computer can aid reading:

- incidental reading
- reading comprehension
- text manipulation.

The incidental reading they referred to occurs in all kinds of software, from word processors to programmes designed to actually teach reading. It occurs in the instructions, in the menus, in the help files. All of these actions require reading skills, and the learners are exposed to written language without being conscious of it. The purpose of such reading is in relation to the actual task they are pursuing, and of course, there is the implication here that learners need to understand a metalanguage that is beyond the texts themselves. Reading comprehension is obvious. It is very easy to get computers to replicate traditional reading comprehension exercises including wh- questions, true or false or multiple choice. Such tasks may be part of language teaching software or provided by publishers on web sites accompanying coursebooks; they may also be developed by the teacher. This latter activity is not difficult with various authoring softwares such as Hot Potatoes (http://hotpot.uvic. ca/) or Clarity English (http://www.clarityenglish.com/). Text manipulation involves the 'degrading' of a text in some way, requiring the learner to 'restore' it to its whole. This works on the basis of a template. A text is typed into the computer software, and the software applies a systematic manipulation to that text. Some software can operate more than one manipulation, for example, jumbling the sentences, removing all punctuation, removing all of the text (total text deletion).

In identifying the three areas of reading practice cited previously, Jones and Fortescue (1987) suggested very much a summary of the types of reading 'task' that we find in our coursebooks. However, at the time the classification neglected a huge area of reading nowadays which is that provided by the potential of the World Wide Web. This has brought learners increasingly into contact with authentic resources that require skills and strategies to cope with the demands of sifting and processing information. Such information in a hypertext world can be complex and media rich. There is also a strong interest in how engaging with these different texts affects our perception of literacy and challenges the very world of reading.

As explored earlier in this book, reading is acknowledged to be a complex process. Reading involves strategies that encourage interaction between reader and text. That interaction involves the use of various schema which may be resident in the L2 reader from L1 experience or be developing as they encounter texts in L2. It also involves approaching the text in different ways. If we consider the nature of reading skills work in our 'paper-based' classrooms, depending on the text-type (e.g. whether a book, an article, a magazine extract, a story, a newspaper item), engaging with a text might include locating the resource; reading with a purpose; making predictions; skimming and scanning; determining text structure/frames; interpreting graphic information; drawing inferences; analysing voice. These skills, familiar to all of us as reading teachers, are clearly related to the nature of textual data in its paper-based format either in journals or in books. They are also closely related to literally 'handling' the text. It is relatively easy to have a feel for a full article or book when we hold it in our hands. We can take in titles, introduction, conclusion, headings, subheadings, general content in seconds. There is no reason why such skills should still not be part of accessing online texts. It is clear that this can be done on screen.

What specific skills do you employ as part of your online reading behaviours?

Think about
- locating a resource;
- locating information within a resource;
- making predictions;
- skimming and scanning;
- determining text structure/frames;
- interpreting graphic information.

Thinking about these behaviours gives us opportunities to create particular tasks. Information searching, for example, involves thinking round a particular topic and is a highly 'lexical' activity, seen, for example, as we 'google' keywords or use menu systems to find our way to specific information. Raising awareness of such linguistic clues is a cognitive strategy that will make for more efficient information location.

Konishi (2003) and Anderson (2003) also observe the relationship between effective Web-based reading and the use of metacognitive strategies, arguing that for learners to fully exploit the wealth of authentic texts offered on the Web, they need to be aware of how they are reading the screen. This can be built into task design at an evaluation stage (e.g. see Slaouti, 2000). An example of such approaches is what is known as a webquest (Dodge, 1997). This is an enquiry task, which typically sees learners working collaboratively to research information towards a given outcome. Learners share the load by taking on specific roles in the enquiry, looking for particular information, or undertaking specific micro tasks such as monitoring progress of the activity or managing the final display of the outcome. Dodge (1997) describes their attributes:

- An introduction that provides background and aims;
- A doable, motivating task that draws on Web-based resources;
- A set of information resources, providing pointers so that learners are not immediately lost in cyberspace;
- A description of the process that scaffolds the achievement of the task (steps; roles);
- Guidance on organizing information (supporting documents to record information);
- Concluding guidance to bring the task to a close; often involves evaluation of both process and product.

The final outcome may in turn make use of specific technologies depending on its purpose and on the technology context: a printed poster giving information about an outdoor pursuit; a presentation delivered in a face-to-face setting, supported by presentation software in which the group shows their peers where they have travelled on a 'virtual trip'; a video clip produced in multimedia editing software such as Windows Moviemaker, showing how learners would introduce their locality to visitors.

Explore this webquest to identify elements which correspond to the attributes described by Dodge http://www.teacherweb.com/IN/PNC/Cassady/

Browse this 'Webquest Taskonomy' http://webquest.sdsu.edu/taskonomy.html to identify different aims of a webquest.

The challenges of working with authentic resources on the Web means we have to think about how we scaffold reading activity, achieving a balance between overly prescriptive 'reading comprehension' and what can sometimes seem rather open and unsupported project work. A webquest aims to achieve this. Brandl (2002) looks at three different approaches to the inclusion of authentic Internet-based reading materials into lessons: teacher-determined, teacher-facilitated and learner-determined. Brandl argues that all three approaches may be employed depending on the 'teacher's pedagogical approach, her/his technological expertise, and the students' language proficiency' (Brandl, 2002: 87).

Read Brandl (2002), Integrating Internet-based reading materials into the foreign Language curriculum: from teacher to student-centred approaches. *Language Learning and Technology*, 6(3), 87–107 (http://llt.msu.edu/vol6num3/brandl/default.html).

• How does thinking about 'control' differ across the approaches?
• What does Brandl see as the advantages and disadvantages of each approach?
• To what extent do you see a role for all three approaches in your own teaching context?
• If you use the Internet for reading skills in your context, which of the approaches is most similar to the one you adopt?
• Use the principles outlined in this section of this chapter to design a Web-based enquiry activity for your learners.

As we look to the Web for such activity, there is no less an interest in the cognitive processes associated with reading; however, the Web also provides texts that are socioculturally situated and we have opportunities to provide learners with access to these as part of real-world discourse communities. We see a similar shift in potential if we look to the roles that computers play in writing development.

5.5   Computers and Writing

The process approach to writing is often juxtaposed with a product-oriented one. White and Arndt (1991: 5) describe how writing

> . . . in a process approach is divergent, with as many different outcomes as there are writers. In a typical product-oriented approach, on the other hand, writing will converge towards a pre-defined goal, with a model text being presented to form the focus of comprehension and text manipulation activities.

This is not say that the process approach is not interested in the product. As White and Arndt (1991: 5) say: 'On the contrary, the main aim is to arrive at the best product possible'. Much of the early understanding of this approach emerged from research into L1 writing development carried out through protocol analysis, that is, the recording and study of verbalized description of the processes writers engage in. One of the earliest models widely quoted in the literature of this process is that of Flower and Hayes (1981). Their model, reproduced below, graphically illustrates the various influences on the writing product and the stages they discovered to be part of real-world writing procedures (figure 5.2).

- Looking at Flower and Hayes' model, where might the word processor play a particular role in the writing process?
- Might other technologies be used to support the same or other stages of this model?

The word processor is the most obvious writing tool. It allows us to generate, develop and make modifications to a text while retaining a 'tidy look' to the page. Resulting text can, importantly, be stored for future retrieval. Because of the flexibility word processors offer to generate and modify text as well as to allow the writer to interrupt, stand back and resume the text as he/she wishes, the process writing approach is inextricably linked to the use

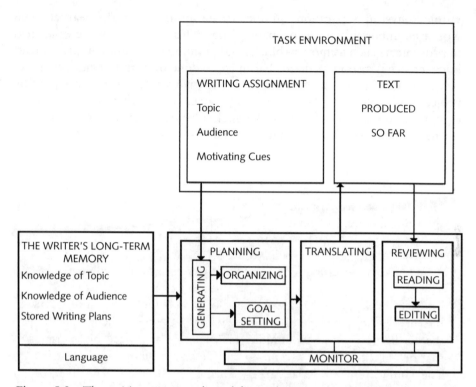

Figure 5.2   The writing process adapted from Flower and Hayes (1981).

of the word processors in the language classroom, whether it be in L1 or L2. Piper's early research (1987) into her learners' use of the word processor reported willingness to spend more time composing, greater concentration on the task in hand, willingness to see the writing as a 'fluid' piece of work, therefore editing where required. We earlier suggested that technology might play a heuristic role, supporting thinking. The functional attributes of the word processor might also be seen to be directly linked to the writing process. Positioning the cursor in the text, deleting, inserting, using copy and paste all relate to thinking about the text in terms of both accuracy and organizational cohesion. As we use these keyboard functions, there is purposeful thinking associated with each decision and the effects of those decisions are seen on screen.

The immediate visualization of text developments is an important attribute of working on screen. Take, for example, paragraphing. Teachers may indicate paragraph breaks in their marking codes, but paragraphing is signalled by 'white space' on the final paper product. Unless the learner rewrites, the full significance of this is not seen. Piper (1987: 121) describes how she was able to illustrate the concept of paragraphing to a learner by introducing the visible, physical separation on the screen in front of the learner. This would be impossible to do on paper. The ability to demonstrate other text improvements such as moving blocks and pointing to resulting improvements in coherence is also immediate. This may be done over an individual's shoulder. It may be achieved by using an interactive whiteboard or a computer projector in a computer lab context or in a classroom where there is teacher equipment at the front of a class. We might also design specific tasks to focus learner thinking on these textual elements.

Here is a task which requires learners to repair a text from which all the verbs have been deleted.

- What is the language focus?
- What keyboard functions would learners use as they problem solve?

These friends of mine a new carpet, so they to the shop and one and the carpet-fitter round to fit it while they out at work. When he, he that there a bump right in the middle. He that this be a pack of cigarettes that he absent-mindedly, so he up and down on the bump until it flat. The family home and the carpet. Then they the man if he their pet canary which missing. It then that he his cigarettes on the hall table!

If we look again at Flower and Hayes' framework, this activity does not really sit within the more obvious stages of 'translating of ideas onto the page' nor in the cyclical revision stages as more text is generated. However, it does contribute to the language element that is part of the writer's long-term memory, informing how subsequent writing takes place. Other text repair or embellishment activities such as this might, for example, focus on the use of cohesive devices in specific text types; or learners might be given a text for reorganization, using copy and paste to see the result of their thinking about text. We see such various activities in our coursebooks, and it may just be that there are opportunities for a computer-based approach, allowing learners to experiment fluidly, review based on teacher or peer feedback and take away a tidy text.

Such activities are also a means of moving learners towards longer texts and of scaffolding writing quality in a more structured way. Research findings in studies of writing quality are generally diverse, however, with numerous variables impacting on outcomes: word processing familiarity, individual

Look at a coursebook that you frequently use.

Are there any activities which focus on elements of text composition, for which you might exploit the particular attributes of the word processor?

writing ability, technology provision (both numbers of computers and regularity of access), curriculum constraints. The latter is a key challenge, and teachers often identify challenges in allocating time to implement a 'process-oriented' approach to writing development – with or without the aid of technology. Acknowledging the mixed findings in this area, Pennington (1996) provides useful food for thought, which may influence our approach to word-processed writing instruction. Her work suggests that improved quality is an outcome over a period of time. She suggests a cause-effect cycle in which we see writing events linked to a series of stages through which the developing computer writer will pass. Pennington sees those developmental stages in terms of four outcomes:

- Writing easier
- Writing more
- Writing differently
- Writing better.

Learners need to be supported towards producing more text in order that thinking *about* text development be activated: without more extensive text, we cannot attend to text cohesion and coherence. These general outcomes describe more specific effects in terms of:

- cognitive/affective effects, 'which impact on the learner's concept of writing and attitudes towards writing';
- process effect, which 'comprise the learner's way or manner of writing';
- product effects which 'are the learner's written texts'.

The word processor can support learners in that development. We started this section, however, by asking whether other tools might play a role, and we return to that question. Look at this description of the stages of a lesson aiming towards a writing outcome. Note which technologies are used, and how uses might support specific stages of the writing process as described by Flower and Hayes.

Task

A number of sports are known as 'extreme sports'. You can practice these in centres with specialist equipment. These are sometimes known as Outdoor Pursuits Centres. You are going to design a poster to tell people attending an Outdoor Pursuits week about one of these sports. You will need to make the sport attractive but give them information about what they need and how to stay safe.

Technologies

Single computer and projection (or interactive whiteboard)

Video clip on topic. (This task used a particular off air video clip, but there are numerous online sources.)

Teacher-created text reconstruction task using WebRhubarb from Text-toys http://www.cict.co.uk/software/textoys/index.htm

Class wiki

Stage	Activity and technology	Purpose (in relation to writing stages)
Stage 1: whole class	Display poster template through computer projection.	Raising awareness of stored writing plan and audience
Stage 2: whole class	Display still frame from start of video; encourage prediction of sport; learners contribute personal experiences.	Schema raising
Stage 3: whole class	Learners view first part of video clip and complete guided note taking task on the equipment and uses.	Generating ideas and knowledge of topic
Stage 4: whole class	Learners collaborate on text reconstruction to complete a description of equipment. Figure 5.3	Rehearsing lexical items and language form for writing

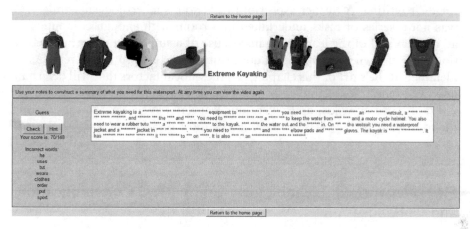

Figure 5.3   Integrating technologies to support the writing process.

| Stage 5: pairs | Pairs watch remainder of video and note dangers and safety precautions. | Generating ideas |
| Stage 6: pairs (home task) | Pages in wiki divided into sections according to poster template. Pairs use class wiki to collaboratively draft the poster content, choosing sections to draft individually before coming back to edit together for display and evaluation in the following lesson. | Translating ideas; reading, reviewing, editing |

If we think back to the two questions posed by Salaberry (2001), the specific attributes of the tools cited here support learners both in the writing process and in attention to the written product. A wiki is an interesting replacement for the word processor here. Its most notable attributes are the collaborative writing functions that allow learners to not only edit each other's texts, but to see a history of those edits. These also provide the teacher with a picture of the collaborative processes. In research doing just that, Kessler (2009) found that, despite such attributes, wiki use without teacher intervention did not necessarily result in focus on form in meaning-focused writing activity. In this task sequence, text reconstruction goes some way towards raising awareness of the writing plan, that is, the language and form of the end product; the public display of the final outcome both within the wiki and shared with the whole class also reminds learners of an audience for their writing. A further aspect of this lesson is its ecological setting. This was not a series of tasks undertaken in a room with enough computers for all or even half of the learners; it makes use of a single computer and projection, with the wiki writing being done outside the classroom context. As we identified at the start of this chapter, it is these local factors that will determine how we orchestrate technology-supported learning. With the growth of Web 2.0 tools such as wikis, and where our learners have access to the Internet, the four walls of the classroom seem to almost disappear.

5.6   Networked Technologies: Computers, Communication and Collaboration

Warschauer and Kern (2000) emphasize the links between developing communicative competence and real-world needs, with language use being described as 'helping students enter into the kinds of authentic social discourse situations and discourse communities that they would later encounter outside the classroom' (Warschauer and Kern, 2000: 5). The speedy developments in global networking have resulted in a focus on the potential of establishing opportunities for such encounters with other language users through computers, not only because computer-mediated communication offers such opportunities but also because learners are, in the main, users of the associated tools. Kern and Warschauer (2000: 13) argue that:

> if our goal is to help students enter into new authentic discourse communities, and if those discourse communities are increasingly located online, then it seems appropriate to incorporate online activities for their *social* utility as well as for their perceived particular *pedagogical* value.

We have already suggested that approaches to using computers for reading and writing reflect similar thinking. In terms of computer-mediated communication, we identify a number of familiar tools: synchronous technologies such as messenger applications and asynchronous tools such as email or discussion forums. Increasingly, audio and video capability is part of both of these communication modes. We are also talking about Web 2.0 developments, which have broadened our thinking beyond 'online conversations' to revolutionary ways of building community, sharing content such as podcasts and vodcasts via YouTube; negotiating content collaboratively through wikis; creating networks of shared knowledge through tagging (labelling content so that semantic relationships can be both retrieved and added to by others); organizing such content in social bookmarking tools such as *del.icio.us* (http://delicious.com/) or *Diigo* (http://www.diigo.com/).

Networked technologies put social interaction at their centre. The contributions that such technologies can make to language learning have been explored from both second language interactionist and sociocultural perspectives. We start by taking a look at 'online conversations' to explore how these might be understood through an SLA lens.

Premised on the fact that input alone is not sufficient, the acquisition perspective addresses how learners might be provided with opportunities to engage in authentic interaction. Its pillar is how language is made salient. Negotiation of meaning is central to this process; this accounts for how interlocutors make adjustments in their interactions to negotiate mutual understanding. As they engage in such adjustments, language features are highlighted, directing attention to form. In research into CALL the interaction account of SLA has enlightened what happens in face-to-face interactions *around* the computer, that is, seeing the computer as a catalyst, and *through* the computer. Second language research in this area has largely been in relation to synchronous communication (e.g. Smith, 2005), where real-time conversation has been explored as an approximation to face-to-face interaction. Jepson (2005) identifies this as 'a wellspring for negotiation of meaning, a communicative exchange that sustains and repairs conversations'.

Chapelle (1998, 2001) outlines the conditions for SLA in her review of arguments for SLA and multimedia:

1   the linguistic characteristics of target language input need to be made salient;
2   learners should receive help in comprehending semantic and syntactic aspects of linguistic input;
3   learners need to have opportunities to produce target language output;
4   learners need to notice errors in their own output;
5   learners need to correct their linguistic output;
6   learners need to engage in target language interaction whose structure can be modified for negotiation of meaning; and
7   learners should engage in L2 tasks designed to maximize opportunities for good interaction.

The synchronous conversation on the next page demonstrates the opportunities that exchange with other L2 users can bring. In exploiting computer-mediated communication (CMC), it is worth reflecting on the nature of the tool and the type of language we tend to see within. Other CMC tools have different attributes to the chat tool that was used in this encounter, and these impact on the characteristics of the language generated. Asynchronous tools such as email or forum spaces provide more thinking time, allowing learners to rehearse language use before committing to sharing their ideas (Slaouti, 2000). Thinking more broadly about how available tools can support interaction then brings us to further dimensions of this networked picture. There

Look at this extract from an exchange between an L2 learner and an L1 speaker of English. How many of the 'conditions' would appear to be accommodated through this communication opportunity?

rachaelegray2003: Hello!
hoontaek_yang: hello
rachaelegray2003: Hope you have not had a very busy day at University today
hoontaek_yang: Next week is Middle exam, it's unhappy
rachaelegray2003: I don't enjoy exams either
hoontaek_yang:^^
rachaelegray2003: ^^ ?
hoontaek_yang: Do you know this emoticon? ^^
hoontaek_yang: ^^ is smile.
rachaelegray2003: Ah!
hoontaek_yang: My teacher told is smile in England
hoontaek_yang: What time is there?
hoontaek_yang: What time is it?

hoontaek_yang: Is this correct text?
rachaelegray2003: Yes perfect. It's evening in Korea isn't it?

rachaelegray2003: It's 12 noon here.
hoontaek_yang: Thank you ^^. Yes, I ate dinner before just.
rachaelegray2003: Anything nice?
hoontaek_yang: I ate Kimchi soup
rachaelegray2003: Whats that made from
hoontaek_yang: Kimchi is main source of Kimchi soup
rachaelegray2003: I've never heard of Kimchi – is it a vegetable
hoontaek_yang: yes
rachaelegray2003: Very healthy. Students in England are known for eating lots of 'junk' food
rachaelegray2003: It's cheap here but it means we all get very fat ^^
hoontaek_yang: Like burger?
rachaelegray2003: yes and chips
hoontaek_yang: I like that too
hoontaek_yang: Kimchi is pickled cabbage in dictionary
rachaelegray2003: I like soup too but I have not tried cabbage soup
hoontaek_yang: Kimchi soup's taste is a little hot.

are various examples of exchange projects that have aimed at developing both language and intercultural awareness through computer mediated collaborative activity using both longer standing CMC tools and Web 2.0 spaces (see e.g. Liaw and Johnson, 2001; O'Dowd, 2007; Lee, 2009). We turn our attention to the collaborative activity itself.

The synchronous extract we have just read is from the early stages of a collaboration in which the two participants explored each other's shared and diverse perspectives on cultural values. This was not an open discussion, but framed by a staged process. They were encouraged to 'meet' synchronously to get to know each other and to negotiate their project focus. This involved individually brainstorming associations with keywords such as 'family' and 'the Internet', and then deciding on one theme which they mutually found interesting to explore together. They used different technologies to support that exploration: the generation of 'word clouds' around their theme using http://www.wordle.net/ (figure 5.4); the sharing of anecdotes, interesting online texts, YouTube clips or other media content.

The learners in their international settings were brought together via a class wiki built using http://pbworks.com/ (figure 5.5).

This latter was not only a home base for all of the different project pairs, but the location for their negotiation of the final project outcome, a summary of their explorations to their class colleagues. From each wiki page, learners provided a link to a short online presentation of what they had learnt from each other using *Prezi* (http://prezi.com/).

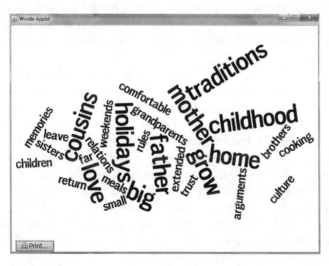

Figure 5.4   Wordle cloud – 'family' http://www.wordle.net/.

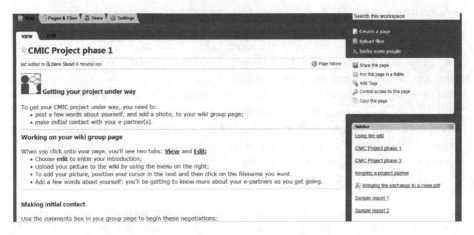

Figure 5.5   A wiki home base for an intercultural collaboration.

This brief description exemplifies learning through social interaction (Vygotsky, 1978). Vygotsky's contribution to our understanding of learning places the social as a precedent to the individual; language is a mediating tool, allowing access to higher level learning. In this theorization, it is not only the teacher but also peers who play a role in scaffolding learners to a point at which they become able to use language independently. Of interest to CALL practitioners is also the fact that different technologies also play a mediating role; as we identified earlier in this chapter, tools can provide heuristic frames for thinking and problem solving (see e.g. Gutierrez, 2003). Such sociocultural perspectives on learning thus provide us with a useful framework for thinking about the opportunities that specific technologies and particular collaborative learning activities bring to our classroom settings, whether physical or virtual.

Such activities do need careful planning, however. Talking of CMC, Stockwell and Levy (2001: 420) warn us that 'learners tend to use this medium of communication more substantially in the early stages and reduce their usage as the initial excitement wears off'. Figure 5.6 illustrates how online collaboration is facilitated by various tools that are freely available to the teacher; it also illustrates, however, an approach to harnessing specific tools for specific purposes. Thinking about the attributes of specific technologies in relation to language learning activity also lies behind this mapping of an exchange between teenagers in Spain and the United Kingdom. This staged exchange gave the children in the two locations an opportunity to find an authentic audience for their language use; it also involved close integration into their class activity.

The two projects described are clearly realized in different ways, each taking account of the local realities of the curriculum, the age of the learners,

Time	Curriculum activity	Project activity	Technology
Week 1	Teachers introduce children to project; background research on exchange location; tasks to check comfort receiving and sending emails		
Weeks 2–3	Review talking about yourself and family; question formation	Initial email contact Manchester - Spain; getting to know you	Email; digital camera
Weeks 4–5	Talking about someone; use of third person	Individual writing about partners; ask for more information by email	Word processing; digital photo from partners; share on class wall poster
Weeks 6–7	Describing a place; my school; my town	Children in both locations take photos through the school window, moving out into the local community; mount and describe in Powerpoint	Email; digital camera; Powerpoint
Weeks 8–9	Food; favourite food; food at Easter	Exchange of information; recipe	Email; present recipe to class (and make if possible!)
Week 10	Closing the project	Children create class video message	Video recorded by school technician; sent on DVD (due to size of file)

Figure 5.6 Stages in an exchange project between teenage English L2 and Spanish L2 learners.

their capacity for independent activity, and each demonstrates different decision-making in terms of the specific technology use. Of note in the planning of the exchange activities illustrated in figure 5.6 is the fact that the teachers made use of tools which were not only fit for purpose, but which were a focus of ICT skills development elsewhere in the learners' secondary school curriculum.

The examples here illustrate the potential of technology to create bridges out from our learners' cultural contexts. They also exemplify technology as a vehicle for extending the locus of language learning activity. Such thinking is not exclusive to intercultural exchanges. As identified earlier in this book, much of our work as language teachers involves encouraging and scaffolding learning which extends beyond the bounds of the physical classroom. Many institutions have a virtual learning environment which they may have

Figure 5.7　A listening blog with embedded video clips, tagged for theme and language level.

purchased; they may alternatively use Moodle, which is a well-known open source environment, and teachers are usually invited to populate these with materials and activities that may either be used in class, or as a self-access resource – very often both. Many teachers harness the tools we have mentioned earlier to provide a more local, personal home base for independent learning. In figure 5.7 we see a teacher blog, created using https://www.blogger.com, and dedicated to listening sources, a combination of embedded video clips from Youtube and RSS feeds to podcasts, for example, from the BBC Learning English web site. Each of these is tagged, that is, labelled, according to recommended minimum language level, general theme and specific source, allowing learners to navigate their way through. Guidance can be provided through a comment feature on each post; a widget is added to poll on what they would like to see more of. Thoughtful planning around available functionality soon allows for a simple but effective resource to be easily built.

As we consider how these find a place in our practice, we would do well to reflect on the words of Cochran-Smith, reviewing the research literature in 1991 on word processing and writing, who wrote that computer use

> is dependent on the learning organisation of the classroom which, in reciprocal fashion, may also be shaped and changed by the capacities of computer technology to accommodate new patterns of social organisation and interaction. (Cochran-Smith, 1991: 122)

We have illustrated in this chapter how the technology itself is not only able to accommodate new patterns of previously unanticipated patterns of interaction; it is in fact beginning to have a very firm influence on where our classroom practice is going. As we also suggested, more and more learners have access to computer-mediated communications technologies outside their learning environment. The fact that networked technologies exist, and that more people access them as authentic tools as part of their lives, is resulting in teachers looking for ways in which to accommodate the patterns of interaction the technology brings.

5.7   Teachers and Technology in Context

We started this chapter by flagging context-sensitive integration, and we finish with this perspective. Having reviewed various theories that frame thinking about technology and language learning, Levy and Stockwell (2006: 141) conclude that theory should not 'replace a principled approach', and this is a position that we hope to have exemplified in this chapter. Principled approaches can, however, be informed by an understanding of how what we do in a specific context is likely to impact on learning.

It is an awareness of contexts of learning that may also determine where research into language learning and technology use continues to move. Many of the classrooms in which we find ourselves may already be equipped with a computer, projection, Internet access; our institutions may already have virtual learning environments; the ubiquitous nature of Web 2.0 tools will also help to expand those classroom boundaries. How we use technology on a daily basis will no doubt influence learner expectations of how and where learning takes place; growth in wireless connectivity brings further implications for where learners potentially learn. Our very classrooms are likely to straddle the physical and the virtual, or even move ever more into the virtual such as Second Life, (http://secondlife.com/) where language learning communities are establishing themselves (see e.g. http://www.avalonlearning.eu/) (figure 5.8).

We also take you back to our two framing questions from Salaberry (2001):

- What technical attributes specific to the new technologies can be profitably exploited for pedagogical purposes?
- How can new technologies be successfully integrated into the curriculum?

We have rehearsed ways of thinking about the attributes of specific technologies, and how these relate to views of technology-supported pedagogy. There are of course many more specific tools which we have not mentioned here. However, understanding the attributes of available tools is one part of our decision-making. We have also emphasized how decisions to use

Figure 5.8   Virtual learning spaces: Second Life.

technology will be filtered by various factors, not least your own beliefs about teaching and learning language, your confidence in using specific tools, your understanding of learner needs. Importantly, Kennedy and Levy (2009) advocate that those seeking to integrate technology into their teaching should see such projects as an iterative process of 'tailoring and integration' (Kennedy and Levy, 2009: 460). As you look for opportunities to use technology in principled ways either in following ideas illustrated in this chapter, or in supporting activities which you have seen and reflected on in the rest of this book, you might be guided by these questions:

Learning assumptions (current approaches to teaching and learning a second or foreign language)

Think about your own perspectives on language teaching. What approach(es) do you take to orchestrating specific aspects of language learning? What do your learners feel comfortable with? Does using a specific technology in a specific way shake learner expectations? Does a specific technology seem to 'fit' with your own pedagogical approach?

Learner needs

Can you identify a gap between needs and response? How can technology provide opportunities to satisfy those needs? For example, can it extend the learning context beyond classroom hours in specific ways; do learners need more opportunities to interact with authentic texts, with other learners or L2 users; can technology-supported activities motivate learner engagement with particular aspects of learning?

Context (teaching and technology)

What sort of technology infrastructure do you have: a computer room or computer in the classroom; how many machines; how does this impact on task organization?

How hard does the syllabus drive you in terms of time for creativity? What ways can you find to integrate technology into textbook tasks?

5.8   Further Reading

Our professional community is also a very active one. The teacher interested in exploring the use of technology can look to the various sources cited in this chapter for practical inspiration, special interest groups in professional organisations such as IATEFL http://ltsig.org.uk/, and practitioner-maintained initiatives such as ICT for Language Teachers founded and developed by Graham Davies at http://www.ict4lt.org/, Nik Peachey's Learning Technology Blog http://nikpeachey.blogspot.com/ or Larry Ferlazzo's http://larryferlazzo.edublogs.org/. We also recommend regular browsing of the online journal *Language Learning and Technology* http://llt.msu.edu.

1   Beatty, K. (2010): *Teaching and Researching CALL*. London: Pearson Education, 2nd edition.
2   Dudeney, G. (2007): *The Internet and the Language Classroom*. Cambridge, UK: CUP, 2nd edition.

Part II

Teaching Language Skills

6

Reading Skills

In Part I of this book, we examined in detail the issues involved in principles of materials design. In this second part of the book, we devote a chapter to each language skill in turn with a final chapter that examines the concept of integrating language skills in the classroom.

According to Alderson (2000: 110), 'The notion of skills and subskills . . . is enormously pervasive and influential, despite the lack of clear empirical justification'. As for the definition of skills, there are many different versions in the research literature and teaching materials. Richards and Schmidt (2010: 532) provide a definition that seems to us to reflect current thinking in that a skill is 'an acquired ability to perform an activity well, usually one that is made up of a number of co-ordinated processes'.

In language teaching, skills are often discussed in terms of four different modes – that is, reading, listening, speaking and writing. The division of each language skill into separate chapters in this book is intentional and is not intended to reinforce the notion of the skills being taught in isolation, but rather is a way of devoting sufficient space to each one to further our original intention throughout the whole book – that of linking key principles to instances of classroom practice. Cross-referencing (both explicit and implicit) occurs often within this part of the book.

6.1 Introduction

We shall begin this chapter by thinking about the different types of material that we read and how these are linked to the purpose that we have in reading.

Materials and Methods in ELT: A Teacher's Guide, Third Edition.
Jo McDonough, Christopher Shaw, and Hitomi Masuhara.
© 2013 John Wiley & Sons, Inc. Published 2013 by John Wiley & Sons, Inc.

After this, we attempt to show how advances in our conceptual knowledge about the reading process have changed some of our approaches to designing and using materials for the teaching of reading. We then look at different ways of providing feedback to learners on their reading. The final part of the chapter is devoted to vocabulary and vocabulary teaching.

As a skill, reading is clearly one of the most important; in fact, in many instances around the world, we may argue that reading is the most important language skill, particularly in cases where students have to read English material for their own specialist subject but may never have to speak the language. English has also been the main driving language of the Internet. Though multimedia-based interaction over the Internet is becoming common nowadays in a resource-rich environment (as described in Chapter 5 of this book), basic Internet communication continues to assume reading skills as the primary mode of communication. Furthermore, from a language acquisition point of view, reading can be a major source of comprehensible input (Krashen, 2004) especially in countries where English is rarely used outside the classroom.

Even though we are looking at each language skill independently in these chapters, there is clearly an overlap between reading and writing, in that a 'text' has to be written down before we can read it. In many societies, literature is still seen as the prime example of writing and therefore, one of the first things a student is asked to do is to read. In classroom terms, one of the reasons for this is partly practical: it is often thought to be easier to supply a written text to be read than a spoken one to be understood.

6.2   Reasons for Reading

Much of the current thinking tends to focus primarily on the purpose of reading because our reading processes will vary according to our purpose. Let us consider how this may be so.

> Think of some materials you have read during the last week, both in English and in your own L1. Make a list of them.

The list that you have drawn up may include newspapers, letters (personal and formal), leaflets, labels on jars, tins and packets, advertisements, magazines, books and so on. Some people may add emails, text messages and all kinds of texts from the Internet (e.g. news, online shopping, poems and stories). Do you read these different kinds of texts in the same way?

Williams (1984) usefully classifies reading into (1) getting general information from a text, (2) getting specific information from a text, and (3) for pleasure or for interest. Which of the texts you listed in your reflection task would require the kinds of reading identified in Williams' categories? How similar or different do you think the reading processes are from one category to another?

Think about how many of these different types of reading materials you will find in your teaching textbook.

What kinds of reading do your students have to do in their L1? How about in the L2?

Do the textbooks satisfy the needs and wants of your students' lives? The EFL learners in your country may not have many opportunities to read any kind of texts in English. If so, what kinds of reading texts and reading experience should materials offer?

Some global ELT materials include reading texts such as newspaper and magazine articles, advertisements, web materials (for examples, see a review of eight global coursebooks published in the United Kingdom in Masuhara et al., 2008). Tomlinson (2008) provides a useful collection of critical evaluations of coursebooks used around the world. Some other textbooks may contain more of what we might call more 'traditional' types of texts, especially longer stretches of narrative and descriptions. We shall look at the implications of this later in the chapter.

6.3   Changes in the Concept of Reading Skills

We have looked at some of the purposes and reasons for reading which we may wish to develop with our learners. Let us now look at how the concept of reading as a skill has evolved in recent years and how this in turn has come to be reflected in the types of ELT materials available.

The traditional way of organizing materials in a unit is generally to begin with a piece of specially written material, which is then 'read' by the student. Such an arrangement essentially focuses on items of grammar and vocabulary that are then to be developed during the unit. This is inadequate if we are attempting to teach reading skills, as students are not being exposed to the variety of styles we would expect with a variety of texts – a scientific report is not written in the same way as a personal letter or instructions on a medicine bottle.

Hence, in reading classes we sometimes have a confusion of aims: often the students are not being taught reading and how to develop reading abilities per se, but rather a written text is being used as a vehicle for the introduction of new vocabulary and/or structures. It is fairly common for such texts to begin along the following lines:

It is eight o'clock in the morning. Mr Smith is in the dining room of their house. Mr Smith is sitting at the table reading his newspaper. He is waiting for his breakfast. Mrs Smith is in the kitchen cooking breakfast for Mr Smith, her husband, and their two children. John and Mary. . . .

The text would then continue in a similar way.

As reading material it seems artificial because the intention is to draw learners' attention to items of structural usage rather than to the authentic features characteristic of 'real' text, or what makes texts 'hang together'. Many teachers, however, still work with this type of material. In this particular passage the sentences are strung together in isolation with little attempt at coherence. The same structures are repeated several times in a rather contrived way, making the whole text feel awkward and inauthentic. Another problem associated with these specially prepared texts, when it comes to the choice of topic, is that the learners are either presented with overfamiliar material that does not focus on what they can bring to the text, or the content is inconsequential for them. No real interaction takes place between writer and reader as the artificiality of the text means that no real message is being communicated. As we shall see later in relation to the overfamiliarity issue, comprehension questions on a text can sometimes be answered without having to look at the text at all! The essential purpose of all reading generally is to get new information and/or for pleasure, not to go over what is known already or what is inconsequential to the reader in the first place.

A good many of the so-called traditional reading materials do not provide learners with useful texts or effective strategies to improve their reading abilities; and if we are to improve the teaching of reading skills, then research into the reading process may well be of some use. However, research tends to show that we know more about what skilled readers can do, rather than how they do it with any real degree of certainty.

Traditionally, and this is borne out in many of the materials, the reader was seen as the 'recipient' of information or as an 'empty vessel' who brought nothing to the text. This notion of 'text as object' (figure 6.1) is now frequently discredited in reading circles as readers are not entirely passive.

This 'text as object' viewpoint regards the reader as having nothing to contribute to the reading process as such; the writer provides information for

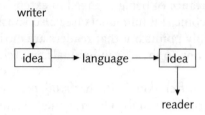

Figure 6.1   The text as object viewpoint.

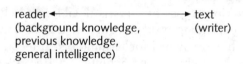

Figure 6.2   The text as process viewpoint.

the reader who is seen as an 'empty vessel' that merely receives information. We may liken this to a one-way traffic system in which everything flows in one direction only (see also Nuttall, 2005 for a similar argument).

In recent years, however, an increasing number of ELT materials that profess to develop reading skills have moved from the 'text as object' viewpoint shown above, to that of the 'text as process', by encouraging close interaction between the reader and the text (figure 6.2).

6.4   Types of Reading Skills

Ur (1996) suggests various criteria that distinguish efficient from inefficient readers: efficient readers can access content more easily by changing reading speed according to text, they can select significant features of a text and skim the rest, they can guess or infer meaning from context, they think ahead by predicting outcomes, they use background knowledge to help them understand the meaning, they are motivated to read the text as they see it as a challenge and the text has a purpose, they can switch reading strategy according to the type of text they are reading and so on.

Eskey (2005: 571), on the other hand, acknowledges the idiosyncratic and unpredictable nature of individual reading preferences and styles, '. . . readers differ in what they read, how much they read, how well they read, and how much they depend on or care about reading'. He then emphasizes the importance of being engaged in extensive reading experiences for the learners to become skillful readers (see also Krashen, 2004 for empirical evidence). He rightly points out that readers are most likely to be engaged if the texts are interesting to them as individuals and relevant to their particular needs and wants.

Classroom teachers often complain that students view reading as tedious and therefore low priority simply because they do not feel challenged or involved in the text. This may be overcome if the text is (and also perceived as) relevant to them. The learners can also be encouraged to 'dialogue' with the writer by expecting questions to be answered, reflecting on expectations at every stage, anticipating what the writer will say next and so on.

It is generally recognized now that the efficient reader versed in ways of interacting with various types of texts is flexible, and chooses appropriate reading strategies depending on the particular text in question. 'Strategy' is another term which is renowned for terminological inconsistency but we go with the definition by Richards and Schmidt (2010: 559–60) that strategies mean 'procedures used in learning . . . which serve as a way of reaching a goal'. McNamara (2007) reports how research confirms the importance of strategy use in L1 reading and how successful readers know when and how to use appropriate strategies. We also need to help our learners become aware that they should match reading strategies to reading purpose. We do not, for example, read seventeenth-century poetry in the same way as we read the television page in our newspaper. Skilled readers scan to locate specific information in a text and skim to extract general information from it. These strategies are quite widely practised in many contemporary ELT reading courses (see the example from a textbook on pp. 115–6).

Literature in mind

THE NUMBER ONE BESTSELLER

YANN MARTEL

Life of Pi

winner of
THE Man BOOKER PRIZE 2002

7 Read

Life of Pi

After the tragic sinking of a cargo ship which was carrying an entire zoo, one lifeboat remains on the wild, blue Pacific. The only survivors from the wreck are a sixteen-year-old boy named Pi, a hyena, a zebra (with a broken leg), a female orang-utan… and a 450-pound Royal Bengal tiger. The tiger eats the other animals – and then there's only it and the boy.

In this extract, the boy Pi has seen a petrol tanker coming towards the lifeboat that he is on, and believes at first that he and the tiger are going to be saved.

(a) **Read the extract quickly to find the answer to these questions.**

1 Who is Richard Parker?
2 Does the tanker hit the lifeboat or not?

I realised with horror that the tanker was not simply coming our way – it was in fact bearing down on us. The bow was a vast wall of metal that was getting wider every second. A huge wave girdling it was advancing towards us relentlessly. Richard Parker finally sensed the looming juggernaut. He turned and went 'Woof! Woof!' but not doglike – it was tigerlike: powerful, scary and utterly suited to the situation.

'Richard Parker, it's going to run us over! What are we going to do? Quick, quick, a flare! No! Must row. Oar in oarlock … there! *HUMPF! HUMPF! HUMPF! HUMPF! HUMPF! HUM–*'

The bow wave pushed us up. Richard Parker crouched, and the hairs on him stood up. The lifeboat slid off the bow wave and missed the tanker by less than two feet.

The ship slid by for what seemed like a mile, a mile of high, black canyon wall, a mile of castle fortification with not a single sentinel to notice us languishing in the moat. I fired off a rocket flare, but I aimed it poorly. Instead of surging over the bulwarks and exploding in the captain's face, it ricocheted off the ship's side and went straight into the Pacific, where it died with a hiss. I blew my whistle with all my might. I shouted at the top of my lungs. All to no avail.

Its engines rumbling loudly and its propellers chopping explosively underwater, the ship churned past us and left us bouncing and bobbing in its frothy wake. After so many weeks of natural sounds, these mechanical noises were strange and awesome and stunned me into silence.

In less than twenty minutes a ship of three hundred thousand tons became a speck on the horizon. When I turned away, Richard Parker was still looking in its direction. After a few seconds he turned away too and our gazes briefly met. My eyes expressed longing, hurt, anguish, loneliness. All he was aware of was that something stressful and momentous had happened, something beyond the outer limits of his understanding. He did not see that it was salvation barely missed. He only saw that the alpha here, this odd, unpredictable tiger, had been very excited. He settled down to another nap. His sole comment on the event was a cranky miaow.

'I love you!' The words burst out pure and unfettered, infinite. The feeling flooded my chest. 'Truly I do. I love you, Richard Parker. If I didn't have you now, I don't know what I would do. I don't think I would make it. No, I wouldn't. I would die of hopelessness. Don't give up, Richard Parker, don't give up. I'll get you to land, I promise, I promise!'

(b) **Read the extract again. Put the statements in the order in which they occur in the extract.**

a Pi starts to row the lifeboat. ☐

b Pi realises that he has positive feelings about the tiger. ☐

c Pi fires a flare but it isn't seen. ☐

d Pi realises that the tanker might be going to hit the lifeboat. `1`

e Pi blows a whistle and shouts but no one hears him ☐

f The tanker disappers out of sight. ☐

g Pi thinks that Richard Parker sees him as a kind of tiger. ☐

h The noise of the tanker is strange to Pi after weeks at sea. ☐

i The tiger goes to sleep. ☐

j The wave of the tanker lifts the lifeboat up. ☐

(c) **Replace the words in italics with a word or phrase from the box. Use the text to check the meanings of the words in the box.**

> to no avail   relentlessly   speck   looming   anguish   crouched
> with all his might   languishing

1   I trudged on *in an extreme way* through the heavy rain to get back to our warm camp.

2   The *large and frightening* shape of the oncoming ship was clearly visible to us all.

3   We *bent our knees and lowered our body* behind a tree and kept quiet hoping not to be found.

4   The sick man had been *existing in an unpleasant situation* in a tent in the desert for almost a month.

5   Joseph tried *as hard as he could* to move the fallen tree from the road.

6   We advised Paula and George not to travel when they felt so ill, but it was *with no success at all*.

7   Helen's house is so clean; there isn't a *tiny spot* of dirt anywhere!

8   In Josie's *extreme unhappiness*, she forgot her suitcase when she left for the airport.

(d) **Answer the questions.**

1   Why do you think the tiger has not eaten the boy?

2   Why do you think the tanker didn't stop and help them?

3   Why do you think Pi says 'I love you, Richard Parker'?

Source: H. Puchta, J. Stranks and P. Lewis-Jones, From Exercise 7b, c and d on pp 66–67, *English in Mind Level 5 Student's Book*. Copyright © Cambridge University Press, 2008. Reprinted with permission of Cambridge University Press.
Source: Excerpt from *Life of Pi* by Y. Martel. Copyright © 2001 by Yann Martel. Reproduced with permission of Houghton Mifflin Harcourt Publishing Company, Random House of Canada Limited, Westwood Creative Artists Ltd, and Canongate Books UK.
Source: Illustration of the book cover *Life of Pi* by Y. Martell, illustration by Andy Bridge. Copyright © Andy Bridge, reprinted with kind permission of the illustrator.

All that we have mentioned thus far tends to confirm the now generally accepted view that efficient readers are not passive and do not operate in a vacuum: they react with the text by having expectations (even though these might in fact have nothing to do with the content of the text) and ideas about the purpose of the text, as well as ideas about possible outcomes.

Efficient readers also interrogate materials of all types by looking for 'clues' in titles, subtitles and within the passage itself. Pre-reading questions can be useful because they focus learners' attention on the types of information that they are about to read.

Getting the learner to interact with different types of text as outlined above does not necessarily mean that learners will have to understand the whole text immediately. They may, for example, be able to understand and to extract specific information from the text as in the example on p. 118.

Global English

Sports English
by David Crystal

Sports commentary is very familiar these days but it only arrived with the start of radio and television broadcasting. The term *sports announcer* was first used in 1923, soon followed by *sporting commentator* in the UK and *sportscaster* in the US. The modern British term, *sports commentator*, dates from the 1930s.

5 Sports commentating sounds easy, but it's difficult to do well, especially on radio, where a long silence can mean disaster. Detailed knowledge of the sport, keen observational skills, the ability to **think on your feet**, and above-average linguistic skills are essential. To make the job easier, commentators can use 'tricks of the trade' such
10 as formulaic expressions. In horse racing there are certain things commentators always say at particular moments such as *They're off!*, *in the lead*, and *into the straight they come*. This means there is less for them to remember and it helps with fluency.

Each sport has its own style, reflecting the atmosphere and
15 momentum, from the wild excitement of football (*It's a GO-O-O-AL*) to the quiet tones of snooker. There's distinctive grammar and vocabulary too. Commentaries are the perfect place to find the English present tense, both simple and continuous (*he's looking for a chance ... he scores ...*), and incomplete sentences (*Beckham to Kaka ... back to Beckham ...*).

20 But if you're looking for new vocabulary, you'll find more in the keep-fit disciplines, such as yoga (with its hundreds of words taken from Sanskrit), Pilates (with its unusual pronunciation taken from the name of its founder, Joseph Pilates, 'puh-<u>lah</u>-teez'), and the combination of yoga and Pilates *yogalates*. And that's just **the tip of the iceberg** of new linguistic blends. If
25 you're into *exertainment* (exercise + entertainment) you'll know about the many kinds of *exergaming* (exercise + gaming). The neologisms keep your tongue linguistically fit too.

Glossary

above-average (*adjective*) – good, better than normal

discipline (*noun*) – a subject or sport

formulaic expression (*noun*) – an expression that has been used lots of times before

keen (*adjective*) – very strong

linguistic blend (*noun*) – a mixture of two or more words

neologism (*noun*) – a new word or expression, or an existing word with a new meaning

sports commentator (*noun*) – a person whose job is to give a description of a sporting event on television or radio as it happens.

Warm up

Read the definition of *sports commentator*. Are there any well-known sports commentators in your country? What are they famous for?

Reading

1 Read the text *Sports English*. Tick (✔) the topics that are mentioned. There are two topics you do not need.

a different words for sport
b sports commentary
c style of speaking
d winners and losers
e English grammar
f new vocabulary

2 Read the text again and find examples of ...

a something you need to be a good sports commentator.
b a 'formulaic expression' that helps commentators sound more fluent.
c an examples of an incomplete sentence used in sports.
d a 'keep-fit' sport.
e a neologism.

Language focus

1 Look at the expressions in **bold** in the text. Answer the questions below.

1 If you *think on your feet*, you ...
  a are a very quick runner.
  b have good ideas and make decisions quickly.
  c get nervous in a difficult situation.
2 If we say something is *the tip of the iceberg*, it means ...
  a there is a lot more of it that you can't see.
  b there is only a little bit of it.
  c it is a very dangerous thing.

2 Put each of the expressions into an example of your own. Tell a partner.

Speaking

1 Work in pairs and ask each other the questions.

• Do you enjoy listening to commentators?
• What sports do you like to watch?
• Do you do any *exergaming*?

Global English Unit 9   **111**

Source: L. Clanfield and A. Jeffries, p. 111, *Global Pre-Intermediate Student Book*. Oxford: Macmillan Education. Text © David Crystal, Instruction © Lindsay Clanfield and Amanda Jeffries 2010. Design & Illustration © Macmillan Publishers Limited 2010. Reprinted with permission of Macmillan Publishers Ltd. All rights reserved.

6.5   Schema Theory

Another major contribution to our knowledge of reading, with many implications for the classroom, is provided by Schema theory. Bartlett (1932) first used this particular term to explain how the knowledge that we have about the world is organized into interrelated patterns based on our previous knowledge and experience. According to the proponents of Schema theory, these 'schemata' also allow us to predict what may happen. Taking the idea of the interactive reading process a stage further, efficient readers are able to relate 'texts' to their background knowledge of the world. Brown and Yule (1983b), McCarthy and Carter (1994), Cook (1997) and Nunan (1999) all provide accounts of how this background knowledge can influence the comprehension process. Clearly it can sometimes be based on previous knowledge of similar texts. In this sense 'Formal Schema' seems useful as well as 'Content Schema' (Carrell et al., 1988). For example, if we are reading a newspaper, we know from previous experience about the typeface, the layout, the order in which the information is presented and so on. We share cultural background material with others. As Nunan (1999: 256) writes, 'We interpret what we read in terms of what we already know, and we integrate what we already know with the content of what we are reading'. The word 'wedding' in a British context could engender a complete schematic framework to accompany it; that is, 'last Saturday', 'Registry Office', 'Best Man' and so on. This is why reading something written by someone in a language with different cultural assumptions from ours can be difficult. Overseas teachers and students sometimes complain that reading literature in an L2 is problematic not just because of the language, but also because shared assumptions or different schemata do not always match up. Grabe (2002: 282) warns that 'schema theory is hardly a theory, and there is very little research which actually explores what a schema is and how it would work for reading comprehension'. He does, however, value schema as 'a useful simplifying metaphor for the more general notion of prior knowledge'.

In many cases an efficient reader appears to use what are called 'top-down' and 'bottom-up' strategies. This means that the reader will not just try to decipher the meaning of individual lexical items but will also have clear ideas about the overall rhetorical organization of the text. With the influence of Schema theory, 'top' has come to mean not only linguistic elements such as discourse but also conceptual elements such as associated background knowledge in our memory. The essential features of the bottom-up approach are that the reader tries to decode each individual letter encountered by matching it to the minimal units of meaning in the sound system (the phoneme) to arrive at a meaning of the text, whereas with the top-down approach, the interaction process between the reader and the text involves the reader in activating knowledge of the world, plus past experiences, expectations and

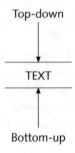

Figure 6.3   Top-down and bottom-up processing of a text.

intuitions, to arrive at a meaning of the text. In other words, the top-down process interacts with the bottom-up process in order to aid comprehension (figure 6.3).

We might further illustrate this by looking at a speaking/listening analogy first of all. If someone asks us, 'Have you got a light?' and we get stuck at the level of the bottom-up process by working out each individual word, then clearly we are missing the top-down request, that the speaker is in fact asking for a match.

Let us look at a newspaper extract about education in Britain in order to see how some of these principles may operate in reality.

> From the title, can you predict what the passage will be about? As you are reading the text, think about how you are reading it.

Paying to Learn: Is It Snobbery?

The British social system is probably the most snobbish in the world but that does not necessarily mean – since it is perfectly natural for parents to wish to give their children the same or a better education than they themselves received – that those who choose to educate their children privately are all snobs. Thus, many upper class families who were forced to send their children to boarding schools at the height of the British Empire because they were often out of the country for years, naturally wish to continue the tradition, although nowadays it involves great financial sacrifices. Even today many pupils in boarding schools are still opting out of what may be the best state education system in the world. Some of these are obviously doing this for snobbish reasons – believing that to have been educated privately is to be socially 'one-up' and that children thus educated, whatever their ability, will have an advantage over their state-educated contemporaries. The less said about this type of parent the better. Fortunately, most parents who choose private education have very good reasons for doing so.

A good start to a child's education is vital and, since the war, classes in many primary schools have been very large so that nervous children or those of average or below average ability could easily get lost in the crowd and miss out on education altogether. This explains the popularity of the small private preparatory school in which a child has more individual attention and help with particular difficulties. Some children of very good ability certainly do not need to be educated privately: my own children have all been educated in the state system and have all gone on to higher education.

However, this is a free country and parents who wish to pay for education are perfectly entitled to do so – they could spend their money much less wisely. There are, nonetheless, two great dangers in having a private system running alongside the state system. One is the development of a privileged class, with the result that people get the top jobs not on the basis of ability but of who they are and where they went to school. If this country is to survive, we must educate our best brains to the highest possible standard – irrespective of their social and financial standing. The other is that we shall need a highly skilled and adaptable workforce capable of dealing with the advanced technology of the future, and this will require an efficient state system of education possessing all the necessary advanced equipment.

> Where did you look on the line? Did you skim/scan? Did you go backwards/forwards? Did you stop to look at every word? Did you stop to think at all?

As teachers we may want to offer our learners one effective reading strategy, which might be to approach this text by noting the title first of all. This clearly points ahead to what the writer will be saying and how the argument develops at various stages in the text itself, when the author is giving approval and disapproval to various types of parent. The reader may also put 'schematic' knowledge into operation: in other words, an understanding of the background to the British education system, the state-versus-private-education debate, the British Empire, the class system. This 'top-down' processing would interact with the text as would the 'bottom-up' processing at the lexical level. The reader may also get through the passage by means of what are sometimes referred to as the discourse signposts in the text: expressions such as 'however', 'fortunately', and 'there are, nonetheless', which are meant as a useful guide for the reader.

6.6 Implications

Teachers should provide students with a purpose for reading by supplying materials that stimulate interest and do not have an overfamiliar content. Of all the language skills, reading is the most private, and there is a problem in getting feedback on a private process. The notion of privacy in reading can sometimes be related to learner needs: a learner may need material of a different level and topic to other learners in the group, which may involve the teacher in the provision of some individualized reading in the programme. Reading practised with reading laboratories and/or self-access centres may well be more pertinent to some learners' needs. (For a full discussion of individualization and self-access systems, see Chapter 12.) We also have to be able to assess the difficulty of the materials for our own learners and to grade them according to familiarity of topic, length and complexity of structure and possible number of unfamiliar words/expressions, as overloading learners with too much may involve them in decoding vocabulary at the expense of reading for meaning. We can also develop and foster appropriate skills according to reading purpose, for example by encouraging students to read quickly when it is appropriate to do so. Timed activities or 'speed reading' can be related to the private nature of the reading process that we mentioned earlier. In other words, reading quickly with good overall comprehension does not necessarily have to be made competitive with other students as the individual student and/or the teacher can keep a record of how long it takes to extract information from a given source. Consequently, the transferability of principled flexible skills to different types of reading materials is one of the most effective things to develop in the reading skills class.

6.7   Classroom Practice and Procedure

On a worldwide level, the format of teaching reading skills may vary according to local circumstances. Many teachers consider dividing reading into intensive, classroom-based work with an adjunctive extensive reading programme to give further out-of-class practice. Some classes will be called 'reading' and will therefore focus primarily on the development of reading skills. Sometimes teachers include reading skills as part of another class either for reasons of expediency – because there is only one timetabled period for English – or for reasons of principle – because they believe that reading is best integrated with the other skills such as writing. The following suggestions for classroom practice and procedure will be of interest to teachers of reading skills.

After reviewing all the recent developments in reading pedagogy, Eskey (2005: 574) argues that 'People learn to read, and to read better, by reading'. He wisely points out that 'The reading teacher's job is . . . not so much to teach a specific skill or content as to get students reading and to keep them reading – that is, to find a way to motivate them to read, and to facilitate their reading. . .'.

R. V. White (1981) makes some suggestions that are still applicable today about the stages and procedure of a reading lesson that may help us (1) to put the skill into a classroom context, and (2) to see some of its possible relationships with the other language skills:

Stage 1   Arouse the students' interest and motivation by linking the topic of the text to their own experience or existing knowledge. Give some pre-reading/focusing questions to help them to do this.
Stage 2   Give them points to search for in the reading text, or ask the students to suggest the points.
Stage 3   After reading, encourage a discussion of answers.
Stage 4   Develop into writing by using the information gained for another purpose.

Tomlinson (2003b: 113–21) offers a detailed account of his flexible text-driven framework, which facilitates the development and teaching of materials based on engaging texts. He then provides an actual example of a text and how it can be exploited using his framework. The teaching procedure involves five stages (see the original article for a complete version for materials development):

Stage 1   Readiness Activities – Help the learners achieve readiness for experiencing the text prior to reading by raising curiosity and motivation through activating their existing knowledge or experience.
Stage 2   Experiential Activities – Help the learners to process the text in an experiential way through while-reading activities.
Stage 3   Intake Response Activities – Help the learners to articulate and develop their mental representation of the text through articulating which facilitates the development and teaching of materials based on their impressions or reactions to the text.
Stage 4   Development Activities – Help the learners to use their representation of the text as a basis for creative language production activities.
Stage 5   Input Response Activities – Help the learners to go back to the text and to discover patterns and regularities of language use in the text.

After exploring the texts in Stage 5, Tomlinson encourages revisiting and improving the work produced in Stage 4. What emerges from his description and example is an overall sequence of starting from the learners' minds to text exploration and back to the learners' minds, thus encouraging the integration of new with existing knowledge and experience.

> Look at the reading passage 'Paying to Learn' on pp 120–1. How could you develop it within the framework outlined above?

Davies (1995) argues the case for providing reading classes and texts that allow students to interact and question the text and to ask about what they do not know, in the belief that this will foster critical readers. Janks (2009) further explores critical awareness elements in literacy and links theory and practice in relation to how language is used by different users for different purposes in diverse social contexts.

Finally, there are teachers who may want or need to design their own reading course within a particular institution. In some cases, L2 readers may require more fundamental literacy education prior to skills/strategy or extensive reading programmes. Reading experts have come to realize that phonological competence is a prerequisite for fluent reading through the neurobiological studies of poor L1 readers (Shaywitz and Shaywitz, 2008). Masuhara (2007), based on her comparative review of L1 and L2 reading acquisition and development, points out that in L1, children spend about five years in aural-oral language acquisition prior to learning how to read whereas in the L2, the learning of language and reading takes place at the same time. She points out the remarkable resemblance in study results of reading difficulties of L1 poor readers and L2 readers and makes some recommendations that incorporate recent insights into reading programmes (see also Masuhara, 2003 and 2005 for examples). Tomlinson (2001) proposes ways of making a smooth transition from an aural/oral phase to effective reading.

Nunan (1999) considers five essential steps involved in designing reading courses:

1   Decide the overall purpose of the reading course within a wider pedagogical framework.
2   Identify the types of texts and tasks that the course requires.
3   Identify the linguistic elements to be covered (consider what is going to be important: grammatical items/lexis/discourse/specific purpose etc.).
4   Integrate texts and tasks into class-based work units.
5   Link reading to other language skills where pertinent (reading as a mono-skill is only taught in some very narrow-angle library language situations. Hence, it is useful to think how reading can usefully be integrated with the other language skills. (See Chapter 10 for further discussion.)

Now let us look at a range of ways for developing reading skills in the classroom and the principles behind each of them:

1   Practising specific strategies such as skimming/scanning with a particular text. The idea behind this is to enable the learner to read and select specific information at the expense of other (redundant) information.

2   One effective way of developing reading skills, which gives the learner a reason for reading, is to use the information gap principle often associated with communicative language teaching. In the materials that use information gap principle, the information required for the completion of a target task is distributed among two or more sources. Each subgroup only has part of the information required to complete the task. The subgroups consequently have to exchange their information so that the information gap is filled and the target task completed. This activity links reading with other forms of communication, for example, speaking/discussion or listening/writing, and can thus provide a reading-driven integration of the language skills.

3   Several of the more recent materials for reading contain what are sometimes referred to as 'text scrambling' activities. The principle behind this type of material is that students can be taught to have an awareness of the discourse or cohesive features of reading materials. If a passage is clearly written, then it can be 'scrambled' and reassembled in the correct order if the learner can recognize the discourse patterns and markers in the text.

4   Some reading materials are constructed along the lines that the learners bring not only background knowledge to reading but emotional (affective) responses as well, and will want to talk about their reactions to various texts.

5   In some instances, depending on the learners and their proficiency, it is feasible to ask the learners themselves to provide reading texts or to research their own material for analysis and discussion in class, particularly in an EAP (English for Academic Purposes) context. Learners often need to read through a lot of material before they select an appropriate piece of material or article. With the advent of the World Wide Web, teachers working in institutions with computers may wish to encourage this. (See Chapters 5 and 12 for more discussion of Web-based teaching and learning.)

6   Teachers need to think about choosing reading passages that provide learners with a way of questioning and interacting with the text (Davies, 1995) to ascertain for example what the writer thinks, not necessarily explicitly, about an issue or topic.

1   Examine your own materials for reading. To what extent do they incorporate these principles? Which are different?
2   Decide which types of reading skills you could develop with the following materials. Start with the nature of the text and then look at what kinds of skills could come from it.

9 Tall stories

Here are four 'tall stories' – stories which are probably not true, but people enjoy telling them. Sometimes they are called urban myths. Read them and decide whether you think they really happened or not.

Safety first!

Did you hear about the plane which crashed somewhere in South America as it was coming in to land?

Apparently, it was fitted with a device which warns the pilot that he is approaching the ground – a Ground Warning Alarm (GWA) system. Some pilots find this warning irritating so they switch it off.

When the black box was examined, the crash was blamed on pilot error. The decision had been easy to reach. When the plane had been coming in to land, the GWA had gone off, telling the pilot he was too close to the ground. On the tape the pilot can be heard saying, "Shut up, you stupid machine!" Then you hear the sound of the crash.

True story or myth?

What a rat!

Then there was the story of the couple who were in Thailand on holiday. The morning after they arrived, they found a thin little cat sitting on their balcony. They immediately fell in love with it. They cleaned it and fed it. By the time they were ready to leave, they couldn't bear to be parted from it.

They arranged for the cat to come home with them. Waiting at home was their pet poodle. The poodle and the cat seemed to get on together very well, so the couple decided to go out for dinner. When they got back, they found their sitting room covered in poodle hair and the dog halfway down the cat's throat!

It turned out the cat was not a cat, but an enormous Thai water rat!

True story or myth?

Drowned in a drain

A man from Wakefield in Yorkshire went out one night for a few drinks at his local pub. He left his car in the street near the pub. When he decided to go home, he went out to his car, took out the keys, and then accidentally dropped them down a drain in the road.

He could see the keys down the drain on top of some leaves. So, he managed to lift the drain cover, but the key was too far down for him to reach. He lay down in order to reach them.

Suddenly, he fell into the drain head first. Just as he did that it started to rain heavily. Nobody heard his cries for help. The next morning he was found drowned, his head down the drain, his legs sticking up in the air.

True story or myth?

Sunk by flying cow

A few years ago, the crew of a Japanese fishing boat were rescued from the wreckage of their boat in the Sea of Japan. They said that their boat had been sunk by a cow falling out of the sky. Nobody believed them.

A few weeks later the Russian Air Force admitted that the crew of one of their planes had stolen a cow in Siberia and put it into the plane's cargo hold.

At 30,000 feet the cow started to run around the plane out of control. The crew decided there was only one thing they could do. So, they opened the cargo door and the cow jumped out, landing on top of the Japanese fishing boat.

True story or myth?

Read one of these stories again at home. You will be asked to tell it to the class at the next lesson. If you like this kind of story, they are all on the Web. Find them under 'urban myths'. Bring one in to class!

Source: Wellar/Walkley/Hocking, From p. 98, *Innovations Intermediate* 1E. Copyright © 2004 Heinle/ELT, a part of Cengage Learning, Inc. Reproduced by permission (http://www.Cengage.com/permissions).

Task 3 (Pairs)

Work in pairs, A and B.

Student A: Read Text 1. Note briefly in your section of the table the 'orthodox' view on the three aspects of work listed in the text.

Student B: Read Text 2. Note briefly in your section of the table the author's view on the three aspects of work listed in the text.

	Text 1	*Text 2*
NATURE OF WORK		
EFFECT OF WORKING CONDITIONS		
MOTIVATION FOR WORK		

Text 1 'Orthodox' view

THE orthodox view of work which has been accepted by most managers and industrial psychologists is a simple one, and fifty years of industrial psychology and more than a century of managerial practice have been founded upon it. Regarding the *nature* of work, the orthodox view accepts the Old Testament 5
belief that physical labour is a curse imposed on man as a punishment for his sins and that the sensible man labours solely in order to keep himself and his family alive, or, if he is fortunate, in order to make a sufficient surplus to enable him to do the things he really likes.* Regarding the *conditions* of work, it is 10
assumed that improving the conditions of the job will cause the worker's natural dislike of it to be somewhat mitigated, and, in addition, will keep him physically healthy and therefore more efficient in the mechanistic sense. Finally, regarding the *motivation* of work, the carrot and stick hypothesis asserts that the main 15
positive incentive is money, the main negative one fear of unemployment.

Brown, J.A.C. (1954) *The Social Psychology of Industry*, p. 186 (London: Penguin).

Text 2 Author's view

(1) Work is an essential part of a man's life since it is that
aspect of his life which gives him status and binds him
to society. Ordinarily men and women like their work,
and at most periods of history always have done so.
When they do not like it, the fault lies in the psy-   5
chological and social conditions of the job rather than
in the worker. Furthermore, work is a *social* activity.

(2) The morale of the worker (i.e. whether or not he works
willingly) has no *direct* relationship whatsoever to the
material conditions of the job. Investigations into   10
temperature, lighting, time and motion study, noise,
and humidity have not the slightest bearing on morale,
although they may have a bearing on physical health
and comfort.

(3) There are many incentives, of which, under normal   15
conditions, money is one of the least important.
Unemployment is a powerful negative incentive, pre-
cisely because (1) is true. That is to say, unemployment
is feared because it cuts man off from his society.

Brown, J.A.C. op cit., p. 187.

Task 4 (Pairs)

Find out from your partner the views expressed in his or her text. Note
them in the appropriate section of the table in Task 3.

Now read each other's text to check if anything has been missed out.

Task 5 (Groups)

Work in groups. Discuss your own views and those expressed in the texts.
Do you agree with either text? Have your views changed through reading the
texts?

Source: E. Glendinning and B. Holmstrom, *Study Reading, A Course in Reading Skills for Academic Purpose*, excercise from pp. 104–5. Copyright © Cambridge University Press, 1992. Reprinted with permission of Cambridge University Press.
Source: J. A. C. Brown, *The Social Psychology of Industry*, p. 186. London: Penguin, 1954. Reprinted with permission of Penguin Books, UK.

6.8   Feedback to Learners

Earlier in the chapter we mentioned that reading is essentially a private activity. However, it remains a fact that as we 'teach' reading skills in the classroom, this often requires us to have some sort of observable (testable) outcome. In its most extreme form, this may be embodied in the materials themselves, which sometimes do little more than test the students rather than helping them to develop different, relevant reading skills.

Questions to learners can be in either written or spoken form and it is generally thought that a balance of the two is appropriate for most learning situations.

One way of thinking about reading comprehension questions is to consider the form of the question; for example, yes/no, true/false, multiple choice, non-verbal matrix to be completed, open-ended question and the type of question, what the question is trying to get out of the reader.

Nuttall (2005) identifies five basic question types commonly used for reading. The first of these is literal comprehension. By this she means that if readers do not understand the literal meaning of a particular text, then they are probably not going to get very much else out of that text. The second is reorganizing or putting the information in the text into a different order. Then come questions of inferring or 'reading between the lines'. Writers do not always state explicitly what they mean. An efficient reader can infer meaning not explicitly stated in the passage. This may be seen as an intellectual skill as opposed to a reading skill by some, although there is clearly a measure of overlap. Question types requiring a measure of personal response are often to be found in literary passages where the reader has to argue for a particular personal response supported by reference to the text. The last type of question is quite sophisticated and not all students would need it. Questions of evaluation would require the reader to assess how effectively the writer has conveyed her intention. If the writing is intended to convince or to persuade, how convincing or persuasive is it?

When evaluating questions for use with particular learners, there may not be enough of the right type or form to match their purpose or what the teacher knows about their personal background. A variety of different question forms and types that enable learners to use their different reading skills in appropriate ways is of most use.

Look at the following question, which accompanies the passage 'Paying to Learn' on pp 120–21. What form and type of question is it, according to Nuttall's classification outlined above?

'Complete the following chart with reasons why parents send their children to private schools and state whether the author considers each reason valid or not'.

Reason	Valid? Yes/No
a.	
b.	
c.	
d.	

Asking questions of the learner is not the only way to check comprehension. It is increasingly common to find materials that require the learner to extract meaning from them and then to use that information in order to do something else – such as jigsaw reading or tasks such as assembling an object from a set of instructions. Successful reading thus enables a certain task to be completed. In many respects, this is more akin to what most people do in their L1 or in the 'real' world; it is rare for people to have to answer questions on what they have read (see Van den Branden, 2006 for a general introduction to task-based approaches and also for actual examples of materials for different kinds of learners).

6.9　Vocabulary and Vocabulary Teaching: Recent Developments

A knowledge and understanding of vocabulary is often considered to be an integral part of a reader's overall competence in a foreign or second language, and the explicit teaching of vocabulary (sometimes linked to a reading class) has enjoyed something of a revival in recent years. Some teachers prefer to include vocabulary as part of their reading class as the following material helps to illustrate. Other teachers prefer to think of vocabulary as an area that merits its own syllabus and materials.

2 Before reading

After you have matched these words with their meanings, look them up in your dictionary to check that you fully understand them.

1. suspend
2. container
3. controversial
4. motive
5. consent
6. protester
7. pickled
8. formaldehyde

a. permission
b. very likely to cause an argument or protest
c. hang
d. reason for doing something (often criminal)
e. a bottle, can, jar or similar thing
f. a liquid used to preserve things
g. a person who disagrees in a public way
h. preserved (often in vinegar)

ART ATTACK

A man almost destroyed a work of art, worth £25,000, in a London art gallery yesterday. The work of art consisted of a glass container with a dead sheep suspended in formaldehyde.

The protester poured black ink into the case while it was on display at the Serpentine Gallery. Gallery staff were shocked as they saw the protester run away after first changing the name of the work to 'Black Sheep'.

The controversial work was originally called 'Away from the Flock'. It was the latest in a long line of animals pickled by famous British artist Damien Hirst. Neither the police nor gallery staff could think of a motive for the attack, other than the fact that it might be a protest about its controversial nature.

Hirst spent last night emptying the case and cleaning the animal in the hope that it might be repaired. Hirst said recently of the sculpture "I don't think it's shocking. It gets people interested in art. The worst thing is if someone just walks through a gallery without seeing anything." However, he went on to say, "People can't come in and mess about with exhibits without the artist's consent. But it could have been worse. Someone could have come in with a hammer."

Hirst has stated that he intends to pickle his grandmother in formaldehyde when she dies, but only if she gives her consent!

Source: Wellar/Walkley/Hocking, From p. 113, *Innovations Intermediate* 1E. Copyright © 2004 Heinle/ELT, a part of Cengage Learning, Inc. Reproduced by permission (http://www.Cengage.com/permissions).

Since the 1990s, language teachers have been able to benefit from the growth in computer-generated corpora, which has provided information about word frequency and how these words can be used in a range of spoken and written situations. The COBUILD Bank of English Corpus, the British National Corpus and the Cambridge International Corpus have already been referred to in Chapter 2. Major dictionaries nowadays are based on the new understanding of language which results from surveying corpus data. In the Longman Dictionary, for example, the 3000 most frequent words in writing and speech are given special attention. (Refer to Chapter 2 again for a full discussion of the lexical approach.)

Research into vocabulary and vocabulary acquisition shows that we have not explicitly been taught the majority of words that we know in a language (Carter, 2001). This raises some interesting questions for the teaching of vocabulary. Beyond a certain point of proficiency in learning a foreign or second language, the acquiring of any new vocabulary is probably going to be implicit rather than explicit. Many practitioners believe that vocabulary development is essentially what is known as an explicit–implicit continuum, where learners may benefit from explicit or implicit learning depending on the stage of their language learning career.

6.10   Vocabulary: What to Teach?

What is your overall approach to vocabulary and vocabulary teaching? Do you teach vocabulary in your reading classes or devote separate lessons to it? Why is this?

Teaching vocabulary in its narrowest sense is teaching the individual words of the language that we expect learners to acquire. However, we know from our knowledge of language that an understanding and production of any sort of 'text' normally involves more language than using a simple word in isolation. Hence, learners may need to progress beyond the basic grammar of regular and irregular verbs and nouns, for example, and be taught more complex multi-word verbs and idioms in context such as 'put someone through on the phone' or someone who 'puts in for a promotion' or 'decides to call it a day'. Lewis (1993) argues that prepositions, modal verbs and delexical verbs (take a swim, have a rest) need to be taught as part of vocabulary development. Lewis (2000) contains chapters which suggest some classroom activities that will help learners to become aware of collocation, to learn general strategies and to use collocation dictionaries. Ur (1996: 60–3) advocates a type of 'mini-syllabus' of vocabulary items that ideally need to be taught to the majority of foreign language learners. These items would typically include collocations such as to 'throw a ball' but to 'toss a coin'. Learners could work with dictionaries to see how collocations are listed and treated. O'Keeffe et al. (2007) provide a comprehensive account of how corpus data can inform the teaching of vocabulary.

Definitions, connotations and appropriateness

Many learners will need to define various concepts as part of their course. If we define a dog as a common, domestic carnivorous animal to some people, the connotation will be friendly and loyal, whereas to others it will mean perhaps dirty and inferior. Taboo words and slang expressions may have their place in some vocabulary classrooms. Stylistic appropriateness is another aspect of vocabulary work that can be stressed: when to use a formal or informal version of a word, for example.

Other areas to look at may include words of the same or similar meaning (synonyms) and those that mean the opposite (antonyms). Superordinates or words used to denote general concepts to cover specific items can also be useful (see Thornbury, 2002 for practical suggestions).

Teachers might also need to teach the component parts of words and multi-words, particularly prefixes and suffixes, so that learners can readily interpret words in context such as 'disrespectful', 'ungrateful', 'mismatch'.

6.11 Vocabulary: Other Possibilities

Depending on the types of learners we are dealing with, there is also the possibility of looking at lexical fields in a subject area such as economics or science where associated vocabulary items are linked to a wider picture. New inventions lead to the introduction of neologisms or new words and expressions in the language, which can be a rich source of vocabulary development work. In recent years, we have seen the introduction of new subjects and expressions such as 'ecommerce'; 'email virus'; 'surfing the Net'; 'wading through a ton of emails' and so on. Given the nature of English as a global or international language, some teachers may wish to concentrate on aspects of vocabulary that differ in, say, British and American English.

New innovations in learning technologies over the past decade or so have also opened up possibilities for teachers to link vocabulary work to computers and the Internet. The corpus-based dictionaries allow further permutations for teachers organizing classroom work, as learners can work individually or in pairs with online versions of these dictionaries (for useful classroom activities, see Fox, 1998; Reppen, 2011 and Willis, J 2011 in Tomlinson, 2003a). These online versions often have task sheets or worksheets incorporated so that learners can approach vocabulary from a wide variety of perspectives. Learners may also wish to keep a learning diary of their progress and feelings about their vocabulary development. This idea is explored further in Chapter 12.

6.12   Conclusion

We began this chapter by examining some of the reasons why we read, as well as the types of material we might typically read in our daily lives. We then considered how our understanding of the reading process and how changes in the concept of reading skills have affected approaches to the design of materials for the teaching of reading, particularly the insights offered by Schema theory. We then looked at these implications for classroom practice and procedure and discussed a range of approaches and materials that feature in reading classrooms. Next we looked at some of the different ways available to teachers for providing feedback to learners on their reading. Finally, we considered some of the different approaches involved in teaching and learning vocabulary.

> In what ways might your approaches to the teaching of reading be modified as a result of this chapter?

6.13   Further Reading

The following books provide a useful insight into the area:

1   Alderson, J. C. (2000): *Assessing Reading Summarises Various Ways of Assessing Reading Skills.*
2   Birch, B. M. (2006): *English L2 Reading: Getting to the Bottom Looks onto the Influence of L1 in Linguistics Processing During Reading.*
3   Grave, W. (2009): *Reading in a Second Language: Moving from Theory to Practice*. This gives a theoretical and pedagogical overview.
4   Nuttall, C. (2005): *Teaching Reading Skills in a Foreign Language*, 3rd edition.

7
Listening Skills

7.1 Introduction

The previous chapter has pointed us in the direction of several themes, both of principle and practice, that will be relevant for the consideration of listening skills to which we now turn. Most obviously, we are dealing with the other key skill under the heading of 'comprehension', and it is simple common sense to assume that reading and listening will share a number of underlying characteristics. The language teaching world turned its attention to listening rather later than it did to reading comprehension (see Rost, 2001 for a brief but useful background of how teaching listening evolved; see also Field, 2008 for a more extensive account). This was due in part to the relevance of quite a large body of research on reading: more importantly, the 'library language' perspective was significant in English language classrooms long before a shrinking world and increased international interdependence led to a greater focus on face-to-face language skills. Even now, however, many learners do not have much opportunity to interact with native speakers, let alone travel to English-speaking countries, so this time lag in the attention given to the different skills is readily understandable. This lack of opportunities, however, should not result in neglect of this fundamental source of language acquisition. As Rost (2005: 503) confirms, 'In L2 development, listening constitutes not only a skill area in performance, but also a primary means of acquiring a second language (see also Masuhara, 2007 for a review of studies that investigate how listening skills are a prerequisite in acquiring reading skills). Recent listening skills publications (Flowerdew and Miller, 2005; Field, 2008;

Materials and Methods in ELT: A Teacher's Guide, Third Edition.
Jo McDonough, Christopher Shaw, and Hitomi Masuhara.
© 2013 John Wiley & Sons, Inc. Published 2013 by John Wiley & Sons, Inc.

Wilson, 2008) reflect the awareness in the field of English language teaching of the important role that listening plays in language acquisition.

This chapter will first briefly consider the similarities between reading and listening comprehension, and the ways in which they differ. We shall then examine the nature of listening as a skill and the features of the spoken language to which the skill is applied. Implications for the classroom will be looked at in detail, together with an exploration of how teaching materials reflect the current state of knowledge. As with reading, we shall concentrate somewhat artificially on listening as an individual, discrete skill (although it should be evident that the chapter both looks back to reading and ahead to speaking skills). It is important to be able to pick out the key characteristics of a particular skill, and the integration of skills is to be given explicit treatment in the final chapter in Part II of the book.

7.2   Reasons for Listening

Pause for a moment and jot down the kinds of things you have listened to in the last few days, both in English and in your own L1.

Do you listen in the same way? If not, why not? Try to think what makes the difference.

The authors' own list is set out here in the order in which the items came to mind:

- Listening to the radio: news, a play, Parliament, a comedy programme (sometimes on a car radio).
- Conversations with neighbours, colleagues, friends.
- Answering the telephone at home and at work.
- Overhearing other people talking to each other: on a bus, in the office.
- Attending a lecture.
- Listening to arrival and departure announcements at the railway station.
- Watching TV.
- Listening to a list of names being read out at a prize-giving.
- While working in the library, trying not to listen to other people talking.

There are several points that we might notice here and that will recur in the course of this chapter. Firstly, there is great range and variety in the type of 'input' – in length or topic, for example. Secondly, in some situations we are listeners only, in others our listening skills form just a part of a whole interaction, and an ability to respond appropriately is equally important. Listening, in other words, may or may not be participatory and reciprocal. Thirdly, there are different purposes involved (to get information, to socialize, to be entertained and so on), so the degree of attention given and possibly the strategies used will differ. A related point is whether we are listening in a face-to-face situation, or through another medium such as the radio or a station intercom system: in some cases, interference or background noise may affect our ability to process what is being said. A fifth factor is to consider the people involved in the listening context – how many of them, their roles, and our relationship with them. Finally, we should note that in many situations, a visual element gives important clues beyond the words used.

7.3   The Relationship between Listening and Reading

It is useful now to highlight some of the ways in which reading and listening comprehension are both related and different. This short section will therefore act as a bridge, linking our earlier consideration of reading with a framework for thinking about listening skills.

What do reading and listening have in common?

We have seen that the traditional labelling of reading as a 'passive' skill is both misleading and incorrect: this is now well recognized as being equally so for listening. Like the reader, the listener is involved, for instance, in guessing, anticipating, checking, interpreting, interacting and organizing. It is worth quoting Vandergrift (1999: 168) in full to reinforce this point:

> Listening comprehension is anything but a passive activity. It is a complex, active process in which the listener must discriminate between sounds, understand vocabulary and structures, interpret stress and intonation, retain what was gathered in all of the above, and interpret it within the immediate as well as the larger sociocultural context of the utterance. Co-ordinating all this involves a great deal of mental activity on the part of the learner. Listening is hard work. . . .

Rost writes that 'Listening consists of three basic processing phases that are simultaneous and parallel: decoding, comprehension and interpretation'. He provides a brief summary of each phase:

> *Decoding* involves attention, speech perception, word recognition, and grammatical parsing; *comprehension* includes activation of prior knowledge, representing *propositions* in short term memory, and logical inference; *interpretation* encompasses comparison of meanings with prior expectations, activating *participation frames*, and evaluation of discourse meanings. Each of

these phases contributes to the larger goal of finding what is relevant to the listener in the input, and what kind of response may be required. (2005: 504, italics in the source)

In addition to this psycholinguistic account of the listening process, Flowerdew and Miller's (2005) listening model pays attention to more individualistic and variable dimensions such as the learners themselves, social contexts and cross-cultural interactions.

Rost (1990) even sees the listener in certain circumstances as 'co-authoring' the discourse, not just waiting to be talked to and to respond, but by his responses actually helping to construct it. There are of course times when we choose to 'switch off' and pay no attention to what is being said to us, in which case we have decided not to engage our capacity. In other words, we can make the following distinctions, with their reading skill parallels:

Attention	Recognition
Listening	Hearing
Reading	Seeing

So just as we might see an object but either not recognize it or regard it as significant, so we can distinguish 'Can you hear that man?' from 'Listen to what he's saying.'

What human beings seem to have, then, is a general processing capacity that enables them to deal with written and spoken input. (See Rost, 2005 for further discussion of this point.) The nature of the processing mechanism for listening comprehension, and how it interacts with what is being listened to, will be discussed a little later. We shall also examine some of the potential difficulties for learners of English: just because a general capacity can be identified does not necessarily mean that the two skills can be activated and 'learnt' equally easily. First of all, we shall look at the most obvious differences between reading and listening.

How do they differ?

The clearest way of distinguishing between listening and reading is to think of the medium itself, and the nature of the language used. The next chapter will be concerned in detail with features of the spoken language, but we can introduce some of them here because they affect the listener's – and especially the learner's – ability to understand:

- The medium is sound, and not print. This self-evident statement has a number of implications. We are dealing, for example, with a transient and 'ephemeral' phenomenon that cannot be recaptured once it has passed (unless it is recorded, or we ask for repetition).

- A listening context often contains visual clues, such as gesture, which generally support the spoken words. More negatively, there can also be extraneous noise, such as traffic, or other people talking, which interferes with message reception.
- Information presented in speech tends to be less densely packed than it is on the page, and it may also be more repetitive.
- There is evidence to show that the spoken language is often less complex in its grammatical and discourse structure. At the same time, however, much speech shows unique features of spoken discourse, with new starts in mid-sentence, changes of direction or topic, hesitation and half-finished statements. This is more often observed in informal than in formal speech. Carter and McCarthy (2006) and O'Keeffe et al. (2007) contain a full discussion of the features of spoken English, and will be referred to at greater length in Chapter 8.

These are significant distinctions, which were often blurred in traditional language teaching materials that took the written medium to be necessarily dominant. More recent materials claim to be sensitive both to the skill itself and to the spoken medium. Here are some typical instructions for types of activities and exercises taken from recent coursebooks.

Predicting What People Will Say
Listening for Specific Information
Example:
With a partner, discuss what you think the people in the pictures do for a living....
Listen and see if you were right. (*Innovations Intermediate*, 2004, p. 36)

Fill In the Gaps with the Missing Words
Example:
Now listen again and complete the gaps in these sentences. (*Innovations Intermediate*, p. 36)
Source: Wellar/Walkley/Hocking, From p. 36, *Innovations Intermediate* 1E. Copyright © 2004 Heinle/ELT, a part of Cengage Learning, Inc. Reproduced by permission (http://www.Cengage.com/permissions).

Listening for Gist
Example:
Listen to Michael and Irina. Mark the things in the box they mention, I for Irina and M for Michael. (*New Cutting Edge Intermediate*, p. 30)

economic problems	street names
tourists	language(s) spoken
how clean/dirty the city is	pace of life
new shops and buildings	traffic and driving
standard of living, prices etc.	

Source: S. Cunningham and P. Moor, Extract from p. 30, *New Cutting Edge Intermediate Students' Book*. Pearson Longman, 2005. Reprinted with permission of Pearson Education Ltd.

Listen and Write the Information in the Chart
Example:
Listen to the two journalists talking after the first treatment and write the information in the chart. Listen again to check. (*New English File Intermediate*, 2006. p. 74)
Source: C. Oxenden and C. Latham-Koenig, Unit 5, p. 74, from *New English File Intermediate*, 2006. Copyright © Oxford University Press.

	Stephen		Joanna	
	Marks out of 10	reasons	Marks out of 10	reasons
1 The body polish				
2 The facial				
3 The foot treatment				

Notice in particular that many of the tasks are based on what people do when they listen – on the processing of meaning that we commented on earlier in relation to both reading and listening comprehension. This may be listening to get the general idea, listening to catch something specific, or anticipating what comes next. Again, although content is clearly important, several of the tasks use tables and other ways of recording information, rather than just requiring a (written) full-sentence answer. Nevertheless, as G. White (1998) reminds us, listening to taped material still tends to treat students as passive 'overhearers', even if task types themselves have become increasingly realistic.

We shall now turn to a more detailed consideration of the skill of listening, and to its pedagogic implications.

7.4   The Nature of Listening Comprehension

Product and process

Implicit in what has been said so far is the distinction, already made in Chapter 6, between the twin concepts of 'product' and 'process'. This distinction has become an important one for all language skills, particularly those labelled 'receptive', and it signals an increasing recognition that language as a fixed system, a 'finished product', is just one part of the picture. It was a major characteristic of language teaching methodology in the 1980s, and more so in the 1990s onwards, that much more attention was paid to human beings as language processors than was previously the case, when 'texts' (whether written or spoken) were presented as objects to be understood. It is arguably with the skill of listening that a 'processing' focus is most crucial, given the transient nature of the language material compared with the relative stability of written texts. Later in this chapter we shall look at how process considerations might come together in different ways for different kinds of learners. For the moment, let us review the nature of the product, and then ask ourselves what proficient listeners actually do.

We have already noted some of the features of authentic spoken language. It varies, for example, in degrees of formality, in length, in the speed of delivery, in the accent of the speaker, in the role of the listener, and according to whether it is face to face or mediated in some way. A number of writers (for instance Brown and Yule, 1983a) make a basic distinction between 'transactional' speech, with one-way information flow from one speaker to another, as in a lecture or a news broadcast, and two-way 'interactional' speech. Rost (1990, 1994) makes an important point in relation to the latter: he refers to it as 'collaborative' and argues that, in such a setting, where we are both listener and speaker, the 'product' cannot be entirely fixed, because we have a part to play in shaping and controlling the direction in which it moves. Carter and McCarthy (2006) and O'Keeffe et al. (2007) provide considerable evidence from corpus data for this collaborative nature of human communication even in formal business communication.

1   If you overheard the following while you were out shopping, how would you interpret it, and what else would you want to hear in order to be able to interpret these words?
    'Really? I didn't know that. How long has she been there?'
    And what would be happening if the shop assistant said to you, 'Five?'
2   Look back at the list you made earlier of the kinds of things you have listened to recently. Take any one of them, and ask yourself how you came to understand what was being said. For example, what aspects do you think you concentrated on? It might have been on the vocabulary, or the speaker's intonation, or some visual element, for instance. Did you understand everything and, if not, what interfered with 'perfect' comprehension?
3   How do you think your own learners would have managed listening to the same thing in English?

Listening skills

As a proficient listener, you will obviously not have achieved understanding in any of these illustrative situations by simply 'hearing' the sound: you will have been processing this stream of noise on a number of levels, which, taken together, make up the concept of 'comprehension'. Let us now look at each of these levels in turn. The first two see the listener as a processor of language, and require a consideration of the micro-skills – the various components of this processing mechanism.

Processing sound   Full understanding, we have noted, cannot come from the sound source alone, but equally obviously, it cannot take place without some processing of what one student of our acquaintance has called a 'word soup'. At its most basic, a language completely unknown to us will sound to our ears like a stream of sound.

Assuming, however, that listeners can identify which language is being spoken, then they must have the capacity to do at least the following (see Field, 2008 for more detailed discussion):

- Segment the stream of sound and recognize word boundaries. This is complicated in English because of the phenomenon whereby, in connected speech, one sound runs into the next. For example, 'I like it' sounds like/ ai'laikit/ ('I li kit'), 'my name's Ann' like/maineimzæn/ ('My name zan') and so on.
- Recognize contracted forms. 'I'd have gone to London if I'd known about it' sounds very different from its 'full' printed form in many grammar book examples.
- Recognize the vocabulary being used.
- Recognize sentence and clause boundaries in speech.
- Recognize stress patterns and speech rhythm. English sentence stress is fairly regular, and tends to fall on the main information-carrying items (nouns, main verbs, adjectives and adverbs) rather than on articles, pro-nouns, conjunctions, auxiliaries and so on. Thus, 'I went to the town and had lunch with a friend' gives a standard mix of 'strong' forms (marked with stress) and 'weak' forms (and, a) where the sound is often reduced to /e/. We shall comment later on the language learning difficulties this can cause. Stress patterns can also be systematically varied, to accom-modate a particular, intended meaning by the speaker. For example, 'I wás there' (no weak form) carries a tone of insistence; 'Whát did he say?' perhaps suggests surprise or disbelief.
- Recognize stress on longer words, and the effect on the rest of the word. Think of the sound of 'comfortable' or 'interesting', for instance.
- Recognize the significance of language-related ('paralinguistic') features, most obviously intonation. Falling intonation, for example, may indicate

the end of a statement; a rise, that an utterance has not yet been completed and the speaker intends to carry on.

- Recognize changes in pitch, tone and speed of delivery.

None of the micro-skills of listening is used in isolation, of course, and those listed so far merge into the second major processing category, the processing of meaning.

Processing meaning   If you think back to something you listened to earlier today, perhaps a news item that you found particularly interesting, it is extremely unlikely that you will be able to remember any of the sentence patterns, or much more than the vocabulary generally associated with the subject matter. You will, however, be able to recall in some sense what it was 'about'. (We are not referring here to a stretch of language learnt 'by heart', such as a poem.) Research on listening has shown that syntax is lost to memory within a very short time, even a few seconds, whereas meaning is retained for much longer. Richards (1985: 191) comments that 'memory works with propositions, not with sentences', and Underwood (1989) draws a familiar distinction between 'echoic' memory (about one second), 'short-term' memory (a few seconds) and 'long-term' memory. What seems to emerge is that the linguistic codes are processed to create some kind of mental representation in our minds as we construct meaning. White (1998: 55) quotes Kaltenbrook (1994): 'The organisation of a text into message units has an immediate impact on intelligibility. . . . Students need to be shown that spoken language consists of *chunks* rather than isolated lexical items and complete sentences' (italics added).

What listeners appear to be able to do here is

- Organize the incoming speech into meaningful sections. This involves the ability to use linguistic clues to identify discourse boundaries. For example, a person giving a talk may signal a new point by explicit markers such as 'Next' or 'My third point' or 'However'; alternatively, a change in direction or topic may be indicated by intonation, or pauses. Related to this is the use of 'co-text' which means the wider linguistic environment. For example, cohesive clues can be used to establish links between different parts of a spoken 'text'.
- Identify redundant material. Speakers often repeat what they say, either directly or by making the same point in different words. Efficient listeners know how to turn this into a strategy to gain extra processing time to help organize what they hear.

(*Continued*)

- Think ahead, and use language data to anticipate what a speaker may be going on to say. For instance, a lecturer who says, 'So much for the advantages', is obviously going on to talk about disadvantages; a change in intonation may mark a functional shift in a conversation, perhaps from an explanation to an enquiry.
- Store information in the memory and know how to retrieve it later, by organizing meaning as efficiently as possible and avoiding too much attention to immediate detail.

Finally, processing skills are often discussed under two related headings, which are tabulated below (the equivalences are not exact, but they capture the points made in this section):

Processing sound	Processing meaning
Phonological	Semantic
Lower-order/automatic skills	Higher-order skills of organizing and interpreting
Recognition of sounds, words	Comprehension
Localized: the immediate text	Global: the meaning of the whole
Decoding what was said	Reconstruction after processing meaning
Perception	Cognition

We can now summarize the discussion so far. The strategies used for processing meaning are not themselves merely skills of recognition. Although they depend on an ability to recognize key aspects of the sound system, they require the listener to combine, interpret and make sense of the incoming language data. In other words, as we saw in relation to the teaching of reading, we are dealing with the interaction of both 'bottom-up' and 'top-down' processing skills.

In the spirit of the introductory remarks in this chapter and the previous one, the two sets of micro-skills just discussed certainly view the listener as 'active'. However, taken alone, they might imply that listening is an internal processing mechanism, a cognitive device disembodied from everyday life. This is clearly not the case, and as social beings we are equipped with other kinds of capacities, which can be thought of as (1) sensitivity to context, and (2) knowledge. Both are to do with the way in which expectations are set up by the non-linguistic environment. For convenience, we shall take them together.

Context and knowledge   Most statements, taken out of context, are open to a number of interpretations (and incidentally offer a rich source of humour). A simple 'I spoke to him yesterday' may indicate a justification, doubt, a proof that the other person was where he was supposed to be, straightforward information, a statement on which further action will be based and so on. Its meaning will usually be clear from the context in which it was said. 'Context' here is taken to cover physical setting (home, office, school etc.), the number of listeners/speakers, their roles and their relationship to each other. Rost refers to this as 'pragmatic context', distinguishing it from syntactic and semantic. He is critical of the information-processing model of comprehension where the listener is seen as 'a language processor who performs actions in a fixed order, independently of contextual constraints' (Rost, 1990: 7). He pushes the significance of the social context further in an interesting discussion of 'collaborative' or 'interactional' speech (see also Chapter 8 of this book). His point, essentially, is that the listener interprets what is being said, constructs a meaning and responds on the basis of that interpretation. The listener is therefore a key figure in the shaping of the whole interaction: in this view, the listening context is open-ended, likely to change direction and not fixed in advance.

Finally, we turn to the knowledge that listeners bring to a listening experience. This may be knowledge of a topic or a set of facts. A student following a course in (say) computing, will gradually accumulate a body of information and technical vocabulary to which he can 'refer' in each new class or lecture; if my neighbour has a new grandchild and comes to tell me about it, then I have some idea of the direction the conversation will take. Previous knowledge is not necessarily as detailed as in these examples. Schema theory, as we saw in Chapter 6, highlighted the fact that we are equipped with pre-organized knowledge of many kinds. It may be that we simply have a set of general expectations when entering a listening situation. If we switch on the TV news, we can probably anticipate both its format and the kind of topic that will occur; if we go to a children's tea party, we expect certain behaviour patterns, and are unlikely to hear a discussion on nuclear physics. These frames of reference are also social and cultural. As members of a particular culture, we have learned the rules of conversational behaviour, and specific topics 'trigger' specific ideas and images.

Listening comprehension, then, is not only a function of the interplay between language on the one hand and what the brain does with it on the other: it also requires the activation of contextual information and previous knowledge. White (1998: 8–9) lists under the following headings all the subskills that go to make up the overall skill of listening,

- perception skills
- language skills
- knowledge of the world

- dealing with information
- interacting with a speaker

and comments that 'good listeners need to be able to use a combination of sub-skills simultaneously when processing spoken language: the skill they will need at any particular moment will depend on the kind of text they are listening to, and their reasons for listening to it'.

At this point you might like to think back to the tasks early in this section, and look at your comments in the light of the present discussion. There is no 'right answer', except to tell you that when the shop assistant said 'Five?' she knew that I always bought a certain kind of bread roll and a certain number. Her one-word query was enough to trigger the frame of reference for both of us, and a simple 'Yes please' was all that was required.

Many of these points are explicitly acknowledged in materials for the teaching of listening. In the *Introduction to Intermediate Listening* (Brewster, 1991: 2), for example, the writer makes the following points:

- We sometimes have an idea of what we are going to hear.
- We listen for a variety of reasons.
- Important information-carrying words are normally pronounced with more stress.
- In face-to-face interaction, gestures and expression are important, as well as the actual words used.
- Natural speech is characterized by hesitation, repetition, rephrasing and self-correction.

These observations still stand in the light of current thinking.

7.5   Listening Comprehension: Teaching and Learning

Before reading on, consider your own situation. To what extent do any of the materials you use to teach listening take into account the components we have been discussing? How might the various components of listening comprehension help your learners to listen more effectively?

In a competent listener, the micro-skills we have been surveying are engaged automatically. Language learners, however articulate in their L1, are confronted with a rich and complex medium, a daunting array of skills and a foreign language. We shall first comment briefly on the kinds of difficulties that learners typically experience in relation to what proficient listeners appear to do. We shall then raise some issues about the application of the discussion so far to the classroom environment. Finally, in this section, we shall explore the ways in which teaching materials have developed in line with an increased understanding of the nature of the skill.

Learners

There is, of course, no such person as the 'typical learner'. Learners are at various stages of proficiency, and they differ across a range of characteristics – age, interests, learning styles, aptitude, motivation and so on. The only claim that can be made is that learners, by definition, are not fully competent listeners in the target language. We can suggest, in other words, that they will be operating somewhere on a scale of approximation to full proficiency. With this in mind, several general observations can be made, which at the same time are not true of all learners everywhere.

Firstly, it seems that there is a tendency to focus on features of sound at the expense of 'co-text' – the surrounding linguistic environment. For example, in 'The East German government has resigned. Leaders are meeting to discuss the growing unrest in the country' the learner heard 'rest' and did not notice the prefix, despite the clear implication of national instability coming from the passage. A second, related point is that previous knowledge and/or context may be largely ignored in the interests of a mishearing. One student, rather improbably, claimed to have heard 'fish and chips' in a talk on telecommunications. Celce-Murcia and Olshtain (2000: 103) give a similar example of a student hearing 'communist' when the lecturer had said 'commonest'. This kind of listening error can be difficult to separate, thirdly, from mishearings caused by using an inappropriate frame of reference: another student, possibly thinking of a sadly familiar problem in her own country, heard 'plastic bullets' for 'postal ballots' in a text that was explicitly about electoral procedure. Fourthly, there is sometimes a reluctance to engage other levels of the listening skill to compensate for not understanding a particular stretch of language. For example, a learner may be unwilling to take risks by guessing, or anticipating, or establishing a framework for understanding without worrying about details, perhaps by using, in Rost's terms, 'points of transition relevance' (Rost, 1990: 100). The most frequently quoted example here is that of a teacher beginning a lesson by saying, 'First of all . . .'. If this is not processed phonologically, learners often do not understand at all, or sometimes suppose that a holiday is being announced, having heard 'festival'. Either way, the lesson cannot proceed until the misunderstanding is cleared up.

Underwood (1989) looks at the same points from another angle, and suggests that potential problems arise for seven main reasons:

1   The learner–listener cannot control speed of delivery.
2   He/she cannot always get things repeated.
3   He/she has a limited vocabulary.
4   He/she may fail to recognize 'signals'.
5   He/she may lack contextual knowledge.
6   It can be difficult to concentrate in a foreign language.
7   The learner may have established certain learning habits, such as a wish to understand every word.

What all this amounts to is that learners sometimes 'hear' rather than 'listen'. They appear to suspend their own mother tongue skills, which would allow them to approach a listening task as a multilevel process. Instead there is a marked tendency to depend too much on the lower-order skills, leading to attempts at phonological decoding rather than attention to the wider message. It is interesting, however, to note a recent counter argument. Field (2008), based on his review of research, argues that what distinguishes expert listeners from unskilled ones is their ability to decode with ease. The expert listeners seem to seek contextual clues when there is a problem in decoding (e.g. noise in the environment). Consistent heavy reliance on contextual clues may be a characteristic of unskilled listeners, compensating for their under-developed decoding skills. It seems that learners need to be able to do both bottom-up and top-down processing.

Classroom applications: some issues

How, then, can the points that have been made in this chapter be reflected, directly or indirectly, in the classroom? Every classroom has its own set of objectives and its own 'climate' and patterns of relationships, all within a specific educational environment. It is therefore not surprising if the principles of language and language processing are taken only variably into account. Imagine the classroom as a filter for some of the following issues, which are set out as questions to consider for your own situation rather than as a 'recipe book' of ready answers. The section on materials will refer to these points again.

• Research into listening comprehension has shown that we are dealing with a complex skill. At the same time, our job is to teach language. What is a suitable balance for the classroom between 'tasks' (the skill) and 'text' (the language material)?
• How closely should the classroom attempt to replicate authentic language and authentic listening tasks? As we have seen, a real-life listening experience is highly complex and is unlikely to transfer easily to the classroom, except perhaps with advanced learners. Mishan (2005) argues that the results of current research appear to favour the use of authentic texts for

language learning in comparison to using simplified texts. She then suggests various ways of designing authenticity into language learning materials using various texts such as newspapers, songs, films and ICT (i.e. Information and Communication Technologies), principally the Internet and email.

- To what extent should spoken material be modified for presentation in the classroom?
- Is it more appropriate to grade tasks (using the micro-skills of listening as a starting point) from 'lower' to 'higher order', or is it preferable to make sure that global understanding has been achieved before focusing on detail? In other words, should we first make sure that learners can listen 'for gist'?
- What resources do we need to teach listening comprehension effectively? Is audio equipment sufficient, or does it leave out the non-linguistic information that video or TV might capture? Is it possible that sometimes the teacher may be more effective in creating a listening environment than the availability of a piece of electronic equipment?
- We can think of the listener's role on a scale of decreasing involvement from participant to addressee to overhearer (adapted from Rost, 1990). Is it possible that the classroom stresses the last of these at the expense of the others? We typically expect our students to listen to (perhaps taped) conversations between other people. We mentioned White's (1998) criticism of this earlier in the chapter. She goes on to propose some extensive possibilities for developing an alternative approach, where students can become participants and even develop their own tasks and materials.

7.6   Materials for Teaching Listening Comprehension

What materials, if any, do you have available for teaching listening? Do you have special supplementary materials, or is listening practice incorporated into a main coursebook? Is it necessary to devise your own listening exercises?

Traditionally, much classroom practice consisted of the teacher reading aloud a written text, one or more times, slowly and clearly, and then asking a number of comprehension questions about it. The skill itself was not given much attention, nor were the characteristics of natural spoken English. The objective was to provide an alternative way of presenting language and testing that it had been understood.

There is nothing wrong with this approach in itself, but it could not claim to be teaching listening comprehension. Many current materials, on the other hand, manipulate both language and tasks, and take into account a range of micro-skills, listener roles, topics and text types. There is space here only to illustrate the main trends. Many more examples will be found in the further reading listed at the end of the chapter (see particularly White, 1998 and Field, 2008).

The first thing to say is that the components of listening – processing sound, organizing meaning, and using knowledge and context – provide a convenient way of laying out the issues, but they are not there to be transferred directly to a teaching sequence. The way they are used depends on the objectives and levels of particular courses, although certain kinds of tasks draw more heavily on some micro-skills than on others.

It is now conventional – and helpful – to divide activities into pre-, while- and post-listening. Wilson (2008) provides a lot of hands-on examples for each stage.

Pre-listening activities

The principal function of these activities, which are now common in teaching materials, is to establish a framework for listening so that learners do not approach the listening practice with no points of reference. This perspective is clearly in line with the use of 'knowledge schema' and the establishing of a context. Activities include the following:

A short reading passage on a similar topic
Predicting content from the title
Commenting on a picture or photograph
Reading through comprehension questions in advance
Working out your own opinion on a topic

Any such activity is bound to generate language. However, in some cases, more explicit attention is given to language practice, particularly to the activation and learning of topic-related vocabulary. Clearly a reading activity can serve both functions of framework-setting and language practice quite well, provided that it does not become too important a focus in its own right.

Listening activities

By this we mean tasks carried out during or after listening that directly require comprehension of the spoken material. We find here a basic and quite standard distinction between 'extensive' and 'intensive' listening.

Extensive listening, or whatever term is used, is mainly concerned to promote overall global comprehension and encourages learners not to worry if they do not grasp every word. Renandya and Farrell (2011) argue for the value of extensive listening to facilitate language acquisition even at lower level by providing experience of listening to meaningful, enjoyable and comprehensible spoken text. They list various online sources that teachers can access. The range of possible activities for extensive listening is enormous, and which ones are selected will depend largely on proficiency. In the early stages, learners may well need support in a non-verbal form:

Putting pictures in a correct sequence
Following directions on a map
Checking off items in a photograph
Completing a grid, timetable or chart of information

As proficiency develops, tasks can gradually become more language based, eventually requiring students to construct a framework of meaning for themselves, and to make inferences and interpret attitudes as well as understand explicitly stated facts. (Rost, 1990 offers a scale from 'closed' to 'open' tasks.) For example:

Answering true/false or multiple-choice questions
Predicting what comes next (preceded by a pause)
Constructing a coherent set of notes
Inferring opinions across a whole text

Intensive listening, as the name implies, deals with specific items of language, sound or factual detail within the meaning framework already established:

Filling gaps with missing words
Identifying numbers and letters
Picking out particular facts
Recognizing exactly what someone said

Note that sequencing and grading can be carried out using both linguistic and psychological criteria: in other words, grading only according to some notion of syntactic complexity is no longer regarded as satisfactory. Further possibilities for grading include (1) task complexity, whether global → specific or vice versa, or indeed global → specific → global (this last technique is evident in the second sample Unit printed at the end of this chapter); (2) varying the amount of language to be processed, for example, from shorter stretches to longer ones; and (3) using a range of authentic and specially written material.

Language material

Two of our earlier observations are relevant here. Firstly, we distinguished 'interactional' and 'transactional' listening. Secondly, we saw that listeners can have a number of roles, on a scale from participant to addressee to overhearer. Both these elements are represented in listening materials. The most straightforward case is where the learner is an addressee or overhearer in a transactional context, such as:

Attending a lecture
Following instructions or directions
Listening to an interview, or a story or to people describing their jobs

At the same time, it is clearly important that learners are exposed to the interactional nature of everyday conversation (quite distinct from fixed 'dialogues' to be read aloud). This is rather more difficult to construct in the classroom environment, except artificially. In a way it is a paradox that students may overhear on tape what others say when it would be more 'natural' for them to participate. (This is not always negative, however: learners have the opportunity to listen to the spoken language in an unthreatening situation.)

Post-listening activities

We shall only comment briefly here on these activities, because they are usually not listening exercises as such. The category is open-ended, and looks ahead to our discussion on the integration of skills at the end of this part of the book. Essentially, the post-listening stage is an opportunity for many kinds of follow-up work – thematic, lexical, grammatical, skills developmental and so on. Here are just a few examples:

Using notes made while listening to write a summary
Reading a related text
Doing a role play
Writing on the same theme
Studying new grammatical structures
Practising pronunciation

Field (2008) suggests a diagnostic approach in which far more weight is given to the post-listening stage where learners are encouraged to reflect where they had problems to find solutions in their subsequent learning.

7.7 Conclusion

Listening comprehension has a number of roles to play within a language course, and its importance clearly depends on the aims of the programme as a whole. It may only be a minor feature, just to give learners exposure to what English sounds like: alternatively, it may have a major function for someone planning to study in an English-speaking country or to interact extensively in the language. Whatever its purpose, we have tried to show in this chapter how views on the learning and teaching of listening have developed from a growing understanding both of the nature of the skill itself, and of the variety and range of language on which it can be practised.

1 A unit from a popular coursebook is printed on the following pages. How closely do you feel that the listening process is mirrored in these materials (at least in so far as you can judge without having the tapes available)? How suitable would they be for your own class?
2 If you had no recorded material available, how could you convert a reading text into a listening exercise? Choose a text originally intended to be read and try to make some practical suggestions.

Listening: storyteller

12 Look at this picture. Where do you
Think this woman is from?
What do you think she does?
Listen to Track 74. Were you right?

13 Listen to Track 74 again. In your own
words, say what Jan thinks stories are
for. Do you agree?

unit fourteen 147

14 **Read through the following questions and then say what you think Jan will say in Track 75.**

a What did Jan do at the age of 19?
b Why did she go to a group called *Common Law*?
c What three things did she have to do for her audition?
d What story did she tell?
e Where did she get the song and game from?
f How did she learn it?
g What happened when she told it?

◀)) **Listen to Track 75. Were you right? Answer the questions.**

🎧 15 **Listen to Track 76 and answer these questions.**

Who or what:
a ... is *The Spitz*?
b ... has a reputation for being late?
c ... plays the drums?
d ... said he was tired and had to lie down?
e ... explained the stories five minutes before the show?
f ... was on the edge of creativity?
g ... weren't very enthusiastic at first?
h ... spoke to the audience to encourage them?
i ... had a fantastic experience?

Tell the story of Jan and Crispin's evening in your own words.

Language in chunks

16 **Look at the Audioscript for Tracks 74–76 and find's phrases (a–i). What do the phrases in italics mean? What was she talking about in each case?**

a *a tried and tested theory*
b *Does that make sense?*
c something ...*I can't put my finger on*
d the opportunity to *delve deep* into your own consciousness
e I couldn't learn the whole story *word for word*
f from that moment *I haven't looked back*
g I kind of *went through the sequence of events*
h we were *on the edge of* our creativity
i I'm slightly *off kilter*

17 **Translate the phrases into your language so that they mean the same as they do in the context that Jan used them.**

18 Noticing language **Look at these phrases from Tracks 74–76 which contain direct and indirect speech. Find examples of things people actually said (direct speech) and of people reporting what other people said (indirect speech).**

a I said oh oh where can you earn some decent money then and she said oh as a storyteller so I said what's that and she said oh I'm a storyteller I think you'd be really good, I think you should come along to *Common Law* and you should audition.
b ... and he was like Oh God my brain and the traffic's awful and just let me lie here for five minutes, and I said we're on in five minutes and he said er yeah just give me five minutes ...
c I asked the audience to join in and sing it and they weren't giving us themselves and I said to them look you know, he was late, he was late...

19 Storytelling **When Jan told the story of *Why cat and dog are no longer friends*, she 'read that and read it and read it and read it', before she told her story. Choose one of the following topics and then make notes about it. Think of ways to make it as exciting or funny as possible. Then write out a version as correctly as you can. Read it and read it and read it.**

Without looking back at what you have written, tell your story to a neighbour. Now tell it to another neighbour, practise it and then tell it to the whole class.

Topics:
• my most embarrassing moment
• my favourite story from a book, TV or the movies
• my most memorable injury
• why I was late
• any other story from your life

148 unit fourteen

Source: J. Harmer and C. Letherby, From Unit 14, pp. 147–8, *Just Right Upper Intermediate – Teachers Book* 1E. Published by Heinle/ELT. Reprinted with permission of Cengage Learning Inc. (http://www.cengage.com/permissions).

7.8   Further Reading

Both these books offer a wide range of examples of listening comprehension tasks and exercises in the context of a clear discussion of the principles of the listening skill.

1   Field, J. (2008): *Listening in the Language Classroom.*
2   Wilson, J. J. (2008): *How to Teach Listening.*

Source: Substitute: J. Harmer and C. Letherby, Unit 14 pp. 147–8, *Just Right Upper-Intermediate*. Marshall Cavendish.

8

Speaking Skills

8.1 Introduction

As a language skill, speaking has sometimes been undervalued or, in some circles, taken for granted. There is a popular impression that writing, particularly literature, is meant to be read and as such is prestigious, whereas speaking is often thought of as 'colloquial', which helps to account for its lower priority in some teaching contexts.

However, as we shall see in this chapter, speaking is not the oral production of written language, but involves learners in the mastery of a wide range of subskills, which, added together, constitute an overall competence in the spoken language.

With the growth of English as an international language of communication (Graddol, 2006, 2010), there is clearly a need for many learners to speak and interact in a multiplicity of situations through the language, be it for foreign travel, business or other professional reasons. In many contexts, speaking is often the skill upon which a person is judged 'at face value'. In other words, people may often form judgements about our language competence from our speaking rather than from any of the other language skills.

In this chapter we shall look at some of the reasons that we might have for speaking in a variety of contexts. Then we shall examine how our concept of speaking has evolved over the last two decades. Next, we investigate the characteristics of spoken language, including pronunciation and conversation analysis, in order to see what their implications might be for language classrooms, and, finally, we consider various types of activity that we can use to promote speaking skills in the classroom.

Materials and Methods in ELT: A Teacher's Guide, Third Edition.
Jo McDonough, Christopher Shaw, and Hitomi Masuhara.
© 2013 John Wiley & Sons, Inc. Published 2013 by John Wiley & Sons, Inc.

What are your learners' speaking needs? Do you feel that your materials fulfil them?

8.2 Reasons for Speaking

As a skill that enables us to produce utterances, when genuinely communicative, speaking is desire- and purpose-driven; in other words, we genuinely want to communicate something to achieve a particular end. This may involve expressing ideas and opinions; expressing a wish or a desire to do something; negotiating and/or solving a particular problem; or establishing and maintaining social relationships and friendships. To achieve these speaking purposes, we need to activate a range of appropriate expressions.

List the different kinds of things you have talked about in the last few days both in English and in your own L1.

Our own list came out as follows, not in any particular order of priority:

Asking for assistance and advice in a shop
Asking for directions in a different town
Making an appointment by telephone
Discussing and negotiating arrangements
Talking socially to a variety of people
Sorting out arrangements for a car to be serviced

These are just a few of the reasons why people may wish to speak in any language. If we are hoping to make our learners communicatively competent in English as a foreign or second language, then it seems fair to assume that speaking skills will play a large part in this overall competence.

Speaking is a process difficult in many ways to dissociate from listening. Speaking and listening skills often enjoy a dependency in that speaking is only very rarely carried out in isolation; it is generally an interactive skill unless an uninterrupted oral presentation is being given. This notion of interaction is one of the key features in spoken corpora (O'Keeffe et al., 2007; McCarten and McCarthy, 2010). What is said is dependent on an understanding of what has been said in the interaction. Speakers listen, interpret what has been said, and adapt how and what to say according to the other speakers/listeners, and it is this reciprocal exchange pattern which becomes important for learners to be exposed to and to practise at various stages of their foreign language career.

There is clearly an overlap in the interaction that takes place between the speaker/listener and the writer/reader, for the listener has to interpret the speaker just as the reader has to interpret the writer. The essential difference, though, is that speaker–listener interaction takes place in real time, thereby allowing very little time for the speaker to respond to the listener if the flow of a conversation is to be maintained. In the writer–reader relationship, however, the reader usually has the opportunity of rereading what has been written, time and time again if necessary.

Spoken corpus studies show how speakers place prime importance on establishing interpersonal relationships during listening and speaking. McCarten and McCarthy (2010: 17), for example, explain, '. . . speakers might adapt or construct their talk in relation to a specific listener or listeners and this includes the obvious areas of politeness strategies and levels of formality'. They provide examples from actual corpora data showing not only how speakers organize their talk according to the listeners' responses but also how they use strategies such as showing good listenership by vocalizing acknowledgement (e.g. huh, uh-huh) or by giving affective responses such as 'exactly', 'wonderful' and 'that would be nice' (McCarten and McCarthy 2010: 19).

All these points obviously have important classroom implications which will be explored later. Let us now turn our attention to how advances in our understanding of speaking have evolved over the last two decades.

8.3   Speaking Skills and Communicative Language Theory

In their analysis of the theoretical base of communicative language teaching, Richards and Rodgers (2001: 161) offer the following four characteristics of a communicative view of language:

1   Language is a system for the expression of meaning.
2   The primary function of language is for interaction and communication.
3   The structure of language reflects its functional and communicative uses.
4   The primary units of language are not merely its grammatical and structural features, but categories of functional and communicative meaning as exemplified in discourse.

When we ask our students to use the spoken language in the classroom, we require them to take part in a process that not only involves a knowledge of target forms and functions, but also a general knowledge of the interaction between the speaker and listener in order that meanings and negotiation of meanings are made clear. For example, listeners may give the speaker feedback as to whether or not the listener has understood what the speaker has just said. The speaker will then need to reformulate what was just said in order to get the meaning across in a different way.

We shall shortly see how some recent materials that have been produced for speaking skills often try to encapsulate these views by trying to promote the expression of meaning, interaction and general communicative use on the part of the speaker.

8.4   Characteristics of Spoken Language

It is useful for the teacher of speaking skills in the classroom to look at the characteristics of the spoken language. The binary distinction of speaking skills made by Bygate (1987: 5–6) still seems helpful in shaping our discussion. He calls the first category 'motor-receptive' speaking skills which involves linguistic elements such as pronunciation, vocabulary and chunks (several words customarily used together in a fixed expression) and structures. The other kind refers to social and interactional skills that relate to what and how to say things effectively in specific communicative situations. In the classroom, the former would involve the learner, for example, in activities that require pronunciation development work or the frequent use of target expressions in meaningful and varied contexts. On the other hand, our understanding of real-life spoken discourse will help us guide our learners to learn how to manage a conversation appropriately and to achieve purposes of conversation effectively. In this part of the chapter we shall firstly examine some of the issues involved in teaching pronunciation and then move on to consider how the development of conversation analysis and of spoken corpora has affected our approach to the teaching of speaking skills. Although the motor-receptive elements of speaking skills are obviously important, the area of communicative interaction in particular has nourished an approach to the teaching of speaking skills in a communicative way.

8.5   Teaching Pronunciation

The teaching of pronunciation is carried out in many different ways, and for different reasons. Sometimes whole lessons may be devoted to it; sometimes teachers deal with it simply as it arises. Some teachers may like to 'drill' correct pronunciation habits, others are more concerned that their students develop comprehensibility within fluency. Behind such different approaches to teaching pronunciation lie different beliefs and attitudes towards the kind of English that is the target of learning. Traditionally, 'a native speaker model' (itself a complex notion for a language like English with so many varieties) seems to have been regarded as ideal by many EFL (English as a Foreign Language) teachers and learners. Many tests and examinations seem to be based on such beliefs. English nowadays, however, has come to be used globally as a contact language (i.e. English as a Lingua Franca (ELF)) for communication by speakers of different languages (Jenkins et al., 2011). In ELF, native-speaker norms become less relevant. Imagine an international convention held in China where medical experts from various continents gather. Would it matter at all if an NNSE's (non-native speaker of English) pronunciation does not simulate a particular variety of NSE (native speakers of English)? Will these medical experts be considered as failed NSEs when they are eloquently and effectively speaking in one of their world Englishes? Jenkins et al. (2011: 284) point out that non-native speakers can be in fact '– more often – highly skilled communicators who make use of their multi-lingual resources in ways not available to monolingual NSEs, and who are found to prioritize successful communication over narrow notions of "cor-rectness" ' (see also Seidlhofer, 2010). If we are to embrace this new notion of fluid and dynamic varieties of English used by NNSEs as a Lingua Franca (ELF), many assumptions of English language teaching will have to be recon-sidered. Jenkins et al. (2011: 297) reflect thus: 'The challenge for ELF researchers and, even more, for English teaching professionals then is to find ways of dealing with this variability so that it can be incorporated into teach-ing in ways that are digestible for learners'.

Challenged by such new insights and situations, no one approach can be said to be universally applicable. As Dalton and Seidlhofer (1994: 6) write: 'the task of pronunciation teaching . . . is to establish models for guidance, not norms for imitation'. Certainly a native speaker model is unrealistic for the great majority of learners, and 'perfection' is an unattainable goal.

There are, nevertheless, a number of key aspects of pronunciation and the English sound system that a teacher can in principle attend to. Some of them are 'bottom-up', dealing with both forming and hearing sounds as 'intelligi-bly' as possible; others are 'top-down', where a learner's pronunciation is part of a broader communicative approach. This is a balance, in other words, between 'accuracy' on the one hand and 'intelligibility' on the other.

Common advice on how to increase intelligibility includes the following:

- Individual sounds, including areas of difficulty for speakers of particular languages (e.g. l/r for Japanese, p/b for Arabic speakers), minimal pairs (bit/bat, hit/hate etc.). This may also be accompanied by ear training, and sometimes by teaching students to read the phonemic alphabet – useful of course for dictionary work.
- Word stress, which exhibits a number of key patterns in English.

- Sentence stress and rhythm. In a stress-timed language like English, this is of particular importance, because both 'regular' and 'marked' stress patterns essentially carry the message of a stretch of speech: Harmer (2001b: 193) gives the example of 'I lent my sister 10 pounds for a train ticket last week' as spoken with regular stress patterns, and then with varying the stress to emphasize different words. Again, it is useful to link this to listening practice as well.
- Intonation, significant in conveying messages about mood and intention. We might consider the different meanings in varying the intonation in such a simple sentence as 'that's interesting': we can sound bored, ironic, surprised or, indeed, interested.
- Sound and spelling, which in English are in a complex relationship.

Jenkins (2007) and Deterding (2010), based on their research on successful users of ELF, identify features of pronunciation that contribute to intelligibility in various world Englishes:

> It has been shown that, although there are substantial differences between the Englishes . . . , some features seem to be shared, particularly the avoidance of the dental fricatives, . . . the use of full vowels in function words and the unstressed syllables of polysyllabic words, and syllable-based rhythm. We might note that all these features fit in perfectly with the Lingua Franca Core (LFC), the set of pronunciation features which Jenkins (2007) suggests as essential for successful international communication. (Deterding, 2010: 396)

If we place intelligibility as the target, then some of the common advice on pronunciation seems to lose its full force. For example, should or should not a teacher emphasize the importance of sentence stress and rhythm (i.e. stress-timed rhythm) when recent research seems to show that syllable-based rhythm is sufficient for successful communication? Jenkins et al. (2011) warn against the prescriptive use of research findings:

> ELF research, then, is not about determining what should or should not be taught in the language classroom. Rather, ELF researchers feel their responsibility is to make current research findings accessible in a way that enables teachers to reconsider their beliefs and practices and make informed decisions about the significance of ELF for their own individual teaching contexts. (Jenkins et al., 2011: 306)

More detailed discussion on the teaching of pronunciation is to be found in Kelly (2000) and Burns and Seidlhofer (2010). Kelly (2000) has a chapter on spelling and pronunciation. Coursebooks include Hancock and Donna (2012) and Hewings (2004). Those who would like to read further on ELF should see Seidlhofer (2011). Kirkpatrick (2010) tackles very similar issues from the perspectives of World Englishes.

8.6   Conversation Analysis

Carter et al. (2011: 78) point out that 'Descriptions of the English Language, and of English grammar in particular, have been largely based on written sources and on written examples'. One consequence of such a tradition, they explain, is that the norms of written language and its grammar have been regarded as a benchmark for spoken language. As a result, 'many perfectly normal and regularly occurring utterances made by standard English speakers (of whatever variety – not just standard British English) have, by omission, come to be classified as 'ungrammatical' (Carter et al. 2011: 78). They show how coursebook dialogue resembles written discourse rather than spoken discourse.

Angouri (2010) compared data taken from a sample of meetings in seven multinational companies in Europe with transcripts of business meetings in best-selling Business English textbooks.

Compare the extract from a Business English coursebook and a transcript of a real-life interaction. Note down the differences in the table below:

	Excerpt X	Excerpt Y
Context	The first part of an authentic brainstorming meeting between three employees. No information is given regarding their relationships or details of the meeting such as objectives.	Three senior managers have just conducted internal job interviews. They are discussing whom to promote as Project Leader based on the performances at the interviews. Manager L is chairing the meeting.
Characteristics of their conversation		

Excerpts

2.3 (P = Paul, S = Stephanie, C = Courtney)

P - OK, thanks for coming along this morning. As I said in my e-mail, the purpose of the meeting this morning is for us to brainstorm ideas, promotional activities that we are going to carry out to make sure that the launch of the Business Solutions website is a success from the start. I'm going to open up to you to come up with the ideas that you've formulated over the past couple of weeks. Anything goes, we've got no budget at the moment but you know, fire away.

S - Oh great, no budget constraints.

C - That's great. Television and radio.

S - Well, it's starting big.

P - Excellent.

C - Well, we haven't got a budget, err, well, I think we could reach a wide audience, something like that, and err, we could focus on some of the big sort of business financial network television if we want to reach a global market, if that's what we're working to do and extending to all areas I think.

S - Yeah, that's been quite successful for some of the banks and stuff.

P - That's right, but definitely focused advertising.

C - Focused on specific networks that would reach, that you know … businessmen are watching network television.

S - Well, I've been working more on cheaper solutions than that just in case there are budget problems. I thought we could do some effective online promotion, which is actually very cheap, and I think we should aim to do anyway. Direct mailing but also register the site effectively with search engines so anybody who goes onto the Internet and is looking for business solutions would come up with our website.

C - Yeah, we should definitely do some of that.

P - Absolutely, yes.

C - What about press advertising, traditional newspapers, business magazines, journals?

P - Yes.

S - Yes, great, I mean we've done that very effectively in the past.

P - Yes, we've had some very good response rates to for the ads we've placed before.

S - Yes, and that could be something we could do, not just once but a kind of campaign over a period of time.

C - Yes, build it up.

P - Yes, use a campaign, OK.

Excerpt 16.1: Transcript from *Market Leader* (Cotton er al. 2001: 157). © Pearson Education Limited 2001.

Source: Cotton, Falvey and Kent, 16.1 from *Market Leader Upper Intermediate Coursebook*, p. 157. Pearson Education, 2001. Reprinted with permission of Pearson Education Ltd.

382 *Jo Angouri*

88 L - --- =yeah I mean it could
89   be in an trading center of somet[hing   ]
90 N --[hmh [ye]ah   ]
91 S - ---[hmh yea]h I mean
92   exactly why was she avoiding the question
93   lik [e that   ]
94 L - --- [I mean i]t's fine her work b[ut   ]
95 N – ---------------------------------------[y[eah] of] c[ourse   ]
96 S - -- [hmh   ]
97 L - ---[is she re]ady
98   to face problems [like this   ]
99 S - ---------------------[and to comm]it to these pr[oblems]
100 N- --- [hmh yea]h yeah
101   that's true I agree w[ith you   ]
102 L - ----------------------[hmh yeah [ri]ght   ]
103 N - -----------------------------------[and I mea]n I thought as you
104   did that she was arrog[ant]
105 S - ------------------------ [hmh] (.) h[mh   ]

Excerpt 16.2: Transcript from a Cassiopeia meeting

Source: J. Angouri, From p. 382, 'Using textbook and real-life data to teach turn taking in business meetings'. In N. Harwood (ed). *English Language Teaching Materials: Theory and Practice*, Cambridge University 2010. Reprinted with permission of Cambridge University Press.

Angouri (2010: 382) observes in Excerpt X that 'the meeting is rather smooth flowing and collaborative, as there is explicit agreement and all interactants work together. Interestingly, however, the participants do not share the floor and the turn-taking patterns follow a rather linear procedure . . .'. She adds that the audio recording features a small amount of overlapped talk though the transcript does not include any. In comparison, Excerpt Y shows many instances of

- overlapping for the purposes of completing or extending other's utterances
- explicit agreement

- positive reinforcements of the previous speaker's utterances
- continuous back channelling (e.g. hmh yeah, hmh).

McCarten and McCarthy (2010: 23) propose general principles that can be applied to reflect the features of real conversation:

- Keep turns generally short, except for narratives. Where one speaker 'holds the floor', build in listener back-channelling (e.g. hmh yeah, hmh) and non-minimal responses (i.e. True, Exactly, Lovely, Absolutely).
- Allow speakers to react to the previous speaker.
- Do not overload speech with densely packed information; ensure a balance of transactional and relational language and an appropriate lexical density.
- Include some repetition, rephrasing, fragmented sentences and other features of speech, but maintain transparency.
- Keep speakers 'polite' . . . and not confrontational or face-threatening.

Go back to the previous task on p. 162 and see if Excerpts X and Y conform to McCarten and McCarthy's general principles.

Based on extensive studies of English from British, American and other varieties, O'Keeffe et al. (2007) describe the spoken corpora in different contexts including everyday, academic and business situations. Burns (2012) also provides a useful summary of typical features of speech.

In sum, spoken interactions often show the following features:

- ellipsis (i.e. incomplete utterances)
- use of conjunction (e.g. and, so) to add information and achieve continuity; very little subordination (subordinate clauses etc.)
- very few passives
- not many explicit logical connectors (moreover, however)
- use of topic head and/or tail (e.g. 'that restaurant yeah the food was great that restaurant'); the syntax of the written language would probably have a subject–verb–predicate structure
- replacing/refining expressions (e.g. 'this fellow/this chap I was supposed to meet')
- the use of vague language (e.g. thing, nice stuff, whatsit)
- repetition of the same syntactic form
- the use of pauses, 'fillers' and lexical phrases (e.g. 'erm', 'well', 'uhuh', 'if you see what I mean') in order to not only help oneself organize what to say but also to strengthen interpersonal relationships.

If your L1 is not English, what similarities and differences would there be to the forms outlined above?

As we have seen so far, spoken language shows regularities and patterns that help speakers organize their turn and maintain social relationships with their listeners. Being aware of possible grammatical choices in relation to spoken grammar will help L2 learners sound fluent, appropriate and effective. Carter et al. (2011) add

> Learners need to be helped to understand the idea of variable patterns. Classroom activities should therefore encourage greater language awareness and grammatical consciousness-raising on the part of the learner and try to stimulate an investigative approach so that learners learn how to observe tendencies and probabilities for themselves. (Carter et al. 2011: 98)

Next, within the 'framework' of the conversation, 'turns' have to take place if the conversation is not to be totally one-sided. Certain strategies have to be put into operation by the speaker. In practice, this may mean trying to 'hold the floor' for a while in the interaction, which will also involve knowledge of how 'long' or 'short' the turn can be; interrupting the other speaker(s); anticipating and inferring what is about to happen next; changing the 'topic' if necessary; and providing appropriate pauses and 'fillers' while processing the language.

The essential thing to note from the foreign language teaching perspective is that what may appear to be casual and unplanned in a conversation may nonetheless follow a deeper, organized pattern the learner has to be made aware of.

Do you think it is useful to apply native speaker strategies directly to classroom use?

8.7   Classroom Implications

If what we have seen above shows native speaker behaviour in conversations, research indicates that the non-native speaker is often reluctant to use some of these strategies when speaking. One such area is the use of pauses and fillers, which, as we have seen, enable the speaker to hold the floor by filling in the silence at that particular moment.

This can often be a cultural phenomenon: some otherwise proficient L2 speakers find this 'switch' a difficult one to accomplish if they come from an L1 culture where silences in conversations are more acceptable. Another area that some non-native speakers tend to neglect is that of making encouraging noises to the speaker such as 'yeah', 'I see', 'aha', 'that sounds fun' during the conversation, which enables the other speaker(s) to see that the conversation is being followed and processed.

One implication of such routines is that there is a need for speaking skills classes to place more emphasis on the 'frames' of oral interactions. We know that conversations have to be started, maintained and finished. The phrases that we use to accomplish this are called 'gambits'. An example of an opening gambit could be 'Excuse me. Do you happen to know if . . .'. Within the framework of the conversation the speakers also take 'turns' and, where pertinent, change the topic under discussion. This is not always an easy task to accomplish successfully. However, if sensitivity to how these conversation 'frames' work can be encouraged from the early stages of language learning by exposing near beginners to samples of natural speech to develop their awareness of conversational features and strategies, then learners will find themselves much more able to cope later on when they need or want to take part in real conversations outside the classroom.

Look at the extract on the next page from materials designed to provide a frame of conversation. How effective might it be for your own learners?

6A Work in pairs and role-play the situation.

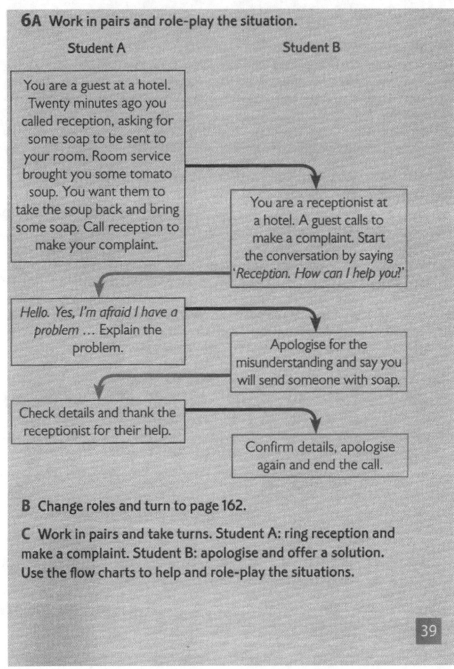

Student A

Student B

You are a guest at a hotel. Twenty minutes ago you called reception, asking for some soap to be sent to your room. Room service brought you some tomato soup. You want them to take the soup back and bring some soap. Call reception to make your complaint.

You are a receptionist at a hotel. A guest calls to make a complaint. Start the conversation by saying *'Reception. How can I help you?'*

Hello. Yes, I'm afraid I have a problem ... Explain the problem.

Apologise for the misunderstanding and say you will send someone with soap.

Check details and thank the receptionist for their help.

Confirm details, apologise again and end the call.

B Change roles and turn to page 162.

C Work in pairs and take turns. Student A: ring reception and make a complaint. Student B: apologise and offer a solution. Use the flow charts to help and role-play the situations.

39

Source: A. Clare and J. Wilson, Speaking 6A from p. 39, *Speakout Intermediate Students Book*. Pearson Education, 2001. Reprinted with permission of Pearson Education Ltd.

What has happened in materials and classrooms in recent years has clearly been influenced by a number of the findings we have outlined above. In what might rather loosely be termed 'pre-communicative' language teaching, dialogues were often used in class, but the purpose was not to teach the rules of communication, appropriateness and use: the focus was nearly always a structural one, and learners were rarely given an information gap task that would have enabled them to engage in some real communication. No account was offered as to how a sentence takes on meaning from its relation to surrounding utterances and to non-linguistic factors. It was also rare for attention to be drawn to who was actually speaking to whom.

In the light of what we have mentioned above, look at the following examples. How would you characterize each as spoken language? How do they differ?

Example 1:

GARY: And how's work?
RITA: Yeah, (it's) fine.
GARY: And your mum? (Is) She any better?
RITA: (She's) Much better, thanks.
GARY: Did you go and see her last week?
RITA: No, I meant to. (I'm) Going (on) Wednesday though. (I) just couldn't get any time off work last week. I tried to, but we were too busy.
GARY: Right.
RITA: So what have been up to this week?
GARY: Oh, er, (I) went to see the Degas exhibition at Tate Modern. (Have) You seen it?

(Taken from the Recording Scripts by C. Redston and G. Cunningham, 2007: face2face Upper Intermediate. Copyright © Cambridge University Press.)

Example 2:

JOHN: Hello, how are you?
TOM: I'm fine thank you. How are you?
JOHN: I'm also fine thank you.
TOM: How's your wife?
JOHN: She's very well thank you. How is your wife?
TOM: She's also very well thank you.

The first example shows two people who have a desire to communicate; they have a purpose; there is an information gap to fill in because both speakers need to listen to find out what the other person will say. They are also selecting appropriate language for their relationship and their informal chat. The second example is rather artificial as conversation and sounds more like a script than a piece of spontaneous language.

So how can we make optimal use of our understanding of real spoken interactions in classroom practice? Nunan (1999) suggests that teachers need to be aware that motivation is a consideration in determining whether or not learners are willing to communicate. Clearly, the more meaningful the materials and tasks are for the learners involved, the better the outcome will be. Ur (1996) develops this further by suggesting that good speaking skills classrooms are ones where learners talk a lot, participation is even, motivation is high and the language is at an acceptable level. Thornbury (2005) advocates three key elements of teaching speaking: 'awareness' in which learners are encouraged to notice features of the spoken language and interactions; 'appropriation', where learners try out their heightened awareness and integrate the new with existing knowledge 'autonomy', in which learners move towards independence and achieve automaticity in their use of skills or strategies.

Tomlinson and Dat (2004) report a longitudinal research project which investigated adult Vietnamese students' apparent reticence in speaking in English in class. The data provided evidence for the students' performance anxiety, low self-esteem, linguistic limitations, negative conceptions of the learning process and so on. The observation data of speaking classes showed the teacher-centred style and rare instances of spontaneous discourse or of oral interactions that involved the students' individual thoughts or elaborated responses. The surprising findings included evidence which revealed that the students actually welcomed opportunities for interactions that led to deepen social relationships in the classroom and that the teachers tended to underestimate learner competence and willingness. Tomlinson and Dat (2004: 215) suggest ways of counteracting various difficulties learners face in speaking and point out that '. . . students will only reveal their real ability to speak in English if their teachers encourage and value oral participation, foster a positive and supportive atmosphere, provide constructive feedback, encourage peer interaction and give thinking and rehearsal time'.

The implication for teachers, therefore, seems to be to devise meaningful activities that will motivate students to speak within a supportive environment.

> Consider your own speaking skills classes with respect to the information above. Does this tell you anything about your approach to teaching speaking skills or the approach favoured by the materials?

8.8   Types of Activity to Promote Speaking Skills

In this section of the chapter we examine some activities used in the classroom to promote the development of speaking skills in our learners. For focusing purposes, we shall begin by looking at an example of some 'pre-communicative' materials and then move on to consider what might broadly be termed 'communicative' activities or games. After this, we shall examine some oral problem-solving activities, role play and simulation materials for decision-making, and materials requiring personal responses from the learners. We finish this section by discussing materials designed to raise awareness of regularities and patterns of conversation.

In recent teaching materials, a lot of attention has been paid to designing activities that focus on tasks mediated through language or that involve the negotiation and sharing of information by the participants. The idea behind this thinking is that learners should be provided with the opportunity to use the language they know in meaningful activities they feel motivated to talk about.

Many of the pre-communicative materials used guided dialogues as a way of trying to develop oral practice with learners. Conversations were frequently structurally graded. Let us look at an imagined example designed to practise the 'not enough' structure:

A: Can John paint the ceiling?
B: No. He can't reach. He isn't tall enough.
A: What about if he uses a ladder? Will he be able to do it then?
B: I should think so.

The pattern practice that learners have to follow, which can then be applied to other conversations, is as follows:

A: Can X do Y?
B: No. He/she isn't tall enough.
A: What about if he/she uses a Z? Will he/she be able to do it then?
B: I should think/imagine so.

In contrast to this, we now turn our attention to materials for the teaching of speaking skills that form part of the communicative approach, beginning with communication games.

Communication games

Speaking activities based on games are often a useful way of giving students valuable opportunities to use English, especially, although by no means exclusively, where younger learners are involved. Game-based activities can involve practice of oral strategies such as describing, predicting, simplifying, asking for feedback, through activities such as filling in questionnaires and guessing unknown information. Even though these activities are called games, thereby implying fun, they are also communication-based and require the learners to use the information they find out in a collaborative way for successful completion of a particular task.

One such activity can be found in the Teaching English web site developed by the British Council and BBC (http://www.teachingenglish.org.uk/try/ activities/getting-whole-class-talking (accessed 10 September 2011)). The game is called, 'Something in Common or "Give Me Five"'. The objective of this game is to discover as many things as possible the learners have in common with fellow students and the one who finds the most common things is the winner. If the teacher limits the common things to five, then the first person to shout out 'Five' is the winner.

A slightly more systematic game may involve using a questionnaire with a potentially engaging topic (e.g. how to give a good first impression, how to prepare for an exam). The class is divided into groups of four. The teacher gives some possible topics as stimuli for the students to come up with their own ideas. The groups then come up with questions, compile lists of answers and prepare a presentation. The students can vote for the best presentation. If possible, the presentations can be recorded for later discussion and suggestions for improvements. Successful completion of this type of activity clearly depends on the effective communicative use of the language and of the sharing of information among the participants.

The 'describe and draw' principle is based on a series of plans and diagrams one student has to describe to another so that the latter can complete the task. The idea behind this 'describe and draw' communication activity is to give learners practice in handling, by means of oral description and drawing in pairs, a core of material of non-verbal data, that is, maps, plans, shapes, graphs. The activities are motivated by the fact that many EFL learners have difficulty when trying to handle these sorts of data in the spoken form. This activity is also a useful way of conversational negotiation in that the 'listener/ drawer' can ask for further clarification if something has not been understood. A typical example would be as follows:

> Learner A has a plan of a town centre containing the High Street, churches, school, library, shops, houses or the floor plan of a building such as a school or a company. Learner B then has to draw the plan as accurately as possible from the description given by learner A.

Ur (1996: 124) has some variations on the picture idea, but in this instance learners are issued with pictures everyone can see. They then have to describe the pictures by saying as many sentences about them as possible. A 'secretary' then marks down the number of utterances. After this, a second picture is provided and learners have to try to beat their first number of sentences produced.

Problem solving

Many speaking skills materials start from the premise that a communicative purpose can be established in the classroom by means of setting up a problem.

An example of a problem-solving principle can be seen at work in materials described by Mishan (2010). Her materials involve reading a mystery story about a man who was found wandering on a seafront road in the South East of England. He was drenched in the cold rain in his formal black suit. He could not speak or would not speak a word and all the labels on his clothes had been cut off. When provided with a grand piano, he amazed everyone with his two-hour virtuoso classical music performance. Mishan uses a maze format in which students develop this story by choosing a plausible option for solving this mystery. The problem-solving principle is used all the way until the final task:

> The main problem/task that the students are given . . . is to decide on an ending, then make a film based on the story. This 'problem' can range, depending on the time available, from drafting the screen-play, choosing a director, actors, etc., to a full-blown project, with students making the film themselves the final stage. (Mishan, 2010: 360)

The students have to share with their peers the stories their group has developed in order to build up a complete picture of that particular situation.

Mishan (2010) gives two further examples of materials using problem-solving principles. One of them involves the 'Whodunit?' genre, where the students have to solve a mystery that led to the death of a person. She makes use of a novel, an audiobook and a film in giving clues as necessary. The main objective is to create motivations and opportunities for communication while working out the likely plot based on the character profiles. The other example involves the students in developing a web site (e.g. Wiki, Blog) to help future Erasmus European Exchange Programme students to understand the host country and people in order to reduce the impact of having culture shock.

Think of how you might set up speaking skills activities using problem-solving principles in your own classroom.

Simulation/Role-play materials

One way of getting students to speak in different social contexts and to assume varied social roles is to use role-play activities in the classroom. Materials are generally aimed at the more proficient EFL learner, although this is not always the case, as they can be set up in a highly structured way with a lot of teacher control. At the other end of the spectrum, however, a considerable amount of choice may be exercised by allowing the students more freedom in what they will say. Role-play activities are also a pertinent way of integrating skills in the language classroom, and therefore we examine them from this perspective in more detail in Chapter 10.

Role plays require a situation, a profile of the people and an outcome for the interaction. It may be a simple one of which the main objective is to practise English expressions. The role cards may be for a shop assistant and for a customer. The card would have what kind of shop it is and it may include useful expressions for the participants. The participants can negotiate the process of buying or not buying.

Role-play materials are often written specifically to get learners to express opinions, to present and defend points of view, and to evaluate arguments for which there is no one objective way of demonstrating the outcome as right or wrong. For example, learners may be asked to consider the planning of a new motorway that would have to go through farmland, some country-side of outstanding beauty, as well as through the outskirts of a large town. The learners' role cards would be written from the various points of view of all the parties concerned in the planning project, and each learner (or pair or group, depending on the number of people in the class) would be asked to prepare notes to speak from in a meeting. This role play makes use of a problem-solving principle and comes from a controversial topic you may come across in real life. There is not one answer to this type of negotiated activity, and in this sense, the outcome of the discussion is very much up to the learners themselves. Viney's (1997) role play uses a critical incident and offers opportunities for the whole class to consider how to negotiate in a reasonable manner without being aggressive or offensive. The role play takes place at a Lost Property Office of a bus company between a day tripper who wants to retrieve a lost bag on the same day and a customer service employee who wants the customer to come back the next day for personal reasons. The rest of the class are given an evaluation sheet for observation of effectiveness of the interactions. The role plays can be recorded for further discussions not only of the expressions but also of the effectiveness of the social interaction.

Materials requiring personal responses

Some speaking materials have been designed for learners to talk about more meaningful things in order to increase the probability of language acquisition. Though this chapter has paid attention to implications of recent corpus studies, as McCarten and McCarthy (2010: 20) explain,

> '. . . very often real conversations pose problems for materials writers for several reasons'. Conversation in the corpus is not meant for appreciation by third parties. The language may not be appropriate. Above all, 'most conversa-

tions are not particularly interesting in themselves (except perhaps to those involved in them originally) and teaching materials needs more than anything to capture students' interest in some way. . .'.

From the point of view of ELF, we might question the legitimacy and appropriateness if we are to set native speaker usage norms as the models of language education. There are ideological issues here.

A logical extension of this would then be to get outside the materials themselves and to use the learners' own backgrounds and personalities in speaking classes so as to give them more genuine reasons for wanting to communicate with each other. One example of such materials is by Rea et al. (2011):

a   Have you ever regretted something that you've said or done? Think of three
     or four stories about
     Things you've said to: a friend, a colleague, a stranger, a teacher
     Things You've done: buying things, education, work, friends and family
     1   What did or didn't you do?
     2   Why was it a mistake?
     3   What should or shouldn't you have done?
     4   What could you have done differently?
b   Talk together. What do you think your partner should or could have done?
     (Rea et al., 2011: 103)

Tomlinson (2011b) stresses the importance of materials being underpinned by learning theories and proposes a flexible text-driven framework in which engaging spoken or written texts drive the sequence of materials (Tomlinson, 2003b). The learning principles Tomlinson (2011b) identifies include

- Provide extensive, rich and varied exposure to language in use
- Ensure affective and cognitive engagement to maximize the likelihood of intake
- Facilitate hypothesis forming, trialing and revising
- Provide opportunities to use the language for outcome-orientated output.

Look at the following speaking materials that aim to achieve personal engagement to create the needs, wants and readiness for language acquisition. The materials try to satisfy Tomlinson's learning principles summarized above and reflect the sequence advocated by Tomlinson (2003b).

1   Do you find the texts and activities engaging?
2   Consider what kinds of learning principles may lie behind each
     activity.

The Bully Asleep

Level: Lower-Intermediate
Class profile: Young adult – adult from mixed culture

1. Look at the photograph.

2. Form groups of three and discuss what you think is happening in the picture.
3. In groups, guess why do you think the conflict occurred? Write a few plausible reasons.
4. You are the boy in the middle in this picture. In groups, decide what to do.
5. What do you think could help to prevent such situations? In groups, list some ideas.
6. Listen to your teacher read the poem 'The Bully Asleep' by John Walsh. Try to see what is happening in the poem.
7. Was there anyone in the poem you sympathised with?
8. Listen again. After listening, form groups of three and try to draw an illustration of the poem. Include the following characters:
   • Miss Andrews
   • Bill Craddock
   • Jimmy Adair
   • Roger
   • Jane
9. Read the poem. In groups, add some more details to your drawing in 7 above.

The Bully Asleep

One afternoon, when grassy
Scents through the classroom crept,
Bill Craddock laid his head
Down on his desk, and slept.

The children came round him:
Jimmy, Roger, and Jane;
They lifted his head timidly
And let it sink again.

'Look, he's gone sound asleep, Miss,'
said Jimmy Adair;
'He stays up all the night, you see;
His mother doesn't care.'

'Stand away from him, children.'
Miss Andrews stooped to see
'Yes, he's asleep; go on
with your writing, and let him be.'

'Now's a good chance!' whispered Jimmy;
And he snatched Bill's pen and hid it.
'Kick him under the desk hard;
He won't know who did it.'

'Fill all his pockets with rubbish
paper, apple-cores, chalk.'
So they plotted, while Jane
Sat wide-eyed at their talk.

Not caring, not hearing,
Bill Craddock he slept on;
Lips parted, eyes, closed –
Their cruelty gone.

'Stick him with pins!' muttered Roger.
'Ink down his neck!' said Jim.
But Jane, tearful and foolish,
Wanted to comfort him.

John Walsh (from *The Roundabout BY the Sea*)

10. Find a partner, do one of the following:
    a) You are Bill. Draw a picture of a typical scene at your home.
    b) Write a short diary of Jimmy Adair, who is normally bullied by Bill. He wrote
       the page of his diary on the day before Billy fell asleep during Miss Andrews'
       class.
    c) You are Jane who is sympathizing with Bill, the bully. Write a letter to Miss
       Andrews, explaining to her what you know about Billy and asking her to be
       kind to him.

11. Miss Andrews asked Bill Craddock to remain after school.
    Choose one of the roles below and prepare for your meeting:
    a) You are Bill. Think of how to explain to her why you bully other pupils.
    b) You are Miss Andrews. You are having a meeting with Bill after school.
    You know that he finds it difficult to explain the reasons why he bullies
    other students. Write down some questions that could help him.
    Find a partner who has chosen the other role. Form a pair and start the meeting.
12. Form groups of four. Find out from members in your groups if:
    a) bullying happens in their cultures
    b) how people deal with the problems in their cultures
13. Individually, in pairs or in groups, try to write a poem about bullying in your
    culture.
14. In groups, prepare a short presentation for the class on one of the following topics:
    • What causes bullying
    • Solutions
    • Bullying – case studies
    • Advice on what to do when bullied

Source: J. Walsh, 'The Bully Asleep', from *The Roundabout By the Sea* by John
Walsh. Published by OUP, 1960. Photograph © iStockphoto.com/1MoreCreative.

Materials illustrating tendencies/patterns of conversation

As discussed earlier, we know a lot more about features of spoken English,
thanks to corpus-based studies since the mid-1990s. Do teaching materials
reflect what we have come to understand about spoken interactions? Cullen
and Kuo (2007) report the results of their extensive survey that investigated
how spoken corpus research may have influenced 24 general EFL coursebooks published in the United Kingdom since 2000. Their survey reveals that
the influence can be observed (e.g. wider use of lexical chunks such as 'you
see', 'I mean'), but the range is somewhat restricted. As for the methodology,
McCarthy and Carter (1995) advocate i-i-i (illustration – induction – interaction) approaches to teaching spoken grammar in contrast to widely used
P-P-P (presentation – practice – production) (see also Carter
et al., 2011). Cullen and Kuo (2007) note some similarity in the teaching
approaches among the materials they analysed: learners are firstly exposed
to listening text that shows some typical features of spoken English with a
focus on its overall meaning. Secondly, the learners are encouraged to find
the tendencies and patterns of spoken grammar. The learners are then given
opportunities to use such features of spoken English in some production
activities.

Timmis (2012) makes a further useful evaluation of two coursebooks that
pay close attention to spoken English: *Touchstone* (McCarthy et al., 2005)
and *Innovations* (Dellar and Walkley, 2004). Timmis describes *Touchstone*
as corpus-informed whereas *Innovations* is intuition-informed. The overrid-

ing principle behind both coursebooks is to try to make learners sound more natural when participating in conversations and discussions. People who never use strategies or well-accepted spoken expressions may be interpreted by the other participant/s as being abrupt, direct or even rude in some cases. For example, we do not generally go into a shop and ask, 'How much is this?' but would probably say, 'Could you tell me how much this is please?' Similarly, we may want to introduce a piece of surprising news with 'You may not believe this, but . . .'. If we are in a shop and wish to leave without purchasing something we may say 'I'm afraid I can't make up my mind at the moment', or 'I'll have to give it some thought'. The two coursebooks mentioned above contain advice and exercises that allow learners to experiment with common features of spoken English.

Materials to enhance academic speaking skills

The materials we have examined thus far have been largely within the general language teaching framework. However, some learners need to speak in an academic community, especially if they are studying their specialist subject in an English-speaking country. *Study Speaking* (Anderson et al., 2004) is widely used in this pedagogical context and provides speaking tasks on topic areas such as types of courses, accommodation, teaching and research and health issues. Bell (2008) introduces language and skills necessary for oral presentations by going through each stage of the process. Schmitt and Schmitt (2005) and McCarthy and O'Dell (2008) explain and offer practice for useful academic vocabulary and expressions.

8.9 Feedback to Learners

In all of the activities outlined above, teachers may wonder how to correct errors produced by learners during the oral skills class. Generally we tend to correct oral mistakes through speech, but the 'how' and 'when' obviously requires a great deal of sensitivity on the part of the teacher. If we are trying to encourage our learners to become fluent in the spoken language, correcting regularly during oral work will tend to inhibit further those learners who may already be rather taciturn in class. Most teachers feel that correcting a student in mid-sentence is generally unhelpful unless the student is floundering and is giving the teacher signals that she wants some help. Some teachers prefer to 'log' oral mistakes in writing and hand these to a student at the end of a class in the belief that learners may 'learn something from their mistakes'. Learners are individuals, and it may be helpful for teachers to work out the kinds of corrections students find most useful, perhaps even linking these to tutorials and diary work (see Chapter 12). Tomlinson (2007b) discusses the value of 'recasting' by the caretakers (e.g. parents in L1, teachers in L2) in facilitating language acquisition with reference to studies in both L1 and L2 language acquisition. Just as a parent interprets the child's intended meaning and then echoes by providing more effective and richer models, teachers' affirmative and supportive rephrasing in response may be beneficial and also welcomed by the learners.

8.10   Conclusion

We began this chapter by examining the needs that learners may have to speak in a foreign language in the first place. Then we discussed some of the background to speaking skills by emphasizing speaking as an active skill. Subsequently we looked at the ways in which speaking and listening interact and how research into communicative language theory and the characteristics of spoken language has had important classroom implications over the last two decades. Finally, we offered a brief overview of the design principles underlying some of the speaking skills materials that have been produced over the last 20 years.

8.11   Further Reading

1   O'Keeffe, A., M. McCarthy and R. A. Carter. (2007): *A comprehensive coverage of corpus studies with some pedagogical considerations.*
2   Thornbury, S. (2005): *How to Teach Speaking.* This book is primarily written for practicing teachers, but it discusses theories behind the practice and provides example worksheets.

9

Writing Skills

9.1 Introduction

Along with the other three skills, writing has developed and accumulated many insights into the nature of language and learning. However, as well as having much in common with other skills, we shall see that writing differs in some significant ways to do with the purpose of writing in class and in everyday life, and the relationship between these two settings.

This chapter will first survey the reasons for writing and the different types of writing associated with them. The central section will focus on a number of approaches to teaching writing, particularly as expressed in teaching materials, and will try to show how perspectives have gradually changed. We shall then move on to the classroom environment itself, including some possibilities for writing-related activities, the issue of error correction and the role of the teacher.

9.2 Reasons for Writing

1 At this point it would be helpful to note down your reasons for needing – or wishing – to write in the course of a typical week, and the form that your writing takes. Try to think of all possible contexts. Can the kinds of writing you do be grouped together in any way?

2 How do you think your own list might compare with that of other people you know: perhaps a friend who is not a teacher, or your students?

Materials and Methods in ELT: A Teacher's Guide, Third Edition.
Jo McDonough, Christopher Shaw, and Hitomi Masuhara.
© 2013 John Wiley & Sons, Inc. Published 2013 by John Wiley & Sons, Inc.

Our own list included the following, not in any particular order:

Shopping list	Notes from a book	Official forms
This chapter	Parts of a prospectus	Letter requesting tourist information
Telephone messages	'Reminder' lists	An essay
Letter to a friend	A meeting agenda	Business letters
Comments on student work	Invitations	Diary (narrative and appointments)
Birthday card	Office memoranda	Map showing how to get to our house
E mails	Text messages	Word and phrase searches on the Internet

We can now make a few initial observations arising directly or indirectly from thinking about the kinds of writing we do. The implications of these points for the teaching of writing are taken up below.

1   A typical 'writing profile' covers a great range of styles. We may just write a list of nouns, or a number, or even simply a visual representation (a list, taking a phone message, drawing a map). Alternatively, taking notes from a book or a verbal message will require some facility with reducing language structure into note form in the interests of speed and efficiency. Discursive writing has many different functions (narrative, persuasion, setting out an argument etc.) and makes considerable demands on our ability to structure an extended piece of writing carefully. Email writing is more often conversational, even when done for professional purposes, and is more immediately interactive.

Moreover, in some cases, we ourselves initiate the need to write – different kinds of letters, a shopping list, or a short story, perhaps – whereas in other cases, the writing is a response to someone else's initiation, as when we respond to an invitation or a letter. The final point to make here is that our writing has different addressees: family, colleagues, friends, ourselves, officials, students and many more.

Reasons for writing, then, differ along several dimensions, especially those of language, topic and audience.

2   In straightforward terms of frequency, the great majority of people write very much less than they talk and listen, although the amount of writing may be increasing as people have more access to computers and to email communication. It is, for example, not unusual to find emails taking over

from telephone calls. Nevertheless, it is still the case that many adults do not need to write much in their everyday lives: and if there are few 'real-world' reasons for writing in our L1, there are even fewer for doing so in a foreign language. Writing for most of us only happens to any significant extent as part of formal education. This dominance of oral/aural over literacy skills holds even for those of us for whom writing is an integral part of our professional lives.

Types of writing

Personal writing	Public writing	Creative writing	

diaries
journals
shopping lists
reminders for oneself
packing lists
recipes
	letters of
	  —enquiry
	  —complaint
	  —request
	form filling
	applications (for memberships)
		poems
		stories
		rhymes
		drama
		songs
		autobiography	

Social writing	**Study writing**	**Institutional writing**	

letters
invitations
notes
  —of condolence
  —of thanks
  —of congratulations
emails
telephone messages
instructions
  —to friends
  —to family
	making notes while reading
	taking notes from lectures
	making a card index
	summaries
	synopses
	reviews
	reports of
	  —experiments
	  —workshops
	  —visits
	essays
	bibliographies
		agendas
		minutes
		memoranda
		reports
		reviews
		contracts
		business letters
		public notices
		advertisements
		emails
			posters
			instructions
			speeches
			applications
			curriculum vitae
			specifications
			note-making
			(doctors
			and other
			professionals)

Source: T. Hedge (2005), *Writing*, 2nd edition, p. 87. Oxford University Press.

3   Some ways of classifying types of writing can be suggested. Hedge (2005: 87) offers a more detailed breakdown under the six headings of personal, public, creative, social, study and institutional. Her checklist is self-explanatory, and is reproduced above in full. We shall refer back to it when discussing the 'products' of writing appropriate to the language classroom. In the meantime, you will certainly recognize some elements of your own list here. You might like to see whether your writing fits into the categories that Hedge uses.

9.3   Writing Materials in the Language Class

It is now time to ask what part writing can and does play in the language class, given its more limited role for most people outside an educational setting. We have seen in previous chapters that some attention to 'real-world' language and behaviour is regarded as increasingly important in the current English language teaching climate. It would be difficult to argue the case that writing in the language class should only mirror the educational function (writing essays and examination answers, taking notes from textbooks etc.) except perhaps in certain 'specific-purpose' programmes such as English for Specific Purposes (ESP) (e.g. nursing, business) or English for Academic Purposes (EAP). At the same time, it is not immediately obvious how the notion of 'authenticity' and the opportunities for transfer from real world to classroom can be maintained to the extent that this can be done for speaking and listening skills.

These two issues – the possibilities for reflecting communicative criteria, and the treatment of the skill of writing resulting from its general educational role – have been significant in the development of materials and methods. We shall now go on to look at how writing has been handled in English language teaching, attempting as we do so to pick out the major trends.

> The titles, with dates, of several popular writing courses are listed below. Pause for a moment to look through the list. Then, as you read the rest of the chapter, ask yourself what significance the titles might have. For example, can you discern a shift in the approaches to the teaching of writing? Do the dates of publication approximately parallel what you know of changing perspectives on language and language learning?

These are speculative questions, and we certainly do not wish to suggest that there is a rigid relationship between a title, a date and a 'movement' in language teaching. We shall make a few comments in the conclusion to this chapter.

Guided Composition Exercises (1967)
Frames for Written English (1966/1974)
Guided Course in English Composition (1969)
Guided Paragraph Writing (1972)
From Paragraph to Essay (1975)
Think and Link (1979)
Communicate in Writing (1981)
Writing Skills (1983)
Pen to Paper (1983)
Freestyle (1986)
Word for Word (1989)

Outlines (1989)
Process Writing (1991)
Feedback (1994)
Better Business Writing: An Interactive Course (1996)
Reasons to Write: Strategies for Successful Academic Writing (2001)
Skills in English Writing (2004)
Writing for the Real World (2005)

'Traditional' writing activities

There are a number of types of writing task that most of us will be familiar with, both as teachers and from our own language learning experience. Simplifying for the moment, they can be listed under three broad headings.

Controlled sentence construction   If the focus of a language programme is on accuracy, then schemes for controlling learners' writing output will obviously predominate. The range of activity types is considerable, and typical approaches include

* providing a model sentence and asking students to construct a parallel sentence with different lexical items
* inserting a missing grammatical form
* composing sentences from tabular information, with a model provided
* joining sentences to make a short paragraph, inserting supplied conjunctions (but, and, however, because, although . . .).

Free composition   Apparently at the other end of the spectrum, a 'free writing' task requires learners to 'create' an essay on a given topic, often as part of a language examination. Sometimes students are simply invited to write on a personal topic – their hobbies, what they did on holiday, interesting experiences and the like. Other materials provide a reading passage as a stimulus for a piece of writing on a parallel topic, usually with comprehension questions interspersed between the two activities.

   Although 'controlled' and 'free' writing appear to represent very different approaches, they are not in fact mutually exclusive, and many writing schemes lead learners through several stages from one to the other. A typical example is provided in Jupp and Milne's (1969) *Guided Course in English Composition*: each 'composition' begins with structure practice, continues with a sample composition, and then uses this material as a basis for students' own compositions.

The 'homework' function   Particularly in general coursebooks (as distinct from materials devoted specifically to the skill of writing), it is quite common to find writing tasks 'bunched' at the end of a unit, either as supplementary work in class or set for homework and returned to the teacher for later correction.

This brief and generalized summary indicates several trends in the 'traditional' teaching of writing from which current views have both developed and moved away:

- There is an emphasis on accuracy.
- The focus of attention is the finished product, whether a sentence or a whole composition.
- The teacher's role is to be judge of the finished work.
- Writing often has a consolidating function.

In her summary of the historical development of writing pedagogy, Reid states that

> In the 1970's many English L2 language programme writing classes were, in reality, grammar courses. Students copied sentences or short pieces of discourse, making discrete changes in person or tense. The teaching philosophy grew directly out of the audiolingual method: students were taught incrementally, error was prevented and accuracy was expected to arise out of practice with structures. (Reid 2001: 28)

Tribble (1996) makes a distinction between 'learning to write' and 'writing to learn'. A concise account of the differences can be found in Tribble:

> . . . In the former, an apprentice writer is learning how to extend his or her textual knowledge, cognitive capacities, and rhetorical skills in order to take on (usually prestigious) social roles, which require the production of certain kinds of text. In the latter, language learners are using the writing system to practice new language knowledge or are using writing to demonstrate their knowledge in the context of assessment.
>
> One of the problems facing the writing instructor of EFL is the fact that all too often, learners' main experience of EFL writing has been in *writing to learn* and that they have had few opportunities to extend their literacy in the target language. . . . (Tribble, 2010: 161)

Note that in many earlier materials, the 'product' did not on the whole reflect the kind of real-world writing discussed earlier, and the 'process' was not given much explicit attention.

9.4   The Written Product

We commented earlier that traditional writing classes were product-oriented. When teachers look at students' written work, they usually pay special attention to sentence structure, spelling, word choice and possibly paragraph construction. Notions of 'correctness', however, have broadened since the 1980s. As one such change, we will examine levels of writing in the next section.

Note that current literature on teaching writing (e.g. Hyland, 2003; Hedgecock, 2005; Hyland and Hyland, 2006; Tribble, 2010) also considers elements that go beyond linguistic domains, such as genre, purpose and socio-cultural factors, in describing L2 writer's texts.

We now look at some selected examples of activities in materials for the teaching of writing. Many more examples will be found in the books listed under 'Further Reading' at the end of the chapter. We shall focus on (1) levels of writing and (2) audience.

Levels of writing

Look back again at your personal list of writing activities. Most teachers, for example, write comments on student work as a regular part of their jobs. You may well recognize this style:

> This is quite a good summary, but it would have been a good idea to include more of your own opinions. Think more carefully about tenses. Your handwriting is also sometimes difficult to read.

From a different sphere, in a letter home from holiday you will probably include something about what you have been doing, details of people and places, and perhaps some information about travel arrangements. As you write, you will certainly have been operating on a number of different and interacting levels, not necessarily consciously, of course, and moving between 'top-down' and 'bottom-up' strategies discussed in Chapter 6.

We saw in Chapter 2 how the advent of the 'communicative approach' had far-reaching implications, including an extension of the size of language stretches that can be dealt with from sentence to discourse level. The two outer layers on figure 9.1 will certainly require consideration of both 'cohesion' – linking devices – and 'discourse coherence' – the ways in which a text forms a thematic whole. Such criteria are now well-established in the teaching of writing. Typical organizational principles for materials include paragraph structuring, particularly related to functional categories, and the use of a range of linking devices. Sentence-level and grammar practice is not omitted but, as the diagram suggests, is set in the context of a longer and purposeful stretch of language. Writing, then, is seen as primarily message-oriented, so a communicative view of language is a necessary foundation.

Some of the trends in the teaching of discourse-level writing, and the techniques used, are readily discernible from a glance at many of the published materials of the 1980s.

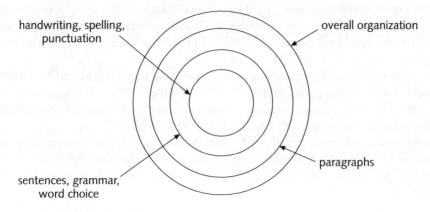

Figure 9.1   Levels of writing.

Functional categories include:

sequencing; chronological order
comparison and contrast
classification
cause and effect
description of objects and of processes
definitions
writing instructions
predicting and speculating
expressing opinion
expressing reasons
discursive essays
   writing narratives, for example, of events
   Nunan (1999: ch. 10) makes a number of proposals for developing what
he terms 'discourse writing'.
   Linking devices covered include the various connectives associated with
these functional categories, and the notions of lexical cohesion, referencing
using pronouns and the article system, ellipsis and substitution.
   The techniques used are many, and you will notice that they usually require
learners to understand the overall purpose of a piece of writing, not just the
immediate sentence-bound grammatical context. Here is a small selection of
some of the possibilities:

- Providing a text to read as a model for a particular function.
- Answering questions on a text, then using the answers as the basis for a
  piece of writing.

- Using non-verbal information in many forms. This may be a simple visual, such as a picture or a drawing; or a table, a graph, a diagram. Alternatively, the overall structure of a text may be represented visually, as an 'information-structure' diagram. The last of these is particularly common with classifications.
- Selecting appropriate connectives in a paragraph.
- (Re)constructing a paragraph from sentences given in the wrong order, or a whole text from a set of jumbled paragraphs. This technique is usually referred to as 'unscrambling'.
- Paragraph or story completion, which can be done by adding not only an ending, but also a beginning or a middle section.
- Parallel writing.
- Choosing an appropriate title for a piece of writing, such as a newspaper article.
- Working on identifying and creating 'topic sentences' as the basis for developing paragraphs.

Many other techniques are developed from pre-writing tasks carried out in the classroom: we shall look at these a little later in this chapter.

Audience

It is now widely accepted that writing is a process of encoding (putting your message into words) carried out with a reader in mind. Certainly the outermost layer of figure 9.1 – the overall organization – is best considered in relation to audience and purpose. The degree of 'crafting' that needs to be done, and at what level, will also be determined to some extent by the addressee. Stylistic choices, in other words, depend on why and for whom we are writing.

It is likely that, in the great majority of situations, our students still write primarily for their teachers, or perhaps for an examiner, both acting in the role of evaluator. Hedge (2005) makes the very useful point that, although transferring real-life writing directly to the classroom is problematic, what we should be aiming at is at least the creation of 'plausible contexts'.

Would you say that your students do most of their writing for their teacher, or are there other 'plausible contexts' that you have introduced into your classroom? When you have read through the following suggestions for extending the range of possible recipients for your students' writing, consider to what extent your own materials or classes could be adapted to accommodate them.

As we have noted several times, the classroom has its own purpose and structure, and is not simply a reflection of the outside world. In this sense, we can think of writing activities both from the 'instrumental' perspective of what is useful for external purposes, and also in terms of their educational function and the reality of the classroom itself. The following audience suggestions reflect this dual aspect. We have listed addressees along with a few suggested topics, but of course the possibilities are considerably greater than this. Our students, then, can write

- to other students: invitations, instructions, directions
- for the whole class: a magazine, poster information, a cookbook with recipes from different countries
- for new students: information on the school and its locality
- to the teacher (not only for the teacher) about themselves and the teacher can reply or indeed initiate (Hedge, 2005, for example, suggests an exchange of letters with a new class to get to know them)
- for themselves: lists, notes, diaries (for a fuller discussion of diary writing see Chapter 12)
- to penfriends
- to other people in the school: asking about interests and hobbies, conducting a survey
- to people and organizations outside the school: writing for information, answering advertisements
- If the school has access to a network of computers, many of these activities can be carried out electronically as well.

So far we have looked at the 'what' of writing, particularly at the nature of text and the importance of writing with a readership in mind. Writing continues to serve as a vehicle for language practice, and necessarily so, but this function should be integrated into a broader and more diversified perspective. As Hyland puts it:

> While every act of writing is in a sense both personal and individual, it is also interactional and social, expressing a culturally recognized purpose, reflecting a particular kind of relationship, and acknowledging an engagement in a given community. This means that writing cannot be distilled down to a set of cognitive or technical abilities or a system of rules, and learning to write in second language is not simply a matter of opportunities to write or revise. (Hyland, 2003: 27).

We now turn to the 'how'.

9.5   The Writing Process

One of the aims of this book is to trace the changes of focus in materials and methods for English language teaching, and to show how different approaches have gained prominence at different times. A characteristic of the 1980s–1990s was a growing interest in what a language skill entails. Initially, attention was focused on the receptive skills, especially reading: more recently, research into writing – much of it concerned with writing in the mother tongue – has become more accessible to second-language teachers, and is beginning to have a significant impact on the design of materials and on attitudes to teaching writing. Stylistic factors, whether grammatical, discoursal or lexical, are now set alongside a concern for how writers go about the socio-cultural performance of the task itself. A detailed discussion of the research base is outside the scope of this chapter but readers interested in pursuing the L1/L2 parallels further are referred to a brief but useful overview in Reid (2001) or a slightly more detailed one in Hedgecock (2005). Hyland (2010) discusses the current applications of research in terms of courses, materials, teaching practices and software. Silva and Matsuda (2010) provide a good overview of a number of L2 writing theories as well as the aspects of L2 writing that are currently attracting the interest of researchers.

We shall now look at the writing process from the two related points of view of the writer and the classroom.

The writer's perspective

> Try to note down the various stages that you think you go through when producing a piece of continuous text, such as a letter, a report, an essay, a story and the like.

Except perhaps with something as straightforward as a shopping list, it is unlikely that your text will appear directly on the page in its final form without any intervening stages. Even with a shopping list you may decide to reorder it, and categorize items in terms of different types of shop or different sections of the supermarket. Writers, it seems, do a great number of things before they end up with the final version – the 'finished product'. For instance, they jot down ideas, put them in order, make a plan, reject it and start again, add more ideas as they go along, change words, rephrase bits, move sections around, review parts of what they have written, cross things out, check through the final version, write tidy notes, write on odd pieces of paper as thoughts occur to them, write directly into a typewriter or a word processor if they are lucky enough to have one, look at the blank page for a long time, change pens, refer back to something they have read – and many more things, some of them quite idiosyncratic.

Tribble reminds us of the fact that not all L1 users write extensively.

> . . . as teachers of writing, we need to be aware of what exactly we are asking of our students. We may be (a) asking learners to take on roles that they do not normally have access to in their first language . . . ; or (b) asking learners to engage with literacy practices that they consider to be superfluous to their primary need to engage with the target language as a medium for spoken interaction. (Tribble, 2010: 160)

The demand must be particularly severe if students are expected to turn in a perfectly polished piece of work. Even if accuracy is an important and legitimate requirement, it is only achieved after a rather untidy and stumbling set of procedures, and the nature of the process itself needs to be acknowledged. We shall return to this point from a different angle when looking at attitudes to the correction of written work.

Hedgecock explains how developments in related disciplines have led to promoting 'process-orientated writing instruction' in recent years:

> . . . process-oriented pedagogies are marked by the following features, among others:
> * Discovery and articulation of writers' authorial voices.
> * Free writing, journaling, and private writing activities designed to enhance writer's fluency, creativity, and exploration of source texts.
> * Localization of writing process and texts in authentic contexts to develop the writer's sense of audience and reader expectations.
> * Constructing purposeful tasks that engage writers and promote their investment in creating meaningful texts.
> * Modelling and monitoring of invention, prewriting, and revision strategies.
> * Recursive practices such as multidrafting, which demonstrate that writing for an authentic audience is often a nonlinear, multi-dimensional process.
> * Formative feedback from real readers in peer response workshops, student-teacher conferences, collaborative writing projects, and so on.
> * Provision of meaningful content for writing tasks, with a corresponding emphasis on representing ideas, rather than solely on producing grammatically accurate prose. (Hedgecock, 2005: 604–5).

Materials for teaching writing are increasingly beginning to incorporate these process-based insights in various ways.

Hedge (2005) provides a comprehensive range of process-oriented classroom procedures teachers can make use of. Her book on teaching writing consists of four sections: Communicating, Composing, Crafting and Improving. *Communicating* represents the first stage of the writing process. The activities suggested in this section are designed to help learners become used to writing as self-discovery and as a means of communication. Examples of activities include producing a class magazine, exchanging letters with teachers and peers and writing a newscast, all of which require the learners to write within a specific genre and context to a specific real-life audience.

Composing is the second stage in which the learners experience the mental processes of gathering and organizing ideas before actually starting to write. Activities in this stage include making mind maps, using a diagram of ideas, brainstorming and cubing (i.e. considering a topic from six different points of views, such as description, comparison and application).

Crafting is the third stage, in which learners are guided to produce well-structured written work. Activities involve writing a book review, a description of a person, a biography and an essay with contrast and comparison. In these activities the learners are provided with opportunities to raise their awareness of how written language (e.g. paragraph, discourse) is organized in different kinds of texts.

The final stage is *Improving*, when the teacher and the class collaborate to improve the quality of writing through awareness activities such as conferencing on plans and drafts, peer editing, reformulation and checking accuracy.

Before leaving this section, it is worth noting that some practitioners involved in EAP or ESP may argue that their approaches to writing should differ from those for General English. For example, EAP classes aim to facilitate the more specific academic literacy skills necessary for undergraduate and graduate study in English-medium institutions, and both EAP and ESP are likely to be more obviously goal-oriented.

Writing in the classroom

Writing, like reading, is in many ways an individual, solitary activity: the writing triangle of 'communicating', 'composing' and 'crafting' is usually carried out for an absent readership. However, we must remember that our students are language learners rather than writers, and it would not be particularly helpful to have them spend all their time writing alone. Although process research points to a need to give learner-writers space and time to operate their own preferred individual strategies, the classroom can be structured in such a way as to provide positive intervention and support in the development of writing skills. We shall comment only very briefly here on possible classroom activities – they look directly ahead to the next chapter on the integration of language skills, and to the management of classrooms that will be the focus of the third part of this book: Aspects of Classroom Methods.

The classroom can provide an environment for writing at each of the three main stages of (1) gathering ideas: pre-writing and planning, (2) working on drafts, and (3) preparing the final version. The primary means by which this can be done – leaving aside for the moment the teacher's role of marking and commenting – is by establishing a collaborative, interactive framework where learners work together on their writing in a 'workshop' atmosphere. A few typical examples, all involving oral skills, must suffice:

- 'Brainstorming' a topic by talking with other students to collect ideas.
- Co-operating at the planning stage, sometimes in pairs/groups, before agreeing a plan for the class to work from.
- 'Jigsaw' writing, for example, using a picture stimulus for different sections of the class to create a different part of the story (Hedge, 2005: 40–2).
- Editing another student's draft.
- Preparing interview questions, perhaps for a collaborative project.

The 'Computers and writing' section of Chapter 5 in this book provides an overview of the literature on using computers for writing and discusses process-oriented approaches to writing using computers. Kervin and Derewianka (2011) list various computer-based writing activities including discussion forums (e.g. WebCT and blogs), interactive texts (e.g. hypertexts) and collaborative writing using Internet resources (e.g. wikis and web quests). They also discuss feedback, revision and assessment using computers.

In the multidimensional view of writing explored in this chapter, there are clearly a number of different possibilities available for the sequencing of materials and activities. We can reduce these to three:

1   Varying/increasing the size of the linguistic 'building blocks', from single lexical items → sentences and sentence joining → the construction of paragraphs and finally → whole texts. This requires attention to all levels of language, from sentence and text structure to a sense of the coherence of a completed piece of writing. This is related, of course, to the more traditional progression through a writing scheme from 'controlled' to 'guided' to 'free', though we now have a much wider range of descriptive tools available for the language material.

2   Paralleling the stages in the process of putting a whole piece of writing together. Although writing processes have little in themselves to do with proficiency – an elementary learner can in principle plan, draft and redraft, and edit as well as an advanced one can – the degree to which the process can be put to use obviously does have.

3   Task complexity. It can be argued – although it is a point that needs further exploration – that personal (expressive) writing is in some sense 'easier' than its institutional or professional counterpart. A letter to a friend, or a short story, while they obviously have their own structure, nevertheless are not as constrained by rules as, say, a business letter or a report or an essay.

9.6   Correcting Written Work

> 1   What is your usual and preferred method for correcting student work?
> 2   What do you see as your main role in relation to the writing your learners produce?

Obviously, teachers' attitudes and methods are determined to a certain extent by their approach to language teaching (whether chosen or imposed), and by the whole educational climate in which they work. We commented earlier that the most common role for the teacher in traditional writing classes is to be a judge, a critical evaluator of the finished product. Work is returned to students with mistakes indicated or corrected: the legendary red pen has always been a tool of the teacher's trade. Error feedback or correction assumes that teachers' marks and corrections are understood and learned by the students. Whether this assumption holds true or not has been an ongoing debate in second language acquisition (SLA) and in writing research. Truscott (1996) examines such a belief based on his critical review of L2 error treatment research and argues that there is no evidence that error feedback in L2 writing instruction is effective. He asserts that 'correction is harmful rather than simply ineffective' and that 'error correction should be abandoned' when there are no convincing reasons for doing so (Truscott 1996: 360). Ferris (1999: 1) describes the shortcomings of Truscott's reviews and says they are based on 'limited, dated, incomplete, and inconclusive evidence' and criticizes his conclusion as 'premature and overly strong'.

The controversies continue. Hedgecock (2005: 606) reports that '. . . studies have shown that expert feedback may not convert to intake or long term uptake. Furthermore, expert feedback may not necessarily improve text quality or develop a writer's autonomous revision skill' (F. Hyland, 2000).

Ferris (2006), after summarizing the studies that support the effectiveness of teacher feedback, reports the results of her own carefully controlled study. She points out that teacher intervention in terms of expressiveness and accuracy seems to have some effect: a more evident short-term effect but a less convincing long-term effect. She observes that the influential factors on feedback effectiveness include

- Learners' proficiency
- Manner of feedback (e.g. direct correction, indirect indication of problems for the learners to solve)

- Kinds of errors (e.g. treatable ones that the learners can overcome, untreatable errors)
- Timing of feedback (i.e. formative feedback during the writing process, post-feedback on errors).

The approaches to writing that we have looked at, from the perspective of both 'product' and 'process', inevitably lead to a much more varied view both of the role of the teacher and the classroom environment, and of the criteria for marking and assessing students' written work.

Process considerations suggest the usefulness of intervention at all stages of writing, not just at the end. It is unlikely that a draft will need to receive a grade, so the teacher, by commenting and making suggestions, becomes a reader as well as a critic. Harmer (2001b: 261–2) regards the teacher as 'motivator' and 'feedback provider'. The feedback given to students is in this view both 'formative' – concerned with a developmental process – as well as 'summative' – the evaluation of the end-product. Secondly, this feedback, whether summative or formative, takes place at a number of different levels of writing, and sentence grammar is not the only subject of attention. We need to take into account the appropriateness of the writing to its purpose and intended audience as well as topic and content criteria. Several marking schemes along these lines are now used by individual teachers, in materials, and by some examination boards. These schemes typically involve

Communicative quality
Logical organization
Layout and presentation
Grammar
Vocabulary
Handwriting, punctuation and spelling

You might like to 'weight' these in terms of their importance in your evaluation of your own students' writing.

After a close evaluation of error correction and feedback research, Ferris (2003: 118), emphasizes the importance of principled feedback. For example, she proposes feedback guidelines that remind teachers to

- Prioritize
- Treat students as individuals
- Be encouraging
- Be clear and helpful
- Avoid imposing their own ideas on student writers, leaving the final decisions in the hands of the writer.

The red pen method is inherently negative, but there is no reason why feedback should not be positive as well: for example, 'communicates effectively', 'excellent control of appropriate vocabulary' and the like. The issue here is what we see to be the overall function of correction. A distinction should be made between 'mistakes', when learners are not using correctly the language they already know, and errors, which, as we have seen, are largely the outcome of a learner's developing competence. Mistakes may require direct feedback and remedial treatment, and largely relate to language points already covered; errors may be more appropriately used for the planning of future work.

Ferris (2003: 122) provides an example of process-orientated feedback procedures:

1st draft – in class peer response
2nd draft – expert feedback
3rd draft – focused editing workshop
Final draft – careful editing and proof-reading
Grade and final comments.

There is an interesting further dimension to the notion of 'correctness' that derives from research into the notion of 'Intercultural rhetoric' (Connor, 2004). This refers to the idea that, at least to some extent, thought patterns are culturally determined, and that these will be expressed in styles of writing. Hyland comments:

> . . . L2 writers are unique because of their bilingual, and biliterate experiences, and these can facilitate or impede writing in various ways. . . .
>
> L2 learners' cultural schemata can impact on the ways they write and the writing they produce.
>
> Effective L2 writing instruction can make schemata differences explicit to students, encouraging consideration of audience and providing patterns of unfamiliar rhetorical forms. (Hyland, 2003: 50)

Whether such sets of cultural schemata exist is controversial. It is more widely accepted that writing is socially situated: each situation requires special consideration of audience, purposes and level of perfection. L2 writers need to understand expectations and norms of discourse communities or communities of practice of the target communities as well as their own.

Finally, there are implications for the role of people other than the teacher in the feedback process. Using other class members as addressees, and the classroom as a co-operative working environment, automatically means that students are involved in the production of each other's written work. There is then a natural extension to peer editing and revision, as well as the more established procedure of peer 'correction'. Clearly all these aspects will only be effective with guidance and focus, but potentially they can help students to develop a critical stance towards their own work as well. Several other procedures might be developed to involve learners in what is presumably the ultimate aim of self-monitoring and self-correction. These include marking schemes that indicate mistake type, leaving the learner to identify the specific problem; the establishment of personal checklists, which of course change as proficiency grows; and the technique of 'reformulation', in which the teacher suggests another wording for what the student is trying to express. It is important to recall that self-evaluation too will require different criteria at different stages in the writing process: there is little point in too great a concern for accuracy when gathering ideas, formulating a plan and establishing readership, whereas correctness has a vital role as the final draft takes shape. Hedge (2005) prefers to think of 'correction' under the more general heading of 'improving', a cover term that stresses the interacting of marking procedures with processing categories.

9.7   Conclusion

Earlier in this chapter we asked you to consider the titles of some published teaching materials to see if any trends were discernible. Although it is much too simplistic to suggest that the date of publication can be directly linked to a particular approach, it is probably true to say that there is a gradual shift from guiding learners through grammatical patterns against the background of 'composition' requirements, to a concern with paragraph and text structure from a communicative perspective, to titles that reflect ways in which we think about the activity of writing – 'outlining', 'putting pen to paper' and so on – to those that refer explicitly to strategies and to the role of the teacher, and awareness of real-life practices outside the classroom. Materials for the teaching of writing, then, do not neglect the basic skills, but are increasingly likely to see writing in terms of purpose, audience, and the development and organization of thinking, for real world, for learning and for educational purposes.

1   If you are a regular user of email, make a list of the main ways in which email differs stylistically from more conventional writing. If you use (or plan to use) email writing in your own teaching, in what ways might your attitude to 'correctness' change?
2   Consider the unit provided here from as many angles as possible, for example, subject matter; 'authenticity'; level; types of writing task; sequencing of activities; suitability for your own students. If it is not suitable, what would you wish to change?

Writing Portfolio

Getting ideas

In this unit, you are to write an explanation, but with a choice of three very different approaches.

Organising your explanation

A Write an analysis of an advertisement of your choice. Describe the advertisement, explain who you think it is aimed at and how it works on the customer — both the visuals and the text.

B You are a journalist writing an article about advertising. You can describe some of your favourite advertisements and brands and explain how they affect you and your friends. Come to a judgement by the end on whether you think advertising is harmful or beneficial to you and to others. Use the internet as a resource for ideas and examples.

C Write about the thought and discussion processes which led you to design your own group advertisement. Explain why you chose the product and why you decided to advertise it in a particular way. Explain how the visuals and words contribute to the overall effect, who your target audience is and how your advertisement tries to get their attention.

Choose the appropriate template from Unit 1 in workbook 3A to plan your writing. Refer to Unit 1 of this Textbook to refresh your memory of the structure, function and features of the text type you have chose. After you have jotted down some initial thoughts and ideas, use the Pre-writing Checklist provided in 'The Write Track' on page 106 to ensure that you are on the right track.

Revising and editing

Use the appropriate Writing Checklist from 'The Write Track' on pages 107 –112 to revise your first draft and produce an improved final draft.

Writing your final draft

Use the Checklist for Final Draft in 'The Write Track' on pages 113 to revise your final draft and make any last corrections before submission.

Remember to file all your drafts in your Writing portfolio.

Source: C. Davies, F. Tup and D. Aziz, 2003.Writing Portfolio of Unit 4, p. 84, *Life Accents*. Copyright © Times Media Private Limited in Singapore. Reprinted with permission of Marshal Cavendish International (Singapore) Pte Ltd.

9.8   Further Reading

1   Hedge, T. (2005): *Writing*. A rich source of ideas for the teaching and learning of writing skills, using a framework that includes both 'process' and 'product' considerations.
2   Hyland, K. (2009): *Teaching and Researching Writing 2nd edn.* Covers the teaching of writing from the perspective of both theory and practice.

10

Integrated Skills

10.1 Introduction

So far in this section of the book we have been devoting a chapter to each of the four language skills in order to give each one some in-depth treatment. In this final chapter of Part II, we consider some of the different ways in which these language skills may be taught in an integrated way in the classroom. Some of the natural overlap of the language skills has already been examined in Chapters 6–9, particularly with regard to speaking and listening and to reading and writing, although there are situations where either three or all four language skills can be integrated effectively, and in this chapter we intend to examine some of these. We start by examining situations that require an integration of skills in order for them to be completed successfully. After this, we consider some different approaches to the integration of language skills in materials. Finally, we look at skills integration in the classroom by discussing a broad range of different materials from the teaching of General English (GE) to the teaching of English for Academic Purposes (EAP). We also consider project work and role play/simulation in relation to the concept of integrated skills.

Let us begin by trying to clarify the concept of integrated skills by looking at the definition provided by the Longman Dictionary of Applied Linguistics. According to Richards and Schmidt (2010: 288), an integrated approach means 'the teaching of the language skills of reading, writing, listening and

Materials and Methods in ELT: A Teacher's Guide, Third Edition.
Jo McDonough, Christopher Shaw, and Hitomi Masuhara.
© 2013 John Wiley & Sons, Inc. Published 2013 by John Wiley & Sons, Inc.

speaking in conjunction with each other as when a lesson involves activities that relate listening and speaking to reading and writing'. This definition is widely accepted and used, especially in relation to various varieties of communicative language teaching. Note that, nowadays, 'integrated skills' may also be used to include some other kinds of skills as well as the four language skills in different contexts. For example, in the context of Content and Language Integrated Learning (CLIL), integrated skills may include cognitive skills such as doing research and problem solving. By the same token, when discussing Computer-Assisted Language Learning (CALL), we may refer to integration of some skills deriving from Information and Communication Technologies (ICT) within language curricula, such as multi-modal literacy and navigation skills.

If we look around us in our daily lives, we can see that we rarely use language skills in isolation but in conjunction, as the definition of integrated skills suggests. Even though the classroom is clearly not the same as 'real' life, it could be argued that part of its function is to recreate it. If one of the jobs of the teacher is to make the students 'communicatively competent' in the L2, then this will involve more than being able to perform in each of the four skills separately. By giving learners tasks that expose them to these skills in conjunction, it is possible that they will gain a deeper understanding of how communication works in the foreign language as well as becoming more motivated when they see the value of performing meaningful tasks and activities in the classroom. These are points made by Oxford (2001: 5) when she describes the advantages of the integrated skills approach:

> The integrated-skills approach, as contrasted with the purely segregated approach, exposes English language learners to authentic language and challenges them to interact naturally in the language. Learners rapidly gain a true picture of the richness and complexity of the English language as employed for communication. Moreover, this approach stresses that English is not just an object of academic interest nor merely a key to passing an examination; instead, English becomes a real means of interaction and sharing among people. This approach allows teachers to track students' progress in multiple skills at the same time. Integrating the language skills also promotes the learning of real content, not just the dissection of language forms.

1   Reflect on your current teaching approach and evaluate the extent to which the skills are integrated.
2   Select one of your instructional materials or textbooks and evaluate how the four skills are taught.

Integration of the four skills can be achieved through various approaches. In fact, even if a given course is labelled as one skill, it is possible to integrate the other language skills through appropriate activities. Teachers are encouraged to familiarize themselves with different options to enrich their repertoire. For instance, Oxford (2001) in the quote above refers to content-based language teaching (CBLT), task-based language instruction or some hybrid form. Coyle et al. (2010) explain how cross-curricular approaches to subject and language teaching in CLIL – CBLT in the European context – can provide an effective platform for learning integrated skills. We will be showing some examples of task-based materials in Section 10.3. Tomlinson (2003b) introduces a flexible framework for developing materials using what he calls the Text-Driven Approach. The framework is designed to help teachers develop integrated skills materials in a principled way in accordance with current learning theories. The Text-Driven framework helps teachers to develop materials in a short time even from a single engaging text (e.g. a poem, extract from a newspaper, video, teacher's anecdote), which could be used even in a resource-poor environment. If you are interested in CALL, Chapter 5 of this book and also Kervin and Derewianka (2011) provide examples and theoretical explanation for how integrated skills teaching could take place.

10.2   Situations Requiring Skills Integration

Let us now examine some situations that require an integration of at least two language skills in order for the task to be completed successfully.

> As you are reading, note down the different language skills involved at each stage.

From the skills integration point of view the situations may be quite simple – such as speaking on the telephone and taking down a message or taking part in a conversation – or, alternatively, they may be much longer and involve more skills integration, as we can see in the following examples:

1   We may read about a film or a concert in a newspaper or magazine:

We ask a friend if they would like to go.
We search the Internet if we have easy access to it.
We phone the box office to reserve tickets.
We drive to the cinema/concert hall with the friend.

We ask the clerk for the tickets.
We watch the film/concert.
We discuss the film/performance with the friend on the way home.
Some of us may write about our experience in a blog, by Twitter, on Facebook and so on to communicate with a larger number of people.

2   We may need to read lecture notes/articles/a paper in order to write a composition or an essay:

We discuss it with other learners/the teacher.
Some of us may do an additional search by using library facilities or by going on the Internet.
We compose a draft.
Some of us may show the draft to other learners or to the teacher for advice.
We rewrite it until we have a final version.
We read the teacher's feedback.
We speak to other learners/the teacher about the feedback.

The two situations we have illustrated above show how, in our daily lives, we are constantly performing tasks that involve a natural integration of language skills. They also show that none of these stages is completely predictable. For example, in the first situation described above, all the seats may have been sold for that particular performance or our friend may reply that she cannot go to the film or the performance on that evening for whatever reason. However, at each stage, there is a reason for using that particular skill.

Exposure to this type of 'natural' skills integration will hopefully show learners that the skills are rarely used in isolation outside the classroom and that they are not distinct as such, but that there is considerable overlap and similarity between some of the subskills involved (e.g. in previous chapters we saw how the subskills of reading and listening involved purpose and anticipation).

The notion of 'appropriacy' will, we hope, be developed in learners if they can see how the four skills can be used effectively in appropriate contexts. As we said earlier in the chapter, overall competence in the foreign language is going to involve more than performing in the four skills separately: it will also involve them in effective, combined use of the skills, which will depend on the nature of the interaction taking place. We might also argue that as integrated skills materials are more likely to involve learners in authentic and realistic tasks, their motivation level will increase as they perceive a clear rationale behind what they are being asked to do.

Let us consider one more example of the integration of skills in a real-life situation: we may see an advertisement for a product that interests us in a newspaper or in a magazine; then we may wish to talk to a friend about it to see if she thinks it would be a good buy. If after some discussion she thinks not, we might decide to leave it there, or we might decide to search the Internet to compare prices. We might phone the company offering the product to get further details. Next, we might write an email or a letter (enclosing a cheque) that will be read by somebody at the company who will despatch the product, possibly with a covering letter enclosed.

We can break this down into the different language skills that it would generate: reading, speaking/listening, writing, reading and writing. Again, one important point to note is that none of the events in this particular scenario is entirely predictable, but will depend very much on individual circumstances as to how and when the outcome will be reached.

Another variation on this theme is provided by Harmer (2007b) who introduces a seven-stage activity for integrating skills, which involves the following sequence:

1 Learners read an advertisement for a public relations job with a major airline.
2 Learners write an application.
3 The teacher divides the class into small groups and distributes letters from the other learners.
4 Each member of the group reads each letter and scores each one from 0 to 5 depending on the quality of the letter.
5 The scores are added up and the winner chosen.
6 The group writes a letter to the winner and another letter to the unsuccessful applicants.
7 The letters are read out to the class and feedback and comments are obtained.

The overall aim and rationale of the activity is to provide solid integration of skills plus the notion that learners are writing for a purpose.

> If you teach integrated skills in your own situation, pause for a moment and think about how you do it. In what ways are your integrated skills activities similar to/different from the ones outlined above?

In their survey review of eight recently published global adult EFL (English as a Foreign Language) courses submitted by eight different publishers, Masuhara et al. (2008) point out that they noticed a general tendency towards 'the scarcity of real tasks which have an intended outcome other than just the practice of language forms'. Rather than the four skills being introduced and established naturally, or as naturally as is possible within a classroom context, integration as found in these coursebooks typically involves linking the language skills in such a way that what has been learned and practised is reinforced/extended through further language activities. In some cases, this would involve a focus on listening and speaking first, followed by reading and writing, as this would provide a convenient class-plus-homework pattern. However, this kind of integration would not expose learners to contexts where the four skills are established naturally and could deny them the opportunity to use the four skills with a measure of communicative effectiveness. Let us look at how this might occur in an example from a typical EFL textbook where a writing activity is rather artificially 'grafted on' to the rest of the unit as an extension activity rather than being designed to fit in with the rest of the unit as a whole as illustrated below (Abbs and Freebairn, 1977):

MAN: What do you do Miss Jones?
SALLY: I'm a secretary.
MAN: Oh, a secretary.
SALLY: That's correct.
MAN: Where?
SALLY: At Midtown Council.
MAN: I see.
SALLY: I'm looking for a small one-bedroom flat near my office.
MAN: Now let's see. Ah yes, here's one. It's in Billington Road, and it's a one-bedroom flat.
SALLY: Billington Road? Where is Billington Road exactly?
MAN: Here, look at the map. Billington Road is just here, next to the Town Hall.
SALLY: Oh, that's wonderful.
MAN: Yes. Well here's the address and the telephone number. 23, Billington Road, London, NW7. 234-8181
SALLY: Thank you very much. Goodbye.
MAN: Goodbye.
MAN: (phones) Hello, hello! 234-8181, Mrs Johns? A young woman called Sally Jones is coming to view the flat this afternoon. She's a secretary at Midtown Council. Thank you Mrs Johns. Goodbye.

And the extension:

Sally's mother, Mrs Jones, is in London. She wants to see Sally for lunch. Sally invites her for lunch. Sally writes her a message:

Mum,
Please meet me outside the Shakespeare pub at 1pm. You can't miss it. It's next to the Odeon cinema.

Love, Sally.

This example also adds evidence to another tendency observed by Masuhara et al. (2008: 310) in their survey of adult global courses when they comment on 'the neglect of the value of extensive writing as a means of self-expression, creativity, and life skills. Writing could give purpose to reading and language discovery. Feedback and revision provides individual development opportunities'.

Let us now look at another example of integrated skills material on p. 208. This unit of material is based on a Text-Driven Approach to CLIL lessons at secondary high school level in Malaysia.

1 Analyse which skills each activity is likely to require in the material.
2 Consider if this unit achieves authentic skills integration by evaluating the materials according to the following criteria. To what extent does this material
   i.   provide opportunities to expose learners to language in real life use?
   ii.   provide opportunities to use language in a meaningful way for the learners?
   iii. make use of the four skills as we are likely to do in real communication to achieve communication outcomes?
   iv.   help the learners to use English effectively outside the classroom?

Water Conservation

1 • Think of an idea to conserve water.
  • Tell a partner of your idea.
  • Form a group of four and share your ideas for conserving water.

2 • Read the passage on *Water conservation* from Wikipedia. As you read it
    decide which you think is the best idea for conserving water at home, for
    commercial conservation of water and for agricultural conservation of water.
    Don't worry about any ideas which you don't completely understand.

3 • In your group share your decisions about the best ideas.
  • In your group help each other to understand any ideas which were not
    completely clear. You can also ask your teacher to help you.

4 • Use the Web references in the Wikipedia passage to help you to read more
    about water conservation.
  • Tell the other members of your group anything interesting which you've found
    out from your reading.

5 • In your group write a one-page leaflet advising people in Malaysia how to
    conserve water. Make the advice clear, useful and memorable.
  • Put your group name on your leaflet and then stick your leaflet on the wall.
  • Walk around and look at the other groups' leaflets. Use the evaluation sheet from
    your teacher to evaluate each leaflet.

6 • In your group invent a device for conserving water.

7 • Write a letter to an international company in Malaysia telling them about your
    invention and asking them for an opportunity to demonstrate your invention.

8 • Prepare a 10-minute presentation on your invention to give to the company
    you wrote to. Aim to make it clear and persuasive.
  • Practise answering questions on your presentation.
  • Give your presentation.

Source: 'Water Conservation' activity written by Brian Tomlinson. Unpublished.
© Brian Tomlinson. Reprinted with kind permission of the author.

10.3   Integrated Skills in the Classroom

Ellis (2010: 52) explores applications of second language acquisition (SLA)
research to language teaching materials through specific examples of task-
based materials. He summarizes the implications as follows:

> I began this chapter by noting the reservations SLA researchers have voiced
> about the applicability of their theories and research to language pedagogy. I
> noted also that, despite the reservations, applications are needed and desirable.

The question is what form the applications should take. The approach that I favor is of viewing SLA as a source of ideas for fine-tuning materials options that have originated from elsewhere (tasks being a good example) and, also as a source of new ideas for teaching grammar (e.g., interpretation activities and consciousness-raising tasks).

Ellis (2010: 52) adds that 'The proposals that emanate from SLA are research- and theory-based, . . .' but that 'it does not obviate the need for teachers to test them out in their own classrooms and reach a decision about their suitability and effectiveness'.

Tomlinson (2011b: 7) argues for a compilation of learning principles and procedures which most teachers agree contribute to successful learning. After warning that 'Such a list should aim to be informative rather than prescriptive and should not give the impression that its recommendations are supported by conclusive evidence and by all teachers and researchers' (Tomlinson 2011b: 7), he summarizes his own six basic principles as a guide for materials development:

1   A prerequisite for language acquisition is that the learners are exposed to a rich, meaningful and comprehensible input of language in use.
2   In order for the learners to maximise their exposure to language in use, they need to be engaged both affectively and cognitively in the language experience.
3   Language learners who achieve positive affect are much more likely to achieve communicative competence than those who do not.
4   L2 language learners can benefit from using those mental resources which they typically utilise when acquiring and using their L1.
5   Language learners can benefit from noticing salient features of the input and from discovering how they are used.
6   Learners need opportunities to use language to try to achieve communicative purposes.

As teachers we have a variety of ways of integrating the language skills in the classroom, and in this section of the chapter, we shall be examining some of the possibilities for different types of EFL classroom. We shall begin by looking at examples of general EFL materials; then we shall look at an example of skill integration from some EAP materials. Then we shall proceed to look at some task-based materials, oral presentations, project work, and role play and simulation.

General materials

Masuhara and Tomlinson (2008) report the results of their survey among teachers and learners who use GE coursebooks in the United Kingdom and some overseas countries. They also show the results of their criterion-referenced evaluation of seven randomly selected GE coursebooks published between 2001 and 2006. Their 14 criteria are based on a selection of learning principles as discussed above. They find that in general, GE coursebooks provide a variety of authentic contemporary topics, texts and genres for exposure to language in use (e.g. stories, news, magazine and book extracts, emails, blogs, SMS messages). They note, however, a lack of extensive texts even at upper-intermediate level, which results in the learners and teachers in the survey commenting that there are 'too many activities to go through' due to a snappy succession of unconnected short texts and activities. One of the major problems that EFL teachers face at all levels is a gap between their learners' intelligence and language level. The most common solution offered by GE coursebooks, according to Masuhara and Tomlinson (2008), seems to be to resort to simple and short texts.

The example of the text-driven integrated unit we have just looked at in Section 10.2, however, tackles this problem of imbalance between cognitive and linguistic levels among learners in a different way. It starts with what Tomlinson (2003b) calls readiness activities in Activity 1 in which the learners come up with their own ideas to conserve water firstly as individuals and then as groups. These readiness activities are thinking and speaking activities that are meant to prepare the learners for the next reading stage in Activity 2 in a non-threatening, personal and thought-provoking way. The sequence of Activities 1–4 involves reading, discussing and re-reading for different purposes, and it takes a problem-solving approach. The best way to conserve water is the 'problem' and the learners are to find the solution through collaboration. The problem of water conservation is a real-life issue, and the solution will come from the learners with the support of reading materials on Wikipedia. The gradual sequencing of Activities 1–4 and the collaboration are intended to help the learners to manage the amount of input and speed of processing to a little bit beyond their own level (cf. i+1 in Krashen, 1982; Krashen and Terrell, 1983).

Using a variety of affectively and cognitively engaging input is one factor to consider, but how the texts are exploited may be even more vital to language acquisition and development. The evaluation of seven GE coursebooks by Masuhara and Tomlinson (2008) further reveals that the input in most cases seems to be presented as opportunities to experience teaching points using the PPP approach (present, practise and produce) together with stock examination-type exercises (e.g. true/false, multiple choice, matching, gap filling, sentence completion). They suspect that 'the authors may be focusing on providing predetermined input rather than facilitating intake, language acquisition and development' (Masuhara and Tomlinson, 2008: 31). Note that a similar tendency was confirmed in Masuhara et al. (2008) with four evaluators from different countries with a larger set of criteria (i.e. 104) in evaluating eight global coursebooks, which did not include the seven in Masuhara and Tomlinson (2008).

In the example of integrated skills material on water conservation in Section 10.2 above, Activity 5 uses a task-based approach in the sense that the learners are asked to write a one-page leaflet in groups advising people in Malaysia how to conserve water. Activity 6 is another related but further development activity of designing a device for water conservation in groups. This task involves a group drawing of the device and should generate focused, spontaneous and purposeful speaking and listening as is likely to happen in real-life communication. What follows next is another writing task in Activity 7: writing a letter to an international company in Malaysia, describing the invented water conservation device and requesting an opportunity to demonstrate their inventions. Finally Activity 8 is an oral presentation of the device in a simulated situation in the company using a role-play format with the inventors making a presentation to company executives. In all the output activities, there is a clearly defined audience and target, and there are outcomes for the communication activities which reflect authentic situations in real life. The skills are integrated, and this material tries to offer opportunities for the personalization and for the approximation important for language acquisition.

You are encouraged to evaluate available GE materials to see how integrated skills are taught and to decide for yourselves how the materials may help your learners in using English effectively in an appropriate manner. The latest GE books at Intermediate level (CEF B1+) include:

English Unlimited (Rea et al., 2011)
Just Right 2nd edition (Harmer, 2012)
Outcomes (Dellar and Walkley, 2010)
Speakout (Clare and Wilson, 2011)

EAP materials

Materials practising integrated skills can be very useful in a number of academic and educational contexts, particularly for EAP students who will be going on to study their specialist subject through the medium of English.

Mol and Tan (2010) evaluated three widely used EAP materials in university foundation courses in New Zealand and Australia. They firstly summarized the required EAP skills recognized in many institutions. They were:

Listening/Reading

- Understanding academic texts
- Taking notes
- Identifying relevant information

- Interpreting information
- Recognizing point of view and bias.

Speaking

- Negotiating
- Paraphrasing and using evidence
- Participating in formal and informal discussion
- Arguing a point
- Expressing ideas.

Writing

- Structuring academic essays and presentations
- Using academic style (writing and speaking)
- Arguing a point
- Expressing ideas.

Other

- Thinking clearly and critically
- Extending learners' awareness of cross-cultural differences and of how to use language appropriately to negotiate these differences
- Developing strategies appropriate for independent and collaborative learning in a university. (Mol and Tan, 2010: 75–6)

They also add that 'some EAP courses stress the importance of specific tools for university study: writing bibliographies and referencing, computing skills for study purposes, library research skills and using study resources' (Mol and Tan, 2010: 76).

> 1 List the kinds of activities you would like to see in EAP materials.
> 2 Read the suggestions by Mol and Tan (2010) below in relation to what EAP materials should provide. Compare their list with what you have written in 1 above.

Mol and Tan (2010: 90), having evaluated the three most popular EAP materials, list the kinds of activities necessary in Australia and New Zealand. Their list includes the following:

- Developing students' awareness of different academic cultures and practices.
- Giving them plenty of opportunities for making discoveries about academic English and academic practices.

- Giving students an opportunity to make discoveries about the host country's academic culture and about their subject-specific academic practices.
- Giving students an opportunity to link the academic English and practices they learn in the EAP coursebooks or courses with the real academic context outside the class. For example, projects can be designed, encouraging students to make discoveries about the academic practice and English used in the subject discipline they will be studying.

Here are a few examples of current EAP materials for you to consider issues we have discussed:

Access EAP: Foundations Course Book (Argent and Alexander, 2010)
Communicative Activities for EAP (Guse, 2010)
EAP Now! (Cox and Hill, 2011)

Task-based materials

As was discussed in Chapter 2, tasks provide an excellent platform for meaning-focused language learning opportunities involving integrated skills activities with a possible language awareness embedded in the sequence. After looking at various definitions of task, Van den Branden (2006: 4) defines a task as 'an activity in which a person engages in order to attain an objective, and which necessitates the use of language'. In the example of Water Conservation in Section 10.2, the students were given a task of writing a one-page leaflet advising people in Malaysia how to conserve water. They were given another task of designing a water conservation device followed by further related tasks of writing to an international company about their device and of preparing a 10-minute presentation. The students have to read, listen, speak and write with clear task objectives, target audience and outcomes in mind. Van den Branden (2006: 1) is a unique addition to the accumulating literature on Task-Based Language Teaching in that all the chapters are based on empirical studies 'where tasks have been used as the basic units for the organization of educational activities in intact language classrooms'. It also contains reports from infant, primary, secondary, science and vocational training, and ICT areas. The book looks at needs analysis, syllabus design, assessment and teacher training. A few examples of kinds of materials are introduced in the following pages.

62   *Goedele Duran and Griet Ramaut*

Show an example of the pen case to the pupils and make clear that they can use it to put in their pens and pencils. When they have made their own pen case, they can put it on their desk.

Give each pupil a page with the visual instructions (see below) and carry out the instructions one by one together with the pupils. Meanwhile provide language input by describing what you are doing:

Draw the plan of the pen case on a sheet of paper.

Cut off the grey parts.

Cut the parts indicated by a dotted line.

Fold the sides upwards, fold the cut pieces and the back and front inwards as indicated on the instructions.

Cut out a double bottom and put it in the box.

Let the pupils further decorate their own box.

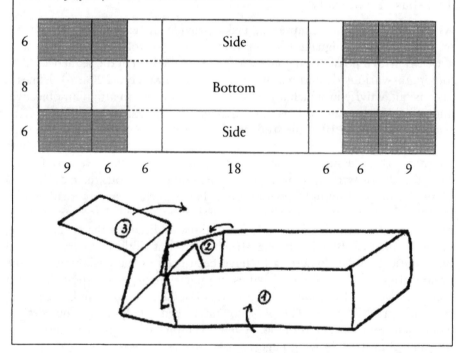

Example 2   Make your own pen case (task taken from the teacher manual of a task-based syllabus for newcomers in Flemish education: *Klaar? Af!* Centre for Language and Education, Leuven)

Source: G. Duran and G. Ramaut, Scanned image of p. 52 from 'Tasks for absolute beginners and beyond: developing and sequencing tasks at basic proficiency levels'. In K. van den Branden (ed), *Task-Based Language Education, From Theory to Practice*. Cambridge University Press 2006. Reprinted with permission.

88   *Koen Van Gorp and Nora Bogaert*

Can you see through your hand?

        Maybe this experiment will help you ...

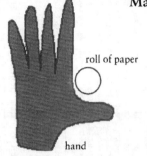

roll of paper

hand

Take a thin magazine and roll it up into a cylinder with a diameter of about 2.5 centimetres. Raise your left hand about 10 centimetres from your face. At the same time, hold the roll of paper in your right hand, and put it between your index finger and the thumb of your left hand, as shown in the picture.

Next, briefly look through the roll with your right eye and look at your left hand with your left eye. Close both your eyes and then open them again. What do you see when you look at your left hand?

Figure 2   A hole in your hand. A task taken from a task-based syllabus for Dutch language education at the level of secondary education. (From: *KLIMOP+TATAMI*, Centre for Language and Education, Leuven)

Source: G. Duran and G. Ramaut, Scanned image of p. 62 from 'Tasks for absolute beginners and beyond: developing and sequencing tasks at basic proficiency levels'. In K. van den Branden (ed), *Task-Based Language Education, From Theory to Practice*. Reprinted with permission of Cambridge University Press.

92   Koen Van Gorp and Nora Bogaert

A Gruesome Performance

The teacher introduces and reads the following story:

Just before sunset, a fakir calls the passers-by to come and watch his performance. Seated in a circle with torches, the audience watches the fakir take a length of rope from a wicker basket and throw it into the air. He repeats this action a couple of times to demonstrate that it is an ordinary rope. But then, as he throws the rope into the air again, it suddenly coils up in the darkness, until the top is no longer visible and then miraculously stays there. The fakir's assistant, a slim young boy climbs the rope and is seen to vanish into thin air. He ignores his master's calls to come back down. Impatiently, the fakir draws a sharp knife, clenches it between his teeth, and clambers up after the boy – and also vanishes from sight. Then there is a series of blood-curdling yells, and various dismembered limbs of the young boy fall to the ground, followed by his head. The fakir then slides down the rope, which falls down behind him. He joins his other assistants, who are standing in tears around the remains of the young boy. They put the parts of the body into a basket. When the fakir claps his hands, the young boy emerges from the basket, smiling, miraculously reassembled and with no apparent damage.

Task: How does this work? How do you think this 'miracle' can be explained?

Here are a number of possible explanations. Which one do you think is the correct one?

- *The fakir has magic powers: he defies the laws of gravity and has the power to resuscitate the dead.*
- *The fakir is in fact an extraordinary hypnotist: through mass hypnosis he makes the audience believe that certain things happen which in reality do not happen at all.*
- *The fakir uses a trick.*

After ticking the answer of your choice, ask your neighbour whether s/he has chosen the same answer or another one.

Who is right and who is wrong? Find out by reading the text opposite.

Tasks for primary and secondary education   93

Text

The trick – for a trick it is – is performed at twilight, before a background of nearby hills or trees. The fakir relies on a thin but strong black cord slung between two high points about fifteen meters above ground level. The rope, which has a small but heavy black ball at the end and which is strong enough to support the weight of the slim boy, is thrown up over the cord. The boy climbs up the rope. The public is blinded by the light of the torches and cannot see boy high up on the rope in the dark sky. Once the boy reaches the top, he attaches the rope to the horizontal black cord, which can then take the weight of the magician.

And the boy's dismembered body parts? When the fakir climbs up, hidden under his wide robe there are shaven monkey limbs, dressed in clothes similar to the boy's, and with a bit of red sauce splattered around. The boy's head is a wooden model fitted with a turban. When the fakir reaches the top, the boy climbs into his robe and throws down the limbs. When the fakir descends and goes to the basket, the boy disappears into it. The limbs then go into the basket, the lid is put on, the fakir claps his hands, and – presto! – the boy pops out.

Figure 3 A gruesome performance. A task taken from a task-based syllabus for Dutch language teaching at the level of secondary school. (Form: *KLIMOP+TATAMI*, Centre for Language and Education, Leuven)

Source: Figure and activity 'A gruesome performance taken from a task-based syllabus for Dutch Language education at the level of secondary education', from *KLIMOP+TATAMI*, Centre for Language and Education, Leuven. Reprinted with permission.

Willis and Willis (2007) is written as an introductory book with teachers new to Task-based Teaching in mind. There is useful discussion of procedures and of examples of tasks submitted by teachers.

Oral presentations

Preparing learners to give short oral presentations in class to the rest of the group is another useful way of achieving skills integration in the classroom. One way to begin this activity is to take cuttings from newspapers, magazines and topics included in existing teaching materials. In some cases, reading material can be used as an initial stimulus, and the activity can be graded to give lower proficiency learners an opportunity to work with less exacting materials. The learners can then take notes and try to pinpoint aspects of what they have read that will be worth discussing. They are then given time to prepare a short talk in front of the class and are encouraged to use maps, diagrams, charts and visual equipment if these can help to make the talk clearer to the group. During the presentation, the other learners are required to take notes so that they can ask questions and/or raise pertinent points during a plenary discussion after the talk has finished.

As teachers, we can sometimes experiment with student assessment at this stage by asking the students to assess each other's work (peer assessment). It is possible to devise a fairly rudimentary evaluation sheet where small groups of students are asked to answer questions that might cover the following: what they thought of the presentation; was it well organized and were they able to follow the main points; could they summarize the talk for someone who was not present; did the speaker make effective use of visual support material; what advice would they give to the speaker for future presentations. This activity can thus interrelate the reading, writing, speaking and listening skills in a motivating way. For further reading, see Bradbury (2010).

Project work

Projects with integrated 'themes' that entail integrated skills can provide a pertinent way of giving learners an effective forum in which to develop these skills. Let us consider an example that takes the overall theme of 'Civilization' as its starting point and examines how it may be seen from opposing points of view. Viewpoint A is concerned with becoming better acquainted with it; viewpoint B is concerned with escaping from it, as shown in figure 10.1.

One suggestion for reading materials for viewpoint A would be magazine articles or books and booklets on the 'Grand Tour', a popular phenomenon in the eighteenth century, when certain young men visited classical areas and cities in Europe. For viewpoint B, materials from magazines and newspapers on 'getting away from it all' and 'living on a desert island' could be provided. The reading component could be designed so that a 'jigsaw' pattern is established (see Chapter 6), which would enable learners to piece together information from both parts to get a complete picture of the theme.

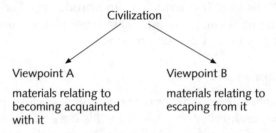

Figure 10.1   Different interpretations of civilization for materials selection.

Possible listening activities might include interviews with a man on his reactions to the Grand Tour and a woman/group on living a communal experience on a desert island. Speaking could involve discussion prompts such as 'what problems do you think people would have on a Grand Tour/desert island?' (e.g. reference might be made to health, money and safety); and 'is living on a desert island escaping responsibility?' The level of difficulty and amount of guidance offered could be varied according to the level of the learners.

For a more advanced group, Gairns and Redman (1998) suggest producing a magazine of short stories as a class project with learners having to decide in pairs or small groups the topics to be included. They also comment that learners might wish to divide tasks into some to be carried out in class and others to be accomplished at home. The final outcome of the project might be a wall display or in booklet form or indeed a combination of both.

> Think of some ways of integrating writing skills into the project work outlined above.

The scheme outlined above is relatively teacher-led. In some cases it may be possible to allow learners to work on projects by collecting data themselves and, where they have access to native speakers, to devise questionnaires and interviews they can then feed back into the group. Skills integration should develop naturally from the tasks that the learners are asked to complete.

Materials to Products (2011) is part of the Oxford Read and Discover series and is a non-fiction graded reader aimed at age eight and older. It provides educational texts and an Audio CD with activities and project work. The topic areas include: the World of Science and Technology, the Natural World, the World of Arts and Social Studies. Teachers involved in CLIL may find the series useful.

Some teachers may not be too familiar with procedures associated with Project work. *Searching* (2010), a successful secondary school coursebook in Norway, provides a useful example of instructions to the students in conducting projects with suggestions for possible topics and outcomes.

Focus on Writing
Project Work

At school – and later at work – you will often be asked to do projects. Very often that means that you work in groups, but you can also do a project on your own. Here we will be dealing with group work at school.

Planning the project

- Plan your project carefully. Freedom to do your own project is not the same as freedom to do nothing.
- Very often you have a general topic, for example "The 1960s". The first thing you have to do, is to decide what you want to do a project on (for example music, fashion, hippies, the Vietnam War, etc.).
- All proposals from the group members are important and should be discussed.
- Time is important. How many lessons or weeks have you got?
- Where are you going to work? Do you have to stay at school or can you work at home, take a trip to a library, etc.?
- What are you going to do at school, and what are you going to do at home?
- How are you going to present your project? See below.
- What material or resources do you need, and where do you find them?
- How will you keep track of your progress? Writing a diary?
- If it has not been said, ask your teacher about how the project will be evaluated.

Doing a project

- You must agree in the group about who will be responsible for what.
- Make a timetable for how you are going to work. How many lessons should be used to get materials, for individual tasks, etc.? When are you going to get together the next time? Etc.
- Remember that your teacher has a supporting function. Ask him or her for help if necessary.

Presenting a project

You will normally have many possibilities when it comes to presentation. Which is the best way to present the outcome of your work? Here are some ideas:

Some ideas for presenting your work:

- posters for the classroom
- a Power Point presentation
- a dramatic performance
- a fashion show
- a mini musical
- a talk
- an interview
- a song contest
- a (music) magazine

Here are some topics for project work from this chapter:

- Famous People in the Sixties
- Space Exploration
- The Vietnam War
- Fashion in the Sixties and/or Today
- Pop Music in the Sixties and/or Today
- The Hippies

Some other writing tasks

L7

Write a text about fashion. Choose one of the following tasks or decide for yourself what you want to write about.

A Do you follow fashion? Why/why not? Describe someone who is a "slave of fashion".

B Have you ever been to a fashion show? Describe it.

L8

Write a text about music. Choose one of the following tasks or decide for yourself what you want to write about.

A Write about what music you enjoy listening to and what music you really dislike. Give examples.

B Write about how important music is in your life and how much time you spend listening to music.

Questions to ask yourself:

1 What new things have I learnt about the Sixties?
2 What do I know about space exploration?
3 What is a musical?
4 Which version of the text *Growing Up in the 1960s* did I read? Why?
5 Do I know how to use relative pronouns?
6 What have I learnt about project work?

Source: A.-B. Fenner and G. Nordal-Pedersen. 'Focus on Writing: Project work', from pp. 148–9, *Searching 9, Learner's Book.* Copyright © Gyldendal Norsk Forlag AS 2008. Printed by permission.

Role play/simulation

Role play and simulation activities are often thought to be one of the most effective ways of integrating language skills in the language classroom. Though the terms 'role play' and 'simulation' have been interpreted in many different ways by both teachers and textbook writers, both activities offer a flexible yet principled way of tailoring integrated skills to learner needs.

It is generally the case that role-play activities involve the learner in 'role assumption'; in other words, the learner takes on a different role (and perhaps identity) from his or her normal one by 'playing the part' of a different person. Role play is used more frequently in the general EFL classroom, that is, in the teaching of English for General Purposes (EGP), where the ultimate goals for learning the language are not necessarily specified in advance, if at all. It may be desirable, however, to give learners more practice in language 'use', even though it may be argued that the communication which ensues is not entirely natural, as the learners may not really empathize with the character whose role they have been asked to assume.

Simulation work, on the other hand, usually requires the learners to take part in communication that involves personal experience and emotions. Because of this, simulation is often seen as being central to English for Specific Purposes (ESP) situations where the task/s to be worked upon can be related directly to the learner's actual or intended occupation. As a consequence, the learners will not only learn more about the communicative use of language in the L2, but will learn more about the setting/scenario relevant to their occupational field. For example, as well as building up competence in the use of the foreign language, a business person taking part in a meeting may well learn more about negotiation strategies in an international context.

Both types of activity clearly have their place in the classroom – be it for general purposes or for learners with more specific goals in learning the language – as they offer a flexible approach to integrating the skills, and involve learners at all stages by stimulating their creativity and responding to their needs and interests.

What are the advantages to learners and to the teacher of using role play/simulation activities in the classroom? Are there any potential problems to using them?

According to Jacobs (1988–1999) these types of group activity encourage positive student attitudes towards the target language, their peers, and the teacher, since 'the mutual dependence that co-operative structured activities require would lead to more communication among students because they need to exchange information and advice in order to succeed in achieving their goals'. They can also release the teacher from the centre stage position for a lot of the time, thereby allowing the possibility of more individual help if necessary. If we manage the activity effectively, we can possibly overcome problems of introversion and lack of fluency in learners by designing tasks that all learners can participate in. A model for structuring simulation (and role-play) activities in the classroom is offered by Herbert and Sturtridge (1979). They explain how tasks can be graded, the role of the teacher during the activity and the type of material to be used. They suggest a three-phase sequence for staging a role play/simulation in the classroom. In the first phase, learners are given the informational input. In the second phase, the learners work on the activity by discussing the task or the problem set. The simulation may involve role play, debate or discussion. In the third phase, the teacher gives learners feedback on the activity just performed, possibly discussing effective strategies and language use and suggesting follow-up work if appropriate.

In the first phase, for example, the informational input can either be in the form of a memorandum to read or perhaps it could be listening based. The linguistic input can be graded so that preliminary work can be done on the material in class before the role-play/simulation activity proper or, if the teacher thinks that the learners have had enough training, they can be presented with a 'deep-end strategy' in which they are given informational input but then move straight into the second phase, the language work being dealt with as an 'outcome' in the third and final phase.

As an illustration of this, let us consider a role play/simulation in which learners have to discuss some cost-cutting measures in their firm, company or school – a fairly typical situation. A task for the first phase of the simulation may involve the reading of a memorandum regarding an imminent meeting for the heads or representatives of different divisions/departments/ sections in the company or school. The participants can be divided into small groups for each division or section (or run separate simulations), and are given a memorandum to read and think about, plus some notes that summarize the present situation in their own division.

However, all participants could be given different information about their respective divisions and a 'jigsaw' is thus established, which will be pieced together when this information becomes disclosed during the second (main) phase. For example, what might be an effective measure to implement in one section of the school or company could prove disastrous for another section. Ensuing interaction is therefore going to focus heavily on negotiating suitable outcomes for as many parties involved in the discussions as possible.

The information that the other learners have will be similar with respect to some of the measures above, and very different in other cases. Hence, much of the meeting will focus on the negotiation and management of potential conflict. In the first phase it may be an idea to 'tease out' some of the language that the participants will need in the second phase. In this second phase the simulation itself takes place, and the main focus is one of fluency. The teacher may wish also to take notes, operate audio/video equipment or intervene in the simulation if so required. At the conclusion of the meeting, one of the managers can be asked to write a report to head office summarizing the decisions that were agreed upon in the meeting. This type of simulation is thus a highly effective way of integrating reading, listening, speaking and writing skills.

The third phase, that of 'feedback', has to be handled carefully so as not to become a negative account of what went wrong. For error analysis, it might be possible to give a report on general types of mistakes made in the group, or where and how communication broke down, as well as giving individualized feedback to learners. The simulation should also provide many ideas to the teacher for future language work. Other types of role-play/simulation work might include setting up a committee to consider the applications of several candidates for a grant or scholarship, which only one of the candidates can obtain. In another type of activity, students could enact roles in an imaginary courtroom by trying to solve a particular crime. Other useful references and materials include

Role Play (Porter-Ladousse, 1987)
Language-Learning Simulations: A Practical Guide (Hyland, 1993)

> If your textbook does not provide any material for role-play/simulation work, would you be able to incorporate some of the above suggestions into your lessons?

10.4   Conclusion

This chapter has attempted to unify some of the issues raised in previous chapters by considering different permutations of integrating language skills in the classroom. First of all, we attempted to define integrated skills and the advantages to the learner of working with integrated skills materials. We saw that some activities and materials only develop the skills in an 'additive' way and are somewhat removed from the ways in which we might use the skills in the 'real world'.

Finally, we considered some class activities which offer different permutations of the skills: GE; EAP; task-based; oral presentations and role-play/simulation activities. This chapter concludes the second part of the book. In Part III we shall examine different ways of organizing the resources and management of the classroom.

In Chapters 6–9 we looked at each language skill in turn. Review these chapters and see what implications there are for the integration of skills across the chapters.

10.5   Further Reading

Nowadays, integrated skills are discussed in terms of different teaching contexts: CLIL, task-based, EAP, projects and so on. We have given recommended further reading in each section above.

1   Oxford, R. (2001): *ERIC Digest*. It compares single skill teaching and explains the strengths of integrated skills teaching.

Part III

Aspects of Classroom Methods

11

Groupwork and Pairwork

11.1 Introduction: Content and Structure

Various kinds of 'communicative' approaches have influenced the design of materials for English language teaching (ELT) over the last three decades or so. As a result, it is clear that a broader view of the nature of language and language learning has permeated language teaching. From the perspective of methods used in the classroom, asking students to work in groups or pairs has come to be taken for granted as a natural, integral part of communicative methodology and language learning materials. Most teachers are now familiar with these kinds of instructions in their coursebooks:

'Practise the dialogue with a partner'
'Ask your classmates . . . '
'Work in a group of four . . . '
'Give your story to someone else in the class to read'
'Do the quiz in pairs'
'What could happen next? Discuss in groups'
'Discuss your answers with other students'
'Choose a question, and ask as many other students as you can'

We shall see later that, although the relationship between materials and methods is in a sense an obvious one, it is not quite as clear-cut as it might seem, as some of the examples just quoted here imply. We can consider not only the frequency with which a particular activity is used in the classroom, but also to what extent that activity grows out of the materials themselves.

Materials and Methods in ELT: A Teacher's Guide, Third Edition.
Jo McDonough, Christopher Shaw, and Hitomi Masuhara.
© 2013 John Wiley & Sons, Inc. Published 2013 by John Wiley & Sons, Inc.

Check through the coursebook you most frequently use. How often are learners expected to work in pairs or in small groups? What kind of language material is being practised during pairwork and groupwork activities? For example, is it a written dialogue, grammar, free speaking on a given topic?

Richards and Schmidt (2010: 81) define classroom management as:

(in language teaching) the ways in which student behaviour, movement and interaction during a lesson are organized and controlled by the teacher (or sometimes by the learners by themselves) to enable teaching to take place most effectively. Classroom management includes procedures for grouping students for different types of classroom activities, use of lesson plans, handling of equipment, aids, etc., and the direction and management of student behaviour and activity.

It will be useful at this point to make a general distinction in language teaching between content and structure. By 'content' we mean the materials themselves in relation to the selected target for learning: for example, segments of language such as vocabulary and lexical chunks; grammar; discourse; subject matter; genre. 'Structure', on the other hand, is concerned with how classes are managed, and thus with decisions about various classroom options as to who works with whom and in what possible groupings. 'Structure' is procedural, and can be thought of as being content-independent.

This chapter looks at a variety of organizational possibilities for the classroom and also, very selectively, at aspects of classroom methods. Here we discuss, first, the functions of groupwork and pairwork. We then go on to consider the implications of various classroom structures for patterns of interaction between teachers and learners, and of learners with each other. The final section will examine possible advantages and disadvantages in different styles of classroom management. The first part of the chapter is mainly descriptive; the second part, evaluative.

11.2   The Classroom Setting: Functions of Groupwork and Pairwork

The social organization of the classroom

Managing classes so that learners 'work in pairs' or 'divide into groups' is now so much part of the everyday professional practice of large numbers of

English language teachers that the instructions leading to these activities sometimes seem to be 'switched on' automatically, occasionally with a frequency difficult to justify. It happens with all kinds of content – dialogue practice, sharing opinions, reading aloud, comparing answers to questions, doing grammar exercises, formulating questions in an information-gap task – the list could be extended considerably.

While all these can undoubtedly be done in a number of different ways, at least two kinds of objections can be made. The first is the possibility that imposed classroom structures may not always be congenial to the learning styles of individuals in the class: we shall come back to this point in the chapter on individualization that follows this one, and again when considering how teachers, by observing what goes on in their classrooms, can become more sensitive to their students' preferred ways of working. The second objection is that a mechanical organization may pay insufficient attention to the relationship between an activity and its purpose. For example, it may be unhelpful to practise reading aloud in groups or pairs if students are unable to check each other's accuracy. If, however, the aim is to encourage learners to discuss a topic more freely in a personalized way, then a paired format may be the most useful one. The choice of group or pairwork and how we conduct the grouping should be based on sound principles, and the use of grouping should lead to developing real communicative competence.

A more coherent picture of management structure is provided by the notion of the classroom as an aspect of 'social organization' (Dörnyei and Murphey, 2003, provide extensive discussion of group dynamics). Seen from this perspective, any procedural decision by a teacher – asking students to work in pairs, or to divide themselves into groups, or nominating group membership directly – leads to a specific set of interaction patterns and to control of those interactions.

The classroom does not operate in a vacuum, and this patterning is closely related to the role relationships of teachers and learners, and of learners with each other; and thus by extension to the nature of the school and to the whole educational, even socio-cultural, context. We shall need to bear this wider setting in mind when discussing the pros and cons of pair and groupwork. We have already noted similar considerations in relation to some of the cultural implications of communicative language teaching (CLT) more generally, and its appropriacy (or not) both in principle and practice. Dogancay-Aktuna (2005) provides a summary of studies from various parts of the world that investigate whether imported methodologies with inherent assumptions fit with the expectations, attitudes, values, and beliefs of the users in different cultures. Cortazzi and Jin (1996) discuss Chinese 'Cultures of Learning'. Hu (2002) argues that CLT has not achieved the expected impact on ELT in China because of the conflict between the assumptions underlying CLT (e.g. cooperative learning, teacher roles) with the Chinese traditional style of learning (e.g. the importance placed on grammatical analysis, the expected teacher authority as the expert, the reluctance among students to participate in interactive activities such as groupwork and debates, the importance placed on memorization of knowledge). Dogancay-Aktuna (2005) argues for the need to include socio-cultural awareness in TESOL (Teaching English to Speakers of Other Languages) teacher training. Qu and Tan (2010) report the result of pre-use evaluation of one set of Chinese and two of English materials used in China which aims to see if there are marked differences in materials for teaching Chinese and English. Their analysis involves comparing various elements of the books such as aims and objectives, structure, design, instructions for activities and tasks. They report commonality and differences. They did note some evidence of a Chinese 'culture of learning' in the Chinese materials in that 'Chinese traditional culture conceptualizes good learning as learner's hard-working, accumulative effort and refined reflection in the process of reading' (Qu and Tan, 2010: 288). They do, however, point out the danger of ignoring many other possible factors that could influence their findings such as the counterarguments to static interpretations of the studies on 'cultures of learning' (Dogancay-Aktuna, 2005).

Guest (2002) and Littlewood (2000), among others, argue that studies such as those cited above can further the 'othering' of non-western cultures, and reinforce stereotypes at the expense of ignoring individual preferences and the inherently dynamic nature of (sub)cultures.

Functions of groupwork and pairwork

Various 'communicative' approaches require a link between activities and the organizational structures available to teachers. In the first place, if we are to create opportunities for learners to experience language in use rather than studying language as knowledge, we need to create situations in which learners converse. To consider functional meaning (e.g. persuasion, apology, suggestion), learners will need a situation, roles and purpose for communication. In this sense, it is logical to assume a natural link between the learning of functional aspects of language use and a classroom-based behaviour that requires class members to exchange and share information and ideas. Such a link, for instance, may mean that students learn how to give and follow instructions in a paired format; while to respond appropriately in a typical range of practical social situations may involve the exchange of opinions within a small group. As an extension of such use of classroom organization we have looked in Chapter 10 at various approaches that enable optimal use of integrated skills such as Task-Based Learning (TBL), Content-Based Language Learning (CBLL)/Content Language Integrated Learning (CLIL), Text-Driven Approaches, Project Work and Role Play/Simulations. These approaches provide reasons and an environment for communicative interactions. Pair and groupwork fit into these approaches very well and enable various patterns of interaction to take place in order to achieve communicative outcomes.

Second Language Acquisition (SLA) studies also seem to support the use of group/pairwork in that the findings often indicate the importance of

- exposure to comprehensible input of language in use (Krashen, 1994; Ellis, 2008; Ortega, 2010)
- use of language for communication to achieve communicative outcomes (Swain et al., 2002; Swain, 2005)
- negotiation of meaning through social interaction (Long, 1996; Lantolf and Thorne, 2006).

Many teachers across the world face the challenges of mixed ability classes of students with different learning preferences/styles in large classes. However capable teachers may be, it is difficult for a single teacher to provide each individual with a suitable kind and amount of language exposure and use. Group/pairwork enables learners of different levels and learning styles to share and pool their resources (e.g. linguistic knowledge, world or subject knowledge, strategies) in a smaller and informal environment. Learners in groups/pairs are more likely to be able to negotiate meaning in optimal ways that suit themselves. In this sense, regardless of cultural traditions, pair and groupwork may have a place as a fundamental facilitator of language acquisition and development in any language classroom.

Further support for the positive effects of group/pairwork on learning comes from studies on Co-operative Learning (CL) from L1 primary to tertiary levels (Baines et al., 2007; Kutnick and Berdondini, 2009). The classroom is clearly a place where people have to work together, essentially requiring a compromise between their own individuality and the dynamics of the whole group. In other words, it is ideally a co-operative environment where structuring activities in different ways can allow for the establishment of a cohesive and collaborative working atmosphere (see McCafferty et al., 2006; Kagan and Kagan, 2009 for a comprehensive introduction to CL in language teaching). CL does not mean abandoning the teacher-fronted mode but it does involve combining various approaches to learning. If teachers and learners only know the teacher-fronted mode they may find other styles somewhat alien. Some teachers may feel apprehensive about possible pitfalls when they switch to unfamiliar CL approaches. For example, teachers may feel that the students' language ability is too low to be able to manage group tasks or discussions in English. Even if they can carry out a group task in English, what happens if a particular task turns out to be beyond the groups' combined ability? In such a case, the students may resort to their L1 and the whole point of ensuring L2 exposure to language in use vanishes into thin air. What happens if some groups finish their work earlier than the other groups? Moreover, group members may not always get along with each other. There might be some students who do not contribute and leave the assigned task to the rest of the group to complete. If a CL task succeeds in engaging learners, it may result in high volumes of noise which could upset other teachers, parents and even the authorities.

All these apprehensions are understandable, and the literature on CL offers possibilities of learner and teacher development. Mak (2011) reports how trainee teachers in Hong Kong needed training to resolve the conflict between the methods that they were used to and those which they thought were good but unfamiliar. Tomlinson and Dat (2004) report on a survey of the views of 300 intermediate level English as a Foreign Language (EFL) adult learners and 15 teachers in Vietnam in relation to the role of spoken interactions in language lessons. Contrary to teachers' perceptions about learners' cultural reticence, learners were in fact willing to participate but needed support and a relaxed environment to be able to do so. Tomlinson and Bao concluded that pedagogic procedures that have proved effective in one culture may require sensitive and principled adaptation if they are to be readily accepted by users in another culture.

Pairwork and groupwork

Pairwork and groupwork are not synonymous terms: just as they obviously reflect different social patterns, so the ways in which they are adapted and applied in the classroom also have distinctive as well as similar functions. Pairwork requires rather little organization on the part of the teacher and, at least in principle, can be activated in most classrooms by simply having learners work with the person sitting next to them (although other kinds of pairing – for example, according to proficiency – may be more suitable depending on the task). The time taken for pairwork to be carried out need not be extensive, and there is a very large range of possible tasks throughout the whole spectrum of functions we have identified, from fully communicative, 'simulated', structure and vocabulary practice, to those where an important aim is to set up co-operative working habits. The skills chapters in Part II of this book have a number of examples.

A group, on the other hand, even though it can have a comparable range of functions, is by its very nature a more complex structure, which will probably require greater role differentiation between individuals as well as a certain amount of physical reorganization of the classroom. This role differentiation may refer to 'assumed' roles, particularly in a 'communicative' setting (having learners enact a courtroom scene with a variety of 'characters', for example, or 'pretend' to be a town council trying to negotiate a decision about building priorities), or to the structure of the group itself, with members being assigned tasks of chairperson, reporter/note-taker and so on. The timescale often needs to be more extended, to allow for the greater number of interacting participants. Ur (1996: 232–3) makes the point comprehensively: 'The success of groupwork depends to some extent on the surrounding social climate, and on how habituated the class is to using it; and also . . . on the selection of an interesting and stimulating task whose performance is well within the ability of the group. But it also depends on effective and careful organisation.'

Finally, groups and pairs are not mutually exclusive, and there are a number of variations that bridge these two basic structural activities. For instance: individuals out of a pair can re-form to make a different pair; or pairs can 'snowball' by joining other pairs until eventually the whole class may have re-formed.

At this point in the chapter, it will be useful to consider briefly these two issues, one of which summarizes the discussion so far, the other of which looks ahead:

1 Looking at your comments on the first task in this chapter, to what extent does the use of pair and groupwork in your own materials reflect the different functions we have discussed?

2 How much flexibility do you have in your own teaching in the 'management' of your classroom?

11.3   Interaction and Classroom Structure

Arranging the class

Readers may well recognize one or more of the following possibilities for the physical arrangement of their classroom, as shown in figure 11.1 (where T = teacher, S = student, and the lines = main directions of interaction).

Not all possibilities can be covered here, but we have tried to show a representative sample. These arrangements are not necessarily static, and in a flexible classroom may change during the course of one lesson, both physically as well as in terms of roles and interaction. There may, of course, be straightforward physical restrictions on the possibilities, such as room size or the nature of the classroom furniture (tables, benches, worktop space, mobility). Space considerations not only act as obstacles to the establishment of a more communicative and co-operative classroom: a room that is too small for the number of students may actually force participative working patterns even where they are not appropriate.

Interaction patterns in the classroom

Just as a great deal has been written about different organizational structures in everyday classroom practice, so there is a large and rapidly growing

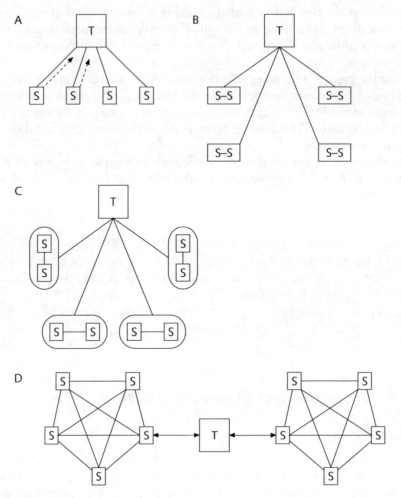

Figure 11.1   Patterns of classroom organization.

research literature concerning the effects of various types of patterning both on aspects of classroom behaviour and on learning outcomes. The research comes particularly from studies in the psychology of SLA, and from work in social psychology and the sociology of small-group behaviour. Here we can only set out very selectively a few of the topics of potential interest to teachers, just to give a flavour of the debate. The bibliography gives several references that go into these topics in more depth, and teachers may wish to evaluate the relevance of these studies to their own classrooms (and ways in which the nature and requirements of research converge and diverge from those of teaching and learning). A further point to consider is how media-assisted language learning might affect group dynamics (see Chapter 5).

Teacher-fronted classes The area that has received by far the most attention to date is that of the quantity and quality of verbal interaction in the plenary class as opposed to the smaller group setting. A lockstep organization of classroom interaction is represented in simple terms by figure 11.1A. The lockstep mode can be explained in terms of a simple sequence of teacher stimulus → student response → teacher evaluation of student response (a traditional pattern of teacher question → student answer → teacher comment). This is, in other words, a situation where the whole class is moving along together, where all the students are 'locked' into the same activity at the same time and at the same pace and where the teacher is the primary, even the only, initiator. Nunan (2005) provides an overview of classroom research for the last three decades. As one of many studies, he refers to Tsui's research (1985) which investigates the amount and types of teacher talk, teacher speech and interaction and student output. Tsui's data from Hong Kong revealed that over 80% of the talk in the classrooms came from teachers. Note here that SLA research seems to indicate the importance of learners' output for communication in class to achieve communicative outcomes (e.g. Swain, 2005; and see discussions on SLA in Section 11.2). Nunan (2005) also refers to Brock (1986) who investigates two kinds of teacher questions: display and referential questions. Display questions are the ones that the teacher knows the answer to (e.g. comprehension questions after reading a text) whereas referential questions means genuine questions where the answer is not known. Nunan (2005: 228) points out that 'The significance of the study was that learners in classrooms where more referential questions were asked gave significantly longer and more complex responses'.

If a teacher-fronted class happens to be a mixed ability large class of 50 students and if the teacher asks questions in a lockstep manner to individual students, it is not difficult to imagine the limited kinds and amount of interactions. In her review of SLA and classroom research, Tsui (2001: 122) offers this summary:

> It was found that compared to teacher-fronted interaction in whole class work, both pair work and group work provide more opportunities for learners to initiate and control the interaction, to produce a much larger variety of speech acts and to engage in the negotiation of meaning.

Before leaving this point, however, we must be careful not to assume that a whole-class, teacher-fronted methodology is necessarily undesirable. Harmer (2007b) offers a common-sense antidote to some of the more negative comments by enumerating a number of positive advantages of the lockstep class, including its practical usefulness when teachers need to give instructions and explanations, but also its affective role in reinforcing a sense of 'belonging' and, for many educational settings, in creating the security of the familiar. Furthermore, in many EFL contexts, English teachers may be the only ones who can provide input in the target language. Teacher-fronted lessons may be a good way of providing the necessary meaningful exposure to language in use if the teacher for example reads stories and poems and performs dramas for the learners to enjoy.

Group structure   Discussion of the nature of classroom organization also draws on very extensive research into the 'social' structure of groups of participants working on specific tasks. It is interesting to speculate what might happen if we simply tell the whole class to divide into small groups in any way they choose: will they do so randomly, or with friends, or with people of similar proficiency? Furthermore, if we imagine giving a free discussion topic to a subgroup consisting of, say, six or seven of our students, and we then leave them to talk with only a small amount of monitoring, it is probable that some will talk more than others, one or two will want to dominate and control, others will react by withdrawing into silence and so on.

These kinds of 'natural' grouping, and relatively spontaneous speech and behaviour patterns within an unmonitored group, are clearly quite different from the other end of the spectrum of control, where the teacher specifies both the group and the nature of the task in detail (e.g. a dialogue rehearsal). The majority of classes fall somewhere between the naturally occurring and the completely structured. Harmer (2007b) lists the principles of friendship, streaming (by ability) and chance, as ways of dividing a class into groups. Jacobs (http://www.georgejacobs.net (accessed in November 2011)) provides useful and up-to-date resources for CL. In his PDF article titled 'Cooperative Learning: Theory, Principles and Techniques', he explains CL principles, including heterogeneous grouping (e.g. gender, ethnicity, language proficiency and diligence). He then gives advice for when students are not happy with unfamiliar members: 'Some ideas for addressing this include helping groups enjoy initial success, explaining the benefits of heterogeneity, doing team-building activities to promote trust and to help students get to know each other, and teaching collaborative skills'.

Learning styles

It is often argued that, in lockstep classes, learners are unrealistically assumed to learn what teachers choose to teach them, leaving no room for individual differences. One basic distinction in learning style research is between 'cognitive' factors (to do with the way people think) and 'affective' factors (to do with emotions and what we feel). There is some attempt to relate these to different types of teaching. There is now quite a long research tradition relating to the strategies apparently used by 'Good Language Learners' (Norton and Toohey, 2001; Griffith, 2008), and to the various cognitive and personality types that affect learning (Robinson, 2002; Dörnyei, 2005). A number of writers are now trying to relate methods, not just to ideas about the nature of communication, but also to what is known about these kinds of psychological variables.

Gardner (2006: 24) warns against 'any belief that all the answers to a given problem lie in one certain approach, such as logical-mathematical thinking' by drawing attention to IQ tests and to the SAT (the college admission test in the United States). His argument seems significant when we use expressions such as 'successful' or 'unsuccessful' learners based on purely linguistic measurement. Gardner (2006: 24) maintains that 'We are all so different largely because we have different combinations of intelligences' and puts forward arguments for multiple intelligences, including 'musical intelligence', 'interpersonal intelligence' and 'intrapersonal intelligence'. If his assertions are right, there are fundamental implications for educational planning, implementation and assessment. In relation to the theme of this chapter, for example, group or pairwork may possibly favour the learners with dominant 'interpersonal intelligence' who are good at working with other people but alienate the learners with 'intrapersonal intelligence' who prefer to work alone. There are other theories of learner differences. Coffield et al. (2004), for example, identified 71 models of learning styles. Behind the theories of learning styles lies an assumption that learners learn best if the ways of learning suit their own styles. Attempts have been made to develop tests such as the VARK (i.e. Visual, Audio, Read/write, Kinaesthetic) questionnaire (Fleming, 1995) in order to identify learning preferences so that learners can learn in the optimal way for fulfilling their potential.

Regarding learning styles, we need to be aware of the danger of careless labelling of student failure: the real cause may be due to incompatibilities between the materials/teaching and the learners' preferred learning routes. It is also necessary, however, to realize that there are many questions that have to be answered in relation to learning styles. After a close examination of 13 influential models of learning styles Coffield et al. (2004) note the lack of consensus among the different models and question the validity and reliability of some models. Pashler et al. (2009) report the results of research commissioned by the Association for Psychological Science (APS) on the scientific validity of learning styles practices. This panel of independent researchers proposes an empirically trustworthy research design on learning styles and examines learning styles studies. Their report reveals that only a few studies use such a research design. Massa and Mayer (2006) is one of the approved studies, but it did not find strong support for giving visual learners and verbal learners different multimedia instructions according to their learning preferences. Pashler et al. (2009) conclude that they see no adequate evidence to justify incorporating learning styles assessments into general educational practice.

So far, we have looked at groupwork and pairwork in the classroom from a number of angles as a procedural, organizational concept, and at some of the related research background. It is now time to turn to an examination of the potential advantages and disadvantages of such procedures.

11.4   Groupwork and Pairwork: Benefits or Drawbacks?

Before you start to read this section (and looking back at some of your comments earlier in this chapter), consider the feasibility and appropriacy of groupwork and pairwork as 'organizational frameworks' for your own classroom. What are the possibilities and limitations? And to what extent do you need to take into account external views and guidelines, rather than organize your class according to your own preferences?

We must be clear that any discussion of the advantages and disadvantages of particular methods is relative. There can be no absolute pros and cons, and we say again that what is appropriate in Mexico may not be appropriate in Japan. This is why the headings in this section are all printed with a question mark against them, to indicate the difficulties of making generalizations. We have stressed many times that any individual teacher with a single class has to be seen in the wider context of the school and its educational and social environment. In many parts of the world, and in the perceptions of many people, the status of 'teacher' commands great respect, and it would not be regarded as appropriate behaviour for the teacher to take a strongly interactive role. In other words, there are many different notions of 'authority' and 'social position', and the expectations of behaviour that go with them. The implications of such cultural differences for whole class versus small groupwork in the language classroom are clear.

Again, it is often the case that 'knowledge' is regarded as content to be transmitted, so that language becomes a curriculum subject similar to history or physics. In such a context, it is unlikely that exploratory, problem-solving activities will fit naturally into educational philosophy and practice. The picture can become very complex when teachers and learners with different backgrounds and preconceptions meet in the same classroom. Consider, for example, the mutual difficulties of a teacher trained in the 'communicative' tradition with an instinctive preference for small groupwork, and a learner who believes that a teacher's role is to be an explicit instructor. Neither side is right or wrong, but a process of adjustment will certainly be necessary.

At the same time, we have also noted that 'the wider context' will include not only local conditions but also the ELT profession as a whole. From this perspective, research and practice are not static, and what is appropriate at a particular point may well be superseded a few years later. Such concepts as 'power' and 'distance' can, in certain circumstances, vary even during the course of a single lesson. To deny the possibility of change, then, is to assume that all development is irrelevant. Neither position – the universal application of certain methods on the one hand, or a lack of openness to new ideas on the other – is realistic (see Tomlinson and Bao, 2004 for useful suggestions).

A final consideration in setting out the framework for discussing the pros and cons of groupwork and pairwork is the question of whose perspective is taken into account. Any teacher will have a view; but so will learners, parents, colleagues, head teachers and education authority personnel, and these views will not always necessarily be in harmony.

We now enumerate, first, some of the more frequently heard points in favour of groupwork and pairwork, and then some of the points against. There is insufficient space here to present argument and counter-argument for each of these points, and readers are invited to consider each argument critically and from their own perspective.

Advantages?

Our earlier discussion of the research base put forward a number of reasons why getting learners to work in subgroups in a plenary class is often to be preferred to 'lockstep' (while also acknowledging that certain kinds of practice may best be handled with the whole class paying attention at the same time):

1   In a lockstep framework, there is little flexibility. Students are frequently 'observers' of others, and work to an externally imposed pace. In small-group and pairwork, on the other hand, the possibility of an individual's learning preferences being engaged is correspondingly increased. (We shall see in the next chapter how the individualization of instruction can take learners even further along this path).

2   Groupwork in particular is potentially dynamic, in that there are a number of different people to react to, to share ideas with and so on: exchange of information is sometimes more 'natural' in smaller-scale interaction. The extent to which this is so, however, clearly depends closely on the nature of the task set.

3   Different tasks can be assigned to different groups or pairs. This may lead to a cohesive whole-class environment if these tasks can be fitted together, perhaps in a final discussion. Alternatively, a teacher working with a mixed proficiency group may have the flexibility to allocate activities according to learners' levels.

4   Each student has proportionally more chance to speak and therefore to be involved in language use. Furthermore, the more varied the types of activity, the greater the variety in types of language used.

5   Groupwork can promote a positive atmosphere or 'affective climate' (Arnold, 1999), as distinct from the more public and potentially threatening 'performance' environment of the lockstep classroom. Motivation, too, is often improved if learners feel less inhibited and more able to explore possibilities for self-expression. Arguably, too, co-operation in the classroom is encouraged. These are undoubtedly positive factors, but the individual classroom still needs to be 'in tune' with its educational environment.

6   There is some evidence that learners themselves favour working in smaller groupings. Millar (2011) reports a case study that investigated the cultural adjustment of four 6–8-year-old Korean school children to studying at an Australian government school. The mothers all suggested that constructivist approaches, cooperative learning and play-centred experiences helped their children adapt easily to the new cultural environment (Hill, 1994; Farver et al., 1995; Okagaki and Diamond, 2000). The children were able to relinquish rote-learning and teacher dependence (Lee et al., 2000) and, once language barriers had decreased, to comfortably participate in open-ended, child-centred learning activities (Farver et al., 1995; Millar, 2011: 6).

Millar (2011) reports how Korean mothers and children commented on the vital importance of interpersonal relationships with other students and teachers as one of the main contributing factors to successful cultural adjustment. According to Millar, the mothers all said strong friendship groups were crucial to their children's academic success, though he does comment on occasional discrepancies between the perceptions of teachers and those of Korean participants in the study. Tomlinson and Bao (2004) also comment on the marked differences in the perceptions of teachers and students in their data about the seeming reticence shown during speaking activities. Spratt (1999) and J. McDonough (2002) discuss a similar phenomenon of how much teachers' ratings of the usefulness of activities differ from learners' preferences. For instance, although 'conversation practice' is rated as 'very high' on both sides, pairwork comes out as 'very high' for teachers but low for learners.

It has to be stressed here that published research data are somewhat patchy, and different contexts might produce differential results. In Chapter 13 we shall be looking at some of the small-scale investigations that teachers can carry out in their own classrooms, and the theme of 'learner preferences' provides us with a good example.

Disadvantages?

Many readers will recognize these kinds of stated objections to groupwork and/or pairwork, and as usual, such objections must be evaluated critically and according to context. Some are practical and straightforward classroom management problems, whereas others are deeper in the sense that they impinge on attitudes to teaching and learning and the whole cultural setting of the classroom.

1   There is some concern that other students will probably not provide such a good 'language model' as the teacher. Barker (2011: 55) reports what happened when he tried to persuade Japanese university students to talk to each other in English outside classes in pairs or groups as a way of compensating for the scarcity of necessary exposure and communication opportunities in an EFL context. The students' objections to his proposal included apprehension such as 'speaking practice is only beneficial if your partner is a native speaker', 'speaking to another non-native speaker is a bad idea because you will 'learn' each other's mistakes' and 'because students won't recognize mistakes, they won't be able to correct each other'.

   It is interesting to note, however, that Barker refers in his chapter to Swain et al. (2002: 181) who state, 'the collaborative dialogue in which peers engage as they work together on writing, speaking, listening and reading activities mediates second language learning'. According to Swain et al. (2002: 18), 'few adverse effects of working collaboratively were noted'. Barker's own study not only confirms the claims of Swain et al. but also shows an increase in self-esteem, confidence and motivation among those who participated in what Barker calls Unstructured Learner Interaction (i.e. learners' regular use of English in pair/group outside classrooms without the teacher's interference).

2   There are several possible institutional objections to rearranging the classroom and to an increased communicative environment. Furniture, for example, may be impossible to move around or may encourage static interaction patterns (such as students sitting in rows on long benches fixed to the floor). Sometimes, too, school authorities or other colleagues may react negatively to what they perceive to be the increased noise levels that come from an active class.
3   Some monolingual classes readily use their mother tongue instead of the target language, particularly where discussion is animated and even more so when the teacher shares the same L1. It is not surprising that interacting in English in these circumstances may initially be perceived as artificial.
4   Learners often have strong preferences, and it is not unusual to find a stated wish for teacher control and direct input of language material. It

is even an expectation in many cases, and there is a point at which a teacher's doubts about its pedagogical effectiveness need to be matched by learners' perceptions of the 'best way' to learn.

5   If the class is divided into smaller units, there may be problems of 'group dynamics' where, for example, students may not wish to work with those of their peers assigned by the teacher to the same group. This may be compounded by feelings of being 'better than' or conversely 'worse than' others.

6   By far the most commonly heard objection to 'alternative' classroom arrangements, and in some ways underlying all the others listed here, is that of class size. It is all very well, the argument runs, to conduct group-work and pairwork if you have only a small, multilingual class of co-operative adults working in a comfortable, modern environment, but 'try doing it with a class of forty!' This is the title of an article by Nolasco and Arthur (1986), in which they try to meet the 'large class' objection head on. Using their experience of teacher training in Morocco, they first of all list nine reasons for teacher resistance to what were perceived as 'new' ideas and techniques. These reasons, some of which we have already met, were as follows:

Students not interested in unfamiliar materials and methods
Discipline problems
Physical constraints
Problems of duplicating material
Students prefer grammar and exam practice
School administration objects to noise
Students talk in L1 in pairs
Students complain they are 'not being taught'
Enthusiasm causes problems of class control.

The authors are sympathetic and sensitive to these objections, and go on to sketch out a phased plan whereby teachers and learners can gradually be introduced to the advantages of groupwork and pairwork. The plan starts from the basis of familiar materials and working patterns, and slowly increases learner responsibility, initiation and control.

The perceived problems by the teachers in Morocco in the 1980s listed in Nolasco and Arthur (1986) include wider issues than just those of groupwork and pairwork. The real issue behind these perceptions seems to come from transplanting CLT in its various incarnations (Task-Based Language Teaching, CBLL) to different contexts. Pham (2007), for example, echoes this in addressing similar problems in Vietnam and adds some more to the list of challenges, such as pressure from traditional exams and teachers' limited expertise. He describes the potential conflicts between imported methods and the local context:

When Vietnamese students are asked to use English to conduct a 'real life' game in pairs, the question raised is whether they are really engaged in genuine communication. Furthermore, the use of 'authentic' material, meaning authentic to native speakers of English, can be problematic in the Vietnamese or Chinese classroom. As Kramsch and Sullivan (1996) point out, what is authentic in London might not be authentic in Hanoi. Also, the large class size in Vietnam (between forty and sixty) also challenges the use of pair work and group work. (Pham, 2007: 196).

Pham (2007: 196), however, does not go down the route of negating CLT altogether. Instead he argues that '. . . while there are certainly problems in the transfer of CLT methods from the Western contexts to others, it is questionable whether these problems negate the potential usefulness of the CLT theory'. He believes that the fundamental tenets of CLT theories seem valid and applicable elsewhere:

> CLT sets the goal of language learning to be the teaching of learners to be able to use the language effectively for their real communicative needs, rather than simply to provide learners with the knowledge about the grammar system of that language.
> This goal is consistent with the long-term goal, if not the immediate goal, of English language instruction in many contexts of the world. (Pham, 2007: 196).

Pham (2007) warns against treating CLT as a formulaic, prescriptive classroom technique. Instead he advocates that:

> . . . teachers in Vietnam or elsewhere need to make further efforts to develop and generate, within the communicative approach, classroom techniques appropriate to their conditions. However, teachers should not be left alone in this process. Support from peers, students, from policymakers, from training courses as well as findings from empirical research on the use of CLT in certain contexts, particularly in non-Western contexts . . . is deemed important in this process.' (Pham, 2007: 200).

11.5 Conclusion

In this chapter we have tried to show that dividing a class into small groups, asking learners to work in pairs or, by implication, any kind of 'structuring' decision by the teacher, are not merely a set of alternatives that can be mechanically applied. However sound their justification in principle, all such arrangements have to be assessed in terms of the teaching situation in its widest sense – the existing syllabus and materials, expected roles of teachers and learners, the practicalities of physical space, the institution and the whole educational system. At the same time, we argue again that no teaching environment can be regarded as fixed for all time. New syllabuses are introduced, often in line with shifting perceptions of national and international needs; attitudes of teachers and learners to materials, methods and to each other change; the expectations of individuals develop, both for themselves and alongside wider social changes. As we shall see in the remaining chapters, all these considerations have direct implications for the training and development of both teachers and learners.

1   Draw up a table for your own classroom of the things you like about groupwork and pairwork, and the things you do not like. You will probably be able to think of more points than we have included in our discussion here.

2   If possible, compare your ideas with those of a colleague – it would be particularly interesting if you could work with someone from a different background to your own.

3   What factors do you think influence your opinions? It may be the materials you use, your learners' attitudes, school policy, your view of your own role and so on.

11.6   Further Reading

1   Griffiths, C. (ed) (2008): *Lessons from Good Language Learners*. This provides a comprehensive overview of successful language learning strategies and is useful for learner training.

2   Harmer, J. (2007: ch. 10): *The Practice of English Language Teaching*. This discusses many practical aspects of groups and pairs within some overall principles.

3   McCafferty, S., G. Jacobs and C.D. Iddings. (2006): *Cooperative Learning and Second Language Teaching*. This provides a useful theoretical and practical introduction to the field of cooperative learning (CL) for language teachers with varied experience.

12

Individualization, Self-access and Learner Training

12.1 Introduction

In the last chapter we considered some of the different possibilities of structuring the classroom with groups and pairs of learners in mind. In this chapter we shall be looking at the concept of individualization in language learning and the extent to which this can be implemented both inside and outside the classroom. We shall begin by considering how individualized learning started and the fundamental philosophies behind it. This will help us to see the different strands and understand the somewhat confusing terms associated with individualized learning. We will then think about why we may wish to individualize the classroom. Then we shall examine some issues of individualization, self-directed learning and self-access and try to relate them to actual learning situations. We shall then consider how recent developments in educational technology have provided further possibilities for individualizing language learning. Finally, we consider the area of learner training in relation to individualizing the classroom.

Growth in the phenomenon of individualization began in the 1970s and was nourished by the Threshold proposals of the Council of Europe (Richterich and Chancerel, 1980) and the notion of 'Permanent Education', or Education for Life, with respect to which pioneering work was undertaken at CRAPEL (Centre de recherches et d'applications pedagogiques en langues), a language teaching and research centre at the University of Nancy, France. Smith (2008: 395–6) provides a concise account of how learner autonomy – one of the newer terms for individualization – started:

Materials and Methods in ELT: A Teacher's Guide, Third Edition.
Jo McDonough, Christopher Shaw, and Hitomi Masuhara.
© 2013 John Wiley & Sons, Inc. Published 2013 by John Wiley & Sons, Inc.

In the interests of widening access to education and promoting lifelong learning, CRAPEL began to offer adults the opportunity to learn a foreign language in a resources centre, free from teacher direction. However, it soon became clear that participants did not necessarily – initially, at least – have the full capacity (competence) to take charge of decision-making in all the areas normally determined by an institution, teacher, or textbook, namely:

- objectives
- contents (including materials)
- stages ('syllabus')
- methods and techniques
- pace, time and place
- evaluation procedures.

CRAPEL put in place various kinds of support measures, including learner counselling and 'training', to assist in the 'autonomization' process – the development of learners' abilities to work more effectively in a self-directed fashion.

These pioneering attempts by CRAPEL show various philosophical learner-centred beliefs which have grown into different fields of study. One of these beliefs is catering for individual differences in terms of needs, purpose, preferred ways of learning and timing for learning. Individualization in language learning in this sense is also symptomatic of the development of interest shown in the learner and the learners' needs, particularly, as can be seen in, for example, English for Specific Purposes, which grew apace in the 1980s.

Another of the beliefs underlying the CRAPEL model is a view of learners' innate capabilities to self-direct their own learning. This belief in learners' capacities to conduct and manage their own learning is often referred to nowadays as 'learner autonomy'. The philosophy of learner autonomy has lent its hand to developing terms used for some modes of learning outside classrooms such as 'self-directed learning', 'self-instruction' and 'self-paced learning'.

CRAPEL's beliefs also involved the importance of providing resources for autonomous learners to make use of. This approach is shared among supporters of 'resource-based learning' or 'self-access learning', which we will be looking at later in this chapter. In relation to self-access learning, the use of Information Technology (IT) has been attracting global interest: for example use of multimedia, integrated virtual learning environment, E-learning (i.e. all forms of electronically supported learning and teaching). Furthermore, individualized use of IT in language learning outside institutions seems to be already happening. M-learning, for example, means 'Any sort of learning that happens when the learner is not at a fixed, predetermined location, or learning that happens when the learner takes advantage of the learning opportunities offered by mobile technologies' (Wikipedia, http://en.wikipedia.org/wiki/MLearning (accessed 08 December 2011)). In M learning, learners are able to choose time, location, sources and even community of learning buddies and teachers (Chinnery, 2006; Goodwin-Jones, 2008). Mobile devices include not only hardware such as handheld tablet computers, MP3 players, netbooks and mobile/smart phones but also any applications that can be uploaded onto these devices. For further discussion and examples of how new technologies can support and enhance individualized learning, see Chapter 5 in this book. Kervin and Derewianka (2011) and Motteram (2011) are also recommended.

Learners may have an innate capacity to be autonomous but, in practice, they may not be able (at least initially) or willing to take on the responsibilities of the whole spectrum of decision-making required for management of their own learning as was observed in the case of CRAPEL. Counselling and training provide necessary support and such guidance is referred to as 'learner training' or 'learner development'. Individual learning with some support schemes outside classrooms may be called 'guided/supported self-study' or 'directed independent learning'. 'Distance learning' can be considered as one mode of directed independent learning. We will discuss Learner Training later in this chapter.

CRAPEL was a case of 'out-of-class' resource centre-based 'directed independent learning'. In comparison, 'Independent learning', 'Open learning', 'Flexible learning' and 'Blended learning' could take various combinations of learning modes: for example, face-to-face teacher-led learning in classes combined with self-directed learning at a resource centre which offers a Virtual Learning Environment as well as hardware such as DVD, books and magazines.

> Why individualize the classroom? Before reading further, think of some reasons why classroom teachers may wish to individualize language learning.

As one of the Good Practice Guide Projects supported by the Centre for Languages, Linguistics and Area Studies (LLAS) in the United Kingdom, Ciel Language Support Network (2000) provides six handbooks. Though the project has now been completed and their handbooks are only available as online archives, the fundamental discussions seem still valid and useful today as they give us a well-considered perspective on evaluating developments in individualized learning. Handbook 1, entitled 'Integrating independent learning with the curriculum', lists some benefits of individualized learning. We will use their categories as a guide to our exploration of possible reasons why we may wish to consider individualized learning as a viable option.

Individualized learning:

1   adds flexibility.

It is still the norm that language learning takes place in groups. Every class is composed of individuals, each of whom will have different capabilities and work rates; and among these heterogeneous groups it can obviously be a problem for the teacher to allow for the variety of pacing necessary if all students are to learn effectively. We sometimes speak of 'teaching up' to some students or, conversely, 'teaching down' to others. It is quite common to hear other teachers speaking about 'teaching to the middle range of the group' hoping that this will best satisfy students' needs. In this context, individualization can help to break the lockstep of the classroom. Individualization is not just limited to language learning either. 'Open learning' centres are sometimes used in industry as part of an in-service or professional development programme for workers, which may be tailored to their own individual needs and to the pace at which they prefer to learn. Many practitioners believe that all learners can make satisfactory progress in learning a foreign language if given sufficient time plus the possibility of developing their preferred learning styles and habits. It is clear that some learners work better in groups, whereas others prefer to work alone. Some learners have a preference for a particular time of the day, and for many, the place of study can be very important, be it in class, in the SAC or anywhere that mobile devices can be used. In some learning contexts, it can be difficult for learners to attend classes regularly, perhaps because of other commitments, and in these situations, an individualized programme may prove to be an effective mode of learning.

2   extends and enhances classroom learning.

In order to ensure language acquisition, learners need a lot of time and a large amount of motivated exposure to meaningful input. Timetabled class hours often are not enough. In individualized learning contexts, learners can consolidate or further explore what they have learned in the face-to-face classroom at their own pace with the kinds of resources that would suit their learning preferences, levels and purposes whenever it is convenient for them. Extensive reading and extensive listening, project work or pair/group tasks can be done in self-access/open learning/resource centres, using various kinds of authentic materials.

3   encourages and develops key transferable skills that could enhance future learning and eventual employability.

Learners can not only learn a language but also acquire life skills such as

- setting targets, planning and organizing their own study without guidance

- managing time and resources required
- conducting research and presenting the results
- using new technologies (e.g. use of multimedia in learning, electronic dictionary, wiki, blog) (See Chapter 5 'Technology in ELT')
- collaborating with peers with or without technology (e.g. pair or group tasks and projects online or offline)
- finding ways of solving problems (e.g. seeking advice, critically evaluating sources of information, self-reflection, coming up with innovative ideas).

4 leads to learner autonomy.

　　Learners learn to be responsible for and manage their own learning.

In sum, individualization as a concept in education including language teaching and learning aims at providing as many permutations as possible to the learner that the traditional lockstep of the classroom cannot in itself provide.

How do you cater for individual learner needs in your classroom at present?

12.2　Individualization: Some Issues

Smith (2003) explores the question of whether learner autonomy is a western concept inappropriate for non-western students. Smith (2008: 396) argues that:

> . . . learner autonomy is not a particular method, nor need it be conflated with individualism. From this perspective, the exercise and development of learner autonomy can be seen as an educational goal which is cross-culturally valid and meets with different kinds of constraint according to context. (Palfreyman and Smith, 2003; Barfield and Brown, 2007)

Though the ideas and earlier attempts originated in the west, as we have seen in Section 12.1, individualization of learning seems to have potential for serving many different contexts. Teachers across the world face many challenges such as limited classroom contact hours, large classes, pressures for improving standards and meeting the demands of new kinds of learners with different learning styles and multimedia preferences and expectations from parents in the global world. Institutions 'in the west' are no exception in sharing some or all of these problems, and this is why individualization has been developed as a possible solution. The interest in individualization has grown to such an extent that the first issue of AILA's (International

Association of Applied Linguistics) Applied Linguistics series is on Learner and Teacher Autonomy (Lamb and Reinders, 2008). It is interesting to note that the AILA book discusses teacher autonomy as well as learner autonomy as individualized learning involves reconsideration and changes of teacher roles. Dixon et al. (2006) is a publication by Arabia Learner Independence SIG based in the United Arab Emirates (UAE) on the theme of Self-Access Centres (SACs) or Independent Learning Centres (ILCs). The editorial note says:

> a universally applicable handbook covering an extensive range of practicalities and issues for consideration when planning, implementing and operating an independent learning facility anywhere in the world. (p. ix)

The contributors to this book are not only from the Gulf countries but also from Japan, Malaysia, New Zealand and the United Kingdom, and the content covers a lot of case studies of building up learner resources in challenging contexts. There is an Independent Learning Association which holds biannual conferences (http://independentlearning.org/ILA/index.html (accessed on 10 December 2011)).

Autonomy and self-directed learning entail individualization but, as Trim (1976: 1), one of the advisors for the Council of Europe, has shown, 'it is possible to pursue individualization within a highly authoritarian framework. The teacher looks at the individual's problems, but decides herself how different types of individual should be treated'. If we consider the implications of Trim's statement, then an individualized programme in this sense would be the very antithesis of self-direction and autonomy. There is consequently an issue between freedom and control, between autonomous, self-directed learning and externally (teacher) directed learning. It may therefore be useful to see the totally externally directed mode and the totally self-directed mode as two polarities in individualizing language teaching, with the majority of programmes occurring somewhere between the two extremes (see figure 12.1).

It is probably fair to state, therefore, that total autonomy is only pertinent if it results in an efficient and satisfying mode of learning for that particular individual. Individualization is also a partial response to the belief that direct teaching in the classroom does not always result in learning taking place. Teaching can take place without learning, whereas learning can often

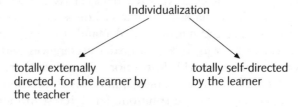

Figure 12.1   An overview of individualization.

occur without any formal teaching. As Riley (1982) points out, learning cannot be done to or for learners; it can only be done by them, and this is one of the basic principles in the definitions of individualization: that learners will assume some responsibility for their own learning at some stage in the process. Whichever approach a teacher chooses, the crucial question to ask is whether acquisition or development of autonomous life skills as well as language skills are taking place. Masuhara et al. (2008) note a trend for global coursebooks to offer multi-component extras on top of traditional paper coursebooks (e.g. audio or video CD, workbook CD, interactive grammar exercises, vocabulary games). Some publishers also offer Web resources for teachers to make use of. Such Internet resources may include photocopiable materials to be downloaded and be used for independent learning outside the class (e.g. extra vocabulary or grammar exercises, interactive quizzes, themes for writing). Some publishers offer teachers authoring software of tests. These ready-made materials may seem enticing to teachers who would like to introduce individualized learning using multimedia or the Internet but do not have time or resources. After reviewing eight recent global adult coursebooks, Masuhara et al. (2008: 310) warn against the danger that 'The ready-made photocopiable materials and tests could lead to unprincipled explicit teaching of discrete item grammar and disguised language drills of trivial content at the cost of overall development of skills and educational development'. Practitioners might like to evaluate these online materials against the philosophies of individualized learning we discussed earlier in this section and ask whether these extra grammar or vocabulary drills are any different from workbook exercises given as homework in the past.

Individualization does not necessarily mean that the students will be working on their own. In some cases, individualization can take place in small groups or pairs where students work on a similar task. At other times the learner may work with a teacher or in a solitary mode.

It is useful to see individualization not as a method per se, but as a possibility of reorganizing the resources and management of the classroom environment, which has many implications for the teacher. Individualization may involve some teachers in hitherto unknown roles such as 'guide', 'helper', 'facilitator'. How we get learners to work in an individualized mode may depend on how much structure we wish to give them. All language learners need to have some purpose to be successful in their learning, and to help in the achievement of this, a teacher may like to analyse the language needs of the learners and then draw up a learning plan with each of them. Points in each plan may include agreement between teacher and learner on learning objectives in relation to different language skills, the level of improvement aimed at, and how and when this may be achieved. After this, it is up to the teacher and learner to decide exactly how to proceed from here. They may decide to allow the learner more or less total autonomy in trying to attain the objectives set, as a teacher from Italy reported to us:

Ideally I wouldn't interfere with what the students select at all, but during the explanation of the materials I would suggest to students that they choose material in areas where they feel they have problems or which are their weakest areas. But after that, I wouldn't interfere at all . . . they can select what they want and proceed with it themselves . . . they know where their weak areas are. Generally students select the material that's most appropriate to their problems.

12.3   Implementation Inside and Outside the Classroom

It is quite common to hear teachers complain about the many reasons why they feel that they cannot individualize their classrooms. These arguments sometimes relate to the fact that they are non-native speakers; that they are under-resourced in general; that the syllabus is strictly controlled; that class size is too large (perhaps even more reason for needing to individualize); that materials are 'fixed'; furniture is screwed to the floor, thereby restricting movement of learners; that they work in a school and not a university. In other words, all the variables and constraints that we mentioned in Chapter 1.

Miller et al. (2007) note that governments in many countries (e.g. Hong Kong, New Zealand, Portugal, Singapore) have acknowledged the importance of learner autonomy in their national curricula of language learning. Miller et al. (2007) then explain how the Education and Manpower Bureau (EMB) of the Hong Kong Government asked a project team to explore ways of implementing autonomous learning in secondary schools. It is interesting to note that three volunteer schools developed different plans as the most suitable:

one school integrated SALL [Self Access Language Learning] into their classroom lessons; the second decided to approach SALL via project work; the third school determined to establish a self-access centre (SAC). (Miller et al., 2007: 221)

The cases in Hong Kong secondary schools that Miller et al. (2007) report are confirmation of how individualized learning can be flexibly incorporated depending on the contexts and the decisions made by the participants (i.e. government, school, teachers and learners in the case of Miller et al., 2007).

In this next section we hope to show that the provision of a measure of individual choice need not entail a full-scale reorganization of the classroom and resources and that individualization may be started in a relatively modest way.

One way of attempting to provide a measure of individual choice in the classroom is to use self-access activities where learners choose the tasks and activities that they wish to pursue with or without the help of a teacher. For example, learner X might have problems with reading skills and might opt to do extra work in this area, while learner Y might have a need to do some extra listening work. Of course self-access activity does not have to be remedial (implying that one is asking the learners to begin from a linguistic lack): some learners want to work in areas they enjoy and where they wish to enhance their performance. Some teachers programme self-access work into their weekly timetable – perhaps for two sessions a week to begin with – and build up from there. Self-access might be offered as integral to a particular course, or in a supplementary mode in a resource or SAC (see later in this chapter).

Something to note at this stage is that a self-access operation does not have to be a full-scale one to begin with. Where resources are limited we hope to show that the provision of a measure of individual choice need not entail a full-scale reorganization of the classroom and resources and that individualization may be started in a relatively modest way.

One way of attempting to provide a measure of individual choice in the classroom is to set up the classroom as a mini SAC with different parts of the room being used for different activities – perhaps reading in one corner, listening with CDs and headphones in another, and some computer-assisted language learning (CALL) in another. As materials and hardware can perhaps be stored easily and transported on a trolley, a small-scale beginning may enable teachers working within administrative constraints or working with sceptical colleagues to start a self-access operation with the hope of extending it later. As teachers we all have to prepare materials for lessons and provide feedback to our learners anyway – either in class or through marked home-work assignments (homework is in any case often set and marked on the lockstep principle outlined above). One suggestion, therefore, might be for two colleagues to collaborate over a mini self-access project by building up a small 'bank' of self-access materials. Dixon et al. (2006) include cases in which teachers began in a small-scale way but succeeded in implementing Self-Access Language Learning (SALL) in classrooms.

> Consider your own teaching situation. What kind of self-access activities would be appropriate for your learners and, if they do not exist already, how could they be set up within your institution?

Reading is one of the areas that provides ample scope for developing self-access work. Teachers can either design their own self-access boxes, perhaps working with other colleagues, as we suggested above, by dividing materials into different levels according to topic and level, or can use and adapt commercially available materials, depending on the types of students in the group, their proficiency level, the purpose of the course and so on. Note here that grading of reading materials can be done intuitively by the teachers and learners rather than following the predetermined grades purely based on vocabulary and structural specifications. Maley (2008) provides an interesting discussion on limitations of Graded Readers which are purely based on linguistic simplification and suitability of the level of reading materials. He rightly reminds us that readability is affected by many factors such as topic familiarity and motivation. In this sense, sensitive and sensible grading done by the teachers and learners who understand the context may turn out to be more theoretically sound than external mechanical grading based on some vocabulary frequency database or readability formulae.

Class self-access is possible even in resource-poor environments. Tomlinson (personal communication) refers to an Indonesian school teacher who asked her students to bring some reading materials in English to fill a class library box. Involving learners in creating their own self-access boxes can lead to raising their affinity with and pride in their own self-access corners so that they may be more likely to use the resources. Moreover, Maley (2008) proposes student- or teacher-generated texts as a possible solution to the problems of lack of appropriate reading materials. Maley (2008: 139) points out that 'One problem for learners, particularly those from non-European backgrounds, is their unfamiliarity with the cultural settings and background assumptions of much of what is available from metropolitan publishers'. He suggests teachers and students write fiction for their own students to read and reports two successful cases in Asia of student- or teacher-generated text projects (Denmark and Miles, 2004–2007; Maley and Mukundan, 2005; Maley, 2007a, 2007b; Maley, 2009). Maley explains why student- and teacher-generated readers make sense:

> The great strengths of this kind of material are that it not only reflects the students' own interests but it also solves at one stroke the issue of language level. Students can obviously only write at their level, which is more or less the level of those who will read the completed books. Bingo! (Maley, 2008: 139)

Maley discusses two modes for extensive reading: in class and out of class. After discussing the pros and cons of each mode, he points out some cases of in-class reading programmes in which institutional constraints distort Extensive Reading (ER) so much that the programme loses its values and effectiveness to facilitate language acquisition and development:

> Real readers read at different rates, with different degrees of attention or commitment, with differential comprehension and interpretation and with different personal preferences for what they read and how they read it. To require everyone to read the same text at the same pace and for the same purpose (usually in order to answer questions about it) is a seriously distorted version of ER. (Maley, 2008: 143)

If teacher intervention is required, Maley (2008) refers to some support that could help the learners to want to read individually. For example, a teacher could regularly read aloud an extract from a story taken from the self-access box. This simulates L1 bed-time story reading by caretakers. The objective is to entice learners to want to continue reading individually. Other suggestions include use of audio books or recording of the story or video or fostering a Reading Circle in which learners in small groups read and discuss the content. Fenton-Smith (2010) provides a comprehensive overview of the ER debate between proponents of 'free, pleasurable reading without any added activities' and of 'extensive reading with added activities (e.g. pre-reading and/or post-reading). He acknowledges that contextual constraints such as assessment requirements and accountability in many institutions means the former (i.e. ER without) is very difficult to realize in the majority of educational settings. After proposing various follow-up activities and evaluating their impact, Fenton-Smith concludes that

> The key point is that ER (as an activity, not a subject) can have a significant, positive effect on a student's second language proficiency, but a poorly designed ER course can negate or disrupt that effect in a multitude of ways (e.g. by decreasing motivation due to boredom, or hampering opportunities to read due to a heavy additional workload). We therefore need materials that satisfy contextual constraints while maintaining the integrity of enjoyable, extensive reading. (Fenton-Smith, 2010: 59–60).

Look at the self-access material in the extract overleaf, which appears in Tomlinson (2011c). Think about how some of his ideas or sequences could be used with your learners. Would any adaptations be necessary, and if so, what would they be?

Ideas for materials development

An example of access-self material
Samples of modern literature
Sample 1 – My Son's Story

Introduction

This is one of a series of units which is based on modern literature and which is designed for learners who are at an intermediate level or above. Each unit introduces you to extracts of a book and aims to give you access to that book in such a way that will help you to develop your language skills and to acquire new language. It is also hoped that the extracts and activities will give you an interest in the book and that you will go on to read the book for yourself.

Try the unit and if you get interested in it, carry on and do most of the activities (you don't have to do them all). If you then want to read the book for yourself, take it, out form the library. If you don't want to read the book, do another of these sample units and see if you want to read that book instead.

You can do this unit by yourself or you can work on it with other learners if you prefer.

Activities

1. You're going to read the beginning of a novel called *My Son's Story*,
The novel begins:
'How did I find out?
I was deceiving him.'
Think of different possible meanings for this beginning of the novel and then write answers to the following questions:
(a) Who do you think 'I' might be?
(b) What do you think the discovery could be?
(c) Who do you think 'him' might be?
(d) What do you think the deception could be?

2. Read the first paragraph of the extract from *My Son's Story* on page 1 of the Text Sheet (see Figure 17.1) and then answer questions 1 (a–d) again.

3. Check your answers to 2 above against those on page 1 of the Commentary [see page 422].

4. Read all of extract 1 form the novel on pages 2–3 [see Figure 17.1] of the text sheet and try to picture in your mind the people and the setting as you read.
If you found the extract interesting, go on to question 5. if you didn't find it interesting, choose a different sample from the box.

420

5. Draw a picture of the narrator's meeting with his father. Don't worry about the artistic merit of your drawing (you should see my attempt); just try to include the important features of the scene.

6. Compare your drawing of the meeting with the drawings on page 1 of the Commentary [see page 425]. what do all three drawings have in common? What are the differences between the drawings?

7. If you're working individually, pretend you're watching a film of *My Son's Story* and act out in your head the meeting between the narrator, his father and Hannah. Try to give them different voices. if you're working in a group, act out the scene together.

8. Compare your scene with the suggested film script for the scene on page 2 of the Commentary [see page 425–6].

9. Imagine that the narrator is talking to his best friend the next day and that he's telling him about the meeting with his father. write the dialogue between the two friends.

10. Compare your dialogue with the suggested dialogues on page 3 of the Commentary [see pages 426–7].

11. Write answers to the following questions:
(a) Why do you think the narrator is so disturbed by the encounter with his father?
(b) How old do you think the narrator was at the time of his encounter with his father and Hannah? Why?
(c) Who does 'us' refer to in 'Cinemas had been open to us only a year or so'?
(d) Explain in your own words the meaning of 'the moment we saw one another it was I who had discovered him, not he me'
(e) Why do you think his father opened the conversation by saying, 'You remember Hannah, don't you –?' Why did he not ask him why he was not studying?
(f) When had the narrator met Hannah before? Why did he not recognise her when he first saw her outside the cinema?
(g) What does the narrator mean by, 'And the voice was an echo from another life'?
(h) What does the narrator's description of Hannah tell you about his attitude towards her?
(i) Why do you think the narrator mentions that his father was wearing 'his one good jacket'?
(j) What does the narrator mean when he says he was 'safe among familiar schoolbooks'?

12. Compare your answers to 11 with the suggested answers on pages 3–4 of the Commentary [see pages 427–8].

421

Ideas for materials development

13. Find examples in the text of the use of the past perfect tense. For each example say why you think the writer used the past perfect instead of the simple past.

14. Compare your answers to 13 with the suggested answers on pages 4–5 of the Commentary [see pages 428–9].

15. Later in the novel, the father asks his son to go on his new motor-bike to Hannah's house to deliver an important parcel to her.
(a) Write the dialogue in the scene in which the father asks the son to deliver the parcel.
(b) Imagine that you are the narrator. write the scene from the novel in which you deliver the parcel to Hannah's house.

16. Compare your answers to 15 to the answers on pages 5–6 of the Commentary [see pages 429–30]. These are answers which were written by other learners.

17. Read Extract 2 from the novel on page 2 of the Text Sheet in which the narrator goes to Hannah's house on his motorbike [see Figure 17.1]. If you'd like any further feedback on any of the written work that you've done in this unit, put your name on it and put it in the Feedback Box.

18. If you're still interested in the story, take the novel, *My Son's Story*, from the library shelf. Write down what you think the significance is of the illustration on the front cover.
Read the novel in your own time and then, if you wish, talk about in with one of the other students who's already read the book (their names are on the back cover). Add your name to those on the back cover.

Source: B. Tomlinson, From 'Openings', Penguin 1994. Copyright © Brian Tomlinson. Reprinted with permission.

Earlier in the chapter we mentioned that self-access work can be done on a larger scale outside the classroom. Ciel Language Support Network (2000) lists six key areas required for successfully implementing SALL:

1   Policymaking
2   Management
3   Staff development
4   Learner development
5   Learning resources
6   Curriculum design and assessment.

In the cases cited in Miller et al. (2007), the government, advisory panel and secondary schools all collaborated. Their report describes how a SAC was established by making sure that stakeholders such as management, teachers and students are all involved from the beginning and that both teacher and learner development take place systematically as the centre is being planned and developed. The project included staff development by the advisory group and teachers, learner development by the teachers and by the students themselves, and materials development by the teachers in order to ensure resources are suitable for their local context. They conclude that SALL implementation requires careful planning based on each context and that inclusion of stakeholders from the beginning helped 'a culture of SALL being promoted very quickly within the school, and a sense of ownership of the SAC among the students' (Miller et al., 2007: 227).

Regarding resources, Cooker (2008), after comparing SACs in Australia, Hong Kong, Japan, New Zealand and the United Kingdom, notes the following software and hardware to be typically housed in resource room/s or in purpose-built centre building:

- Authentic materials such as magazines, television programmes, films and music
- Graded readers (some with audio components)
- Language learning software/Web-based resources (CALL materials)
- Drama-based language learning materials
- Coursebooks
- Texts for specific skills (e.g. listening, reading, speaking, writing, grammar, vocabulary and pronunciation)
- Examination preparation texts.

She establishes criteria for evaluating self-access materials, reports her evaluation results for each kind and makes overall suggestions. The criteria she uses are as follows:

1   Exposure to English in authentic use
2   Meaningful English

  3   Interest
  4   Achievable challenge
  5   Affective engagement
  6   Cognitive engagement
  7   Opportunities for discovery about how English is used
  8   Opportunities for meaningful use of English
  9   Feedback on the effectiveness of use of English
 10   Positive impact
 11   Navigability
 12   Learner training
 13   Attractiveness

In addition to Cooker, there might be other possibilities for SAC resources:

- listening (self-monitoring) section or laboratory
- computer facilities with programmes on vocabulary, testing, reading and communication games
- video/DVD/blu-ray facilities
- wall charts analysing at a quick glance all materials available
- classified folders, drawers or boxes containing all the materials available in the centre as well as online catalogues
- answer sheets or self-correcting keys where appropriate.

Some centres may have consultation room/s for individual counselling with specially trained advisors.

1   If you do not have the possibility of either setting up or using a SAC in your institution, think of ways open to you for reorganizing your resources in small ways to individualize your classroom more effectively.
2   If you do have a self-access facility, think about some of your learners and their individual characteristics, and devise a plan of activities for each learner who will visit the centre for up to six hours per week on three separate occasions.

Once students have found their way around the centre, they can begin to devise an individualized plan that may, for example, include listening to general, social English, listening to lectures, some intensive reading (both general and perhaps subject specific), CALL practice and video listening with note-taking practice.

Many variables are involved in the setting up of a centre of these proportions, not least of which will be a range of staffing and budgetary issues. Materials will have to be prepared and written; the centre will have to be maintained and regularly added to, perhaps by learners themselves in some cases; the centre will have to be supervised and students will have to be advised/counselled.

We have attempted here to show the different proportions that self-access activities might take. As suggested earlier, it is possible for an institution, or even an individual teacher, to start off in a small way to begin with and to develop the facility when circumstances permit.

Advantages and shortcomings

Operating a self-access system will offer learners a wide choice of material and the possibility of becoming much more self-reliant and less teacher dependent. Learners should begin to understand more about their needs and how they prefer to learn. On the other hand, it has to be stressed that setting up a self-access system will involve a lot of time and work, usually on the part of the teaching staff, and that institutional constraints might mean that a full-scale centre will never become operational. However, if it is at all possible, the result is worthwhile.

From the materials point of view, there is a danger in providing too much that is related to classroom work: the materials become 'further practice' or 'follow-up activities' rather than allowing the students to explore and learn new things by themselves.

12.4   Focus on the Learner through Diary Studies

In recent years, some EFL (English as a Foreign Language) teachers have been exploring the advantages offered by learner diaries as yet another way of focusing on the learner as an individual with needs. There is now a growing awareness of how these diaries can establish an effective channel of communication between teacher and learners.

The process works as follows: the teacher enters into an individual 'contract' with each learner in the class whereby the learners keep a daily record of events that happen to them. The teacher will discuss contents of the diary in private with learners, who are free to develop the diary in whatever ways they wish. It may include observations of what they did on a particular day; observations and feelings about classes, teachers, peers, landladies; thoughts on how they feel they are learning with respect to a task, a class or the whole course. It is important for learners to understand the rationale behind the diary writing, and the following example of guidelines developed for learners can be useful in establishing this:

Learner Diary

The diary is a very important part of your studies here and will be of most help if you write it regularly. Your diary will enable you to express your opinions on all the classes that you take, and will help you to understand exactly what you need in your studies, as well as keeping a record of all the work you do. It will also give you valuable extended writing practice.

For the next few weeks we would like you to write each day about the lessons you have taken. There is no limit to the amount you can write, but we suggest that you spend at least 20 minutes a day on the diary. Your tutor will ask you to hand in the diary weekly; it will then be corrected, returned and discussed in tutorials.

It would be useful if your diary could include some of the following information:

- date/lessons followed
- how you think you performed
- what difficulties you had
- how you think that you might overcome these difficulties
- what you found most enjoyable/least enjoyable
- what you found most useful/least useful
- what you feel about a specific lesson/the course/group/teacher/yourself
- what you did in your spare time to practise your English
- any other thoughts, feelings and experiences relevant to your personal progress on the course.

Please look upon the diary as an exercise in writing fluently: your diaries will not be graded or strictly corrected, but frequent and important language errors will be pointed out to you. All diary entries will be treated confidentially.

Diary entries allow learners to report on a range of different observations according to the needs and wishes of each learner. Some learners may offer a simple account of what they have done during a particular day from a general point of view. Other learners, however, prefer to focus on particular classes that they have attended or a specific learning issue, such as how they feel they are progressing with vocabulary or with listening.

Diary writing can be very useful for learners. What sort of information for future work do you think the teacher might be able to get from reading the diaries?

As well as giving each student authentic written practice, these diaries can help the teacher with counselling the learner on specific learning problems that may not have surfaced in the classroom. They can sometimes offer a teacher a fresh insight into the study techniques of a particular learner, which, again, are not always apparent in the classroom, especially when the teacher may be dealing with large numbers. Nunan (1999: 167) provides samples of learner diary entries based on the learners' views of a writing class they had just taken. As a result of reading the diaries, it may also be possible for teachers to adjust materials and methods and to rearrange group dynamics in subsequent classes. For teachers wanting to investigate particular issues within their own classroom, they offer numerous possibilities of looking at the ways that individuals approach tasks and how they conceptualize and categorize teaching and learning events. By adding other data as well, it may be possible for the teacher to do a longitudinal study of a particular learner or small group of learners over a period of time – perhaps four to six months – in order to see what sort of learning/study profiles emerge for these learners.

12.5   Learner Training

We have examined individualization and some of its possible ramifications, such as using self-access activities both within and outside the classroom. We now start to look at other concrete possibilities for helping learners to learn more effectively by making them aware of their different language learning needs. As teachers, many of us have been involved in some aspects of learner training to a greater or lesser extent, by giving suggestions for organizing vocabulary books to using dictionaries more effectively, to how to exploit the environment outside the classroom for learning the target language wherever possible. As learner training can only really work effectively if we have some account of what a 'good' language learner actually does, let us briefly examine what has been studied and what we know. Griffiths (2008a) offers an edited collection of chapters on up-to-date research and pedagogical application, covering a comprehensive range of studies on the 'good' language learner. Attempts to develop systematic learner training can be traced back to research carried out in Canada in the 1970s by Naiman, Fröhlich and Stern into the strategies of 34 adults known to be 'good' language learners. They were interested in finding out the common characteristics of successful learners so that the findings can be applied to the teaching of less successful learners.

Before reading further, what do you feel would be the characteristics of a 'good' language learner?

From Naiman et al. (1975), the following generalized strategies emerge as being of most importance. Good language learners

- are aware of their own attitudes and feelings towards language learning and to themselves as language learners
- realize that language works as an organized system and is a means of communication and interaction
- assess and monitor their progress regularly
- realize that language learning involves hard work and time and set themselves realistic short-term goals
- involve themselves in the L2 and learn to take 'risks' in it
- are willing to experiment with different learning strategies and practice activities that suit them best
- organize time and materials in a personally suitable way and fully exploit all resources available.

Oxford and Lee (2008: 306) provide an update in that subsequent studies since the 1970s have found that

> The assumption of identifiability of a single set of characteristics possessed by the good language learner, and possible transferability of these characteristics to less fortunate learners gradually gave way to the realization that no single ideal set of characteristics existed. Instead, researchers . . . show that many different kinds of successful learners ply their varied talents in a wide range of settings.

Griffiths (2008a) classifies 'good language learner' studies into two sections: one on learner variables such as motivation, age, gender, learning styles, strategies, metacognition, autonomy, culture and aptitude; the other on learning variables such as linguistic content (e.g. vocabulary, grammar, functions), skills, methodology and error correction. Oxford and Lee (2008: 312–31) summarize the implications of all these studies on teaching:

1   Teachers must understand the crucial roots of language learning such as age, gender, personality and aptitude. It is especially important for teachers to remember that a slightly lower aptitude can be balanced by strong motivation and positive use of strategies. Teachers should never assume that a given learner lacks the aptitude to learn a language.
2   Teachers need to recognize that just as there is no single good language learner model, there is no single perfect instructional method or error correction technique that works for all students in all settings. Learners are different, every single one, even though some general categories can be identified. In response to learner diversity, principled eclecticism is required.

3   Because motivation is the fire that creates action, it is crucial for teachers to tend the fire. If learners are intrinsically motivated by challenge, personal satisfaction and interest, they will be active and involved. If they believe that language learning is unimportant, that they have no talent for learning languages, or that their cultural values and personal identity are about to be subverted, they will not have the motivation to learn the language.

4   Teachers must realize that they can provide strategy instruction that empowers and strengthens their students. Strategy instruction can occur in the four skills of reading, writing, listening and speaking, as well as in vocabulary, grammar and pronunciation. Through strategy instruction, teachers can help learners discover how to identify strategies that meet task demands and that relate to learners' styles. In doing so, teachers can become catalysts in the growth of culturally appropriate patterns of learner autonomy. However, strategy instruction must take into account learners' cultural expectations and beliefs; otherwise it will fail. If a shift of beliefs is essential in order for a student to learn new strategies, the teacher must first think carefully whether such a change in beliefs and strategies is necessary, worthwhile, culturally respectful, and linguistically appropriate. Only then should strategy instruction take place, and communication during and around it should be as open as possible. Understanding the cultural context is crucial for strategy instruction, just as it is for any other aspect of language learning and teaching.

It is interesting to note that Oxford and Lee emphasize the role of motivation as the vital driving force to successful learning and pay special attention to studies on volitional strategies. Such humanistic variables have often been neglected in past research due to the difficulties of quantifying such concepts, but they advocate more investigation in the future. We welcome such trends when we think of the fundamental fact that we may be able to help the learners to become aware and able to use strategies, but if they are not motivated to use them, the instructions may fall short of achieving success.

The research base for identifying issues dealing with language learning strategy training developed apace in the 1990s. Griffiths (2008b) provides a historical overview of attempts to classify and define strategies. Anderson (2008) focuses on metacognition and good language learners. According to Vandegrift (2002: 559), 'metacognitive strategies are crucial because they oversee, regulate, or direct the language learning task, and involve thinking about the learning process'.

Materials that purport to help learners for independent learning and autonomy have been developed for classroom use. Lowes and Target (1998) have some practical suggestions for achieving learner autonomy through a series of tasks designed to offer students choices about their learning, particularly in instances where students may come from educational backgrounds with very different cultural assumptions. The material is also designed to help teachers to reflect on the ways in which their teaching might help learners to make choices. The book also contains information on finding and using resources. Brown (2001) provides a very practical guide for teachers and learners in understanding the process of applying learning strategies. G. White (2008) provides a useful list of teachable strategies for listening and discusses an approach to training in strategy development and use. Oxford (2011) provides a comprehensive list of strategies in relation to the Strategic Self-Regulation Models. Her list includes cognitive, affective and socio-cultural strategies. She also discusses practice and theories that support them and provides useful references. Goh (2010) describes in detail a theoretical framework for listening material that is designed to nurture learners' self-regulation and self-appraisal during the listening process. Her framework consists of two major components: integrated experiential listening tasks and guided reflections on listening. In the former, 'learners are encouraged to arrive at an understanding of what they hear but are at the same time supported by activities that enable them to discover and use listening strategies as well as understand the nature of second language listening' (Goh, 2010: 188). The latter, that is, guided reflections 'encourage learners to attend to implicit processes in listening and help them make their knowledge of listening explicit' (Goh, 2010: 195) through, for example, the use of listening diaries or process-based discussions. The box overleaf shows a programme planning sheet for 'listening buddies', one of the integrated experiential listening activities. It shows how a pair of students are guided to collaborate in conducting a self-designed listening programme with a specific goal, plan and appraisal afterwards.

Listening as process: Learning activities for self-appraisal   193

Our personal listening program

Listening buddies: _____ and _____
Week _____
(Write your responses on separate sheets of paper)

Session 1
Listening material: _____
Type of text:
Source:
Equipment:
Date:
Time:
Other considerations, if any:

Our listening goal

    1. Why are we listening to / viewing this recording?
    2. What do we hope to achieve?
    3. How many times should we listen to / watch this recording? Why?

Our listening plan

    1. What do we know about this topic?
    2. What type of information can we expect to hear (and see)?
    3. What words can we expect to hear? (*Use a dictionary, if necessary.*)
    4. What difficulties can we expect?
    5. What strategies should we use when we encounter these difficulties?

Our listening report

    1. Why did we choose this recording / listening text?
    2. What was the most interesting thing about it?
    3. Are we satisfied with what we have understood? Why?
    4. Were we able to make use of our prior knowledge about the topic?
    5. What difficulties did we face? Were our strategies useful?
    6. What did we discuss after our listening?
    7. What did we agree or disagree about?
    8. What have we learned from each other about listening?

Figure 8.3: Outline for a personalized listening program for listening buddies

Source: C. Goh, Figure 8.3 on p. 193 from 'Listening as process: learning activities for self-appraisal and self-regulation'. In N. Harwood (ed), *English Language Teaching Materials: Theory and Practice* (2010). Copyright © Cambridge University Press 2010. Reprinted with permission.

Let us finish this section by looking at the following quotation from an EFL teacher being interviewed by Nunan (1991: 185), whose remark neatly encapsulates the feeling that a growing number of practitioners have with respect to the importance of learner training on their courses:

> As a teacher I see my role as being twofold. One is, yes, I am teaching the language, but I feel my other very important role is to assist the learners to take a growing responsibility for the management of their own learning. Within our programme, learners are with us for only a relatively – a short time, and we have to prepare them so that their learning can continue outside, erm, the length of their course.

On the whole, evidence tends to suggest that teachers are becoming increasingly aware of the various opportunities that individualizing the language classroom can offer to both learners and teachers alike.

> Consider the concept of learner training in your own teaching situation and the extent to which it would be feasible to incorporate it into your regular classes.

12.6   Conclusion

We began this chapter by looking at the concept of individualization by examining some definitions of the term, and have suggested various ways of implementing it both inside and outside the language classroom by incorporating combinations of self-access work, diary writing and learner training. We have tried to show that the most appropriate way of implementing individualization will depend, to some extent, on the context of the teaching operation that we work in. We have also attempted to illustrate that individualization is one way of reorganizing the management and resources of the classroom to try to maximize learning potential for as many people in the class as possible.

12.7   Further Reading

1   Cooker, L. (2008): *Self-access Materials*. This provides useful evaluation results of various kinds of materials for self-access learning.
2   Griffiths, C. (2008): *Lessons from Good Language Learners*. This is a comprehensive account of theories of Good Learner studies since its inception.

3 Kervin, L. and B. Derewianka. (2011): *New Technology to Support Language Learning*.

4 Maley, A. (2008): *Extensive reading: maid in waiting*, is a very informative and stimulating chapter on theories and practice of extensive reading. Useful links and references.

5 Motteram, G. (2011): *Developing Language Learning Materials with Technology* offers plenty of ideas for teachers wanting to explore individualization by the use of technology.

13

Observing the Language Classroom

13.1 Introduction

In this chapter we shall be looking at language classrooms in order to analyse in some detail what occurs in them. We shall begin by considering why the classroom might be a useful place to observe. Then we shall move on to examine, as teachers in the classroom, some of the different issues we might want to look at to become better informed about our own practice, and thus to improve our own teaching. After this we shall look at some of the different methods that have been used by teachers/researchers to gather data from classrooms. Our final aim in the chapter is to make some suggestions for observation tasks that could be of use to teachers working in a wide variety of classrooms, and to apply these tasks to transcripts of actual classroom interaction. We hope this analysis will help teachers to become further informed about their own practice.

13.2 Why Focus on the Classroom?

We noted in the previous chapter that what we teach does not necessarily result in learning taking place, nor does the best prepared lesson plan result in that plan being followed absolutely in the classroom. However carefully and skillfully prepared, the plan may impose a framework upon the class which could restrict rather than aid some learners. Because of this, what is

Materials and Methods in ELT: A Teacher's Guide, Third Edition.
Jo McDonough, Christopher Shaw, and Hitomi Masuhara.
© 2013 John Wiley & Sons, Inc. Published 2013 by John Wiley & Sons, Inc.

often noticeable about classrooms is that they are not necessarily neat, organized places, while interaction patterns that occur in them can be highly erratic and variable as genuine interaction cannot be completely planned for and requires co-operative effort. The co-operation required in the classroom setting involves everyone (teacher and learners) in managing many things at the same time, including who gets the chance to speak, what they speak about, what each participant does with the different opportunities to speak, and what sort of classroom atmosphere is created by learners and the teacher. For us as teachers, it is important to observe the interaction within the classroom because it can determine the learning opportunities that students get. We might also suggest that learners do not learn directly from a syllabus, but what they learn, or not, is the result of the manner in which this syllabus is 'translated' into the classroom environment, in the form of materials but also of their use by the teacher and learners in the class.

Lawson (2011) differentiates between two kinds of observation: 'observation as inspection' and 'observation as CPD (i.e. Continuing Professional Development)'. Observations as part of supportive continuing professional development seem to lead to positive results. For example, Joyce and Showers (2002) report that peer coaching reduces the stress that many of those being observed experience when being watched and is more likely to lead to professional development compared with observation 'as inspection'. Smith et al. (2004) point to the crucial importance of providing teachers with opportunities to participate in professional dialogues during planning, conducting observation and feedback discussion. Observation of this kind can provide opportunities for self-reflection and improvement of practice (Reeves and Forde, 2004).

13.3   What to Observe

> Think about your own classroom situation. If you had the chance to observe your own or a colleague's class, what sorts of things would you want to look at?

Tsui (2001) notes how current trends in classroom research tend to be of a more ethnographic, naturalistic nature rather than being strictly experimental. Within English language teaching (ELT) over the last decade several practitioners have attempted to focus on the language classroom within this perspective. Allwright and Hanks (2009) advocate the value of teachers finding answers through exploratory teaching in which they try out something that has been attracting their attention. Burns (2005) explains the concept of 'action research', which involves teachers asking questions and researching their own classrooms from an angle often empathetic to learners' experiences in the classroom. She reports action research projects in ELT from various parts of the world in which teachers were helped to raise awareness, improve skills and build up confidence. She discusses the strengths of practitioner research and the contribution it could make in supplementing published academic research. For further discussion of the teacher as researcher, see Chapter 14.

As we mentioned in the previous section, the classroom is the basic focus of the teaching and learning process, and there are literally hundreds of different permutations of classroom processes that we may wish to focus on: some of them perhaps very 'macro' or wide-ranging, such as how a particular teacher/group of learners use a textbook during a class; and some very 'micro', such as how a teacher elicits responses with a given class or how a particular learner or small group of individuals initiate turns in an oral skills class. We may wish to classify the information we get from observing the classroom into different areas such as information that focuses primarily on the teacher, the interaction patterns of learners in general, interaction of learners in pairs and/or groups, and the interaction of certain individuals with the teacher. If we wish to focus on the teacher, the following criteria could be offered as factors for observation. We may wish to investigate each one in turn, or we may decide to focus on some or all of them during a particular lesson:

- the amount of teacher talking time (TTT) contrasted with student talking time (STT) during the course of a particular class
- the type of teacher talk that takes place in a given class and where it occurs in the lesson
- the teacher's questioning/elicitation techniques
- how the teacher gives feedback to learners
- how the teacher handles 'digressions' in the classroom
- the different roles a teacher takes on during the class ('manager', 'facilitator' etc.)
- the teacher's use of encouragement and praise with learners
- the technical aids and materials a teacher uses to create learning contexts, and how the teacher involves the learners in these activities
- how 'tightly' a particular teacher corrects the learners' work.

There are many more possibilities, of course.

Think about other criteria that interest you as a teacher and add them to ours.

Nunan (1990) reports on a teachers' workshop where one of the groups participating in the workshop offered the following criteria as aspects of the class that they would like to look at. These were

wait time; repair techniques; 'fun'; questioning; materials; student–teacher interaction; scope of student response; amount of direction offered; class organization; lesson objectives; student and teacher talk time; control and initiative; who asks questions; context for language practice; how language is practised; methods used; digressions; variety of activities; interaction between students; lesson cohesion; teacher language; eliciting techniques; evaluation possibilities.

It is possible, of course, to extend these criteria, or combinations of them, to different classes in order to gain comparative data. For example, we may wish to compare the metalanguage (the language the teacher uses in the classroom to explain things) of the same teacher across a range of different classes – perhaps of different proficiency levels – in order to ascertain what similarities and differences exist across the various groups; or we may wish to observe how different teachers who teach the same class use the textbook or set of materials with that class. Some teachers feel that it would be useful to observe classes with a fundamentally different focus, such as a 'traditional', grammar-based class, in contrast to a more 'communicative' one, to see which could be deemed more successful from the learners' point of view. In a similar vein, we may wish to observe various things that occur in a given classroom with the learners themselves.

As Dörnyei and Murphy (2003) advocate, it may be useful to observe the group dynamics of a particular class during a language lesson in order to observe the interaction patterns that occur as a result of the exercises/tasks that the teacher sets up and manages. We might observe how well the learners seem to work together as a whole group, in small groups, in pairs or, indeed, if some learners prefer to work individually. Allwright and Hanks (2009) comment on the idiosyncratic nature of the language classroom and the fact that from the same lesson different learners will take away very different things. Analysing and perhaps contrasting two or more different learners in a class can help us as teachers to understand how these learners are using the classroom context to maximize their own learning potential, if at all.

To further illustrate the essentially puzzling nature of language learning in different classrooms, Allwright (1992) offers the following comments from teachers and learners, in different contexts, on what they found was particularly bewildering about language learning in their classrooms:

Teachers:

Why do students feel that they have to know all the vocabulary in order to understand a text?
Why do students use so little English in group work?

Do students work better in small groups or pairs?

What do students really want to learn from our lessons?

Learners:

Nobody ever explains the purpose of the exercise.

I don't understand why I don't understand English.

We try to understand the words not the lessons.

Teachers expect us to remember what we did in the last lesson but we don't operate like this.

Why does a teacher only ask me a question when I don't know the answer?

Being armed with an awareness of these factors can make classroom observation highly fruitful in that we may be able to make corrective adjustments to classroom teaching and management as a result of analysing the data we collect.

13.4   Different Approaches to Classroom Observation

We have already examined some recent trends in classroom observation at the beginning of this chapter and, having decided on the criteria we would like to observe in the classroom, we then have to decide which method we would like to use to gain access to the classroom for observation purposes. Allwright and Bailey (1991) list three main approaches classroom observers have typically used in classroom observation. The first of these is an experimental observation in which the teacher/researcher exercises a high degree of control over the classroom and purposefully becomes involved in the setting to try to discover the effects of the intervention. A control group would typically be set up. This 'scientific' approach to observation usually implies a one-way, (usually) top-down approach to classroom observation, since the teacher and class will be observed from the 'outside' by a linguistic 'expert' who will probably distinguish theoretical issues from actual classroom practice. The second main approach is called 'naturalistic enquiry' and may involve observers as participants either in their own or in someone else's class to 'see what happens'. The essential feature of this approach is to act as a fly on the wall and, where possible, not to influence normally occurring patterns of instruction and interaction.

Another way of implementing the approach is to video a class or to have one's own class videoed. However, sitting in on a class and/or videoing the experience are never neutral, because an unaccustomed presence in the class is bound to cause some disruption and alter the normal patterns of interaction. One advantage of this approach is that data from different classrooms can easily be seen and compared.

The third approach, already outlined earlier in this chapter, and an increasingly popular one, may be of more interest to practitioners as a whole as it is performed by teachers themselves from within the classroom.

Wajnryb (1992) comments how classroom observation has often been perceived in judgemental terms of assessment, evaluation or experimentation. Assessment and evaluation through observing the classroom are still an integral part of many teacher training programmes across the world and are deemed useful, especially where it is thought that the trainee might benefit from the evaluation and feedback of a more experienced teacher or trainer. As was discussed in Section 13.2, 'Why focus on the classroom?' Lawson's (2011) overview of teacher observation studies provides evidence of the benefits of observation as part of teacher support and development. In fact, there is a growth of emphasis on extending knowledge and understanding of what happens from inside the classroom (perhaps with some small-scale intervention). This is done by teachers themselves, perhaps collaborating with a colleague, either as part of a teacher development or classroom research project. (Classroom research by teachers is explored in the following chapter.) In this third approach, observation may include some naturalistic observation (perhaps of a colleague's class), but will typically involve teachers in the setting up of some small-scale intervention that will then be monitored by the teachers themselves over a period of time. Topics for this type of classroom research may be the development of oral competence of a learner/ learners, why the content of certain materials appears not to stimulate students, or whether 'active' tasks actually improve language learning.

Although the data for the observation may be gathered over a period of time, the teachers' observations are 'recycled' or fed back into the classroom process. Hence, within this framework, classroom observation does not occur from the outside, but instead the impetus comes from within the classroom in a 'bottom-up' fashion that allows the teachers themselves to decide which areas they wish to investigate. The observation involved in classroom research can be quite small-scale; it does not have to run to the dimensions of a large project. Stillwell et al. (2010) report on a collaborative materials development project in Japan which was combined with self-initiated peer observation and discussion, as part of an action research project. Four colleagues individually developed learner-centred materials. Each of them then invited the others to observe the materials being taught. They then discussed in meetings how the materials and the teaching could be improved. They also kept personal diaries during the process. The testimonials from the participating teachers and from the students seem to indicate that this endeavour resulted in enhanced materials and professional development.

Being observed at some stage during one's career as a teacher is usually mandatory. In the United Kingdom, for example, there is a (non-compulsory) national accreditation scheme for both public and private sector ELT, run by the British Council. Institutions are inspected according to several sets of criteria, one of which covers the expertise in the classroom of the teaching staff. Teachers working on the course are therefore observed during their lessons, inspectors paying attention to such factors as classroom rapport, teachers' knowledge of linguistic systems, involvement of learners in the lesson, monitoring of participation, error correction and so on. Many inspectors or assessors take notes on what they observe in the classroom and a possible 'observation of teaching' schedule is printed below.

> Before reading this observation of teaching schedule, what areas would you want to look at if you were observing a teacher in a class? After reading, see how many similarities and differences you noted.

Observation of teaching (20–30 minutes max.)

Group:

Class/Session:

A. Preparation of lesson

- specification of clear aims
- choice of appropriate material
- choice of appropriate teaching aids

B. Organization of lesson

- introduction
- progression of activities
- management of resources

C. Responsiveness to students' needs

- appropriate teaching techniques
- checking of students' understanding
- provision of helpful feedback
- involvement of students at all stages

D. Links between lesson and overall aims/syllabus
E. Evidence of professional expertise of teacher
F. Overall description of lesson and critical evaluation

> If you have been involved in any type of classroom observation, think about the approach you used. What were the advantages/disadvantages of this approach?

Professional development and peer observation have been attracting attention as they benefit both employers and employees in educational institutions. Some UK universities, for example, offer guidelines for observation on their web sites. The Professional Development page on the University of Nottingham web site, for example, offers advice on ways of conducting peer observation, advice for the observers and those who are being observed, as well as a putative training programme. It also provides an observation form that is much simpler and more flexible to use than many such forms. See http://pd.nottingham.ac.uk/eng/Learning-Teaching/Peer-Observation (accessed 24 January 2012).

Using video/digital recordings

If we are interested in understanding classrooms through observation in a co-operative way outside the realm of experiment/assessment (e.g. within a teacher development programme), there are a number of advantages in using pre-recorded video ('video' also represents various digital devices, e.g. digital video recorder) as a way of stimulating interest in the classroom for observation purposes. Sometimes, various administrative constraints may make it impossible to work with colleagues or in a team, and in such cases, videotaped classes can give teachers access to situations that they would not otherwise be able to observe. Videotaped lessons may also provide a springboard for the teacher-initiated research outlined above, in that the issues raised on the tape may have relevance to the observer's own classroom and could help in the formulation of an action plan for that teacher.

There are a few collections of videotaped lessons available in commercial packages for teacher education purposes as well as somewhat ad hoc collections on Youtube. 'Looking at Language Classrooms' by Lubelska and Matthews (1997) might be useful to teachers as it links topics from Wajnryb's Classroom Observation Tasks (1992) to corresponding video material.

The topics include attending to the learner, the learner as doer, the teacher's metalanguage, the language of feedback to error, lesson planning, grammar as lesson content, eliciting and giving instructions (refer to Lubelska and Matthews, 1997: 110 for more details).

Using video for classroom observation also has the advantage of being easy to set up – you do not have to disturb a class or organize one especially for the purpose, and you, the observer, have total control in that you may view, pause, replay and so on. Videotaped lessons are also useful to the extent that it is possible to focus on a single issue for one viewing, such as teacher talk, and then replay the tape to focus on a different issue, perhaps to observe how a pair of learners work together on an information-gap activity. It can be very motivating to see how other teachers work in the classroom without the threat of being evaluated oneself. When videos are viewed as a group activity with other teachers, any difference in perception and/or opinion that occurs can be usefully discussed. There is sometimes a danger, however, that we might see these lessons as offering a perfect model or, conversely, that we might be overcritical of what we consider to be the shortcomings of a particular teacher, rather than trying to get as balanced a perspective as possible.

As with all media, there are drawbacks to using video. We can rarely see the whole class performing as the camera can offer us only a partial view of the classroom. As lessons are usually edited, this also results in the observer getting an incomplete picture of the whole lesson. Nevertheless, given its versatility as a resource, videotaped material offers many possibilities for classroom observation.

13.5   Devising Classroom Observation Tasks

Earlier in the chapter we suggested that we might wish to observe the 'macro' details of the classroom or to analyse a particular aspect in more depth – such as observing the teacher in as comprehensive a way as possible or looking at a subtopic, such as the amount of teacher talk in a given class. In this section, we shall offer some suggestions for analysing different aspects of one area – that of teacher talk in the classroom – and then consider some criteria that we might wish to include in a general observation task sheet that could be used as an aid to provide an initial 'overview' of a classroom. Later we shall apply some of these details to the analysis of transcripts of English as a Foreign Language (EFL) classes to see how they might operate on 'real' data in practice. Teacher talk in classrooms has been an area of interest to researchers for a long time. What often surprises teachers themselves, as Nunan (1991) points out, is the sheer amount of talking that they themselves do in the classroom, sometimes up to 80% of the total class.

Depending on the aims of a particular lesson, the amount of teacher talk may vary; for example, a teacher may wish to focus on the explanation of a certain function or structure in one class that will entail a high degree of teacher talk, to be followed on by a range of student-centred tasks in the next class, which will include a higher amount of student talk. In the late 1970s, in the heyday of the communicative approach in Britain, it was generally thought that teachers should strive for a high degree of STT and a low amount of TTT in the classroom. However, some practitioners feel TTT is useful, not merely for organizing the classroom, but also because it can offer pertinent language acquisition and development opportunities, since the caretaker's speech used by the teacher can be considered as 'genuinely communicative' and 'comprehensible' and may be of considerable benefit to the learners.

Consider your own teaching situation. Think carefully about how much time you spend talking in the classroom as a proportion of the total lesson. Does this surprise you?

We may wish to observe how the teacher talk relates to the specific function of the teacher in the class at that point in time. Park (2010) describes a study in which she investigated teacher talk, especially in terms of the ratio of display and referential questions. 'Display question' means the asker already knows the answer as in a teacher asking a student, 'What's the opposite of "up" in English?' (Park, 2010: 160). A 'Referential question' is characterized as 'genuine information seeking' – a teacher may ask a student, 'Why were you absent yesterday?' because she does not know the reason and is interested in what the student has to say. Referential questions are considered closer to real-life communication (Ellis, 2008). Park's data provide evidence that the teacher used more display questions when she introduced new vocabulary and more referential questions when she was improvising as part of a drama activity. A similar tendency is reported in Ghosn (2010) when she describes a five-year research project which looked at the differences between literature-based and skill-based ESL courses. Her classroom observation transcripts show a lot more occasions of spontaneous and voluntarily meaning-focused interactions in the literature-based classes than the skill-based classes using a coursebook.

Nunan (1991) outlines three factors that ought to be considered when assessing the appropriateness and quantity of teacher talk. These are the point at which the talking occurs; whether it is planned or spontaneous, and if spontaneous, whether the digression is helpful or not; and the value of the teacher talk as potentially useful input for acquisition purposes. What constitutes appropriacy and quality may be thought of as matters of judgement and may be subject to considerable variation. Evidence also tends to suggest that the questions a teacher asks in the classroom can be extremely important in helping learners to develop their competence in the language. It is useful to observe whether teachers put questions to learners systematically or randomly, how long they wait for a response, and the type of question asked, from that requiring a simple one-word reply to higher-order referential questions where learners can provide information the teacher does not know. Similarly, in the case of feedback and correcting learners, we can observe how and when the teacher does this, and whether all learners receive treatment systematically.

Thus far, we have looked at some of the factors we might wish to observe pertaining to the teacher in the classroom. We could also, for example, turn our attention to one learner or to a pair of learners to compare how each of them tends to individualize whole-class instruction to their own benefit.

Let us now consider some of the general criteria we might find useful in order to observe as many facets of the language classroom as possible in the context of one language lesson. We have set these out in the form of a general observation task sheet as an example, which can be used as a prompt for making notes during an observation session:

1   Focus on Learners
    a)   Group dynamics. How well do they work together as:
        • a whole group
        • small groups
        • pairs.
        Do some prefer to work individually?
    b)   How well do they appear to relate to and interact with the teacher?
    c)   Is the students' apparent interest in learning sustained or enhanced?
2   Focus on the Teacher
    a)   Context of teaching
        How is a context for the lesson established?
    b)   Teacher's role
        What are the different roles assumed by the teacher during the class?
    c)   TTT
        What is the approximate amount of TTT in the lesson? What kind of teacher talk (e.g. display questions vs. referential questions) does she use?
    d)   Clarity
        Were the explanations given readily understood by the students?
    e)   Emotional support
        How much encouragement and care is offered to the learners and how is it done?
    f)   Use of aids/materials
        • If aids/materials are used what is their purpose in the lesson?
        • How effective are the aids/materials in amplifying or reinforcing the teaching points?
        • How effective are the aids/materials in helping the learners to understand and achieve learning?
    g)   Activity
        • What activity/activities are the students asked to perform?
        • Do they seem to be pertinent/useful in realizing the objectives of the lesson?
    h)   Classroom management
        • Are the activities smooth and effectively managed?
        • Do students seem to be clear about what they should be doing?

i) Correction/Feedback
   - How does the teacher give feedback to students at various stages of the activities? (e.g. positive encouragement, supportive reformulation of student's utterances, expansion of student's utterances, responsive and supporting attitudes to students' questions)
j) Motivation
   - How would you characterize the atmosphere of this class? For example, alert, hard-working, good humoured, keenly motivated and so on.
   - Note down any particular motivating features of this lesson.

3 Overall Comments/Observation

> If you have the opportunity, try this observation schedule with a colleague by observing each other's classes and producing feedback to each other. Add any other factors you feel are important to you in your teaching situation.

13.6 Applying the Tasks to Classroom Data

In this section we intend to look at the application to actual classroom practice of some of the observation tasks discussed above. We shall analyse materials and transcripts of different language classes in order to gain an overview of what is occurring in each of the classes. Clearly it would be useful to have access to the video material, but the transcripts also show a lot of detail.

2B   Lesson planning

BEFORE VIEWING

Individual teachers vary in the amount of planning they do.
Look at the following diagram of lesson planning areas:

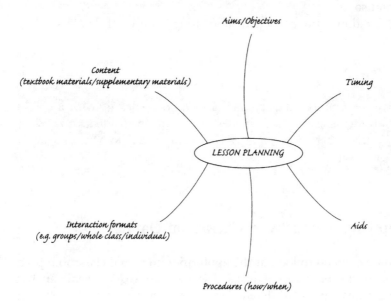

In pairs, rank these areas in order of importance, and discuss the reasons for your decision.
Discuss your ranking with the rest of the group, and add to the diagram any other points which
have come up in your discussion.

Sequence **2B** **Lesson planning**

WHILE VIEWING

1 You are going to watch part of a lesson based on the structures *used to* and *didn't use to*.
Here is an outline plan for the lesson. It contains details about the content, timing and aids, but
no information about interaction formats or procedures. As you watch the lesson, add details to
the outline plan about these two aspects. Then, after comparing your notes with a partner, watch
again to check them.
Note: Some parts of the lesson are not shown in the video extract.

```
                          Lesson plan

Aim:                  By the end of the lesson, learners will be
                      able talk about past habits.
Target structures: Used to / didn't use to
Aids:                 Cassette recorder, cassette
Book material:        Blueprint Two, Unit 31.


1 Present language (5 mins).
  e.g.    I used to live in Cuba.
          I didn't use to be a teacher.
2 Listening and True/False statements (10 mins).
3 Asking and answering questions about past life (18 mins).
          • appearance
          • spare time
          • books
          • places
  e.g.    Did you use to have long hair?
          Yes I did.
          So did I. / I didn't.
4 Game - 'Call My Bluff' (7 mins).
  (Making statements about a partner's past life.)
```

2 Consider the way in which this lesson plan was written.
Would you write out your plan in this way? If not, how would you remind yourself what to do
during the lesson?
Discuss the presentation of plans with the rest of the group.

WHILE VIEWING (40 mins)

1 It will probably be necessary for participants to watch the video twice to do this task. Suggested annotations are as follows:

Lesson plan

```
Aim:                By the end of the lesson, learners will be
                    able to talk about past habits.
Target structures:  Used to / didn't use to
Aids:               Cassette recorder, cassette
Book material:      Blueprint Two, Unit 31.
```

1 Present language (5 mins).
    e.g.   I used to live in Cuba.
           I didn't use to be a teacher.

Write sample sentences on board and <u>leave there</u>.

2 Listening and True/False statements (10 mins).

Individual work: learners write down T or F.

3 Asking and answering questions about past life (18 mins).
        • appearance
        • spare time
        • books
        • places
    e.g.   Did you use to have long hair?
           Yes I did.
           So did I./ I didn't.

Give an example of dialogue orally → Learners practise in pairs →
Some pairs present dialogue to class.

4 Game – 'Call My Bluff' (7 mins).
   (Making statements about a partner's past life.)

Learners prepare sentences about partner (true or false) → Two teams.
One learner keeps score on board.

2B   Lesson planning

School: Escuela Oficial de Idiomas, Las Arenas, Spain
Teacher: Ileana Reguera

Voiceover: At the start of the lesson, the teacher introduces the structure 'used to'.
Teacher: [writes on board] 'I didn't use to' pay attention to the negative. 'Use to', 'use to', hmm? Different from 'used to'. I didn't use to...work...as a teacher.
Tape: Woman 1: Exercise one. Dialogue.
Voiceover: The students then listen to the structure being used in a recorded dialogue, and answer some questions.
Tape: Man: There's the school I used to go to, when I was little.
Woman 2: It looks a bit old and depressing!
Man: I know! But it's all right inside. And you see that house over there?
Woman 2: What, the one with the white fence?
Man: Yes. I used to live there.
Teacher: Now, I would like you to work in pairs, with your partner, and, er...let's try to reproduce, sort of dialogue. [writes on board] You can talk about, er...your appearance...you can talk about, er...your spare time, or...the books...you read, or...the places...you went to...and so on. So thi...there are some cues, but of course you can speak about whatever you like. Er...the dialogue will consist of, er...A, for example, says, er...'What...', make a question...makes a question to B, for example, 'What did you use to look like when you were a little girl?' And B answers, 'Well, I used to have long, curly hair'. And A agrees, or disagrees. Hmm? If she agrees, 'Oh! So did I'. If she disagrees, 'Oh, I didn't'. And then B makes another question, to A; 'And what about you, did you use to wear glasses?' for example, and A answer 'Oh, yes, I did'. Right, so try to use short answers, 'yes I did', hmm? 'No, I didn't', or 'Nor did I'. Hmm? Is it clear? Just two minutes in pairs, and then you will speak aloud. Right? And you want to ask me any question, I will be ready to help you.
[Students work in pairs]
Student 1: What did you use to go, in the...
Student 2: I, er...used, er...to spend my holidays in Bilbao or Palencia because I used to live in Madrid.
[Fade out and in]
Teacher: OK? So, let's begin. Hmm? Let's break the ice. Estivaliz, can you play with, er...Rocio?
Student 3: Er...what did you use to look like as a child?
Student 4: Er...when I was a child...I used to be very fat, but now I don't eat too much, and I was thin.
Teacher: Yes, great! What about you, can you make...?
Student 3: No, I didn't. I was very thin, and...I used to have short, blonde hair.
Teacher: Really?
Student 4: And, what did use to...to do in your spare time?
Teacher: Good!
Student 3: I used to play with my sisters, at home.
Student 4: I...didn't.

Teacher: You didn't?
Student 4: No.
Teacher: Did you like...er...do you have any, I mean, have you got sisters or brothers to play with?
Student 4: Yes, er...I wa...well, *bueno* [=well], I am, er...one, er...sister, but I was, er...ten years, er...he was, er...one year.
Teacher: Oh, I see. So different ages. Good. What about you two, Elisa and, er...Rosa?
Student 5: Er...what did you use to look like as a child?
Student 6: I used to have short hair.
Student 5: Er...oh, I didn't, I used to have long hair.
Teacher: Did you? Long hair? What about now? What have you done with your long hair?
Student 5: Is more...I don't...*comódo* [=comfortable].
Teacher: Comfortable?
Student 5: Comfortable.
Teacher: Yes, good.
Student 6: Er...what did you use to do in your spare time?
Student 5: Er...I used to play tennis.
Student 6: Er...I didn't. I used to go with my friends.
Teacher: Did you? And what did you do with...what did you use to do with your friends? What did you use to play with, er...your friends? Or what did you use to go, or do?
Student 6: Mmm...we used to...to walk, er...
Teacher: Mm hmm. Along...
Student 6: Along, er...Las Arenas.
Teacher: Right. Mm hmm. Did you use to go and...for a picnic, from time to time, with your friends?
Student 6: Yes. Some...sometimes, ermm...on Saturdays, for example.
Teacher: Mm hmm. Yes. Did you enjoy it? Yes?
Student 6: Yes.
Teacher: Right. What about you two?
Student 2: Er...what did you use, er...to...er...spend your holidays?
Student 1: I used to go...Europe...
Teacher: To Europe?
Student 1: French, and...and sometimes, *bueno* [=well]...when I have, er...a big time, I, er...I pass my...my holidays on, er...on climb mountains.
Teacher: Yes, you spend your holidays, ermm...practising exercise, you mean? Climbing up and down the mountains?
Student 1: Yeah.
Teacher: With your friends?
Student 1: Yeah.
Teacher: And you...and you?
Student 2: No, no I didn't.
Teacher: You didn't. You don't look like a...being a climber!
Student 2: No! I spend...I used to spend my holidays in Palencia. Or, er...I used to, ermm...go to know, er...the ous...the outskirts, the...Mad...of Madrid.

Teacher: Good.
Student 2:   Er...the bor...bordering province.
Teacher: Yes. Good. So you...
Student 2:   Such as Toledo, Segovia...
Teacher: Right. It's a very good thing, at least you know places. And, er...anybody can tell me...
[Fade out and in]
Teacher: Right, so...Umm...you are going to...for example, every pair of students, every pair of you, er...is going to think...or to say aloud three...well, three would be too much, two...two each, eh? Two each, four altogether. Two sentences talking about, er...past habits, eh? Past routines. But the more incredible the better, do you know why? Because then the other group, hmm?...has to tell if the sentences they said, hmm?...were true or false. Right?
[Fade out and in]
Student: True. And the second is false.
Teacher: Right, so. You have a...perfectly right. So, er...
Student: Two points.
Teacher: Two points, for group B. Two points. Right, er...Sonia and, er...Fagita. Come on.
Fagita: Er...Sonia w...when Sonia was ten, er...she used to live on a farm.
Teacher: On a farm? Good. Another one?
Fagita: Er...when Sonia was, er...five, er...she used to have bl...very blonde hair.
Teacher: [laughs] Good. What about you? Oh, I have forgotten about yours, Margerita. All right?
Sonia: Er...when Fagita was ten I used, er...to speak five language.
Teacher: She used to speak five languages. Or you? Fagita or you?
Sonia: Fagita.
Teacher: Fagita used to speak five languages. Good. And another one?
Sonia: Er...when she, er...he was, er...four I used to help, ermm...his mother.
Teacher: You used to help her mother.
Sonia: In the cooking.
Teacher: Cooking. Doing the cooking and so on? What's your opinion, er...[inaudible] on Fagita's sentences, true or false?
Student 7:   I think, er...the last sentence in...is true, and, er...first is false.
Teacher: What's your opinion? Were you bluffing, or were you telling the truth? .
Fagita: I, er...wa...bluffing.
Teacher: You were bluffing? Number one? So?
Fagita: No.
Student: Yes!
Fagita: No, the two. The two sentences are, er...bluffing.
Teacher: So, how many points?
Student: One.
Teacher: Only one? OK. But I forgot about Margerita, so I have to for...forget about it. So only one person in each group, all right? What about you two? Come on!
Carmen: When did you...?
Teacher: [laughs] Don't be so impatient, Carmen!

Student 8:   Er...no, er...Carmen, the last year, er...met, er...handsome man, er...and she is going to get married with...
Carmen: Yes! I am going to marry! This year!
Teacher: We are not using 'used to', but it's OK. And the second one? Try to use 'used to'.
Student 8:   OK, er...er...she used to...to have, ermm...ermm...ermm...I don't...know...
Teacher: A small...? Cat, at home?
Student 8:   No...in the...
Teacher: A what?
Student 8:   A snake.
Teacher: A snake?
Student 8:   Yes.
Teacher: My goodness! She used to have a snake at home. Right, remember them. What about you, Carmen? Tell me something incredible about you.
Carmen: I used to, ermm...working a nurse.
Teacher: As a nurse?
Carmen: As a nurse.
Teacher: Oh! Good. She used to work as a nurse. And, er...another one.
Carmen: Er...Santa Marina, er...
Teacher: No, another sentence. A new one. Another one, yes.
Carmen: Only one, now.
Teacher: [laughs] Just one sentence! And enough, for you. A lot of work. All right? Could you tell me if, ermm...just to finish, if, er...it is false?
Student 3:   I think, er...your name?
Student 4:   Arantxa.
Student 3:   Arantxa is bluffing.
Teacher: Yes?
Student 3:   In both.
Teacher: In both?
Student: In both.
Teacher: Were you bluffing?
Student: Yes, I was.
Teacher: So you are completely right. So...
Student: Two points. [pron: as French]
Teacher: Poi...no, two points [pron: correct]. Team B. OK, so we cannot go on, so we can say that...the winner is...group B!
[Fade out]

Talking about teaching

Teacher: Of course, I think, er...drills are very useful. But, er...in some ways, I mean, I prefer to present the new language first...I mean make them feel motivated with, er...the language, try...I...I try to make them, um...use the language, the new language, as their own. So, when I present a...a new passage, hmm?...first of all I...I make, er...questions about, ermm...their own life, their own feelings, their own, ermm...hobbies. Hmm? So I...I force them to use the new language, using them. And, er...well after...presenting the...the, umm...the new language of course, er...I...I made...I made them, er...work in pairs, hmm? So, this is something they like a lot. Because they...they don't feel on their own but, er...with a partner's help they...they

do it much better. And if I play some background
music [laughs]...even better! Because they feel more
relaxed and, er...they...they speak, er...more loudly
and so on.
Of course they commit, ermm...mistakes. But, today
was not the, ermm...the day to force them to speak
accurately. But just should get familiar with, er...the
new structure, the new language, and reproduce it,
and...getting it as their own.

Source: D. Lubeleska, M. Matthews and A. Bampfield, 1999 in the booklet accompanying *Looking at language Classrooms*, pp. 48, 50–51, 126–128. Copyright © Cambridge University Press. Reprinted with permission of Cambridge University Press.

In this first extract we are invited to consider the area of lesson planning. The first task is to 'brainstorm' the topic with a colleague wherever possible.

If you have access to the video, the 'while viewing' task is for teachers to add details of the interaction formats or procedures (the trainers' notes contain answers).

Finally, examine the transcript and reflect on the teacher's comments at the end.

Consider the following questions in relation to the transcript. Again work with a colleague if at all possible.

1   Analyse the four main activities that the teacher asks the learners to perform. Consider them in relation to the concept of integrated skills.
2   Observe what the learners appear to be doing during these activities. Analyse pair/group arrangements in relation to activity.
3   Do the activities seem useful in realizing the objectives of the lesson?
4   How much teacher talk is there in relation to student talk? What are the different functions of the teacher talk and when does it occur?
5   How much correction and feedback does the teacher provide? Does it seem to be equal for all learners?
6   Do you feel that this is a teacher- or a student-centred lesson? Why? Note what the teacher says themself.
7   Allwright and Bailey (1991) mention the 'atmosphere' created in the classroom co-production. How would you characterize the atmosphere of this particular class?

When you have completed the above, read the two transcripts below, taken from Ghosn (2010: 31). The first transcript is taken from a primary school classroom in Lebanon where English is taught as the first foreign language, using a 'communicatively orientated, content-integrated, world-wide marketed ESL course'. The second transcript is also from an equivalent primary school classroom but the material they are using is an American literature-based reading anthology. What differences do you notice in the two transcripts in terms of teacher–student interactions, learner engagement and 'atmosphere' in the classes?

> S1:   Do your parents give you pocket money?
> S2:   My *dad* gives me pocket money.
> S1:   How much do they
> T: He said his *dad* gives him
> S1:   How much he
> T: How much *does* he
> S1:   How much does he give you?
> S2:   He gives me three pounds.

> T: Don't read what Rick's dad gives him! Say how much *your* dad gives *you*.
> S2:   ((I don't get pocket money.)) [in a quiet voice, blushing, looking down]
>   [giggles from some students]
> T: Oh, OK. Pretend that he gives you, say, five thousand pounds.

Source: I.-K. Ghosn, pp. 31–2, Chapter 2. In B. Tomlinson and H. Masuhara (eds) 2011, *Research for Materials Development in Language Learning*. London: Continuum. Copyright © Irma-Karina Ghosn.

> T: [reads] 'I've made some cookies for tea,' said Ma
> S1:   The lady she the mother ((not the maid like Hadia said))!
> T: Right, she is Sam's and Victoria's mother. See the cookies she has made
>   [points to the illustration]. Mmm! That's a big plate of cookies.
> [Several children lick their lips and make 'mmm' sounds.]
> S1:   Miss! Me, my mother she make cookies ((very tasty)).
> T: Uhhuh! Your mother makes delicious cookies too! Did you hear that?
> Ruba's mother also makes delicious cookies, like Sam's and Victoria's mother.

Source: I.-K. Ghosn, Transcript between T and S1 and transcript between T, S1 and S2, from pp. 31–2, Chapter 2. In B. Tomlinson and H. Masuhara (eds) 2011, *Research for Materials Development in Language Learning*. London: Continuum. Copyright © Irma-Kaarina Ghosn. Reprinted with the kind permission of the author and by kind permission of Continuum International Publishing Group, a Bloomsbury company.

13.7   Conclusion

In this chapter we have examined the reasons why classrooms are useful sources of information about teaching and learning and have considered some of the different criteria that we might want to observe in them. After this, we moved on to look at some of the different options open to us for observing the classroom. We then suggested that we might wish to concentrate in some detail on one aspect of the language classroom, such as teacher talk, or that we may wish to observe several criteria together, depending on our purpose. We then proposed a set of general observation criteria that we might find useful in order to get an overview of what is happening in a classroom. Finally, we examined transcribed data from different classrooms and applied focusing tasks to this data to try to gain further access to, and understanding of, what was occurring in these classrooms.

> How might your approach to what you do in the classroom be affected as a result of reading this chapter?

13.8   Further Reading

The following books give a useful overview of the area of classroom observation:

1   Allwright, D. and J. Hank. (2009): *The Developing Language Learner: An Introduction to Exploratory Practice.*
2   Bailey, K. and D. Nunan (eds) (1996): *Voices from the Language Classroom.*

In addition, the following chapter reports how teachers collaborated and used observation for materials and professional development:

3   Stillwell, C., B. McMillan, H. Gillies, and T.   Walker. (2010): *Four teachers looking for a lesson: developing materials with lesson study.*

14

Views of the Teacher

14.1   Introduction

Chapters on 'the teacher' are often, even traditionally, to be found at the end of books concerned with aspects of language teaching methodology. While such a format might be criticized on the grounds of relegating teachers to last place on a scale of importance, with learners certainly, but also materials and methods, having primacy, in the present book this is emphatically not the intention, and the position of this chapter is deliberate. It has been chosen because the teacher arguably represents the most significant factor in any language teaching operation. The teacher is typically a 'constant' in the throughput of different students in the institution, and works in different ways at the interface of several systems – the classroom, the school, the educational environment – all of which affect a teacher's professional attitudes and behaviour. A principal aim of this chapter, then, is to offer a view of the teacher as a synthesizer of all the aspects we have covered, as a professional who has to make sense of the decisions, opinions and perceptions of many different people. Certainly teachers will often experience this as pressure and conflict, which may be difficult to resolve. Nevertheless, we wish to stress the importance of a positive and active professional self-image, rather than a more passive and reactive one.

The chapter is broadly divided into three sections. In the first of these we examine the concept of 'role' and explore its possible dimensions for English

Materials and Methods in ELT: A Teacher's Guide, Third Edition.
Jo McDonough, Christopher Shaw, and Hitomi Masuhara.
© 2013 John Wiley & Sons, Inc. Published 2013 by John Wiley & Sons, Inc.

language teachers in general. We then go on to look particularly at the teacher's classroom role, focusing on the implications of innovation and change in materials and methods. These two sections, in other words, will be concerned first, with contextualizing 'role' and, secondly, with differences over time. Finally, a number of issues to do with the training and development of teachers will be raised, including a brief survey of the growing importance of teacher-research in English language teaching (ELT). We have included more activities and things to think about because of the nature of the topic and its reflective orientation, and the chapter finishes, quite intentionally, on an open-ended note.

14.2   The Teacher's Role

> Make a few notes on what you actually do as a teacher in a regular working week. Keep the notes – we shall refer back to them later.

Our own list looks something like this:

Preparing timetables
Spending a certain number of contracted hours in class
Preparing materials and handouts
Seeing students individually
Attending staff meetings
Arranging out-of-class activities
Writing reports
Marking tests and examinations
Planning courses and their associated teaching activities
Liaison with outside bodies and other institutions.

There are two obvious points to be made here. The first concerns the fact that any job specification is part of a network of interacting and overlapping roles; secondly, and related to the first point, we do our job in the context of a whole 'environment'. This now takes us full circle, and we shall be referring back explicitly to the points first raised in Chapter 1.

The concept of role

The list you have just made will show that you carry out a range of specified tasks within the social framework of an institutional structure. It is, then,

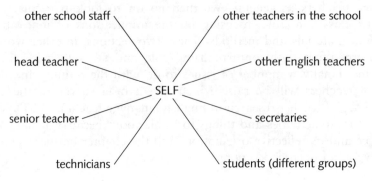

Figure 14.1   The role network.

self-evident that your work is not done in isolation, but that you need to interact, directly or indirectly, with a number of others – with students, obviously, with other teachers, with the head teacher (or head of department/principal), with non-teaching staff and so on. Both in your professional and in your private life you are a member of a role set, the group of people with whom you interact in any particular situation. Taking yourself as the focal person, you might like to represent your own most important role sets in diagrammatic form as in figure 14.1.

You could also do this with family and friends as the set, or alternatively for any leisure activity that you do regularly.

Teacher's roles may also be expressed in some kind of hierarchical relationship to each other where each person accepts or at least understands the organizational chain of authority and accountability. One example of how this view works in practice can be found in the scheme organized by the British Council for inspecting and recognizing private language schools in the United Kingdom. As well as the obvious categories of 'teaching' and 'professional qualifications', the extent to which a school performs its central teaching function is also evaluated in terms of the overall management structures, in addition to resources and the physical environment of the institution. Thus, a classroom teacher might be accountable to a senior teacher and through him to the principal, but also 'laterally', to colleagues with special areas of responsibility such as resource management.

The concept of 'role' has been studied in social psychology and related areas, including the investigation of behaviour in industrial and organizational settings. Dörnyei and Murphey (2003) argue that ELT professionals do not pay enough attention to group dynamics and the various roles that the teacher and the student play in the language classroom. Let us then consider three aspects of teacher roles that follow from the general features that we have just outlined:

1   We noted above the significant members of our own role set in any specific situation. The 'mirror image' of this, of course, is that we fulfil
certain roles in the role sets and networks of other people: we are therefore at any one time colleagues, employees, perhaps authority figures
in the classroom, somebody's superior, a casual acquaintance and so
on. There will also be differences in what is accepted as appropriate
institutional behaviour, and great variation in patterns of power and
authority.

2   There is arguably a great deal of truth in the assertion that 'we are
as others see us'. In other words, our image of ourselves as professionals
will be an amalgam of a whole range of perceptions and expectations,
and this takes us beyond the idea of a role as simply a list of tasks to
be carried out, or an officially issued job description. Bush (1984),
for example, refers to the theatrical image used by several writers in
which the actor plays out a role in accordance with the expectations
of an audience. This implies, however, that the actor is rather a passive
figure: Bush goes on to remind us that a role is not tidy and objective,
but that 'in practice the role-occupant brings to the position his or
her values, perceptions and experience and these will interact with
other expectations to determine the way the part is played' (Bush,
1984: 76). Moreover, the notion of a 'network' indicates that different
people's expectations will carry different degrees of importance: for
instance, an organization with a powerful authority figure at the head
may lead to a reduction in the weight attached to student views and
needs.

3   Most writing in the field of role theory recognizes – as indeed the previous points imply – that people inevitably perceive their own role as
multiple and complex. A number of secondary notions have therefore
evolved that reflect this. Handy's (1985, ch. 3) list is comprehensive, and
makes rather negative but probably realistic reading. He points out that
a role occupant can experience one or more of the following, which are
interrelated:

*   *Role conflict* – for example, our role as a classroom teacher and as
    an institutional examiner may not be fully compatible.
*   *Role ambiguity* – defined by uncertainty as to what is expected at any
    particular time.
*   *Role overload* – not the same as work overload – where the focal
    person is not able to integrate roles that are too many and too varied.
    Many teachers who are required to take on increased administrative
    or external duties may experience this as a problem.
*   *Role stress* – which Handy divides into role pressure (positive, where
    synthesis of roles and expectations remains possible), and its opposite,
    role strain.

Earlier in this section you drew up a simple 'role set' diagram with yourself as the focal person.

Consider now the range of roles that you play in your own institution. To whom are you responsible, and who is responsible to you?

Do any of Handy's points match your own experience, for example, as a result of increasing role diversification? In particular, is your own perception of your role(s) fully in line with what you take to be the expectations of others?

The wider environment

Up to now, we have been thinking of teachers in the setting of their own institutions. However, crucial as that is, the concept of 'role' cannot be restricted to the institution in which we work, and in a sense, our workplace is a microcosm of the wider environment. In the first chapter of this book we proposed a framework for thinking about materials and methods in which a number of contextual variables – management decisions, resource factors, types of learners and many more – were considered. Here we re-examine them from the perspective of the teacher as a 'focal person', and taking into account such factors as the teacher's potentially multiple roles, the expectations of others, and the inherent possibilities for conflict, pressure and so on. We might represent the situation as in figure 14.2 to show both the importance of the teacher as well as the direct and indirect effects of all these different 'layers' on the teacher's role.

Beyond the immediate environment of your own institution/school, try to enumerate from the outer layers in particular (a) the people (the other 'actors') and (b) the variables that you think have most influenced your understanding of your own role.

You may have listed your family and friends, or your own tutors; your students' peer groups and parents; external inspectors or advisers; the authorities who draw up your contract and decide on your salary and conditions; the writers of commercially published materials; agencies and organizations sponsoring students to take your programmes. For example, low pay sometimes indicates low social esteem of the profession and even low self-esteem,

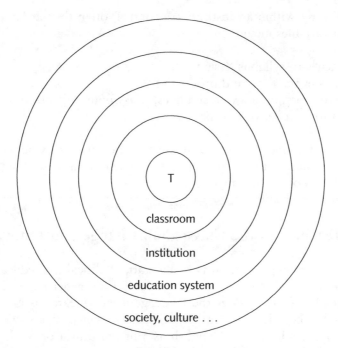

Figure 14.2 The teaching environment.

and may in turn mean there is a need to take on extra work, leaving no time for any more than routine preparation of classes, certainly not professional development. Conversely, the combination of a consultative environment that considers the views of everyone involved both within and outside the institution, and a recognition that teachers may be more active and productive if they are given time to develop resources, for example, will clearly lead to a more positive working atmosphere.

A useful way of looking at these issues from the teacher's point of view may be to differentiate the two broad headings of community-controlled variables and teacher-controlled variables (following Strevens, 1979). A few representative examples are given here. Community-controlled variables include

- cultural norms and restrictions, for instance, on materials or teaching styles
- standards of teacher training
- status of teachers in society
- attitudes to target language.

Under this heading you may also like to include institutional factors, such as class size, resources, time available and so on. Sometimes, of course, these may be directly within an institution's control; often they are not. Teacher-controlled variables include

- approaches to syllabus design
- materials evaluation (and production)
- choice of methodology, techniques, classroom organization (see next section for a fuller discussion).

You may of course disagree with some of the details of where exactly the responsibility lies, but the 'control' notion is helpful in describing the many different facets of a teacher's role.

14.3   Teachers in the Classroom: Change and Innovation

No teaching/learning situation is really static. Political and educational circumstances change, as do resources available for teacher training; views of methodology change, as does the language itself; research is gradually disseminated; teachers develop; learners' expectations change; and we are seeing dramatic changes in terms of English as a lingua franca or world Englishes (Graddol, 2006, 2010; Kirkpatrick, 2010; Jenkins et al., 2011). Most of our discussion in this section will focus on the teacher's classroom role, picking up the key implications for teachers of the materials and methods examined in this book.

> We would like you at this point to try to set out the most important changes in your own job, and role, over the last few years (5–10 years might be a useful period if you have been teaching that long). For example, do you have new areas of responsibility, either administrative or pedagogic? Have there been many innovations in the types of materials used? Have your students' attitudes to learning English changed in any discernible way? Are there any techniques you have adopted in the classroom that you did not use a few years ago, or conversely, have you abandoned any? Some of the changes you identify will be concerned with your role within the classroom, some with your role outside. In so far as they are separable, please take more time to think about the classroom context – learners, materials, methods.

Teachers will all have their own version of changing circumstances. The present writers, who teach English at most proficiency levels to adults coming to Britain for a variety of purposes, noted these general trends:

- Students will often have spent time in an English-speaking country already.
- Classes have become increasingly participatory.
- More detailed attention to needs and expectations is required of us, and for an English for Specific Purposes (ESP) teacher, this often includes some familiarity with learners' jobs or subject specialisms.
- There is a great amount of published material now available, appropriate in varying degrees.
- We spend more time engaged in various forms of individualized instruction.
- We need to respond to learners' needs for different kinds of delivery (e.g. blended learning, distance learning, overseas delivery).

In sum, we think it likely that your role will have become more diversified on many fronts.

Before going on to identify some of the more specific aspects of classroom-based change, it is worth reflecting for a moment on innovation in language teaching. In education we are often expected to adapt to changes and innovations. Such changes may include

- the adoption of new textbooks
- the introduction of pedagogical/methodological 'reforms' that teachers have not been trained to implement
- the establishment of new goals for a language teaching programme
- the prescription of new teacher–learner role relationships (as when a central authority specifies less 'teacher-fronted' and more 'learner-centred' work).

Any of these changes might well involve various small and large conflicts and disturb teachers' mental frames as they can threaten their routines and sense of security. The level of disturbance that teachers feel may be different depending on who proposes the change and how it is implemented and also on teachers' perceptions of how much it is likely to lead to improvements. In figure 14.2 we have shown how teachers are surrounded by various layers of the teaching environment. Waters and Vilches (2008: 20) discuss the '. . ."two cultures" situation, where the policy level "ethos" may exhibit a lack of empathy for that of the implementation level'. The policy level involves curriculum developers, decision-makers and advisors whereas the implementation level involves principals and teachers. The policymakers are not directly affected by their decisions but the implementors are, often significantly within a short span of time. The lack of fit between the policy and its implementation, reported in the recent literature on managing innovation in ELT, could result in unsuccessful, partial or distorted implementation (Waters, 2009; Kennedy and Tomlinson, 2012). Waters (2009) provides an overview of studies on innovation and explores various models of successful management of change. Kennedy and Tomlinson (2012) discuss how innovation may be implemented in materials.

Change, materials and methods

The main purpose of this book has been to survey current trends in materials and methods for ELT, to trace the sources and development of those trends, and to link our everyday practice as teachers with the principles on which that practice is based. Let us now briefly review some of the themes that have recurred with reference to the classroom context.

1   There has been a significant shift towards more 'communicative' views of both language and behaviour.

2   We have a deeper understanding of language and how it is used. An analysis of language goes beyond sentence grammar to the level of 'discourse' – of paragraph structure and longer texts. Corpora studies have shown how spoken and written discourses are different, and what may be regarded as errors in writing may in fact be features of speech. These findings have been filtering through to teaching methods and materials.

3   A variety of classroom 'management' techniques have been introduced to allow for more realistic practice of language in use.

4   Syllabuses and materials are often based not only on one or two, but on several organizing principles linked together in quite complex ways as can be seen in the 'multi-component' construction of recent global coursebooks.

5   Research into the characteristics of language skills has contributed to gradual changes in the materials we use for teaching the four skills. For instance, the range of possible activities has been extended a long way beyond the traditional procedures of reading/listening, followed by a test of understanding through comprehension questions. In other words, we can now work with a notion of language-as-process, as well as language-as-product.

6   Our methodology has also been affected by increased understanding of differences in learning styles and strategies, justifying the distinction between whole-class and smaller group work, and also allowing, where feasible, for the individualization of instruction in various formats.

7   The global trend of English being used as a lingua franca is affecting both theory, practice and materials. What kinds of language? What are the optimal targets for language learning? What kinds of language achievements are acceptable in exams and in the multilingual and multicultural world?

8   Computer-assisted language learning has been developing rapidly not only at an institutional but also at an individual level, as seen in M-learning

where autonomous learners can use mobile technology and manage learning anywhere any time. In resource-rich contexts, teachers need to be aware of possible different modes of delivery inside and outside the class.

Not all of these developments have taken place simultaneously, of course. The various aspects of change have had differential impact and usefulness, and have naturally occurred at different times in different contexts, as you will be well aware from your own teaching situation. Note, too, that sometimes an innovation has direct implications for what a teacher in some sense needs to know (knowledge about text structure, for example, or the psychology of comprehension). At other times it influences attitudes and perceptions about appropriate roles and behaviour as well (such as restructuring the classroom arrangement or introducing self-access material). We can now reflect on how these perspectives have contributed to the diversification of the teacher's role that we referred to earlier.

1 Reflect upon your roles you have considered in Section 14.2 'The teacher's role' earlier in this chapter. You have considered various roles you play in networks and in the hierarchy in the educational system that you belong to.
2 What is your view now in relation to the teacher's overall role?

A number of writers on methodology and teacher training have proposed various ways of labelling the language teacher's potential roles. Harmer (2007a: pp. 108–17) offers these:

1 The teacher as controller of everything that goes on in the classroom.
2 The teacher as prompter who provides sensitive encouragement for the learner to steer their learning.
3 The teacher as participant in student activities.
4 The teacher as a resource who provides information, ideas and advice.
5 The teacher as tutor, particularly useful with small groups and individuals working on longer pieces of work.
6 The teacher as organizer of a range of activities.
7 The teacher as assessor. Obviously the 'examiner' role is one of our traditional functions, but Harmer extends it to include the importance of giving regular feedback, as well as just correction and grading.

8   The teacher as observer, both to give feedback and also to evaluate materials and methods.

Tudor (1993) discusses teacher roles with specific reference to the notion of the 'learner-centred classroom', arguing that this shift of focus will have obvious implications. Far from the traditional conception, then, of 'knower' and 'activity organizer', the teacher will need to

- prepare learners (for awareness of goals, language and so on);
- analyse learner needs;
- select materials;
- transfer responsibility; and
- involve learners

which are challenging roles for many of us.

Finally, Smith (2011), referring specifically to Norway, discusses the multifaceted roles that teacher educators are expected to play in accordance with Norwegian and international innovations in education. Teachers are expected to manage being

- versatile pedagogues who are 'able to build a bridge between theory and practice' (Smith 2011: 342)
- role models 'as teachers and as academic researchers' (Smith 2011: 343)
- researchers as 'consumers of research, producers of research and teachers of research' (Smith 2011: 343)
- administrators who are in charge of planning and delivering the course, who offer support, assess the students' achievement and evaluate the whole course.

In addition she notes that much of the administrative work is now handled with ICT (Information and Communication Technologies), and this requires teachers to be IT literate. Smith (2011: 344) then points out how complex and demanding an ideal educator is expected to be:

> To sum up, the teacher educator should fit into all the roles stated above, and have attributes characterised as self-reflective, empathetic, communicative, collegial, open-minded, flexible, organised and assertive (yet without being perceived as 'difficult'), which leads one to wonder whether this ideal really exists.

Smith also emphasizes the importance of establishing support systems for professional development programmes that build on the strengths of diverse members of staff.

1 Look back over the list of teacher functions that you made earlier: to what extent does it overlap with/differ from the (fairly representative) list that we have just set out?

2 Now try to put the individual points in order of importance for your own teaching circumstances. For instance, are you primarily an instructor/assessor and only secondarily a 'resource' for your students?

3 If you are studying/working with other teachers, it will be interesting to compare your order of priority with theirs. Do colleagues working in the same situation necessarily have identical perceptions? And do teachers from different contexts see things differently from you?

As a short commentary on this activity, and to conclude this section, two observations can be restated. First of all, the roles and tasks that we perform result from a complex network of factors, and an objective definition, however necessary, will not be sufficient. They derive from our own perceptions, from the attitudes and expectations of many others, and not least from the language teaching materials that we are expected (or choose) to work with. Secondly, and finally, it should be remembered that this whole discussion has been based on the assumption that change and innovation are an inevitable part of our professional lives, and therefore no individual role description can be regarded as frozen in time.

14.4 Preparing the Teachers

The 'good language teacher'

In Chapter 12, we discussed recent updates by Oxford and Lee (2008) on 'good language learner' studies. It is now widely accepted that many kinds of successful learners make use of their strengths in various ways to achieve their goals. Researchers have questioned the feasibility and usefulness of trying to identify a single set of characteristics possessed by the good language learner so that they can be transferred to less successful learners.

In a similar vein, the sheer number of variables involved in teaching will probably mean that identifying the characteristics of a good language teacher remains an impossible task, especially when we consider the sheer diversity of teaching contexts around the globe (Canagarajah, 2005). Even if we were to take the very straightforward criterion that a 'successful' teacher is one whose learners achieve good examination results, this in fact tells us rather little: we do not learn much about the relative importance of the teacher's preferred style and method, nor about the role of materials, and certainly nothing specific about the part played by different elements in an individual learner's success. Indeed this may have more to do with motivation, attitude, interest and so on, than with anything the teacher has to offer directly. Nevertheless, and despite the impossibility of precise measurement, most of us will have an opinion as to what constitutes a 'good language teacher'.

Assume that you have some responsibility for the selection of English language teachers for the specific context in which you work. Make a list of the qualities you would be looking for in that selection process.

Your suggested list may contain some of the following, and you may have others that we have not thought of:

Knowledge of the language system
Good pronunciation
Experience of living in an English-speaking country
Qualifications (perhaps further training taken, or in-service development)
Classroom performance
Evidence of being a good colleague
Length of time as a teacher
Ability to write teaching materials
Careful planning of lessons
Same L1 as students, or a sound knowledge of it
Experience of a variety of teaching situations
Personal qualities (outgoing, interested in learners and so on)
Publications
Knowledge of learning theories
Wide vocabulary
Ability to manage a team of teachers.

We should note here that this list includes factors of different kinds: knowledge, skills awareness and personal attributes. Knowledge may include theories and practice of teaching and learning of the English language. Skills may involve planning, delivering the course, managing the classroom, assessment and evaluation. Awareness may derive from experience of working with colleagues and students in a variety of teaching situations. Lastly, but not least, is what the teacher as an individual brings into the classroom (e.g.

personality, enthusiasm). As Oxford and Lee (2008) emphasize, the teacher's ability to 'ignite the fire' seems to help the learners to spark off their own initiative and drive in learning.

Although it is difficult to categorize our list of teacher qualities under one heading or the other in any precise way, the basic distinction of knowledge, awareness, skills and personal attributes is quite helpful when considering the 'training' of teachers, to which we now turn.

Teacher training, teacher education and continuing professional development

Opinions as to the necessary and desirable qualities of a teacher form the basis for the specification (whether by education authorities, training bodies, colleges and so on) of the goals of teacher training and teacher education programmes. Detailed design of such programmes will in turn derive from this setting of aims and objectives.

There is a large literature on the issue of 'training' versus 'education', and on the more concrete design specifications for a variety of training programmes for different levels of experience, different contexts, differing in duration and with varying degrees of generalizability. A few references are given in the further reading section at the end of this chapter. It has not been the purpose of this book to conclude with a detailed proposal for a particular kind of teacher preparation programme, a topic well covered elsewhere (e.g. Harmer, 2007b; Richards and Farrell, 2011; Scrivener, 2011), but rather to trace developments and trends in materials and methods in our field and then to ask, in this final chapter, what might be the most appropriate perspectives on the role and training of teachers. With this in mind we look, firstly, at the relevance of the training/education debate, and secondly, invite you to formulate your own ideas for the in-service preparation of teachers.

Sometimes the notion of 'training' is used to refer to pre-service programmes for new teachers, with 'education' the preferred term for in-service work with experienced professionals. The idea here is that the narrower concept of training is more applicable to people who need to acquire a knowledge of the basic 'tools' of the job, whereas education implies a broader range of knowledge and skills. More usually, it is argued that both beginning and experienced teachers need elements of each, albeit with differing emphasis and depth. If we glance back at the list of possible teacher qualities, it is quite difficult to claim that some are relevant in pre- or, conversely, in-service situations. Pennington (1990: 134) relates the issue to the concept of professionalism, and argues that teachers require both 'a repertoire of skills' and 'judgement to apply these skills'. Richards (1990) puts forward a similar distinction with the terms 'macro' and 'micro' as approaches to teacher preparation. By 'micro' he means techniques – what teachers actually do that is directly observable and quantifiable (amount of teacher talk, questioning techniques, types of classroom tasks and the like). By 'macro' he means a 'holistic' approach that focuses on 'the total context of classroom teaching and learning in an attempt to understand how the interactions between and among teachers, learners and classroom tasks affect learning' (Richards: 1990: 9). In other words, a macro approach is concerned with a teacher's ability to make judgements and inferences, to explore the relationship between different types of activity and their effect on learning, and to raise questions about one's own practice. It is both exploratory and generative. Clearly, a teacher needs to be familiar with both kinds of approach.

1   We would like to ask you now to consider the design of a possible teacher preparation programme. In order to keep the task within manageable proportions, we suggest a number of guidelines.
2   Assume you have responsibility for planning an in-service course for teachers. Think in terms of a short programme of one or two weeks' duration, and relate your planning to a teaching context with which you are familiar.
  • What components would you wish to include?
  • Approximately what proportion of time would you devote to each one?
  • What would be your preferred methodology – lectures, workshops, discussion, observation of teaching?
  • To what extent, if at all, would you give consideration to participants' personal proficiency?
  • If possible, try also to decide whether you are more concerned with 'macro' or 'micro' approaches, and with 'subject matter' or 'action-system' knowledge, as we defined them earlier in this section.

We have worked with a number of different groups of teachers from many different countries, and have also asked them to design a teacher programme along these kinds of lines. Some groups have chosen to work on a specific area or theme only. Examples would be 'Approaches to Skills Teaching and Learning', 'The Development of Self-access Materials' or 'Communicative Methodology'. More often, these teachers have designed a broader-based programme, and the following content headings are typical (the points are not given in any particular order and are illustrative, not rules):

Errors and mistakes: analysis, feedback and guidance
Syllabus design and lesson planning
Materials evaluation
Principles of learning
Audio-visual aids
Observation of teaching (using video if possible)
Preparing supplementary materials
Using English outside the class
Sharing problems
Test design
Sound system of English.

Suggested methodology of presentation is a mixture of lecture input and workshop-discussion, depending on the area under consideration. Our groups have placed particular emphasis on the importance of working out in advance the needs and interests of teachers on such an in-service course, and on the principle that a starting point of enquiry in everyday practice will usually be more fruitful than a rundown of theory for its own sake, however stimulating.

14.5 Teacher Development and Teacher Research

At several points in the preceding section we indicated the importance of seeing language teachers not only as carriers of knowledge about language and techniques, but as active and questioning professionals who are able to make generalizations and inferences from the basis of their own practice. The three overlapping but distinct views of teacher preparation – training, education, development – are seen by Wallace (1991) as three models, which he terms (1) the 'craft' model, where a range of practical techniques is learned from an experienced person; (2) the 'applied science' model, implying a one-way application, and often therefore separation, of theoretical research to practice; and (3) the 'reflective' model, with the teacher as a 'reflective practitioner'.

In Chapter 12 we considered the values of nurturing learner autonomy and ways of helping learners to manage their own learning. Likewise, considering the diverse situations and different teachers' needs, it would be best for each teacher to play an active role in their own development processes. In his state-of-the art review, Mann (2005: 108) discusses teachers' autonomy in this process and points out that 'a number of studies have demonstrated that more reflective teachers are better able to monitor, make real-time decisions and respond to the changing needs of learners than less reflective teachers'. Mann also gives a detailed account and references for various ways of

encouraging reflection, self-evaluation, exploration, research and collaboration in teacher development.

The notion of critical reflection is a rapidly growing area of attention
because it is seen as the first step for teachers to become investigators of
pedagogical issues, that is, classroom researchers. There is a long tradition
in general education of encouraging classroom teachers to be initiators of
research and development, as well as recipients of external investigation and
results (e.g. by professional researchers or educational administrators).
Research, in other words, is done 'by', not only 'on' or 'to' teachers, and is
thus much more readily integrated into questions of practice. Hopkins
(2002) offers a clear overview of 'the teacher as researcher', and also introduces the closely related concept of 'action research' or 'classroom research
by teachers' as he prefers to call it. The key point, in Hopkins's words
(2002: 5) is 'the teacher's ability . . . to think systematically and critically
about what he or she is doing and to collaborate with other teachers. Central
to this activity is the systematic reflection on one's own classroom experience to understand it and to create meaning out of that understanding'.
Richards and Farrell (2005) provide a number of procedures for self-
monitoring and self-evaluation and suggest various forms of lesson reports,
checklists and questionnaires.

In ELT there is a growing literature on ways in which a 'reflective'
approach – put simply, an attitude of curiosity – can lead to teacher-generated
investigations. Burns (1999, 2005, 2010), although referring to 'action
research', makes the following point that is relevant to any kind of teacher-
generated research: 'The major focus of action research is on concrete and
practical issues. . . . It is conducted in naturally occurring settings. . . . Its
approaches are essentially "participatory" in that they are conducted by and
with members of the actual community under study' (Burns, 1999: 24). She
lists a wide range of areas nominated by teachers as starting points for such
research, including affective factors, course design, materials and resources,
learning strategies, classroom dynamics, the teaching of specific skills, and
assessment (Burns 1999: 56–8). A similar perspective is put forward by
Richards and Lockhart (1994), who discuss the following 'dimensions', each
of which can of course be subdivided, as suitable for reflection and practical
investigation:

- Exploring teachers' beliefs.
- Focus on the learner.
- Teacher decision-making.
- The role of the teacher.
- The structure of a language lesson.
- Interaction in the second-language classroom.
- The nature of language learning activities.
- Language use in the classroom.

There is no space here to discuss methods in detail. Briefly, however, all the following methods are possible even within modest and small-scale teacher research projects. In no particular order:

1 Classroom observation (systematic, open, descriptive).
2 Teaching and learning diaries and logs.
3 Introspection and verbal reports (such as think-aloud).
4 Questionnaires and surveys.
5 Interviews (structured, semi-structured, ethnographic).
6 Experiments and quasi-experiments.
7 Case study (not strictly a 'method'; normally uses a mix, to study individuals, groups or specific contexts).

For details of available research methods, and for discussion of both quantitative and qualitative approaches, readers are referred to the references at the end of the chapter.

Finally, teacher development can also be equated with personal development. There are many activities that teachers can in principle engage in if they wish to extend their understanding of their role. They may, for instance, put themselves in the position of their students by learning another language (Gower, 1999; J. McDonough, 2002). They may choose to attend courses or workshops, join a local teachers' network, go to conferences, write a regular teaching diary, learn something about educational management or counselling. Obviously each individual's working environment will determine to what extent these courses of action are realistic. This whole area has been incorporated into various teachers' organizations, including TESOL (Teaching English to Speakers of Other Languages) and IATEFL (International Association of Teachers of English as a Foreign Language). IATEFL, for example, has associate organizations in a number of countries, and also runs several Special Interest Groups (SIGs), one of which in fact is concerned with Teacher Development.

Wallace's (1991: 166) conclusion offers an appropriate ending to this book too, which has throughout attempted to encourage teachers to think critically about the major aspects of their own everyday professional reality. Wallace writes:

> An important aim of the reflective approach to teacher education is to empower teachers to manage their own professional development. Surely few things could be more conducive to raising the standards of teaching than a cadre of teachers who have the skills, ability and motivation to develop their practice. . . . A second aim of this approach is to enable teachers to be more effective partners in innovation. In many situations teachers themselves are not recognized as possible agents of change . . . innovation is always a top-down affair. . . . If foundations have been laid where, during their training period, at least some

teachers have had an opportunity to be reflective and collaborative, then it might be possible for their professional expertise to be harnessed to implement innovation more effectively.

We would like you to consider two final questions here relating to your own development as a teacher:

1   What kinds of activities have you done – or would you like to do – outside the daily classroom context that are of professional interest to you? A little earlier we gave just a few examples, which you might like to refer back to.
2   What are some of the issues that concern you as a teacher? For instance, would you like to have a clearer picture of the contribution of groupwork techniques to learning? Are you interested in the 'acceptability' to different people of the errors that your learners make? Would you like to compare your experiences of a particular class with those of a colleague? How useful are bilingual dictionaries, and do they affect a student's memory for vocabulary? Would it be useful to carry out a longitudinal 'case study' of an individual learner? How can we match more closely the statutory teaching materials to learners' needs and interests?

But these only represent a few of our questions, and we leave you now to generate some of your own.

14.6   Further Reading

1   Hopkins, D. (2002): *A Teachers Guide to Classroom Research*. This book was written in the context of mainstream education. The title is self-explanatory, as a way into issues of professional development.

2   The following books offer an overview for language teacher preparation:

Harmer, J. (2007b): *The Practice of English Language Teaching*.
Richards, J. C. and T. Farrell. (2011): *Practice Teaching: A Reflective Approach*.
Scrivener, J. (2011): *Learning Teaching – The Essential Guide to English Language Teaching*.

3   For practical discussion of teacher reflection and research in ELT, see:

Burns, A. (2010): *Doing Action Research in English Language Teaching*.
Richards, J. C. and T. Farrell. (2005): *Professional Development for Language Teachers – Strategies for Teacher Learning*.

4   For a comprehensive overview of methods in the broader context of the theory
    and principles of research, see:

Cohen, L., L. Manion and K. Morrison. (2007): *Research Methods in
    Education.*
Denscombe, M. (2010): *The Good Research Guide: For Small-scale Social
    Research Projects.*
Dörnyei, Z. (2007): *Research Methods in Applied Linguistics: Quantitative,
    Qualitative, and Mixed Methodologies.*

Bibliography

Abbs, B. and I. Freebairn (1977): *Starting Strategies*. Harlow: Longman.

Alderson, J. C. (2000): *Assessing Reading*. Cambridge: Cambridge University Press.

Allwright, R. L. (1984): Why don't learners learn what teachers teach? The interaction hypothesis. In D. M. Singleton and D. G. Little (eds): *Language Teaching in Formal and Informal Contexts*, Dublin: IRAAL, 3–18.

Allwright, R. L. (1988): *Autonomy and individualisation in whole class instruction*. In A. Brookes and P. Grundy, 35–44.

Allwright, R. L. (1992): *Understanding classroom language learning: an argument for exploratory teaching*. Talk given at Essex University, February 1992.

Allwright, R. L. and K. Bailey (1991): *Focus on the Language Classroom*. Cambridge: Cambridge University Press.

Allwright, D. and Hanks, J. (2009), *The Developing Language Learner: An Introduction to Exploratory Practice*. Basingstoke: Palgrave MacMillan.

Anderson, K., J. Maclean and T. Lynch (2004): *Study Speaking*. Cambridge: Cambridge University Press, 2nd edition.

Anderson, N. (2003): Scrolling, clicking and reading English: online reading strategies in a second/foreign language. *The Reading Matrix* 3/3, 1–33. http://www.readingmatrix.com/current.html [Accessed 8.05.2010].

Anderson, N. J. (2008): Metacognition and good language learners. In C. Griffiths (ed) *Lessons from Good Language Learners*. Cambridge: Cambridge University Press, 99–109.

Angouri, J. (2010): Using textbook and real-life data to teach turn-taking in business meetings. In N. Harwood (ed): *English Language Teaching Materials: Theory and Practice*, Cambridge: Cambridge University Press, 373–94.

Materials and Methods in ELT: A Teacher's Guide, Third Edition.
Jo McDonough, Christopher Shaw, and Hitomi Masuhara.
© 2013 John Wiley & Sons, Inc. Published 2013 by John Wiley & Sons, Inc.

Argent, S. and O. Alexander (2010): *Access EAP: Foundations Course Book*. Reading: Garnet Education.

Arnold, J. (ed) (1999): *Affect in Language Learning*. Cambridge: Cambridge University Press.

Aston, G. (1993): The learner's contribution to the self-access centre. *ELT Journal* 47/3, 219–27.

Bailey, K. (2001): *Observation*. In Carter and Nunan, 114–19.

Bailey, K. and H. Masuhara (2012 forthcoming): Language testing washback: The role of materials. In B. Tomlinson (ed) *Applied Linguistics and Materials Development*. London: Continuum Bloomsbury.

Bailey, K. and D. Nunan (eds) (1996): *Voices from the Language Classroom*. Cambridge: Cambridge University Press.

Baines, E., P. Blatchford and A. Chowne. (2007): Improving the effectiveness of collaborative group work in primary schools: effects on Science attainment. *British Educational Research Journal*. 33(5), 663–80.

Ballard, B. (1984): Improving student writing: an integrated approach to cultural adjustment. In R. Williams, J. Swales and J. Kirkman (eds): *Common Ground: Shared Interests in ESP and Communication Studies*, ELT Documents 118. London: Pergamon/The British Council, 43–54.

Bao, D. (2006): Breaking stereotypes in coursebooks. In J. Mukundan (ed) *Readings on ELT Materials II*. Petaling Jaya: Pearson Longman Malaysia, 70–83.

Barfield, A. and S. Brown. (eds.) (2007): *Reconstructing Autonomy in Language Education: Inquiry and Innovation*. Basingstoke: Palgrave Macmillan.

Barker, D. (2011): The role of unstructured learner interaction in the study of a foreign language. In S. Menon and J. Lourdunathan (eds), *Readings on ELT Materials IV*. Petaling Jaya: Pearson Longman, pp. 50–71.

Bartlett, F. C. (1932): *Remembering: A Study in Experimental and Social Psychology*. Cambridge: Cambridge University Press.

Bartram, M. and R. Walton (1991): *Correction: Mistake Management: A Positive Approach for Language Teachers*. Hove: Language Teaching Publications.

Bax, S. (2003): CALL – past, present and future. *System* 31, 13–28.

Bell, D. (2008): *Passport to Academic Presentations*. Reading: Garnet Education.

Bowers, R. (1980): The individual learner in the general class. In H. Altman and C. James (eds): *Foreign Language Teaching: Meeting Individual Needs*, Oxford: Pergamon, 66–80.

Boyle, R. (1994): ESP and distance learning. *English for Specific Purposes* 13/2, 115–28.

Bradbury, A. (2010): *Successful Presentation Skills*. London: Kogan Page, 4th edition.

Brandl, K. (2002): Integrating internet-based reading materials into the foreign language curriculum: from teacher-to student centred approaches. *Language Learning & Technology* 6/3, 87–107. http://llt.msu.edu.

Breen, M. (1987): Contemporary paradigms in syllabus design. *Language Teaching* 20/2, 81–92, 20/3, 157–74.

Breen, M. and C. Candlin (1987): Which materials? A consumer's and designer's guide. In L. E. Sheldon (ed): *ELT Textbooks and Materials: Problems in Evaluation and Development*, ELT Documents 126. London: Modern English Publications/The British Council, 13–28.

Brewster, S (1991) *Intermediate Listening*. Walton-On-Thames, Nelson.

British Council (1983): *Teaching and Learning in Focus*. London.

Brock, C. A. (1986): The effects of referential questions on ESL classroom discourse. *TESOL Quarterly*, 20 (1), 47–59.

Brookes, A. and P. Grundy (eds) (1988): *Individualisation and Autonomy in Language Learning*. ELT Documents 131. London: Modern English Publications/ The British Council.

Brown, H. D. (2001): *Strategies for Success: A Practical Guide to Learning English*. NY: Pearson Education.

Brown, G. and G. Yule (1983a): *Teaching the Spoken Language*. Cambridge: Cambridge University Press.

Brown, G. and G. Yule (1983b): *Discourse Analysis*. Cambridge: Cambridge University Press.

Burns, A. (1999): *Collaborative Action Research for English Language Teachers*. Cambridge: Cambridge University Press.

Burns, A. (2005): Action research: an evolving paradigm? *Language Teaching*, 38, 2, 57–74.

Burns, A. (2012): Teaching speaking in a second language. In B. Tomlinson and H. Masuhara (eds): *Applied Linguistics and Materials Development*, London: Continuum International Publishing Group.

Burns, A. and B. Seidlhofer (2010): Speaking and pronunciation. In N. Schmitt (ed): *An Introduction to Applied Linguistics*, second edition. London: Hodder Education, 2nd edition, 197–214.

Bush, T. (1984): *Key roles in post-school management*. Management in Post-Compulsory Education. Block 3 Course Materials, Course E324, Milton Keynes: The Open University.

Bygate, M. (1987): *Speaking*. Oxford: Oxford University Press.

Byrne, D. (1981): *Integrating skills*. In Johnson and Morrow, 108–14.

Canagarajah, S. (ed.) (2005): *Reclaiming the Local in Language Policy and Practice*. Mahwah, NJ: Lawrence Erlbaum.

Canale, M. (1983): From communicative competence to communicative language pedagogy. In J. C. Richards and R. W. Schmidt (eds): *Language and Communication*, London: Longman, 2–27.

Canale, M. and M. Swain (1980): Theoretical bases of communicative approaches to second language teaching and testing. *Applied Linguistics 1*, 1, 1–47.

Carrell, F., J. Devine and D. Eskey (eds) (1988): *Interactive Approaches to Second Language Reading*. Cambridge: Cambridge University Press.

Carter, R. (2001): *Vocabulary*. In Carter and Nunan, 42–7.

Carter, R. and D. Nunan (eds) (2001): *The Cambridge Guide to Teaching English to Speakers of Other Languages*. Cambridge: Cambridge University Press.

Carter, R., R. Hughes and M. McCarthy (2011): Telling tails: grammar, the spoken language and materials development. In B. Tomlinson (ed): *Materials Development in Language Teaching*, second edition. Cambridge: Cambridge University Press, 2nd edition, 78–100.

Carter, R. A. and M. J. McCarthy (2006): *Cambridge Grammar of English: A Comprehensive Guide to Spoken and Written English Grammar and Usage*. Cambridge: Cambridge University Press.

Celce-Murcia, M. and E. Olshtain (2000): *Discourse and Context in Language Teaching*. Cambridge: Cambridge University Press.

Chambers, F. (1997): Seeking consensus in coursebook evaluation. *ELT Journal* 51/1, 29–35.

Chapelle, C. (1998): Multimedia CALL: lessons to be learned from research on instructed SLA. *Language Learning and Technology* 2/1, 22–34. http://llt.msu.edu.

Chapelle, C. (2001): *Computer Applications in Second Language Acquisition: Foundations for Teaching, Testing, and Research*. Cambridge: Cambridge University Press.

Chinnery, G. (2006): Going to the MALL: Mobile Assisted Language Learning. *Language Learning and Technology*, 10(1), 9–16.

Clandfield, L. and A. Jeffries (2010): *Global Pre-Intermediate*. Oxford: Macmillan.

Clare, A. and J. Wilson (2011): *Speakout Intermediate*. Harlow: Pearson Longman.

Cochran-Smith, M. (1991): Word processing and writing in elementary classrooms: a critical review of related literature. *Review of Educational Research* 61, 107–55.

Coe, N., R. Rycroft and P. Ernest (1983): *Writing Skills: A Problem-Solving Approach*. Cambridge: Cambridge University Press.

Coffield, F., D. Moseley, E. Hall, and K. Ecclestone. (2004): *Should we be using learning styles? What research has to say to practice*. London: Learning and Skills Research Centre.

Cohen, A. D. (1998): *Strategies in Learning and Using a Second Language*. Harlow: Longman.

Collins (2001): *COBUILD English Language Dictionary*. London: Collins, new edition.

Connor, U. (2004): Intercultural rhetoric research: beyond texts. *Journal of English for Academic Purposes* 3, 291–304.

Cook, G. (1997): Key concepts in ELT: schemata. *ELT Journal* 51/1, 86.

Cook, G. (1989): *Discourse Analysis*. Oxford: Oxford University Press.

Cook, V. J. (2001): *Second Language Learning and Language Teaching*. London: Arnold, 3rd edition.

Cooper, J. (1979): *Think and Link*. London: Edward Arnold.

Cortazzi, M. and L. Jin. (1996): Cultures of learning: Language classrooms in China. In H. Coleman (ed) *Society and the Language Classroom*. New York: Cambridge University Press.

Council of Europe (2001): *Common European Framework of Reference for Languages*. Cambridge: Cambridge University Press.

Cox, K. and D. Hill (2011): *EAP Now!* Harlow: Pearson Longman, 2nd edition.

Coyle, D., P. Hood and D. Marsh (2010): *Content and Language Integrated Learning*. Cambridge: Cambridge University Press.

Cullen, R. and V. Kuo (2007): Spoken grammar and ELT materials. *TESOL Quarterly* 41/2, 361–86.

Cunningham, S. and B. Bowler (2005): *New Headway Pronunciation*. Oxford: Oxford University Press.

Cunningham, S. and P. Moor (1999): *Cutting Edge: Intermediate*. Harlow: Longman.

Cunningsworth, A. (1995): *Choosing Your Coursebook*. London: Longman.

Dalton, C. and B. Seidlhofer (1994): *Pronunciation*. Oxford: Oxford University Press.

Davies, C., F. Tup and D. Aziz (2003): *Life Accents*. Singapore: Times Media Private Ltd.

Davies, F. (1995): *Introducing Reading*. London: Penguin.

Day, R. R. (1990): *Teacher observation in second language teacher education*. In Richards and Nunan, 43–61.

Dellar, H. and A. Walkley (2004): *Innovations Intermediate*. London: Thomson/ Heinle.

Dellar, H. and A. Walkley (2010): *Outcomes Intermediate*. Andover: Heinle, Cengage Learning EMEA.

Dellar, H., A. Walkley and D. Hocking (2004): *Innovations Intermediate*. Andover: Heinle/Cengage Learning.

Denmark, W. and R. Miles (2004–2007): *The Turnabout Series*. Bangkok: Assumption University Press.

Deterding, D. (2010): Variation across Englishes – Phonology. In Kirkpatrick (ed) *The Routledge Handbook of World Englishes*. Oxon: Routledge, 385–99.

Dickinson, L. (1987): *Self-instruction in Language Learning*. Cambridge: Cambridge University Press.

Dickinson, L. (1989): Learning purpose, learning structure and the training of learners for autonomy. In C. Cecioni (ed): *Proceedings of the Symposium on Autonomy in Foreign Language Learning*, Florence: Language Centre, University of Florence, 30–42.

Dixon, D., H. Baba, P. Cozens, and M. Thomas (eds) (2006): *Independent Learning Schemes: A Practical Approach*. TESOL Arabia. Available from: tailearn@yahoo. com.

Dodge, B. (1997): *Some thoughts about Webquests*. http://webquest.sdsu.edu/about_ webquests.html [Accessed 8.05.2010].

Dogancay-Aktuna, S. (2005): Intercultural communication in English language teacher education. *ELT Journal 59.* 2, 99–107.

Donna, S. and M. Hancock (2008): *English Pronunciation in Use*. Cambridge: Cambridge University Press.

Dörnyei, Z. (2005): *The Psychology of the Language Learner: Individual differences in second language acquisition*. Mahwah, NJ: Lawrence Erlbaum.

Dörnyei, Z. and Murphy, T. (2003): *Group dynamics in the language classroom*. Cambridge: Cambridge University Press.

Dubin, F. and E. Olshtain (1986): *Course Design*. Cambridge: Cambridge University Press.

Ducate, L. and N. Arnold (eds) (2006): *Calling on CALL: From Theory and Research to New Directions in Foreign Language Teaching*. San Marco, TX: CALICO.

Dudeney, G. (2000): *The Internet and the Language Classroom: A Practical Guide for Teachers*. Cambridge: Cambridge University Press.

Eastment, D. (1999): *The Internet and ELT*. Oxford: Summertown.

Ellis, B. and G. Sinclair (1989): *Learning to Learn English*. Cambridge: Cambridge University Press.

Ellis, G. (1996): How culturally appropriate is the communicative approach? *ELT Journal 50/3*, 213–18.

Ellis, R. (1997): The empirical evaluation of language teaching materials. *ELT Journal 51/1*, 36–42.

Ellis, R. (2008): *The Study of Second Language Acquisition* 2nd edn. Oxford: Oxford University Press.

Ellis, R. (2010): Second language acquisition research and language-teaching materials. In N. Harwood (ed) *English Language Teaching Materials – Theory and Practice*. Cambridge: Cambridge University Press pp. 33–57.

Eskey, D. E. (2005): Reading in a second language. In E. Hinkel (ed) *Handbook of Research in Second Language Teaching and Learning*. Mahwah, N. J.: Lawrence Erlbaum Associates, pp. 563–79.

Farver, J. M., Y. K. Kim and Y. Lee (1995). Cultural differences in Korean- and Anglo-American pre-schoolers – social interaction and play behaviours. *Child Development*, 66, 1088–99.

Fenner, A.-B. and G. Nordal-Pedersen (2008): *Searching 9, Learner's Book*. Oslo: Gyldendal Norsk Forlag AS.

Fenton-Smith, B. (2010): A debate on the desired effects of output activities for extensive reading. In B. Tomlinson and H. Masuhara (eds) *Research for Materials Development in Language Teaching – Evidence for Best Practice*. London: Continuum International Publishing Group.

Ferris, D. (1999): The case for grammar correction in L2 writing: a response to Truscott (1996). *Journal of Second Language Writing* 8, 1–11.

Ferris, D. (2003): *Response to Student Writing: Implications for Second Language Students*. Mahwah, NJ: Lawrence Erlbaum Associates Inc.

Ferris, D. (2006): Does error feedback help student writers? New evidence on the short- and long-term effects of written error correction. In K. Hyland and F. Hyland (eds): *Feedback in Second Language Writing – Contexts and Issues*, Cambridge: Cambridge University Press, 81–104.

Field, J. (2008): *Listening in the Language Classroom*. Cambridge: Cambridge University Press.

Fleming, N. D. (1995). I'm different; not dumb: Modes of presentation (VARK) in the tertiary classroom. Research and Development in Higher Education, Proceedings of the 1995. Annual Conference of the Higher Education and Research Development Society of Australia (HERDSA) 18: 308–13.

Flower, L. and Hayes, J. R. (1981) A Cognitive Process Theory of Writing, *College Composition and Communication*, Vol. 32, No. 4, pp. 365–87.

Flowerdew, J. and L. Miller (2005): *Second Language Listening: Theory and Practice*. Cambridge: Cambridge University Press.

Fox, G. (1998). Using corpus data in the classroom. In B. Tomlinson (ed) *Materials Development in Language Teaching*. Cambridge: Cambridge University Press, pp. 25–43.

Freeman, D. (1996): *Redefining the relationship between research and what teachers know*. In Bailey and Nunan, 88–118.

Gaies, S. (1980): *Classroom-centered research: some consumer guidelines*. Paper presented at *Second Annual TESOL Summer Meeting*, Albuquerque, NM.

Gaies, S. and R. Bowers (1990): *Clinical supervision of language teaching: the supervisor as trainer and educator*. In Richards and Nunan, 167–81.

Gairns, R. and S. Redman (1998): *True to Life*. Cambridge: Cambridge University Press.

Gardner, H. (2006): *Multiple Intelligences – New Horizons*. New York: Basic Books.

Ghosn, I.-K. (2010): Five-year outcomes from children's literature-based programmes vs Programmes using a skill-based ESL course – The Matthew and Peter effects at work? In B. Tomlinson and H. Masuhara (eds) *Research for Materials Development in Language Learning – Evidence for Best Practice*. London: Continuum International Publishing Group, 21–36.

Goh, C. (2010): Listening as process: Learning activities for self-appraisal and self-regulation. In N. Harwood (ed) *English Language Teaching Materials – Theory and Practice*. Cambridge: Cambridge University Press.

Goh, C. M. and A. Burns (2012): *Teaching Speaking: A Holistic Approach*. New York: Cambridge University Press.

Goodwin-Jones, R. (2008): 'Mobile-computing trends: lighter, faster, smarter'. *Language Learning and Technology*, 12 (3), 3–9.

Gower, R. (1999): Doing as we would be done by. *Modern English Teacher* 8/4, 7–15.

Grabe, W. and R. Kaplan (1996): *Theory and Practice of Writing*. London: Longman.

Grabe, W. (2002) Dilemmas for the development of second language reading abilities. In J. C. Richards and W. A. Renandya (eds) *Methodology in Language Teaching: an Anthology of Current Practice*. New York: Cambridge University Press, pp. 276–86.

Graddol, D. (2006): *English Next*. London: British Council.

Graddol, D. (2010): *English Next. India*. London: British Council.

Grant, N. (1987): *Making the Most of Your Textbook*. London: Longman.

Grellet, F. (1981): *Developing Reading Skills*. Cambridge: Cambridge University Press.

Griffiths, C. (ed) (2008a): *Lessons from Good Language Learners*. Cambridge: Cambridge University Press.

Griffiths, C. (2008b): Strategies and good language learners. In C. Griffiths (ed) *Lessons from Good Language Learners*. Cambridge: Cambridge University Press, 83–98.

Gruba, P. (2004): Understanding digitised second language videotext. *Computer Assisted Language Learning* 17/1, 51–82.

Guest, M. 2002. 'A critical 'checkbook' for culture teaching and learning'. *ELT Journal* 56/2: 154–61.

Guse, J. (2010): *Communicative Activities for EAP (English for Academic Purposes)*. Cambridge: Cambridge University Press.

Gutierrez, G. A. G. (2003): Beyond interaction: the study of collaborative activity in computer-mediated tasks. *ReCALL* 15/1, 60–81.

Haines, S. (1995): For and against: pairwork. *Modern English Teacher* 4/1, 55–8.

Halliday, M. A. K. (1975): *Learning How to Mean: Explorations in the Development of Languages*. London: Edward Arnold.

Halliday, M. A. K. and R. Hasan (1976): *Cohesion in English*. London: Longman.

Hancock, M. and S. Donna (2012): *English Pronunciation in Use Intermediate* (2nd Edition) with Answers, Audio CDs (4) and CD-ROM. Cambridge: Cambridge University Press.

Handy, C. B. (1985): *Understanding Organisations*. London: Penguin, 3rd edition.

Harmer, J. (1998): *How to Teach English*. Harlow: Longman.

Harmer, J. (2001a): Coursebooks – a human, cultural and linguistic disaster? *Modern English Teacher* 10/3, 5–10.

Harmer, J. (2001b): *The Practice of English Language Teaching*. London: Longman, 3rd edition.

Harmer, J. (2007a): *How to Teach English: An Introduction to the Practice of English Language Teaching*. 2nd Edn. Harlow: Longman.

Harmer, J. (2007b): *The Practice of English Language Teaching*. 4th edn. Harlow: Longman.

Harmer, J. (2012): *Just Right Intermediate*. Andover: Heinle, Cengage Learning, 2nd edition.

Hayes, J. R. and L. S. Flower (1980): Identifying the organisation of writing process. In L. W. Gregg and E. R. Steinberg (eds): *Cognitive Processes in Writing*, Hillsdale NJ: Erlbaum Associates, 3–30.

Hedge, T. (1983a): *Freestyle*. Walton-on-Thames: Nelson.

Hedge, T. (1983b): *Pen to Paper*. Walton-on-Thames: Nelson.

Hedge, T. (2000): *Teaching and Learning in the Language Classroom*. Oxford: Oxford University Press.

Hedge, T. (2005): *Writing*. Oxford: Oxford University Press, 2nd edition.

Hedgecock, J. S. (2005): Taking stock of research and pedagogy in L2 writing. In E. Hinkel (ed): *Handbook of Research in Second Language Teaching and Learning*, Mahwah, NJ: Lawrence Erlbaum Associates, Inc, 597–614.

Herbert, D. and Sturtridge, G (1979): *Simulations. ELT Guide 2*. London: The British Council.

Hewings, M. (2004): *Pronunciation Practice Activities*. Cambridge: Cambridge University Press.

Hill, S. (1994): Cooperative communities in early childhood. *Australian Journal of Early Childhood*, 19(4), 44–8.

Hill, D. A. (2003): The visual element in EFL coursebooks. In B. Tomlinson (ed) *Developing Materials for Language Teaching*. London: Continuum, 174–182.

Holliday, A. (1994): *Appropriate Methodology and Social Context*. Cambridge: Cambridge University Press.

Holliday, A. (2005): *The Struggle to Teach English as an International Language*. Oxford: Oxford University Press.

Hopkins, D. (1993): *A Teacher's Guide to Classroom Research*. Buckingham: Open University Press, 2nd edition.

Howarth, P. and R. Hetherington (eds) (2000): *EAP Learning Technologies*. Leeds: Leeds University Press.

Hu, G. (2002): Potential cultural resistance to pedagogical imports: The case of communicative language teaching in China. *Language, Culture and Curriculum*, 15, 2, 93–105.

Hu, G. (2003): English language teaching in China: Regional differences and contributing factors. *Journal of Multilingual and Multicultural Development*, 24, 4, 290–318.

Hubbard, P. and C. Siskin (2004): Another look at tutorial CALL. *ReCALL* 16/2, 448–61.

Hughes, R. (2010): *Teaching and Researching Speaking*. Harlow: Pearson Education, 2nd edition.

Hyland, F. (2000): ESL writers and feedback: giving more autonomy to students. *Language Teaching Research* 4, 33–54.

Hyland, K. (1993): Language-learning simulations: a practical guide. *English Teaching Forum* 31, 4. Available from http://exchanges.state.gov/englishteaching/forum-journal.html.

Hyland, K. (2003): *Second Language Writing*. Cambridge: Cambridge University Press.

Hyland, K. (2010): *Teaching and Researching Writing*. Harlow: Pearson Education Ltd., 2nd edition.

Hyland, K. and F. Hyland (eds) (2006): *Feedback in Second Language Writing: Contexts and Issues*. Cambridge: Cambridge University Press.

Hymes, D. (1972): *On communicative competence*. Philadelphia: University of Pennsylvania Press.

Imhoof, M. and H. Hudson (1975): *From Paragraph to Essay*. London: Longman.

Islam, C. and C. Mares (2003): Adapting classroom materials. In B. Tomlinson (ed): *Developing Materials for Language Teaching*. London: Continuum, 86–100.

Jacob, G. (1988): Co-operative goal structure: a way to improve group activities. *ELT Journal* 42/2, 97–101.

Janks, H. (2009): *Literacy and Power*. New York: Routledge.

Jenkins, J. (2007): *English as a lingua franca: Attitude and identity*. Oxford: Oxford University Press.

Jenkins, J., A. Cogo and M. Dewey (2011): Review of developments in research into English as a lingua franca. *Language Teaching* 44.3, 281–315.

Jepson, K. (2005): Conversations – negotiated interaction – in text and voice chat rooms. *Language Learning and Technology* 9/3, 79–98. [online] http://llt.msu.edu.

Johnson, K. (1981): *Communicate in Writing*. Cambridge: Cambridge University Press.

Johnson, K. (2001): *An Introduction to Foreign Language Learning and Teaching*. Harlow: Longman.

Johnson, K. and H. Johnson (eds) (1998): *Encyclopedic Dictionary of Applied Linguistics*. Oxford: Blackwell.

Johnson, K. and K. Morrow (eds) (1981): *Communication in the Classroom*. London: Longman.

Jolly, D. and R. Bolitho (2011): A framework for materials writing. In B. Tomlinson (ed) *Materials Development in Language Teaching*. 2nd edn. Cambridge: Cambridge University Press, 107–34.

Jonassen, D. (2000): *Computers as Mindtools for Schools: Engaging Critical Thinking*. Upper Saddle River, N.J: Merrill, 2nd edition.

Jones, C. and S. Fortescue (1987): *Using Computers in the Language Classroom*. London: Longman.

Jones, K. (1997): *Simulations: A Handbook for Teachers and Trainers*. London: Kogan Page Ltd., 3rd edition.

Jordan, R. R. (1997): *English for Academic Purposes*. Cambridge: Cambridge University Press.

Joyce, B., and B. Showers. (2002): *Student achievement through staff development*. 3rd edn. London: Longman.

Jupp, T. C. and J. Milne (1969): *Guided Course in English Composition*. London: Heinemann.

Jupp, T. C. and J. Milne (1972): *Guided Paragraph Writing*. London: Heinemann.

Kagan, S. and M. Kagan. (2009). *Kagan cooperative learning, Second Edn*. San Clemente, CA: Kagan Publishing.

Kanan, J. and P. Towndrow (2002): On-line feedback. *Modern English Teacher* 11/1, 62–7.

Karpati, A. (2009): Web 2 technologies for Net Native language learners: a 'social CALL'. *ReCALL* 21/2, 139–56.

Kelly, G. (2000): *How to Teach Pronunciation*. Harlow: Pearson Education.

Kennedy, C. (1983): Video in ESP. In J. McGovern (ed): *Video Applications in English Language Teaching*, ELT Documents 114. Oxford: Modern English Publications/The British Council, 95–102.

Kennedy, C. and M. Levy (2009): Sustainability and computer-assisted language learning: factors for success in a context of change. *Computer Assisted Language Learning* 22/5, 445–63.

Kennedy, C. and B. Tomlinson (2012 forthcoming): Implementing language policy and planning through materials development. In B. Tomlinson (ed) *Applied Linguistics and Materials Development*. London: Continuum International Publishing.

Kern, R. and Warschauer, M. (2000). Introduction: Theory and practice of network-based language teaching. In M. Warschauer & R. Kern (Eds.), *Network-based Language Teaching: Concepts and Practice*. Cambridge: Cambridge University Press.

Kervin, L. and B. Derewianka (2011): New technologies to support language learning. In B. Tomlinson (ed): *Materials Development in Language Teaching*. Cambridge: Cambridge University Press, 2nd edition, 328–51.

Kessler, G. (2009): Student-initiated attention to form in wiki-based collaborative writing. *Language Learning and Technology* 13/1, 79–95. [online] http://llt.msu.edu/vol13num1/kessler.pdf.

King, J. (2002): Using DVD feature films in the EFL Classroom. *Computer Assisted Language Learning* 15/5, 509–23.

Kirkpatrick, A. (ed) (2010): *The Routledge Handbook of World Englishes*. Oxon: Routledge.

Konishi, M. (2003): Strategies for reading hypertext by Japanese ESL learners. *The Reading Matrix* 3/3, 97–119. http://www.readingmatrix.com/current.html [Accessed 8.05.2010].

Kosslyn, S. M., W. L. Thompson and G. Ganis (2006): *The Case for Mental Imagery*. Oxford: Oxford University Press.

Kramsch, C. and P. Sullivan. (1996): Appropriate pedagogy. *ELT Journal* 50/3, 199–212.

Krashen, S. (1982): *Principles and Practice in Second Language Acquisition*. New York: Prentice Hall.

Krashen, S. (1994): The input hypothesis and its rivals. In N. Ellis (ed.) *Implicit and Explicit Learning of Languages*. London: Academic Press, pp. 45–77.

Krashen, S. (2004): *The Power of Reading- Insights from the Research*. 2nd edn. Portsmouth, NH: Heinemann.

Krashen, S. and T. Terrell (1983): *The Natural Approach: Language Acquisition in the classroom*. Menlo Park, CA: Alemany Press.

Kumaravadivelu, B. (1990): Classroom observation: a neglected situation. *TESOL Newsletter* 24/6, 5–32.

Kutnick, P. and L. Berdondini. (2009) Can the enhancement of group working in classrooms provide a basis for effective communication in support of school-based cognitive achievement in classrooms of young learners. *Cambridge Journal of Education*, 39(1), 71–94.

Lamb, T. and H. Reinders (eds.) (2008): Learner and Teacher Autonomy: Concepts, Realities and Responses. *AILA Applied Linguistics Series 1*. Amsterdam: John Benjamins Publishing Company.

Lantolf, J. P. and S. L. Thorne (2006): *Sociocultural Theory and The Genesis of Second Language Development*. Oxford University Press.

Larsen-Freeman, D. and Anderson, M. (2011): *Techniques and Principles in Language Teaching* 3rd edn. New York, NY: Oxford University Press.

Lawson, T. (2011): Sustained classroom observation: what does it reveal about changing teaching practices? *Journal of Further and Higher Education*, Vol. 35, No. 3, 317–37.

Lee, L. (2009): Promoting intercultural exchanges with blogs and podcasting: a study of Spanish-American telecollaboration. *Computer Assisted Language Learning* 22/5, 425–43.

Lee, J., E. Park and H. Kim (2000): Literacy education in Korea: a sociocultural perspective. *Childhood Education*, 76(6), 347–51.

Levy, M. (1997): A tutor-tool network. In M. Levy (ed.): *Computer-assisted Language Learning: Context and Conceptualisation*, Oxford: Clarendon Press, 178–214.

Levy, M. and G. Stockwell (2006): *CALL Dimensions: Options and Issues in Computer-assisted Language*. Mahwah, NJ: Lawrence Erlbaum.

Lewis, M. (1993): *The Lexical Approach: The State of ELT and a Way Forward*. Hove: Language Teaching Publications.

Lewis, M. (ed) (2000): *Teaching Collocation: Further Developments in the Lexical Approach*. Hove, England: Language Teaching Publications.

Liaw, M.-L. and R. Johnson (2001): Email writing as a cross cultural learning experience. *System* 29/2, 235–51.

Littlejohn, A. (2011). The analysis of language teaching materials: inside the Trojan horse. In B. Tomlinson (ed) *Materials Development in Language Teaching*. 2nd edn. Cambridge: Cambridge University Press, 179–211.

Littlejohn, A. and S. Windeatt (1988): Beyond language learning: perspectives on materials design. In R. K. Johnson (ed): *The Second Language Curriculum*, Cambridge: Cambridge University Press.

Littlewood, W. T. (1981): *Communicative Language Teaching*. Cambridge: Cambridge University Press.

Littlewood, W. T. (1992): *Teaching Oral Communication*. Oxford: Blackwell.

Littlewood, W. 2000. 'Do Asian students really want to listen and obey?' *ELT Journal* 54, 1, 31–5.

Long, M. (2005) (ed): *Second Language Needs Analysis*. Oxford: Oxford University Press.

Long, M. (1996): The role of the linguistic environment in second language acquisition. In W. Ritchie and T. Bhatia. *Handbook of Second Language Acquisition*. San Diego: Academic Press, pp. 413–68.

Long, M. H. and P. A. Porter (1985): Group work, interlanguage talk and second language acquisition. *TESOL Quarterly* 19, 211–23.

Lowes, R. and F. Target (1998): *Helping Students to Learn: A Guide to Learner Autonomy*. London: Richmond Publishing.

Lubelska, D. and M. Matthews (1997): *Looking at Language Classrooms*. Cambridge: Cambridge University Press.

Madsen, K. S. and J. D. Bowen (1978): *Adaptation in Language Teaching*. Rowley, MA: Newbury House.

Mak, S. H. (2011): Tensions between conflicting beliefs of an EFL teacher in teaching practice. *Singapore: RELC Journal*, 42/1, 53–67.

Malamah-Thomas, A. (1987): *Classroom Interaction*. Oxford: Oxford University Press.

Maley, A. (2007a): *Asian Short Stories for Young Readers*. Vol. 4. Petaling Jaya: Pearson Malaysia.

Maley, A. (2007b): *Asian Poems for Young Readers*. Vol. 5. Petaling Jaya: Pearson Malaysia.

Maley, A. (2009): Materials writing: By the people, for the people? In Mukundan, J. (ed) *Readings on ELT Materials III*. Petaling Jaya: Pearson Malaysia.

Maley, A. and J. Mukundan (2005): *Asian Stories for Young Readers* Vol. 2. Petaling Jaya: Pearson Malaysia.

Mann, S. (2005): The language teacher's development. *Language Teaching*, 38, 103–18.

Massa, L. J. and R. E. Mayer (2006): Testing the ATI hypothesis: Should multimedia instruction accommodate verbalizer-visualizer cognitive style? *Learning and Individual Differences* 16, 321–36.

Masuhara, H. (2003): Materials for teaching reading skills. In B. Tomlinson (ed) *Developing Materials for Language Teaching*. London: Continuum Press, pp. 340–63.

Masuhara, H. (2005): Helping learners to achieve multi-dimensional mental representation in L2 reading. *Folio* 9 (2), 6–9.

Masuhara, H. (2006): Materials as a Teacher-Development Tool. In J. Mukundan (ed) *Readings on ELT Materials II*. Petaling Jaya: Person Longman Malaysia, 34–46.

Masuhara, H. (2007): The role of proto-reading activities in the acquisition and development of effective reading skills. In B. Tomlinson (ed): *Language Acquisition and Development – Studies of Learners of First and Other Languages*, London: Continuum.

Masuhara, H. (2011): What do teachers really want from coursebooks? In B. Tomlinson (ed) *Materials Development in Language Teaching* 2nd edn. Cambridge: Cambridge University Press. 236–66.

Masuhara, H. and B. Tomlinson (2008): Materials for general English. In B. Tomlinson (ed): *English Language Learning Materials – A Critical Review*, London: Continuum International Publishing Group.

Masuhara, H., N. Hann, Y. Yi and B. Tomlinson (2008): Adult EFL courses. *ELT Journal* 62/3, 294–312.

McCarten, J. and M. McCarthy (2010): Bridging the gap between corpus and coursebook: the case of conversation strategies. In F. Mishan and A. Chambers (eds): *Perspectives on Language Learning Materials Development*, Bern: Peter Lang.

McCarthy, M. and R. A. Carter (1994): *Language as Discourse: Perspectives for Language Teaching*. London: Longman.

McCarthy, M. and R. A. Carter (1995): Spoken grammar: what is it and how should we teach it? *ELT Journal* 49/3, 207–17.

McCarthy, M. and F. O'Dell (2008): *Academic English in Use*. Cambridge: Cambridge University Press.

McCarthy, M., J. McCarten and H. Sandiford (2005): *Touchstone 2*. New York: Cambridge University Press.

McDonough, J. (2002): The teacher as language learner: worlds of difference? *ELT Journal* 56/4, 404–11.

McDonough, J. and S. H. McDonough (1997): *Research Methods for English Language Teachers*. London: Arnold.

McDonough, S. H. (1995): *Strategy and Skill in Learning a Foreign Language*. London: Arnold.

McDonough, S. H. (1999): Learner Strategies. *Language Teaching* 32, 1–18.

McDonough, J. and C. Shaw (2003): *Materials and Methods in ELT* 2nd edn. Oxford: Blackwell Publishing.

McNamara, D. S. (ed) (2007): *Reading Comprehension Strategies: Theory, Interventions, and Technologies*. Mahwah, NJ: Erlbaum.

Meddings, L. and Thornbury, S. (2009): *Teaching unplugged: Dogme in English language teaching*. Peaslake UK: Delta.

Meskill, C. (2005): Metaphors that shape and guide CALL Research. In J. L. Egbert and G. M. Petrie (eds): *CALL Research Perspectives*, Mahwah, NJ: Lawrence Erlbaum Associates.

Millar, N. (2011): Korean children's cultural adjustment during transition to the early years of school in Australia. *Australian Journal of Early Childhood*, 36/3, 10–18.

Miller, L. (2000): What have you just learnt? Preparing learners in the classroom for self-access language learning. *Modern English Teacher* 9/3, 7–13.

Miller, L., E. T. Shuk-Ching and M. Hopkins (2007): Establishing a self-access centre in a secondary school. *ELT Journal*, 61/3, 220–27.

Mishan, F. (2005): *Designing Authenticity into Language Learning Materials*. Bristol: Intellect Books.

Mishan, F. (2010): Withstanding washback: thinking outside the box in materials development. In B. Tomlinson and H. Masuhara (eds): *Research for Materials Development in Language Learning*, London: Continuum International Publishing Group, 353–68.

Mol, H. and B. T. Tan (2010): EAP materials in Australia and New Zealand. In B. Tomlinson (ed): *English Language Learning Materials – A Critical Review*, London: Continuum International Publishing Group, 74–99.

Moody, K. W. (1974): *Frames for Written English*. London: Oxford University Press.

Morrow, K. (1981): *Principles of communicative methodology*. In Johnson and Morrow, 59–66.

Motteram, G. (2011): Developing language-learning materials with technology. In B. Tomlinson (ed) *Materials Development in Language Teaching*. 2nd edition. Cambridge: Cambridge University Press, 303–27.

Mukundan, J. and T. Ahour (2010): A review of textbook evaluation checklists across four decades. In B. Tomlinson and H. Masuhara (eds) *Research for Materials Development in Language Learning – Evidence for Best Practice*. London: Continuum International Publishing Group, 336–52.

Munby, J. (1978): *Communicative Syllabus Design*. Cambridge: Cambridge University Press.

Naiman, N., M. Fröhlich and H. H. Stern (1975): *The Good Language Learner*. Toronto: Modern Language Centre, Department of Curriculum, Ontario Institute for Studies in Education.

Nolasco, R. and L. Arthur (1986): Try doing it with a class of forty! *ELT Journal* 40/2, 100–6.

Nolasco, R. and L. Arthur (1988): *Large Classes*. London: Macmillan.

Norton, B. and K. Toohey (2001): Changing perspectives on good language learners. *TESOL Quarterly* 35, 2, 307–322.

Nunan, D. (1988): *The Learner-Centred Curriculum*. Cambridge: Cambridge University Press.

Nunan, D. (1989): *Designing Tasks for the Communicative Classroom*. Cambridge: Cambridge University Press.

Nunan, D. (1990): *Action research in the classroom*. In Richards and Nunan, 62–81.

Nunan, D. (1991): *Language Teaching Methodology: A Textbook for Teachers*. Hemel Hempstead: Prentice-Hall International.

Nunan, D. (1999): *Second Language Teaching and Learning*. Boston: Heinle and Heinle.

Nunan, D. (2004): *Task-Based Language Teaching*. Cambridge: Cambridge University Press.

Nunan, D. (2005): Classroom research. In E. Hinkel (ed) *Handbook of Research in Second Language Teaching and Learning*. Mahwah, NJ: Lawrence Erlbaum Associates, Inc, 225–40.

Nuttall, C. (1996): *Teaching Reading Skills in a Foreign Language*. London: Heinemann, new edition.

Nuttall, C. (2005): *Teaching Reading Skills in a Foreign Language* (3rd edn) Oxford: Macmillan.

O'Dowd, R. (2000): Intercultural learning via video conferencing: a pilot exchange project. *ReCALL* 12/1, 49–61.

O'Dowd, R. (2007): *Online Intercultural Exchange: An Introduction for Foreign Language Teachers*. Clevedon, UK and New York: Multilingual Matters.

Okagaki, L., and K. E. Diamond (2000): Responding to cultural and linguistic differences in the beliefs and practices of families with young children. *Young Children*, 55(3): 74–80.

O'Keeffe, A., M. J. McCarthy and R. A. Carter (2007): *From Corpus to Classroom: Language Use and Language Teaching*. Cambridge: Cambridge University Press.

O'Neill, R. (1982): Why use textbooks? *ELT Journal* 36/2, 104–11.

Ortega, L. (2010): *Second Language Acquisition. Critical Concepts in Linguistics*. London: Routledge.

Oxford, R. (2001): *Integrated Skills in the ESL/EFL Classroom*. ERIC Digest.

Oxford, R. L. (1990): *Language Learning Strategies: What Every Teacher Should Know*. New York: Newbury House/Harper and Row.

Oxford, R. (2011): *Teaching and Researching: Language Learning Strategies*. Harlow: Pearson Education Ltd.

Oxford, R. and K. R. Lee (2008): The learners' landscape and journey. In C. Griffith (ed) *Lessons from Good Language Learners*. Cambridge: Cambridge University Press. 306–15.

Oxford University Press (2011): *Materials To Products Level 5 (Intermediate) with Audio CD*. Oxford: Oxford University Press.

Palfreyman, D. and R. C. Smith. (eds.) (2003): *Learner Autonomy across Cultures: Language Education Perspectives*. Basingstoke: Palgrave Macmillan.

Park, H-O. (2010): Process drama in the Korean EFL secondary classroom: A case study of Korean middle school classroom. In B. Tomlinson and H. Masuhara (eds) *Research for Materials Development in Language Learning – Evidence for Best Practice*. London: Continuum International Publishing Group, 21–36.

Pashler, H., M. McDaniel, D. Rohrer and R. Bjork (2009): Learning styles: Concepts and evidence. *Psychological Science in the Public Interest 9*, 105–19.

Pattison, P. (1987): *Developing Communication Skills*. Cambridge: Cambridge University Press.

Pennington, M. (1996): Writing the natural way. *Computer Assisted Language Learning 9/2-3*, 125–42.

Pennington, M. C. (1990): *A professional development focus for the language teaching practicum*. In Richards and Nunan, 132–52.

Pham, H. H. (2007): Communicative language teaching: Unity within diversity. *ELT Journal, 61/3*, 193–201.

Pica, T. and C. Doughty (1985): Input and interaction in the communicative classroom: a comparison of teacher-fronted and group activities. In S. M. Gass and C. G. Madden (eds): *Input in Second Language Acquisition*, Rowley, MA: Newbury House, 115–32.

Piper, A. (1987): Helping learners to write: a role for the word processor. *English Language Teaching Journal 41/2*, 119–25.

Porter-Ladousse, G. (1987): *Role Play*. Oxford: Oxford University Press.

Prabhu, N. (1987): *Second Language Pedagogy*. Oxford: Oxford University Press.

Puchta, H., J. Stranks and P. Lewis-Jones (2008): *English in Mind Book 5*. Cambridge: Cambridge University Press.

Pugh, A. K. (1978): *Silent Reading*. London: Heinemann.

Pylyshyn, Z. W. (2002): Mental Imagery: in search of a theory. *Behavioral and Brain Sciences 25*, 157–82.

Qu, J. and B. T. Tan (2010): 'Cultures of learning in three language coursebooks in China – 'Read with your heart, 'Listen and Check' and 'Fill in the blank and use the language. In B. Tomlinson and H. Masuhara (eds) *Research for Materials Development in Language Learning*. London: Continuum International Publishing Group, 273–90.

Ramani, E. (1987): Theorising from the classroom. *ELT Journal 41/1*, 3–11.

Rea, D., T. Clementson, A. Tilbury and L. A. Hendra (2011): *English Unlimited*. Cambridge: Cambridge University Press.

Reeves, J., and C. Forde. 2004. The social dynamics of changing practice. *Cambridge Journal of Education 34*, no. 1: 85–102.

Reid, J. (2001): Writing. In R. Carter and D. Nunan (eds) *The Cambridge Guide to Teaching English to Speakers of Other Languages*. Cambridge: Cambridge University Press.

Renandya, W. A. and T. S. C. Farrell (2011): Teacher, the tape is too fast!' Extensive listening in ELT. *ELT Journal* 65/1, 52–9.

Reppen, R. (2011): Using corpora in the language classroom. In B. Tomlinson (ed): *Materials Development in Language Teaching*, 2nd edition. Cambridge: Cambridge University Press.

Richards, J. C. (1985): *The Context of Language Teaching*. Cambridge: Cambridge University Press.

Richards, J. C. (1990): *The dilemma of teacher education in second language teaching*. In Richards and Nunan, 3–15.

Richards, J. C. and C. Lockhart (1994): *Reflective Teaching in Second Language Classrooms*. Cambridge: Cambridge University Press.

Richards, J. C. and D. Nunan (eds) (1990): *Second Language Teacher Education*. Cambridge: Cambridge University Press.

Richards, J. C. and T. S. Rodgers (2001): *Approaches and Methods in Language Teaching*. Cambridge: Cambridge University Press, 2nd edition.

Richards, J. C. and R. Schmidt (2010): *Longman Dictionary of Language Teaching & Applied Linguistics*. Harlow: Pearson Education Ltd., 4th edition.

Richterich, R. and J. L. Chancerel (1980): *Identifying the Needs of Adults Learning a Foreign Language*. Oxford: Pergamon.

Riley, P. (1982): Learners lib: an experimental autonomous learning scheme. In M. Geddes and G. Sturtridge (eds): *Individualisation*, Loughborough: Modern English Publications, 61–3.

Rixon, S. (1986): *Developing Listening Skills*. London: Macmillan/Modern English Publications.

Robinson, P. (ed.). (2002). *Individual differences and instructed language learning*. Amsterdam: J. Benjamins.

Rost, M. (1990): *Listening in Language Learning*. London: Longman.

Rost, M. (1994): *Introducing Listening*. Harmondsworth: Penguin.

Rost, M. (2001): Listening. In R. Carter and D. Nunan (eds): *The Cambridge Guide to Teaching English to Speakers of Other Languages*, Cambridge: Cambridge University Press.

Rost, M. (2005): L2 Listening. In In E. Hinkel (ed) *Handbook of Research in Second Language Teaching and Learning*. Mahwah, NJ: Lawrence Erlbaum Associates, Inc, 503–28.

Rubdy, R. (2003): Selection of materials. In B. Tomlinson (ed) *Developing Materials for Language Teaching*. London: Continuum, 37–57.

Rubin, J. and I. Thompson (1982): *The Good Language Learner*. Boston: Heinle and Heinle.

Ruehlemann, C. (2007): *Conversation in Context: A Corpus-Driven Approach*. London: Continuum.

Salaberry, R. (2001): The use of technology for second language learning and teaching: a retrospective. *Modern Language Journal* 85/i, 39–56.

Saraceni, C. (2003): Adapting courses: a critical view. In Tomlinson (ed): *Developing Materials for Language Teaching*. London: Continuum, 72–85.

Schmitt, D. and N. Schmitt (2005): *Focus on Vocabulary: Mastering the Academic Word List*. New York: Longman.

Seedhouse, P. (1997): Combining form and meaning. *ELT Journal* 51/4, 336–44.

Seedhouse, P. (1999): Task-based interaction. *ELT Journal* 53/3, 149–56.

Seidlhofer, B. (2010): Lingua franca English – the European context. In A. Kirkpatrick (ed): *The Routledge Handbook of World Englishes*, Oxon: Routledge, 355–71.

Seidlhofer, B. (2011): *Understanding English as a Lingua Franca*. Oxford: Oxford University Press.

Shaywitz, S. E. and B. A. Shaywitz (2008). Paying attention to reading: the neurobiology of reading and dyslexia. *Development and Psychopathology* 20 (4), 1329–49.

Sheerin, S. (1989): *Self-Access*. Oxford: Oxford University Press.

Sheldon, L. E. (ed) (1987): *ELT Textbooks and Materials: Problems in Evaluation and Development*. ELT Documents 126. Oxford: Modern English Publications in Association with The British Council.

Sheldon, L. E. (1988): Evaluating ELT textbooks and materials. *ELT Journal* 42/4, 237–46.

Sherman, J. (2003): *Using Authentic Video in the Language Classroom*. Cambridge: CUP.

Silva, T. and P. K. Matsuda (eds) (2010): *Practicing Theory in Second Language Writing*. West Lafayette, IN: Parlor Press.

Sinclair, B. (1999): Survey review: recent publications on autonomy in language learning. *ELT Journal* 53/4, 309–29.

Skehan, P. (1980): Team-teaching and the role of the ESP teacher. *Study Modes and Academic Development of Overseas Students*, ELT Documents 109. London: The British Council, 23–37.

Skehan, P. (1989): *Individual Differences in Second Language Learning*. London: Edward Arnold.

Slaouti, D. (2000): In search of a role for email and the World Wide Web in improving writing. In T. O'Brien and M. Beaumont (eds): *Collaborative Research in Second Language Education*, Stoke on Trent, England: Trentham Books.

Slaouti, D. (2002): The world wide web for academic purposes: old study skills for new. *English for Specific Purposes* 21/2, 105–24.

Smith, B. (2005): The relationship between negotiated interaction, learner uptake, and lexical acquisition in task-based computer-mediated communication. *TESOL Quarterly* 39/1, 33–58.

Smith, F. (1978): *Reading*. Cambridge: Cambridge University Press.

Smith, R. C. (2003): Pedagogy for autonomy as (becoming-)appropriate methodology. In D. Palfreyman and R. C. Smith (eds.). *Learner Autonomy across Cultures: Language Education Perspectives*. Basingstoke: Palgrave Macmillan, 129–46.

Smith, R. (2008): Key Concepts in ELT – Learner Autonomy. *ELT Journal*, 62/4, 395–96.

Smith, K. (2011): The multi-faceted teacher educator: a Norwegian perspective. *Journal of Education for Teaching*, 37, 3, 337–49.

Smith, F., F. Hardman, K. Wall, and M. Mroz. (2004): Interactive whole class teaching in the national literacy and numeracy strategies. *British Educational Research Journal* 30, no. 3: 395–411.

Spencer, D. H. (1967): *Guided Composition Exercises*. London: Longman.

Spratt, M. (1994): *English for the Teacher: A Language Development Course*. Harlow: Longman.

Spratt, M. (1999): How good are we at knowing what learners like? *System* 27/2, 141–55.

Stern, H. H. (1983): *Fundamental Concepts of Language Teaching*. Oxford: Oxford University Press.

Stevick, E. W. (1972): Evaluating and adapting language materials. In H. B. Allen and R. N. Campbell (eds): *Teaching English as a Second Language*, New York: McGraw-Hill, 102–20.

Stillwell, C., B. McMillan, H. Gillies and T. Walker (2010): Four teachers looking for a lesson: Developing materials with Lesson Study. In B. Tomlinson and H. Masuhara (Eds.) *Research for Materials Development in Language Learning – Evidence for Best Practice*. London: Continuum International Publishing Group, pp. 237–50.

Stockwell, G. and M. Levy (2001): Sustainability of email interactions between native speakers and non native speakers. *Computer Assisted Language Learning* 14/5, 419–42.

Stoller, F. (1984): *Designing an effective reading lab*. TEAM. Dharan: University of Dharan Language Centre, no. 49.

Storch, N. (2001): How collaborative is pairwork? ESL tertiary students composing in pairs. *Language Teaching Research* 5/1, 29–53.

Strevens, P. (1979): Differences in teaching for different circumstances or the teacher as chameleon. In C. A. Yorio, K. Perkins and J. Schachter (eds): *On TESOL '79: The Learner in Focus*, Washington, DC: TESOL, 2–11.

Stubbs, M. and S. Delamont (eds) (1976): *Explorations in Classroom Observation*. New York: John Wiley.

Sutherland Smith, W. (2002): Weaving the literacy Web: changes in reading form page to screen. *The Reading Teacher* 55/7, 662–9. Available http://tapor.ualberta.ca/Resources/e-text%20reading/Sutherland%20-%20Weaving%20-%20RT%2055.pdf [Accessed 8.05.2010].

Swan, M. (1985): A critical look at the communicative approach. *ELT Journal* 39/1, 2–12, 39/2, 76–87.

Swain, M. (2005): The output hypothesis: Theory and Research. In E. Hinkel (ed) *Handbook of Research in Second Language Teaching and Learning*, pp. 471–84.

Swain, M., L. Brooks, and A. Tocalli-Beller (2002): Peer-peer dialogue as a means of second language learning. *Annual Review of Applied Linguistics*, 22, 171–85.

Taylor, R. (1980): *The Computer in the School: Tutor, Tool, Tutee*. Teacher's College, Columbia University, New York: Teacher's College Press.

Thickett, P. (1986): The use of TLF on an RSA preparatory certificate course. *English Teaching Information Circular (ETIC)*, London: The British Council.

Thompson, G. (1996): Some misconceptions about communicative language teaching. *ELT Journal* 50/1, 9–15.

Thornbury, S. (2000): A Dogma for EFL. *IATEFL Issues*, 153, 2.

Thornbury, S. (2002): *How to Teach Vocabulary*. Harlow, Pearson Educational Ltd.

Thornbury, S. (2005): *How to Teach Speaking*. Harlow: Pearson Education Ltd.

Timmis, I. (2012): Spoken language research: the applied linguistic challenge. In B. Tomlinson and H. Masuhara (eds): *Applied Linguistics and Materials Development*, London: Continuum International Publishing Group.

Tomlinson, B. (1999): *Developing criteria for evaluating L2 materials*. IATEFL Issues 47, March.

Tomlinson, B. (2001): *Materials development.* In Carter and Nunan, 66–71.

Tomlinson, B. (ed) (2003a): *Developing Materials for Language Teaching.* London: Continuum.

Tomlinson, B. (2003b): Developing principled frameworks for materials development. In B. Tomlinson (ed): *Developing Materials for Language Teaching,* London: Continuum, 107–29.

Tomlinson, B. (2003c): Materials evaluation. In B. Tomlinson (ed) *Developing Materials for Language Teaching.* London: Continuum, 15–36.

Tomlinson, B. (2007a): *Language Acquisition and Development – Studies of Learners of First and Other Languages.* London: Continuum.

Tomlinson, B. (2007b): The value of recasts during meaning focused communication – 1. In B. Tomlinson (ed): *Language Acquisition and Development – Studies of Learners of First and Other Languages,* London: Continuum, 141–61.

Tomlinson, B. (ed) (2008): *English Language Learning Materials – A Critical Review.* London: Continuum International Publishing Group.

Tomlinson, B. (2010): Principles of effective materials development. In N. Harwood (ed): *English Language Teaching Materials – Theory and Practice,* Cambridge: Cambridge University Press, 81–108.

Tomlinson, B. (ed) (2011a): *Materials Development in Language Teaching.* Cambridge: Cambridge University Press, 2nd edition.

Tomlinson, B. (2011b): Introduction: principles and procedures of materials development. In B. Tomlinson (ed): *Materials Development in Language Teaching.* Cambridge: Cambridge University Press, 2nd edition, 1–34.

Tomlinson, B. (2011c): Access-self materials. In In B. Tomlinson (ed) *Materials Development in Language Teaching.* 2nd edn. Cambridge: Cambridge University Press, 414–33.

Tomlinson, B. (2012a): Materials development for language learning and teaching. *Language Teaching,* 45.2, 1–37.

Tomlinson, B. and B. Dat (2004): The contributions of Vietnamese learners of English to ELT methodology. *Language Teaching Research,* 8/2, 199–222.

Tomlinson, B. and H. Masuhara (2004): *Developing Language Course Materials.* Singapore: RELC.

Tomlinson, B. and H. Masuhara (eds) (2010): *Research for Materials Development in Language Learning – Evidence for Best Practice.* London: Continuum International Publishing Group.

Tomlinson, B., B. Dat, H. Masuhara and R. Rubdy (2001): Survey review: ESL courses for adults. *ELT Journal* 55/1, 80–101.

Tribble, C. (1996): *Writing.* Oxford: Oxford University Press.

Tribble, C. (2010): A genre-based approach to developing materials for writing. In N. Harwood (ed): *English Language Teaching Materials – Theory and Practice,* Cambridge: Cambridge University Press, 157–78.

Trim, J. L. M. (1976): Some possibilities and limitations of learner autonomy. In E. Harding-Esch (ed): *Self-Directed Learning and Autonomy.* Cambridge: mimeo, 1–11.

Truscott, J. (1996): The case against grammar correction in L2 writing classes. *Language Learning* 46, 327–69.

Truscott, J. (1999): The case for 'The case against grammar correction in L2 writing classes': a response to Ferris. *Journal of Second Language Writing* 8, 111–22.

Tschirner, E. (2001): Language acquisition in the classroom: the role of digital video. *Computer Assisted Language Learning* 14/3-4, 305–19.

Tsui, A. B. M. (1985): Analyzing input and interaction in second language classrooms. *RELC Journal*, 16, 8–32.

Tsui, A. B. M. (1996): Reticence and anxiety in second language learning. In K. Bailey and D. Nunan (eds): *Voices from the Language Classroom*, Cambridge: Cambridge University Press, 145–67.

Tsui, A. B. M. (2001): *Classroom interaction*. In Carter and Nunan, 120–5.

Tudor, I. (1993): Teacher roles in the learner-centred classroom. *ELT Journal* 47/1, 22–31.

Tudor, I. (1996): *Learner-Centredness as Language Education*. Cambridge: Cambridge University Press.

Underwood, M. (1989) *Teaching Listening*. London: Longman.

Ur, P. (1996): *A Course in Language Teaching*. Cambridge: Cambridge University Press.

Van Den Branden, K. (2006): *Task-Based Language Education – From Theory to Practice*. Cambridge: Cambridge University Press.

Vandergrift, L. (1999): Facilitating second language listening comprehension: acquiring successful strategies. *ELT Journal* 53/3, 168–76.

Vandergrift, L. (2002): It was nice to see that our predictions were right: Developing metacognition in L2 listening comprehension. *The Canadian Modern Language Review*, 58, 555–75.

Van Ek, J. A. (1977): The Threshold Level for Modern Language Learning in Schools. London: Longman.

Van Ek, J. A., L. G. Alexander and M. A. Fitzpatrick. (1980): *Waystage English*. Oxford: Pergamon (on behalf of the Council of Europe).

Van Lier, L. (1988): *The Classroom and the Language Learner*. London: Longman.

Vilmi, R. (2000): *Collaborative writing projects on the internet: more than half a decade of experimentation*. In Howarth and Hetherington, 28–42.

Viney, P. (1997): Lost property. In B. Watcyn-Jones (ed): *Top Class Activities, 50 Fun Games and Activities by Top ELT Writers*. Book 1. London: Penguin English.

Vygotsky, L. S. (1978): Mind and society: The development of higher mental processes. Cambridge, MA: Harvard University Press.

Wajnryb, R. (1992): *Classroom Observation Tasks*. Cambridge: Cambridge University Press.

Walker, R. (2010): *Teaching the Pronunciation of English as a Lingua Franca*. Oxford: Oxford University Press.

Wallace, M. J. (1991): *Training Foreign Language Teachers: A Reflective Approach*. Cambridge: Cambridge University Press.

Warschauer, M. and R. Kern (eds) (2000): *Network-based Language Teaching: Concepts and Practice*. New York: Cambridge University Press.

Warschauer, M. (2002): A developmental perspective on technology in language education. *TESOL Quarterly* 36/3, 453–75.

Warschauer, M. and D. Healey (1998): Computers and Language Learning: an overview. *Language Teaching* 31, 57–71. Available from http://www.gse.uci.edu/person/warschauer_m/overview.html.

Waters, A. (2009): Managing innovation in English language education. *Language Teaching*, 42, 4, 421–58.

Waters, A. and M. L. C. Vilches (2008). Factors affecting ELT reforms: The case of the Philippines Basic Education Curriculum. *RELC Journal*, 39 (1), 5–24.

Wenden, A. and J. Rubin (1987): *Learner Strategies in Language Learning*. New York: Prentice-Hall International.

White, G. (1998): *Listening*. Oxford: Oxford University Press.

White, G. (2008): *listening and good language learner*. In C. Griffith (ed) *Lessons from Good Language Learners*. Cambridge: Cambridge University Press. 208–17.

White, R. V. (1981): Reading. In: Johnson, K. and K. Morrow (eds): *Communication in the Classroom*. London: Longman, 87–92.

White, R. and V. Arndt (1991): *Process Writing*. London and New York: Longman.

Widdowson, H. G. (1978): *Teaching Language as Communication*. Oxford: Oxford University Press.

Widdowson H. G. (1979): The simplification of use. In H. G. Widdowson: *Explorations in Applied Linguistics*. Oxford: Oxford University Press.

Wilkins, D. A. (1976): *Notional Syllabuses*. Oxford: Oxford University Press.

Williams, E. (1984): *Reading in the Language Classroom*. London: Macmillan.

Willis, D. (1990): *The Lexical Syllabus*. London: Collins.

Willis, J. (1996): *A Framework for Task-Based Learning*. Harlow: Longman.

Willis, J. (2011): Concordances in the classroom without a computer: assembling and exploiting concordances of common words. In B. Tomlinson (ed) *Materials Development in Language Teaching* (second edn). Cambridge: Cambridge University Press.

Willis, D. and Willis, J. (2007): *Doing Task-based Teaching*. Oxford: Oxford University Press.

Wilson, J. J. (2008): *How to Teach Listening*. Harlow: Pearson Education Ltd.

Index

Materials and Methods in ELT: A Teacher's Guide, Third Edition.
Jo McDonough, Christopher Shaw, and Hitomi Masuhara.
© 2013 John Wiley & Sons, Inc. Published 2013 by John Wiley & Sons, Inc.

Printed and bound by CPI Group (UK) Ltd, Croydon, CR0 4YY